MEMOIRS

OF A

HUGUENOT FAMILY.

Jaqueffontaine.

After an Original likeness in the possession of Miss Fontaine Bexley, England.

G P PUTNAM & Cº

MEMOIRS

OF A

HUGUENOT FAMILY:

TRANSLATED AND COMPILED FROM THE ORIGINAL
AUTOBIOGRAPHY OF THE

REV. JAMES FONTAINE,

AND OTHER FAMILY MANUSCRIPTS; COMPRISING AN ORIGINAL JOURNAL OF
TRAVELS IN VIRGINIA, NEW-YORK, ETC., IN 1715 AND 1716.

BY

ANN MAURY.

WITH AN

APPENDIX,

CONTAINING A TRANSLATION OF THE EDICT OF NANTES, THE
EDICT OF REVOCATION, AND OTHER INTERESTING
HISTORICAL DOCUMENTS.

CLEARFIELD

Originally Published
Expanded Edition
New York, 1853

Reprinted
Genealogical Publishing Co., Inc.
Baltimore, 1967

Reissued
Genealogical Publishing Co., Inc.
Baltimore, 1973

Reprinted for
Clearfield Company, Inc. by
Genealogical Publishing Co., Inc.
Baltimore, Maryland
1994, 2002

Library of Congress Catalogue Card Number 67-22179
International Standard Book Number: 0-8063-0553-3

PREFACE.

In bringing before the public this history of a private family, part of which was published some years ago, we feel it to be possible, that in our own admiration of the virtues of our forefathers, and our deep interest in the vicissitudes of their fortunes, we may over-estimate the pleasure a perusal is likely to afford the general reader. There are, however, so many individuals in the United States who are lineally descended from James Fontaine, that we think the publication is required for them alone. We believe, also, that the work will address itself to the hearts of a numerous body of Christians, who glory, like ourselves, in a Huguenot origin, and who, in reading the following pages, may realize, more fully than they have hitherto done, the trials of their own ancestors in leaving the homes of their fathers for the sake of the Gospel, and be thereby incited to more steadfast faith.

We have been so much struck with some remarks upon the benefits to be derived from family history in a preface to the "Lives of the Lindsays," that we venture to make a quotation which we think equally applicable to the volume we are now introducing to the reader.

"Every family should have a record of its own. Each has its peculiar spirit, running through the whole line, and, in more or less development, perceptible in every generation. Rightly viewed, as a most powerful but much neglected instrument of education, I can imagine no study more rife with pleasure and instruction. Nor need our ancestors have been Scipios or Fabii to interest us in their fortunes. We do not love our kindred for their glory or their genius, but for their domestic affections and private virtues, that, unobserved by the world, expand in confidence towards ourselves, and often root themselves, like the banian of the East, and flourish with independent vigor in the heart to which a kind Providence has guided them. An affectionate regard to their memory is natural to the heart; it is an emotion totally distinct from pride,—an ideal love, free from that consciousness of requited affection and reciprocal esteem, which constitutes so much of the satisfaction we derive from the love of the living. They are denied, it is true, to our personal acquaintance, but the light they shed during their lives survives within their tombs, and will reward our search if we explore them. Be *their* light, then, *our* beacon—not the glaring light of heroism which emblazons their names in the page of history with a lustre as cold, though as dazzling, as the gold of an heraldic illuminator; but the pure and sacred flame that descends from heaven on the altar of a Christian heart, and that warmed *their* naturally frozen affections, till they produced the fruits of piety, purity, and love—evinced in holy thoughts and good actions, of which many a record might be found in the annals of the past, would we but search for them, and in which we may find as strong incentives to virtuous emulation as we gather every day from those bright examples of living worth, which it is the study of every good man to imitate. And if the virtues of strangers be so attractive to us, how infinitely more so should be those of our own kindred, and with what additional energy should the precepts of our parents influence us, when we trace the transmission of those precepts from father to son through successive generations, each bearing the testimony of a virtuous, useful and honorable life to their truth and influence, and all uniting in a kind and earnest exhortation to their descendants so to live on earth, that—followers of Him through whose grace alone we have power to obey Him—we may at last be reunited with those who have been before, and those who shall come after us—

> "No wanderer lost,
> A family in heaven."

Be grateful, then, for your descent from religious, as well as noble ancestors; it is your duty to be so, and this is the only worthy tribute you can now pay their ashes."

On the former appearance of a portion of the present book, many supposed it to be a work of imagination merely, presented under the guise of autobiography. It is therefore proper, now, to state that it is in truth what, on the title-page, it purports to be, an authentic narrative of actual occurrences, and is drawn entirely from family manuscripts.

We have translated and printed in an Appendix various documents and edicts throwing light upon the history of the times, some of which, we believe, have not been published at length in the English language for more than a century. We took infinite pains, without success, to procure a translation of the Edict of Nantes, and were therefore induced to translate it for ourselves, and we think it desirable to place it within the general reach of the descendants of Huguenots, as a document in which they cannot fail to take an interest.

CONTENTS.

CHAPTER I.

1*

CHAPTER V.

CHAPTER VI.

CHAPTER VII.

CHAPTER VIII.

CHAPTER IX.

CHAPTER X.

CHAPTER XI.

CHAPTER XII.

CHAPTER XIII.

CHAPTER XIV.

CHAPTER XV.

CHAPTER XVI.

JOURNAL, SERMON, LETTERS, APPENDIX.

MEMOIRS OF A HUGUENOT FAMILY.

CHAPTER I.

LET our beginning be in the name of the Lord who made heaven and earth.

SEVENTY-EIGHTH PSALM.

Give ear, O my people, to my law: incline your ears to the words of my mouth.

I will open my mouth in a parable; I will utter dark sayings of old; Which we have heard, and known, and our fathers have told us.

We will not hide them from their children, showing to the generation to come the praises of the Lord, and his strength, and his wonderful works that he hath done.

For he established a testimony in Jacob, and appointed a law in Israel, which he commanded our fathers, that they should make them known to their children;

That the generation to come might know them, even the children which should be born, who should arise and declare them to their children;

That they might set their hope in God, and not forget the works of God, but keep his commandments. Amen.

I, James Fontaine, have commenced writing this history, for the use of all my children, on the twenty-sixth day of March, 1722; being sixty-four years old.

My dear Children—

Whenever I have related my own adventures to you, or given you details of the incidents that befell your ancestors, you have evinced so deep an interest in them, that I feel I ought not to neglect making a record of the past for your use ; and I am determined to employ my leisure time in this way. I would fain hope that the pious examples of those from whom we are descended, may warm your hearts and influence your lives. I hope you will resolve to dedicate yourselves, wholly and unreservedly, to the service of that God whom they worshipped at the risk of their lives, and that you, and those who come after you, will be steadfast in the profession of that pure reformed religion, for which they endured, with unshaken constancy, the most severe trials. You cannot fail to notice, in the course of their lives, the watchful hand of God's Providence, supporting and preserving them through hardship and suffering.

You need not look farther back than the period over which your own memories can stray, for numberless instances of the providential care of that same God, whose " hand is not shortened."

I have gained the knowledge of those events which occurred before my day from my mother, my older brothers, and my aunt Bouquet, my father's sister ; and I have the most perfect conviction of the truth of all which I relate.

For my own part, I trust that, while recording the past mercies of God for the benefit of my descendants, I may derive personal advantage from the review. The frailties and sins of the different periods of my life, thus brought to mind, ought to cause me to humble myself before the throne of grace, and tremblingly implore pardon for the past, through

the mediation of my blessed Saviour; and the assistance of
the Holy Spirit to make me watchful and circumspect for the
time to come. When I look back upon the numberless, uncommon, and unmerited mercies bestowed upon me during
the whole course of my life, I hope that my gratitude will be
increased towards my Almighty Benefactor, and my confidence in him so strengthened, that I may be enabled for the
future to cast all my care upon him. Great as is my debt of
gratitude for the things of this life, its manifold comforts and
conveniences, how incalculably greater is it for the mercy to
my immortal soul, in God having shed the blood of his only
begotten Son to redeem it! Oh, my God! I entreat thee to
continue thy fatherly protection to me during the few days I
have yet to live, and, at last, to receive my soul into thine
everlasting arms. Amen.

I shall begin the narrative as far back as I have been able
to ascertain the facts with certainty. I must remind you at
the outset, that our name was originally *De la Fontaine*, and
not *Fontaine* only. You might find the original name on record in Rochellé, where my grandfather held some command
in the Tower. I have seen his name, signed *Jaques de la
Fontaine*, to the deed made out when he purchased the house
adjoining the fish-market in Rochelle, which house was part of
the marriage portion of my sister Gachot. My father always
signed his name *De la Fontaine*, during the life of my grandfather, but afterwards, from motives of humility, he cut off
the *De la*, the indication of the ancient nobility of the family.
My brothers wished to resume it when they married, but my
father would not consent, thinking there was more of vanity
than utility in it for one like himself, with a large family and
very little property. You must know that in France, an in-

dividual of noble family cannot engage in trade or the mechanic arts, without forfeiting his claim to nobility.

I have insinuated that our family was of noble origin, and it is true ; but I would not have you glory in that knowledge, but rather in the much greater and more glorious nobility which I am going to lay before you—the suffering and martyrdom for the cause of true religion of those from whom we are descended.

The father of my great-grandfather could not bear the idea of bringing up his sons, according to the usual habit of the nobility, without any employment, and therefore placed his son in the king's service. It is with this son I commence these annals.

John de la Fontaine was born in the province of Maine, near the borders of Normandy, about the year 1500 ; and as soon as he was old enough to bear arms, his father procured him a commission in the household of Francis I., in what was then called "Les Ordonnances du Roi." It was in the tenth or twelfth year of that monarch's reign that he entered his service, and he conducted himself with such uniform honor and uprightness, that he retained his command, not only to the end of the reign of Francis I., but during the reigns of Henry II., Francis II., and until the second year of Charles IX., when he voluntarily resigned. He and his father had become converts to Protestantism on the first preaching of the Reformed religion in France,—about 1535. He had married, and had at least four sons born to him, during his residence in the Court. He wished to retire to private life at an earlier period, but being in the king's service was a sort of safeguard from persecution. He and his family not only ran less risk from his remaining near the king's person, but it

gave him the means of showing kindness to his Protestant
brethren, and oftentimes shielding them from oppression. He
was much beloved by his brother officers, and by the men under his command, which made the Roman Catholic party
afraid of disturbing him ; though, at the same time, his exemplary piety and benevolence marked him as one for whose
blood they thirsted.

You may read in history how the kingdom of France was
laid waste by abominable persecutions and civil wars, on account of religion.* In the interval, between the year 1534

* Open hostilities were occasioned by an event which occurred at the
little town of Vassy, in Champagne, in the year 1562. The Protestants
were engaged in prayer outside the walls, in conformity with the king's
edict, when the Duke of Guise approached. Some of his suite insulted the
worshippers, and from insults they proceeded to blows, and the Duke himself was accidentally wounded in the cheek. The sight of his blood enraged
his followers, and a general massacre of the inhabitants of Vassy ensued.
The report of this roused the suffering Huguenots throughout the kingdom, and a savage and bloody war followed, during which, Anthony of
Bourbon, King of Navarre, fell, fighting in the Catholic ranks, leaving a son
eight years old—the future Henry IV.—that great supporter of the Protestant cause. The constable Montmorency was taken prisoner, and the Duke
of Guise slain : thus the Catholics were without a leader. The Prince of
Condé being also a prisoner, and the Protestant Coligny the only chief remaining on either side, an accommodation appeared indispensable ; and in
March, 1563, an edict was granted, which allowed the Huguenots to worship *within* the towns they were possessed of, up to that day. This permission led some of the bishops and other clergy who had embraced Protestantism, to celebrate divine worship in the cathedrals, according to the
rites of the Reformed Church. Such an extension of the meaning of
the edict had never been contemplated, and it was soon modified by a declaration, that ancient cathedrals should in no case be used as Protestant
churches.

Another edict was passed very shortly, which imposed greater restrictions, and the Huguenots, finding that they were likely to lose by edicts all
that they had wrested from the king by the sword, prepared to take up arms
again, and in 1567 another struggle commenced, which, with a very short
interval of peace, lasted until 1570, when a treaty was concluded upon terms
so favorable to the Huguenots, as to excite some suspicion in their minds
that all was not right. They were to have liberty of conscience, and their

and 1598, when Henry IV. granted the celebrated Edict of
Nantes, the professors of the pure faith were most particularly subjected to every kind of cruelty and injustice. These
persecutions were carried on with some of the forms of law,

worship was allowed in all the towns they had held during the war; and
they were permitted to retain and garrison Rochelle, Montauban, Cognac,
and La Charité, as guarantees for the observance of the treaty. .
  All had now the appearance of peace; but it was the delusive calm
which preceded a storm : vengeance was preparing, and the massacre of St.
Bartholomew's day followed with all its horrors, which are too well known
to need repetition. The number of Huguenots slaughtered, has been estimated at 50,000. Those who survived were for a moment paralyzed by the
blow, and the Catholics themselves seemed stupefied with shame and remorse. Charles was as one struck by avenging retribution; he became rest-
less, sullen, and dejected, and labored under a slow fever to the day of his
death. He tried to excuse his perfidy on the plea of its having been necessary for self-preservation : and he sent instructions to his ambassador
in England, to give such an explanation to Queen Elizabeth. Hume, speaking of this interview, says, " Nothing could be more awful and affecting than
his audience. A melancholy sorrow sat on every face: silence, as in the
dead of night, reigned through all the chambers of the royal apartments—
the courtiers and ladies clad in deep mourning were ranged on each side,
and allowed him to pass without affording him one salute or favorable look,
till he was admitted to the Queen herself."
  The lives of the young Prince of Condé and Henry of Navarre had been
spared, on condition of becoming Catholics, a condition to which they merely pretended to accede, as both attempted to escape from Paris immediately
afterwards. Condé alone was successful, and placed himself at the head
of the Huguenots ; and this sect, which Charles had hoped to exterminate
at one blow, soon mustered an army of 18,000 men, and they had kept possession of Rochelle and Montauban, besides many castles, fortresses, and
smaller towns. Thus Charles, and Catherine his mother, gained nothing
by their infamous treachery, but a character for perfidy and cruelty which
has been unequalled in the annals of history.
  After the death of Charles IX., the condition of the Huguenots was ever
changing ; they were frequently in the field, and when successful, obtained
favorable edicts, which were broken as soon as they laid down their arms,
and then they would resume them, and fight until their success gained
fresh concessions.
  In 1576, the Catholic league was formed, having for its main object
the exclusion from the throne of France of Henry of Navarre, who was
next heir to Henry III., the reigning monarch. War was carried on between
the League and the Huguenots, until 1594, five years after the death of

but the gallows was erected and the fires were kindled, not to support the law, but in the vain hope of striking from the earth the very name of Protestant. The means which were adopted, however, had frequently an effect exactly the opposite of what was intended and expected, increasing rather than diminishing the followers of the true faith. The martyrs, by their constancy, proved, in many cases, the instruments which God made use of to open the eyes of the papists, and it was no uncommon occurrence to see those who had aided in the destruction of others rush to the same martyrdom themselves.

The Protestants, in some of the provinces, were irritated beyond endurance, and took up arms, not against their monarch, but in self-defence against their persecutors. This led to an Edict of Pacification, granted on the 17th of January, 1561–2, commonly known in history as the January Edict. Charles IX. was then in his minority. The Protestants, believing this to be in good faith, very generally laid down their arms.

John de-la Fontaine resigned his commission at this time. He thought himself protected by the Edict in the exercise of his religion, and therefore felt himself no longer under the necessity of remaining in the king's service, to make use of his

Henry III., when Henry IV. from motives of policy, united himself to the Catholic church, and was thereupon generally recognized as the legitimate monarch. He still felt favorably disposed towards his old friends, and in 1598 granted the celebrated edict of Nantes, which allowed them to worship in freedom in all towns where their creed was the prevailing one. They were to pay the regular tithe to the established church, but were permitted to raise money for their own clergy, and to hold meetings of their representatives for church government. In all lawsuits Protestants were to have the privilege of one half the judges being of their own faith, and several towns were left in their possession for a limited time as a surety. The parliament objected to registering this edict, but the king was resolute, and finally overcame their obstinacy.

military profession as a buckler in time of profound peace. He retired to his paternal estates in Maine, where he hoped to end his days peacefully in the bosom of his family, worshipping God according to the dictates of conscience, with those of his neighbors and friends who yet survived. He was greatly mistaken in his anticipations of tranquillity following the Edict: the change was for the worse; whereas, heretofore the proceedings had been openly carried on, and with the semblance of justice, founded upon the king's proclamation against the (so-called) heretics; now, all was secrecy, prisons and judges were alike uncalled for, any wretched vagabond, imbued with the spirit of bigotry, could at once exercise the functions of judge and executioner. Armed miscreants broke into the houses of the Protestants at midnight, they robbed and murdered the inmates with attendant circumstances of cruelty, at which humanity shudders, and they were encouraged in their atrocities by priests, monks and bigots, who made them promises of the tenor of that given to the city watch by the Sanhedrim of Jerusalem, "If this comes to the governor's ears, we will persuade him and secure you."

No inquiry or examination followed these excesses, and the Protestants, in self-defence, were again obliged to have recourse to arms, to repel nocturnal insult and guard against treachery.

John de la Fontaine had long been watched by sworn enemies of God and his Gospel, who hated him on account of his piety and his zeal for the pure worship of God. He was a stanch supporter of the Protestant Church, and occupying an elevated position, it was judged expedient to get rid of such a man as soon as possible, in order the more easily to scatter or destroy the congregation to which he belonged.

In the year 1563, a number of ruffians were dispatched from the city of Le Mans to attack his house at night. He was taken by surprise, dragged out of doors, and his throat cut. His poor wife, who was within a few weeks of her confinement, rushed after him, in the hope of softening the hearts of these midnight assassins, and inducing them to spare the life of her husband; but, so far from it, they murdered her also, and a faithful valet shared the same fate. Oh, my children! let us never forget that the blood of martyrs flows in our veins! And may God of his infinite mercy grant that the remembrance of it may enliven our faith, so that we prove not unworthy scions from so noble a stock.

God has promised to bestow special blessings upon the seed of the righteous, and we can generally see his providential care guarding the children of those whose blood has been shed in his service. He mercifully preserved the lives of the three younger boys, and guided their steps to a place of safety. The oldest was about eighteen, and of his fate I am uncertain, but have reason to believe that he was from home when his parents were murdered, and that he also was massacred. The second son, James, my grandfather, was about fourteen years old; Abraham was about twelve, and the youngest was nine years old, at the time of the murder. They were filled with horror and consternation, and fled from the bloody scene, without any guide save the providence of God, and no aim but to get as far as possible from barbarians who had in a moment deprived them of both father and mother. They found their way to Rochelle, which was then a safe place, and, indeed, for many years a stronghold of Protestantism in France, containing within its walls many devout and faithful servants of the living God. These poor boys were at one blow deprived of parents and property, and from ease and affluence plunged into poverty. They were actually begging their bread when they reached Rochelle, and had no recommendation but their affliction and their prepossessing exterior. I have been told they were fair and handsome, and had evident marks of belonging to a good family, and having been well brought up. Some of the inhabitants took compassion upon them, and gave them food and shelter in return for little services they were capable of performing. A shoemaker, who was a charitable man, fearing God, and in easy circumstances, received James into his house, treated him with much kindness and affection, and taught him his own trade, but without binding him to it as an apprentice. This was no time for pride of birth or titles of nobility to be thought of, but rather to be thankful to God for putting it in his power to earn his daily bread by honest labor. It was not long before he was in receipt of sufficient wages to enable him to support his younger brothers, but in a very moderate way, for they all three lived poorly enough until James reached manhood. He then engaged in commerce, and his after career was comparatively prosperous.

He married and had several children, but only three who lived to be marriageable, two daughters and one son. The latter was my father, and was born in the year 1603, long after the others. He married again, but happily had no addition to his family. It would have been much better for him to have remained a widower, for his last wife was a wicked woman who became tired of him, and tried to poison him, and though she did not succeed, for medical aid was promptly obtained, yet the offence became too notorious to be hushed up, and she was taken to prison, tried, and condemned to death.

It so happened that Henry IV was then at Rochelle, and application was made to him for a pardon. He replied, that before making an answer, he should like to see the husband she was so anxious to get rid of, to judge for himself whether there was any excuse for her. When my grandfather appeared before him, he called out, " Let her be hanged ! Let her be hanged ! Ventre Saint Gris !* He is the handsomest man in my kingdom."

I have seen a picture of him, which should now be in the possession of my sister Madame L'Hommeau's descendants at Jouzac, in Saintonge. That picture represented him as very handsome, with a full face, pure white and red complexion, and a long flaxen beard reaching to his waist, with a few hairs white from age intermixed with it. He was also of a good height, and well proportioned.

He died in the year 1633, at the age of eighty-three. He left property to his family amounting to about 9000 livres.

* The accustomed oath of Henry IV.

CHAPTER II.

I CONTINUE the narrative with what I know of my father, the youngest child and only son of James de la Fontaine, who received his own name, James. He was of delicate constitution, and he was from the earliest age very fond of books, which circumstances decided his father not to bring him up to a trade of any kind, but to make every possible effort to cultivate his taste for study, and to give him an education to fit him for one of the learned professions. He was assisted by several friends in this undertaking, but most effectually by Mr. Merlin, a sincere and worthy servant of God, a Protestant minister in Rochelle, who gave James gratuitous instruction in various branches of knowledge.

My father's inclination towards the office of the holy ministry soon evinced itself, and he did not hesitate to follow the pious impulse, though fully aware of the dangers incident to the vocation. When his education was somewhat advanced, his pious and generous friend, Mr. Merlin, further assisted him by recommending him to the Countess of Royan as a suitable tutor to a young relation of hers. In that capacity he accom-

panied the young man to the college of Saumur, and superintended his studies there, while he availed himself of the advantages, thus opened to him, of completing his own preparation for the ministry.

After leaving college, he travelled with his pupil through
various countries, and he was thus enabled to perfect himself
in several living languages. In the course of their travels
they went to London, and they remained there long enough to
allow my father to fall in love with a very interesting and accomplished young lady named Thompson. She was of good
family, spoke the French language with fluency; she played very
well upon the Spinette, and was altogether a remarkably well
educated person. My father was obliged to return to France,
but before they parted they exchanged portraits, and promised
to be constant to each other until they could meet again.

Very soon after his return home, he received a call from
the United Churches of Vaux and Royan, which met the approbation of the Synod, and by its authority he was installed
as pastor. At that time there was a good church edifice in
each of these small places, and they were united under the
charge of one minister. My father was cherished and tenderly beloved by the whole community, from his first appearance amongst them until he ended his days.

He steadily performed the duties of his sacred office for
one year, and he then requested his flock to grant him a
short leave of absence, to allow him to go to London and
fetch that dear one to whom he had plighted his troth. He
found her, as he expected, true to her promise, ready to fulfil
her engagement, and return with him to his own country.
They were married in London in the year 1628, and immediately returned to the borough of Vaux, where they took up

2

their abode in a small, and not very convenient house, which
they hired. They continued to occupy it until her death,
which took place twelve years after their marriage. They
had þeen very happy together, and were the parents of several
children, five of whom lived to mature age, and perhaps I
may as well name them here, before I proceed to the second
marriage of my father.

1. Jane married unfortunately a Mr. L'Hommeau, a man
of good property, but who turned out to be an idle, drunken
spendthrift, who wasted his substance in riotous living, and in
the end Jane was obliged to maintain herself and family by
keeping a school.

2. Judith married Mr. Guiennot, and was left a widow
with four children. She was seized during the persecution
and confined in a convent, from which she only obtained release
by making a compulsory abjuration. She was so fortunate
as to escape from France, and she and her daughters maintained themselves by needlework in London.

I would here pause, and call your attention to the uncertainty of this world's goods. You may observe, in the short
history I have already given of the fortunes of a single
family, how mutable are all worldly possessions. Who could
have foreseen, when the father of my grandfather was honored
and respected in the Court of Francis I., that three of his
children would have to beg their bread from door to door, and
be glad to learn how to support themselves by mechanical employments; and equally in my father's family; how little
could it have been anticipated, when Jane and Judith married
rich men, that they also would be obliged to work for their
living !

3. James was educated for the ministry, and became pastor

of the church at Archiac, in Saintonge. He had the infirmity of stammering when he repeated any thing that he knew by heart, so he was obliged to employ another person to repeat the Creed and the Lord's Prayer in his church; but he could preach and pray extemporaneously without any hesitation. He died before the great persecution came on, but his widow endured cruel sufferings for the faith. She was imprisoned for three years, and during part of the time she was confined in a dungeon, but at last she was liberated and banished from France. She reached London in safety with three sons, one of whom became a Protestant minister in Germany.

4. Elizabeth, married to Mr. Sautreau, minister at Saujon, in Saintonge, under whom I studied. His church was condemned, and he and his wife and children went to Dublin, where he was urged to receive Episcopal ordination, but he thought the Presbyterian Church more like that to which he had devoted himself in his own country, so he gave it the preference. He determined to take his family to America; and he, his wife and five children were wrecked, and all drowned, within sight of the harbor of Boston, their destined port. I think we may add these seven persons to the list of martyrs in our family, as they had abandoned their home and possessions for the Gospel's sake.

5. Peter, who was also brought up to the ministry, had no sooner completed his preparation than he was appointed to assist my father, as his colleogue, in the church at Vaux; where he succeeded him at his death, and remained until the demolition of the church. When it was about to be condemned, he was served with a "Lettre de Cachet," confined in the Isle of Oleron six months, and then banished from the kingdom, without the possibility of taking his two older

daughters with him, for the law forbade ministers to take out
of the country any of their children who were above twenty
years old; but, by the good providence of God, they were
able to join him afterwards in London, where, as you know,
he spent the remainder of his days, filling the office of minister
or chaplain at the Pest House, beloved and respected by all
who knew him.

His youngest daughter, Esther, became the wife of John
Arnauld, the grandson of my aunt Bouquet, a highly estima-
ble man, of whom I shall have occasion to speak again in the
course of these memoirs. His uprightness and correctness
of judgment caused him to be frequently called upon, to act
as umpire, when differences arose between any of the French
merchants in London.

6. Francis ought not to be passed over without mention,
though he died too young to leave any descendants. He was
gifted with the most astonishing memory. When only six or
seven years old he was much in my father's study, where he
heard the children and other pupils learning their lessons,
and so retentive was his memory, that from simply hearing
them repeat aloud what they were going to recite, he acquired
the whole so perfectly, that when any boy paused for a word,
he supplied the deficiency instantly; and that, not in English
lessons only, but in Latin and Greek. My father became
apprehensive that he would have a jumble of words in his
head, without any ideas attached to them, and therefore posi
tively forbade him to learn the lessons of others. The poor
child, nevertheless, continued to do it, and he excused himself,
saying, he could not help remembering that which he heard
repeated over and over again; so, at last my father thought
it best to begin to teach him Latin, in order that his memory

might be employed connectedly at any rate. He made the most rapid progress, and soon surpassed boys twice his age. In due time, he accompanied his elder brother, Peter, to college, at Saumur, and before he had been there a year, he became an object of admiration to professors and students alike. At the end of the second year, he had distinguished himself so much, that he was looked upon as a prodigy for his years, and great hopes and expectations were raised as to his future career, all of which God saw fit to disappoint by taking him to himself soon after. He was too good for this world.

My father was married to his second wife, Marie Chaillon, my mother, in the year 1641. She was from the neighborhood of Pons, in Saintonge, where her father possessed considerable property, and resided at a country place named Rue au Roy, distant about a mile and a half from the town. She was a handsome brunette, twelve years younger than her husband, to whom she brought a marriage portion of four thousand francs, which was expended, by her desire, in the purchase of the small estate of Jenouillé, and the adjacent manor of Jaffé. My father made an addition of several rooms to the house already built upon the property, so that it might comfortably accommodate a few boarders in addition to his own family; for at that time he received pupils to educate with his sons.

The issue of the second marriage was remarkably similar to the first; five children by each, two sons and three daughters, who lived to a marriageable age.

1. Susan, married Stephen Gachot, a grandson, through his mother, of that most excellent, pious, Christian minister, Mr. Merlin, of Rochelle. This circumstance was not without its influence upon my father, in gaining his consent to what

proved a miserable marriage. Gachot was drunken and dissipated, and treated my sister unkindly. He even threatened
her life with a pistol. He squandered his wife's portion, and
had mortgaged his own property, when he became known to a
man named Jeudy, a collector to the farmers of the Royal
Domain, who, perceiving him to be an acute, clever, and unscrupulous sort of man, engaged his services as a clerk or
assistant collector. They were men of one mind, knowing
how to fill their own purses. They committed acts of violence in making their collections, that made them worthy of
two halters, and it was most fortunate for Gachot, that at
the time he was beginning to tremble for fear of inquiry, a
decree was issued by the Court, which ordered all Protestants
in public employments, either to recant or resign. Gachot
was only too glad to avail himself of the opportunity to give
up his employment, and pretend to be a good Protestant.
Jeudy envied him his escape from investigation of his doings,
and wished that he too had been of a Protestant family.
After a while the dragoons came, and Gachot readily changed
his religion to retain his ill-gotten wealth. He jocularly observed, "I can accommodate myself easily to the Church of
Rome, for I do not understand Latin, and so I cannot be
scandalized by her services, which are all in that language."
He remained in France, and my poor sister with him.

2. Peter was light-complexioned, and of a very pleasing
countenance. He was first appointed minister of St. Saurin,
in Saintonge, and then removed to the church at Salles, in
Aunix. He married, unhappily for himself, a little, ugly,
haughty, jealous, worldly-minded woman of good fortune, who
ruled him. She would not tolerate in him any evidence of
affection to mother, brothers or sisters. She must be all in
all to him.

On one occasion, my mother went to St. Saurin, a distance of four leagues from our house, to visit this dearly beloved son, and she was so much fatigued and exhausted with her ride, that she went to lie down as soon as she alighted from her horse, and begged to have a little herb soup. Her own maid, whom she had taken to wait upon her, was busy preparing it for her, when her daughter-in-law went into the kitchen, in a very bad humor, vexed at her mother-in-law being there, and still more that her husband should have received his mother with evident marks of kindness and affection, and, in this mood, she took a fire-brand out of the fire, and began to stir the broth with it. The servant cried out, "Madam! what are you about? here is a spoon for you." She answered contemptuously, "It is good enough for her." This was very inconsiderately repeated to my poor mother, who was so much wounded by it, that she shortened her visit; she mounted her horse to return home next day, and never again went to the house of this dear son. Peter knew the cause of it, and he was deeply grieved; but still, his wife had become so entirely the governing power in his house, that he made no effort to correct the grievance.

Three years before the Revocation of the Edict of Nantes, he began to collect money with which he intended to leave France. He sold whatever he could, and he had raised about 15,000 francs in gold, when he thought it was time to apply for a passport. He obtained one from the king, in which his wife and two daughters were included, and they all four might easily have quitted the kingdom, but he had still some sums of money due to him, which he hoped to receive, and so he lingered on from day to day, and kept it a secret that he had procured a passport. At length the dragoons made their appear-

ance in Rochelle, and he felt it was high time to make use of
the passport; which he accordingly produced to the Intendant.
He looked at it carefully, and discovered that it was dated
six months before. He exclaimed, " Oh! oh! Sir, you can
derive no benefit from this, it is of old date. We can see
through your designs, you have not used your passport in order
to take time to collect money, to carry out of the country with
you, contrary to law. You must now either change your religion,
or I can tell you the dragoons will soon have your treasure."
He turned round, and gave immediate orders that ten or
twelve dragoons should go to my brother's house. They
went and took possession of every thing they could find, but
the gold was too carefully concealed for them to discover it.
My brother had hidden it in a barrel of wine.

During the succeeding night his wife was a greater torment than the dragoons. She left no argument untried to
persuade him to ask time for consideration on the subject of
religion, and then she told him they could find an opportunity, in all probability, to escape with their gold, before the
time allowed to consider should have expired. At any rate,
she said if he would only get the dragoons out of the house,
she would follow him where he pleased. He resisted all her
entreaties for some time, and told her he would rather beg
his bread in a foreign land, where he could worship according
to his conscience, than have the greatest wealth at home if he
were obliged to abjure his religion to gain it.

The cursed Eve gained her point by morning, and he put
forth his hand to the forbidden fruit. He went to the Intendant at an early hour, and told him he wished for time to
study the subject, and see whether he could change his re-

ligion. The dragoons were thereupon ordered from his house, and fifteen days allowed to him for consideration.

Observe, my dear children, the fatal influence of a bad wife over a too yielding husband. The first step was persuading him to withhold, from his affectionate, widowed mother, that respectful tenderness to which she was entitled The next was to induce him to temporize for the sake of gold, and finally, he was forsaken of God. He, who had been as a shining lamp in the tabernacle, preaching to others, renounced the pure faith he had taught, and signed the act of abjuration. It is always thus; the great enemy of mankind tempts us first to commit small sins, and the downward path becomes easier as we descend. Let us lay to heart the lesson taught in the fall of some members of our family, and learn from it distrust of self and dependence upon God, for the grace of his Holy Spirit, to sustain us through temptation and deliver us from evil. It is a comfort to me to know that my brother had no son; thus there is not one descendant of my father, bearing the honored name of Fontaine, who is now living in France in what I consider idolatry.

3. Mary, married Peter Forestier, a zealous minister, an able preacher and a sound theologian, of whom I shall have occasion to make honorable mention hereafter.

4. Ann, my youngest sister, the light and joy of the house, married Leon Testard Sieur des Meslars. He changed his religion, or pretended to do so, when the dragoons came, but my sister remained firm in her faith, and could not give up the hope of escaping from France, and in about two years after the abjuration it was accomplished. They landed in safety at Plymouth, but my sister's health was much impaired, and she died a few months after reaching England, well satis-

2*

fied to leave this present life and enter upon her heavenly inheritance. She was rejoiced to leave her children in a land where the gospel was preached in all its purity.

I, James, was the youngest child of my parents, but before I narrate my own life I will say something more of my father.

He was a man of fine figure, pure red and white complexion, and of very dignified deportment, commanding the respect of all with whom he came in contact. He was a remarkably abstemious man; he lived chiefly upon milk, fruits and vegetables, during the greater part of his life, but towards its close he lived more generously, in conformity with the advice of his physicians. He was never to be seen amongst his flock at feasts or entertainments, but he made it an invariable rule to pay a pastoral visit to each family twice in the year. He hastened to the sick and afflicted as soon as their sorrows were made known to him. Almost all the people were Protestants in the neighborhood where he lived, so all belonged to his church, and when it was known that he was praying with any sick person, crowds would flock to hear him, and frequently the houses could not contain those who came. He was zealous and affectionate, and employed all his gifts, his time, his knowledge and his talents, in the service of God, for the good of his people, and he was rewarded even in this life by the affectionate attachment of his flock. He was a man of unusual attainments; he had great learning, quick and ready wit, clear and sonorous voice, natural and graceful action; he always made use of the most chaste, elegant and appropriate language; and genuine humility, crowning the whole, gave an indescribable charm to his discourses, and all who heard him were delighted.

The following incident may serve as an example of his facility in preaching. On the afternon of a Communion Sunday he had just given out his text, which had been selected with reference to the services of the morning, when he perceived some Capuchins and Jesuits enter the church. He paused and addressed his own people, saying: "The text I have read to you is of a kind suitable for the edification of those who, by the grace of God, have been already well instructed in pure religion; but I see persons before me whom I believe to be still in a state of superstition and ignorance; I therefore feel it my duty, for this time, to leave the ninety and nine, and strive to bring back the lost sheep to the fold." He then turned over the leaves of his Bible, took a controversial text, upon which he gave an extempore discourse, and treated the subject with so much force and perspicuity, that the Fathers were obliged to confess, on going out, that they had never heard error (as they called it) so well defended.

The Synod thought most highly of his judgment and discretion, and on that account they usually selected him for the difficult task of reconciling differences between pastors and their flocks, when any such occurred.

He generally succeeded in healing the breach, and his eloquence frequently drew tears from the eyes of his auditors, at the same time that it softened their hearts towards each other.

He was invited to take charge of a church at Rochelle, where he was offered a salary just twice as large as that which he was receiving, but he refused decidedly. He had not the heart to abandon a flock who loved him so much.

I have mentioned that he was Pastor of the United Churches of Vaux and Royan. At the commencement of his ministry he preached in one church in the morning, and the other in the afternoon, taking each church alternately for the morning service. They were distant from one another two short miles. In course of time an Order in Council was issued, condemning the church at Royan, and it was pulled down accordingly. My father went there as usual, and persevered in holding services upon the ruins of the church.

The Governor was much enraged when he heard of it, and sent him a summons to appear before him at Brouage, to answer for the offence. My father rested his defence upon the ancient privileges and liberties accorded to the people. The Governor said he knew of no privilege or liberty that subjects could claim but such as had been granted by the king, the council, or the ancient laws. This church had been built, he said, without the king's permission, which was the fact, and therefore, as its erection had been an act of usurpation in the first instance, no one could consider its demolition now to be an arbitrary stretch of power. He added, that the distance was so short from Royan to Vaux, that it could not be considered a great hardship for his followers at the former place to walk to the latter to hear him. My father was obliged to acquiesce.

Another Order in Council was issued soon after, which forbade Protestant ministers to wear their clerical robes in the street. My father looked upon this as an indignity, and appeared abroad in his robe as he had hitherto done. The Governor summoned him to appear before him a second time to answer for this new offence.

He went, accompanied by the elders of his church, and attired in his robe. The wife of the Governor was present at the examination, and so much was she touched with the dignified eloquence of his defence, that she entreated her husband to permit him to continue wearing a garb to which he did so much honor.

The often repeated occurrence of little vexatious trifles, such as those named above, made it evident to my father that more serious persecution was at hand. He did every thing in his power, by prayer and teaching, to prepare his flock for the day of trial. His labors were blessed in no common degree, and the effects of his instruction were visible long after he had been laid in the grave. When the great persecution came on, eighteen years after his death, a most unusual proportion of the Protestant population of Vaux and Royan fled the kingdom for the sake of the truth. There were few parishes in which so small a number of persons abjured their religion under the terrors of the dragonade, and of those who were terrified into doing so with their lips, I believe there are many who still worship God in sincerity around their family altars.

My father was never seen in the transaction of worldly business of any kind. My mother attended to all such matters. She consulted with him in any case where she had doubts, but she alone appeared. She received and paid money, she gave directions to work-people and servants ; thus my father never came in contact with his flock but in the exercise of his spiritual functions, and this circumstance no doubt contributed to the respect with which all looked up to him.

His favorite recreation was gardening, and it was in coming out of his garden, in the year 1666, that he was seized with apoplexy, which proved fatal.

It is impossible to describe the affliction caused by his death to a large circle of mourning parishioners, as well as to his own immediate family. I knew not then the full extent of my personal loss; but I have since thought that I was perhaps the greatest sufferer of all, for, had it pleased God to lengthen his days, what a guide and instructor would he have been to me !

CHAPTER III.

My birth—Lameness—Imitation of my father's prayers—Meditations upon the heavenly bodies—Sent to school—Anecdotes of boyhood—Disgusted with study—Letter to sister—Mr. De la Bussiere—Admirable preceptor—College—Take degree of Master of Arts—My mother's death—Division of property.

I HAVE now arrived at the history of my own life, which I shall give more in detail, as being more immediately interesting to you than the annals of past generations. You will find a varied tissue of adventures, checkered with alternate extremes of prosperity and adversity, but amidst its joys and sorrows, you will not fail to discern the hand of Almighty God leading me by his good Providence, watching over me, and making all things work together for my good.

I was born at Jenouillé, on the 7th April, 1658. The first sorrow of my life proceeded from the carelessness of my nurse: she trusted me to her daughter's care, who was a young and giddy girl, and she played and romped with me, tossing me in the air and catching me in her arms. At last she missed her hold and let me fall on the ground, by which my leg was broken a little below the knee. The nurse lived at Royan, and being desirous to conceal the disaster from my parents, she took me of her own accord to an ignorant surgeon, near at hand, who relieved her apprehension by pronouncing that no harm had been done. He was entirely mistaken, and the bone, not having been set, reunited of itself in process of time, with considerable enlargement at the place, and making the leg shorter and weaker than the other, thus causing lameness for life.

I inherited something of the family beauty of face, and resembled my father more than any of my brothers and sisters, and I was of a very lively and inventive turn. When I was only four years old, I was so taken with hearing my father read the Scriptures and pray with the family, that I had a fancy to imitate him, and I called together the servants and my sisters, and made them kneel down while I prayed. They gave my father such an account of my proceedings, that he and my mother became curious to hear me. I would not proceed until they also knelt down with the rest. My father was much affected by the earnestness of my manner, and he thought he could discover a germ of piety and talent, which he prayed to God to nourish and strengthen so as to produce fruit in due season.

I was seven years younger than any of my brothers and sisters, and I was consequently left much to myself, and used to reflect a great deal upon all that I saw and heard ; and some of the meditations of my childhood were rather unusual, and perhaps worth relating.

You must bear in mind that all my knowledge was derived from what I could see for myself, and learn from the Holy Scriptures, which I heard my father read in the family daily. I beheld the glorious sun arise each morning, rejoicing our hearts by the light and warmth which he imparted ; and when he disappeared, the vault above our heads was enamelled with thousands of stars. I watched another beautiful luminary, which appeared to change its shape day by day ; now it was perfectly round, but each night it became less and less, and then, by the same gradual change, it increased again and returned to its first glory. I was led from these observations to meditate upon the structure of the heavens. I had heard my father read from the Scriptures, that God inhabited a light which no man could approach unto, and also that St. Paul had been caught up to the third heaven. I was satisfied that the dwelling-place of God was above the sun, the moon, and the stars, and all resplendent with the light that his glory diffused around him. I thought that the floor of the third heaven must be of a solid substance, in order to sustain the weight of the celestial court, which I understood consisted of an infinite number of angels and glorified saints. Brilliant as was the sun, I concluded that the light, he shed abroad, only came through a hole in the ceiling of the second or floor of the third heaven, giving us a faint gleam, of the glorious effulgence, which illuminated the abode of saints and angels. The stars were, according to my system, only so many small gimlet-holes in that part of the floor which was most distant from the throne of God. The moon, I supposed, was a large hole, nearly as large as the sun, but, like the stars, away from the immediate presence of God. I had no difficulty in accounting for her changes, because I could produce the same gradually varying shape, by sliding a lid over the top of a pot, and it was easy to imagine it the employment of some of the angels of God, to slide the round cover over the round hole of the moon, according as they were bidden. I thought thunder and lightning were produced by the discharge of guns and pistols in the heavens; the rain was poured through small holes by the angels, whom I concluded were very numerous, and always busily employed in obeying the commands of God. I had

but one difficulty in my system, and that was, how it was possible for the heavens to turn round, without shaking the foundations or pillars, upon which David had said that the earth
rested. But, if my reason proved unequal to the solution,
my faith made up all deficiencies; for I was confident that
every thing was easy to Him, who had made all things out of
nothing. I spent many solitary hours ruminating upon these
subjects, and when I was satisfied with the plan in my own
mind, I propounded it to my sisters and the servants, and as
they saw no difficulty, I was emboldened to submit my astro-
nomical system to my father for his opinion. He saw that I
had taken the Scriptures for my foundation, and as I was too
young to understand the true philosophy of the heavenly
bodies, he thought it best not to undeceive me.

When I was six years old, my father took me to Rochelle,
and placed me under the care of Mr. John Arnauld, who kept
a school there. He was married to a daughter of my father's
sister, my aunt Bouquet, and he lived under her roof. I
learned to read, write, and cipher during two years that I was
his pupil.

Perhaps, as the traits of boyhood prefigure the future character of the man, it may not be amiss to relate two anecdotes
of these early school-days, which indicated resolution. Mr.
Arnauld followed literally the precept of Solomon, not spoil-
ing his pupils by sparing the rod. He always administered
the chastisement in private, from motives of delicacy, because
he had girls as well as boys in the school. We boys were
talking together one day of the severity of our master, and
speculating upon the number of stripes he gave at each whip-
ping, and wishing that some one would count them. No one
else offering to do it, I volunteered to make the attempt on

the next occasion. It was not long before my delinquencies
drew upon me the usual punishment.

I cried and screamed as vociferously as ever during the
preparation for chastisement, but became suddenly silent when
he gave the first stroke, for I found it impossible to cry and
count at the same time. Mr. Arnauld was astonished, and
looked me in the face to see what was the matter; he saw
nothing wrong, so he gave a second blow with more force,
I still kept silence, counting to myself, for I was intent upon
keeping count, and at the same time concealing from him that
I was counting. His astonishment increased, and he struck
again with his full strength, which did not make me lose
count, but forced me to break silence, and cry out involunta-
rily, with a tone so much the louder for having been long suppressed: "THREE." "Ah! you rogue! you are counting, are
you? There, count, count, count;" and he struck me so rapidly, that I must acknowledge I lost the count—but something was gained by the trouble I had taken, for I am sure I
received an extra number of stripes as a reward for my
hardihood.

The other incident was similar. Mr. De la Laude, who
now lives at Port Arlington, in Ireland, was at Rochelle, in
Mr. Arnauld's school, at the same time that I was there. We
became the greatest friends, and we desired some mode of
showing it to each other. We decided, at last, that when
either of us should be taken to the room for chastisement,
the other should follow and call Mr. Arnauld names for his
cruelty, which would, of course, irritate him, and then we
should both be punished together. De la Laude was first
in fault, and no sooner had the master ordered him out, than
I ran after them, and asked Mr. Arnauld why he was going

to whip my friend? what had he done? &c.   The object was
fully accomplished; and after we had both been well whipped,
we fell on each other's neck and embraced, being too full of
joy at having proved the sincerity of our friendship, to mind
the bodily pain.   The time appeared long until the occasion
came round when I could know that my friend would do for
me as I had done for him, but it came at last, and I had the
inexpressible satisfaction of finding that he was sincere, for
he too drew upon himself the anger of our master, by reprov-
ing him for punishing me.

Mr. Arnauld tried to discover what had prompted such
conduct, but we would not have disclosed it for the world.
Some of our schoolfellows, however, let out the secret.   He
tried various expedients to conquer our resolution, but in
vain.   At one time he punished the innocent and allowed the
guilty to go free.   This pleased us mightily, for we were able
to testify our affection by sparing each other from the rod.
At last, his mother-in-law, my aunt Bouquet, persuaded him
to adopt the following plan.   His habit was to keep a record
of the faults of each pupil, and to administer the rod when a
certain number had been committed.   So when one of us
two had reached the limit, his punishment was delayed until
the other had filled up his measure, and then both were whipped at the same time.   This plan worked well, and made us
circumspect, to spare each other.

My mother sent for me from Rochelle, soon after the
death of my father, when I was eight years old.   My dear
young friend De la Laude accompanied me.   We went by sea
to La Tremblade, and spent the night there at the house of
an old woman who had been a servant in my father's family
many years.   She made us very welcome, regaled us with the

best she had, and carried her mistaken kindness so far as to give each of us a goblet of wine. This made us too merry for sleep, and we danced and sang through the night.

My mother only kept me at home two weeks, and then sent me to Mr. Forestier, who had recently married my sister Mary. He was minister of the Church of St. Mesme in Anguomois. I commenced Latin under his tuition, but whether I was wilful, or he negligent, I am unable to say. It is certain, however, that I made very little progress during five years that he was my preceptor.

While I was with him, two sons of the Marquis de Siré were sent to the school, who infected us with a shocking eruptive disease. The drugs and the science of the apothecary were alike exhausted, in vain attempts to cure us. My sister was in despair about it, when a journeyman tailor, at work in the house by the day, told her he could cure the disease. She allowed him to try his skill upon me first. He bought three or four pennyworth of quicksilver, rubbed it smoothly and perfectly into hog's lard, and with this preparation I was anointed from head to foot, before a good fire. The application was thrice repeated, and my skin became as clear and pure as ever. The apothecary had much to say upon the danger of this remedy, and so frightened my sister, that she did not venture to use it for the other boys. Not long afterwards, I was taken very ill with a violent fever, which lasted several weeks, and finally turned to inflammation of the brain. The Doctor attributed the illness entirely to the effect produced by the ointment, that had driven in the eruption. My life was despaired of, and my sister sent an express to inform my mother of my condition. She came off immediately, and so hopelessly had my case been represented to her, that she brought every thing necessary for my burial. God mercifully inclined his ear to her prayers for my life, and raised me from my sick bed, but I had returns of fever from time to time for many months.

I am particular in relating the foregoing, in order to act as a warning to you, in the careful use of remedies for the diseases of your children, and by no means to trust to the prescriptions of presumptuous quacks.

The Church at St. Mesme did not pay Mr. Forestier's salary with punctuality; consequently, the Synod punished them by removing him to Arvêrt. In less than a year the arrears were collected, and the Synod restored Mr. Forestier to them.

I returned home at fourteen years of age, and, after six years of study under Mr. Forestier, I scarcely knew the regular declensions of nouns.

I was thought entirely too wild to be trusted with any but my relations for preceptors, so my mother now tried another brother-in-law for me, Mr. Sautreau, minister at Saujon in Saintonge, the husband of my sister Elizabeth, who was my godmother.

Mr Sautreau had very few pupils, he was extremely severe, he required all lessons to be repeated with the strictest verbal accuracy, but took no pains to explain the meaning of any thing. He inflicted corporal punishment for very slight errors. I was weary of being beaten like a slave, ashamed of my ignorance, and disgusted with study, when I formed an intimacy with a youth who was apprenticed to a druggist, and whose comparatively happy situation I envied. He used to give me a few sweetmeats, and made me long for the abundant supply of such things that he possessed. I thought I would write to my mother and ask her to change my destination, for I saw plainly that I was wasting my youth and exhausting her purse without any advantage. But how could I venture to broach such a subject? I had been devoted to the holy ministry from my birth. My father had been a minister, my three brothers, two brothers-in-law, two maternal uncles, were all ministers of the Gospel. My mother had placed me for tuition with ministers, whom she hoped would lead me in the way she desired. After all this, to tell her that I wanted to be a shop-boy, I dare not do it, I should be afraid of breaking her heart. After much deliberation I determined to write to my sister Anne, and make her my confidante. I first pointed out to her my own miserable deficiencies; I had studied so many years and made so little progress, that I had lost all hope of doing better in future. I told her I had the greatest possible reverence for the ministerial office, I looked up to it as the most honorable of all employments; but then, if it was an undertaking beyond my strength, if I had not the requisite gifts, I ought not to enter upon it; and therefore it would certainly be the best to waste no more time and money in preparing for it. After having, as I thought, made my incapacity appear very plain, I proceeded to open my mind to her upon the plan I had formed for my future career. I then begged her to keep my letter a profound secret, but on some favorable occasion to tell my mother, as it were, of her own accord, how poorly qualified I appeared to be for the important and noble vocation of a minister of the Gospel; and to suggest the expediency of letting me leave off study, and try whether I should not do better at some more common employment. After all this preparation, I disclosed my wish to be placed as an apprentice in a druggist's shop.

Notwithstanding all my precaution, my sister Anne did not keep my secret, she thought it was her duty to make known the communication I had made. Great was the consternation produced by it, and a family council was summoned to deliberate. Peter the elder, and Peter the younger, were both sent for by my mother, and she told them she thought my brother-in-law, Mr. Sautreau, was tired of me, and had dictated this letter in order to get rid of me. The two Peters were of a different opinion, they discovered a fire and vivacity in the style altogether foreign to that of my brother-in-law; they therefore decided that the letter was mine, and mine alone, and it was the unanimous opinion that my mother ought to keep me at study. I had defeated my object by the pains I had taken to accomplish it, for they said that the ingenuity of my arguments to prove incapacity established incontestably the fact that inclination alone, not talent, was wanting.

My mother was so deeply grieved that she fell sick upon it. She sent my brothers with her answer to me, which was to the effect, that if I gave up studying for the ministry, she would give up me. I should experience a change for the worse in every way, they told me; my handsome clothing should be changed for coarse garments, and I should be sent to a school kept by one Perrinet, who was notorious for his mode of imparting instruction by free administration of stripes and frequent fasts; and if I still refused to study I should be sent to sea, and she would see me no more.

I decided to remain at my studies, but I tried hard to gain a change of masters at the least, through the intercession of my brothers. But the answer was, "Stay where you are, or go to Perrinet."

A short time after this ineffectual struggle for liberty, Mr. Sautreau beat me unmercifully, and I felt so dreadfully outraged by it, that I quitted his house next morning, at break of day, and lame as I was, I ran home, a distance of fully six miles. I hoped to soften my mother, but she was immovable; she would not suffer me even to kiss her, but told me to go straight back; she offered me only the old alternative, of going to Perrinet, if I refused. She said she would not allow me to sleep in her house. I had set off from Saujon without having breakfasted, and the only refreshment furnished by my mother was dry bread.

You may imagine, better than I can describe, the feelings with which I commenced my walk back again; but my mother *must* be obeyed, and I can truly say, that the mortification I experienced from her cold reception, was much more painful than the blows or the taunts of Mr. Sautreau.

When I had completed three years at Saujon, my mother heard so much of the great skill of a Mr. De la Bussiere, at Marennes, in imparting learning, that she, most happily for me, determined upon trying what he could do with me, whether he could draw forth the talent, which the family council had decided, that I possessed.

Mr. De la Bussiere was a very eccentric man, a Protestant layman. He was an excellent Greek and Latin scholar; he wrote pretty poetry, and he was withal a good physician. He was as obstinate as a mule; he drank to excess, but did not commence his potations until the labors of the day were ended. He had ten or twelve pupils, but no boarders, for he and his wife had only one small room, which served as kitchen,

3

bedchamber and study; and a little closet or store-room,
which contained only a few plates and dishes. His dress was
a threadbare cloak, once black, now of a reddish brown, and
always covered with dust. He never used a razor, but when
his beard became inconveniently long, he cut it off with a
pair of scissors. Their slovenly apartment did not contain
such a thing as a looking-glass. In short, he was, what is
called in England, "a mere scholar;" he had learning, and
nothing else.

I had hitherto learned from the Port Royal Grammar,
which Mr. De la Bussiere held in perfect abhorrence. He
esteemed the masters who taught with it, and the pupils who
learned from it, as ignoramuses alike. The result of my nine
years' labor was, that I knew the whole of this grammar by
heart. I began then at the age of seventeen "*omne viro
soli*," a fine prospect. His plan was altogether different
from my former teachers; he explained every rule thoroughly
to me, and required me to find twenty examples in some
author. His explanations and exercises soon brought into
play the stores that memory had laid up; I was astonished
to find that I had accumulated such a mass of materials without being able to make use of them until now.

We had no holiday but Sunday. Every Monday morning,
Mr. De la Bussiere expected to receive from his pupils a full
account of the sermon they had heard on the preceding day.

I made rapid progress. In the second year I translated
Du Moulin's French Logic into Latin, and thus became familiar with the terms in Latin. At the end of three years we
parted, and I was well satisfied with what I had acquired.
Mr. De la Bussiere knew human nature well, and he had the
faculty of inciting his pupils to the utmost exertion, and

guiding them as he pleased. A single word of reproof, from him, affected me more than the severe punishments of my former preceptors.

My next step was to the college of Guienne, which was supported by the king, and much resorted to by Protestants.

A great mortification awaited me there; Latin was the only language made use of, and though I was familiar with the best Latin authors, I could not speak it, and found myself unable to follow the lecturers. I did not allow this to discourage me; I was still given to building castles in the air, as in my childhood; in order to make Latin more familiar I resolved to meditate in that language; I forbade my thoughts to clothe themselves in my mother tongue, and thus I succeeded well, and was soon able to reflect upon what I read in Latin, and I could express myself with ease. I also hired a private tutor to assist me in the hours of relaxation, and by these means I could keep pace with the professor. I may say, with truth, that during the two years I remained at college, I spent sixteen hours out of every twenty-four in study.

Fourteen students took the degree of Master of Arts at the same time; I was the second on the list. At the age of twenty-two, I found that five years of hard study had compensated, in some degree, for the previous nine years of negligence.

I am under great obligations to Mr. De la Bussiere for making me what I am, and therefore I feel it is his due to perpetuate the remembrance of his talents amongst my descendants, which I can perhaps do in the best manner by relating something that occurred while I was at college.

His wife died, and he removed to Bourdeaux during my second year there. He was unchanged in his appearance; he

was as slovenly as ever, and was clad in the same threadbare
cloak, and the same little collar.

During the professor's lecture, it was customary for
strangers to occupy a bench, appropriated for their use; and
for one half hour, from half-past eleven to twelve o'clock,
they might argue, if they pleased, upon àny subject connected
with the thesis of the day. One of the students was always
expected to speak in reply to the stranger. A day seldom
passed without some priest, monk, or Jesuit, taking a seat on
the bench.

One morning an Abbé took his seat, who was dressed
with the utmost elegance; Mr. De la Bussiere followed close
after him. The students began to exchange glances and crack
jokes upon the slovenly appearance of the latter, and they
continued to do so, even after the professor had made them a
signal to stop their ill-timed mirth.

I spoke in a whisper to those near me. "Restrain your
laughter," said I, "until you have heard him."

Mr. L'Abbé had prepared himself with three or four arguments in opposition to one of our theses. He gave them out,
and he was answered, in the usual way, by a student. He
then bowed most politely to the professor, and with much
courtesy complimented both him and the students on their
skilful solutions, and he resumed his seat.

Mr. De la Bussiere's turn had now come. He began in
Latin, with a complimentary address to the professor; he then
turned round and said, "Mr. L'Abbé, you have expressed
yourself satisfied with the answers you have received; I am of
opinion that you yielded too soon, for your argument admits
of being carried much further." He then took up the subject
where the Abbé had left it, and handled it in so masterly a

style, that the students were unable to say a word in reply, and the professor was obliged to rise in support of his own thesis. He also actually became cornered, and knew not how to defend his own position, when to his infinite relief the clock struck twelve, which put an end to the discussion.

My mother's death, at the age of sixty-three, took place about the time that I had completed my college course and taken my degree. After she became a widow, she devoted herself with the greatest assiduity to her children, doing all that lay in her power both for their temporal and eternal welfare. She was tender and affectionate to them, but at the same time rigid in requiring from them a strict fulfilment of their duties.

You must know, that in France, a man is considered a minor until he is twenty-five years old. I was therefore, according to law, still in my minority, but my brothers did not want to be troubled with looking after my property ; they therefore made me of age, or free, soon after the death of my mother. My brothers and sisters were all married, and they had long ago received the principal part of their portions, so it did not require very long to come to an amicable arrangement in the division of what was left. I paid to them severally the small sums to which they were entitled, and then I remained sole proprietor of the estates of Jenouillé and Jaffé, by which I possessed, not only a good comfortable dwelling-house for my residence, but an annual income of about 1000 francs.

CHAPTER IV.

HAVING made all necessary arrangements for the management of my property, I went once more to the house of my brother-in-law, Mr. Forestier, at St. Mesme in Anguomois. I knew that I should find in him an able and willing friend, to help me in the prosecution of my theological studies. My sole wish now was to dedicate all the talents, God had bestowed on me, to his glory.

I spent a year with Mr. Forestier, during which time he took great pains with me. He taught me to prepare sermons, and showed me how far it was desirable to use Commentaries for such purposes. When he thought me qualified, he allowed me to preach sometimes in his church.

While I was with him, a complaint was lodged against him that he had received a Papist into the communion of the Protestant Church, contrary to the king's edict. Upon this accusation, he was seized and carried to prison with much degradation: he was placed on horseback, with his legs tied together under the horse's belly.

If you had but seen the Papists of Angoulême collected

úpon the road to enjoy the spectacle! They were in such numbers that I may say they were literally piled up by the way-side; and they were uttering the most horrible maledictions and imprecations, and throwing stones at those who accompanied him to the prison-door. I say, if you had seen them, you would have concluded the prisoner could have been guilty of no less a crime than murdering his father, committing violence on his mother, or attempting the life of the king.

Oh! my God! to what a horrid pitch of barbarity can mankind be borne by the blind zeal of superstition and idolatry.

Through her many severe trials my sister was always resigned to the will of her Heavenly Father, who, she felt assured, ordered all things for the best.

Mr. Forestier had a tedious imprisonment, which was attended with great loss and inconvenience to him, because it obliged him to give up his school. At length he appealed to the Parliament* of Paris, and obtained an acquittal.

The church of St. Mesme soon shared the fate of others, and was condemned. The Synod then removed him to Coses. in Saintonge; and though it is rather anticipating events, I think I had better proceed with his history, before returning to the memoirs of my own life.

The church at Coses had its turn, and was condemned before long. The Papists in the neighborhood had not patience to wait for the day appointed for its demolition, but desired

---

* There were ten Parliaments in the kingdom of France. They were superior courts of judicature, to which appeal was made from the decision of inferior tribunals. They had no legislative functions but that of registering and publishing the Royal Decrees, to which they very rarely raised any objection.

to put a stop to the religious exercises at once. To accomplish this end, they made some frivolous complaint of Protestants who had recanted, having been seen there, and procured a warrant to arrest Mr. Forestier upon this charge. The plot became known by accident to Colonel Boisron, who was at Saintes, and he set off immediately, and rode all night, in the hope of arriving before the Archers, and giving him notice in time to conceal himself.

He reached Coses on Sunday morning, just as Mr. Forestier was going to church. He instantly made known his errand, and begged him not to make his appearance in the church.

Mr. Forestier said : " Can we change the decrees of the Eternal God? No! I hold myself in readiness, therefore, to do my duty, and submit to whatever he thinks fit to bring upon me."

Colonel Boisron still urged him. " Only think, my dear friend," said he, " of the suffering you would bring upon your wife and children, if you should be taken from them."

My sister then came forward, and the Colonel asked her to use her influence to dissuade her husband from showing himself, where he would inevitably be seized by the Archers. With a composed and firm tone she said, " It is the duty of Mr. Forestier to preach to his flock, and it is for God to do as seemeth him good."

Mr. Forestier turned round in triumph, and said to his friend, " You see, sir, we have no Eve here."

He then went forward, with his family around him, to the church. He gave no sign of emotion, he preached with his accustomed energy, and had just concluded the service, and was descending from the pulpit, when the Archers entered, laid hold of him, and carried him off to Saintes. He was confined in the prison at that place for a time, and then he was transferred to La Reolle, where the Parliament of Bourdeaux held its sittings. He was a truly faithful servant of God, and was by him most mercifully preserved through many dangers, and at last brought in safety to England, with his wife and younger children. My sister was near her confinement, and gave birth to a daughter on board the vessel. It is difficult which to admire most, the husband or the wife; the faith of both shone so triumphantly on these trying occasions. I can assure you that my sister's firmness was the result of principle, and did not proceed, as those who were not well acquainted with her, might have supposed, from deficiency of sensibility. She had very warm feelings, strong affections, and great love for her husband and children, but her love to God was even stronger; and when his glory was in question, she held nothing dear in comparison.

Happy couple! their treasure was laid up in heaven, and they could well afford to despise this present life, and its short-lived enjoyments.

I now resume my own history. Soon after the imprisonment of Mr. Forestier, I went to reside at Saintes, in order to avail myself of the assistance of two able and pious ministers, who were settled there, in completing my preparation for the ministry. It is but a repetition of the same story. These two good men, Mr. Mainard and Mr. Borillak were shortly cast into prison likewise, and I returned to my lonely home.

I was not idle there, as you will presently see. My brother Peter had succeeded my father at Vaux, and continued there until about this time, when he was seized, under a "lettre de cachet," and confined in the castle of Oleron.

The church at Vaux was levelled with the ground; most of
the Protestant places of worship in our province had shared
the same fate. My neighbors could not get to any church
without difficulty and extreme fatigue, and I felt compassion
for them, as sheep without a shepherd, and considered it my
duty to invite them to join me in my family devotions. They
came most gladly, and the number increased until it reached
one hundred and fifty. I then recommended them not to
come daily, as they were in the habit of doing, but to come
two or three times a week, which would give me more time to
make suitable preparation for preaching and expounding the
Scriptures to them. I also suggested to them that each
family should only come once a week, and thus our meetings,
being less numerous, would be less likely to attract attention,
and yet each would have their turn. I frequently changed
our days of assembling, giving previous notice to the people,
with the view of escaping observation, and we continued this
endearing intercourse without interruption, during the whole
winter. All who joined in these religious exercises were
known to me and to each other, and we were all equally interested in keeping the secret. My house stood entirely alone,
which was a circumstance much in our favor.

At length, however, a rumor got abroad that meetings
were held in our parish, and that I was the preacher. We
had no traitor in our ranks, and all things were conducted so
quietly that the Papists were unable to discover any thing,
with sufficient certainty, to found action upon it. Some of
my friends, with more of policy than of piety, recommended
me to cease before we were discovered, but I believed I was
in the path of duty, and therefore I did not hearken to their
counsel, but persevered in leading the services.

Our holy meetings continued without molestation or drawback of any sort till Palm Sunday, 1684. Being only a candidate, and not a regularly authorized minister, I judged it best to advise my people to go to some of the few remaining churches, in order to receive the Communion with their brethren. I wished to partake of that holy sacrament myself, and for the purpose I went to the other side of the province, and tarried with friends there, with whom I received the Communion, both on Palm Sunday and Easter Sunday, and remained until ten or twelve days after Easter.

On Palm Sunday, some of the neighbors came to my house as usual, and finding that I was not there, they retired to a wood behind the house for religious worship, and one of their number, a mason by trade, who could read very well, officiated as pastor. He read several chapters from the Bible, the prayers of the Church, and a sermon; and some psalms were sung. This meeting having taken place openly, the report of it was noised abroad, and on Holy Thursday from seven to eight hundred assembled on the same spot, the mason again the pastor. On Easter Sunday the number increased to a thousand.

In the neighborhood there lived a miserable pettifogging attorney, named Agoust, a base deceitful man, who had been a Protestant, but had abjured his religion to retain his employment. His house was within four hundred paces of the high road, by which many persons returned from the meeting, and he seated himself at his window to watch the passers-by, hoping to be able to give information by which he might ingratiate himself with those in power. The services had continued until after dusk, therefore it was too dark to recognize individuals at that distance; nevertheless, he made

out a list of sixty persons, and amongst the names were some
who had, and others who had not, been there, and at the
head he placed Mr. Mouillère and myself. He could form
a very good idea from the general character of his neighbors,
of those who would be likely to attend such a meeting, and
that was about as much as he really did know. On the de-
position of this single witness—a man of indifferent character at best—before the Seneschal of Saintes, warrants were
issued against us.

Two or three days before my return home, the Grand Provost and his Archers were sent in search of us. The country
people had had timely notice of their approach, and had concealed themselves so effectually in the woods that after scouring the country in all directions, the Archers returned with
but one prisoner. They found the mason who had officiated,
and no one else. They seized him, fastened him securely to
the tail of a horse, and thus dragged him all the way to
Saintes, a distance of fifteen miles. They took great delight
in frightening him by the way, telling him all that would be
done to him for his crime. The least he could expect would
be to be hanged as soon as they reached the town.

It was late when they arrived, and they said that nothing
but the lateness of the hour saved him from execution that
night, which fortunately left him a solitary chance for life.
"If," said one of the Archers, "you recant without delay, you
may yet escape, but once get within the prison wall, and a
hundred religions will not save you from death. All that is
asked of you is to renounce the errors of Calvin, and do not
you see how easily you can do that, without wounding your
conscience, be it ever so tender? You only swear to renounce
errors: if Calvin had none, you renounce nothing, it is a

mere ceremony, and if he had errors you would not surely object to renouncing them." Those who surrounded him saw that the specious arguments made an impression, and they followed it up with others based upon his duty to his wife and children, who would be left destitute if he was taken from them. The poor fellow was overpowered by their crafty reasoning, he had no one near to strengthen his weakness, and it is not to be wondered at that he should at last have yielded to the tempter, abjured the errors of Calvin, and obtained life and liberty as the reward. The wakeful monitor, conscience, had slumbered for a short space, but she soon awakened and resumed her power most fearfully. After the recantation, the mason became a prey to the most frightful remorse; he was so wretched that he could not rest or sleep by night or day.

As soon as he heard of my return home, he hastened to me, threw himself at my feet, wept like a child, and declared that he had damned his soul by his weakness. He then related all the circumstances to me; he said it would be impossible to describe to me the torments he had endured, and that he could not pray for himself, but he implored me to pray for him. He looked upon his crime with such utter abhorrence, and was plunged into such depths of despair, that I clearly perceived it was my duty rather to comfort than reprove the sinner. I endeavored to convince him that the mercy of God was open to him, and I urged him to go at once to the Fountain for sin and uncleanness. I drew a parallel between his case and that of St. Peter, from which I thought he might draw consolation, as he had imitated the apostle in his bitter tears of repentance as well as in his fall.

He abjured once more, and this time it was the abjuring

of his abjuration. His penitence was so sincere, that he felt no humiliation too great, and he asked forgiveness of every one he met for the scandal he had brought upon their holy religion. God brought good out of evil on this occasion, for he made the remorse of this unhappy man the means of strengthening the faith of many others, who saw, by his melancholy example, that man, with all his cruelty, can inflict no such torture as God causes to the consciousness of those, who deny him before men.

I was deeply grieved that I had not been upon the spot when this poor man was taken up, for I thought I might have accompanied him and prevented his recantation; and it determined me to do what I could to confirm the faith of the other members of my flock. I was told that there was a warrant out for my apprehension, so I rode over to Saintes to inquire into the truth of the report, and I determined to give myself up to the authorities, if it should be required.

I called upon the Lieutenant-General or Seneschal of the Presidency of Saintes to ascertain the fact, and he was malicious enough to deny that there was any such warrant out, though he was himself the very person who had issued it. He wished me to return home in ignorance of the truth, for the purpose of inflicting upon me the ignominy and mortification, that he supposed would be the result of making me a public spectacle, dragged to prison by the Grand Provost and his Archers. I had a shrewd suspicion that it was so, and therefore went home with the determination to make the most of my time for the benefit of my poor neighbors. During the week I visited from house to house, prayed, and exhorted to the best of my ability.

At length I was informed that the Provost and his Archers

were on the road to our village, and that they were spending the night at Saujon, within two leagues of my house. I sent messengers to warn the people in the surrounding villages, in order that they might hide themselves in the woods. For my own part, my resolution was formed, not to shrink from the threatened danger, be it what it might, but rather to walk boldly forward to justify that which I had done in the fear of God. Some of my friends came to give me notice of the approach of the Archers, and at the same time to offer me their houses as an asylum until the storm had passed over, but I declined their kind offers. I said to them, "It was I who induced the poor people to jeopard their lives for our holy religion. I invited them to my house to join in religious worship, and having acted as their leader when no danger threatened, ought I not to continue at their head in the hour of peril? If I were now to flee, I should consider myself like the shepherd, who is described in the Gospel as an hireling, who fled at the sight of the wolf. Example, my friends, is more powerful than precept. I am determined to share the risks of my poor neighbors, for if I were absent from them, and they abjured their faith for want of the countenance and support that I, as their leader, could give them, I should for ever feel that the sin rested upon my shoulder."

Seeing me so determined, my friends ceased to urge me to go with them, and when they left me I set to work to prepare for the morrow. I gave full directions to my servants for their conduct during my absence. I prepared a bundle of clothing and other necessaries to take with me to the prison, and then before retiring to rest, I knelt down and prayed earnestly to God to give me grace and strength to support and guide me in the step I was taking, and in which

I believed I had a single eye to his glory. My mind became so perfectly composed after this, that I went to bed
and fell asleep almost immediately, and I slept so soundly
that I did not waken until I heard the sound of the Provost
and Archers knocking at the door for admittance. The day
was just breaking when I opened my eyes, and being yet only
half awake, I trembled from head to foot, and felt a vague
sort of alarm at I knew not what, and the thought actually
crossed my mind that I would defend myself with the firearms which I had in my room.

Presently I collected my scattered senses, and knew what
the noise meant, and then I called to mind the thoughts with
which I had retired the night before, and I again implored
the aid of my heavenly Father, which was granted me on the
instant, for I felt tranquillized almost immediately. I was
displeased to hear my servants telling the Archers that I was
not in the house, and I opened the window, and put my head
out to tell them that I should soon be ready for them, having
made my preparations over night. Upon this they retreated
a little, being afraid that I was going to fire upon them, and
I heard the Provost give orders to his Archers to be upon
their guard. I told him he need not fear the weapons I had
for my defence; I relied upon my innocence for protection, and
I hoped to conquer by my constancy. I begged him to wait
patiently a few minutes and I would accompany him. As
soon as I had dressed myself I opened the door to him, and
showed him my little bundle which I had prepared the night
before.

The Provost proceeded to perform what he considered to
be his duty, and he gave me an exhortation, to the effect that I
ought to obey the orders of the king, and make a prompt recan-

tation. He then gave me in charge of two of his Archers, and he went with the rest to look for the other persons, against whom he held warrants. They scoured the country in all directions without finding any of my accomplices in prayer. They seized upon a poor ploughman, whose zeal had never been warm enough to carry him to any illegal assembly, and he felt both pained and embarrassed to be suffering persecution without the consolation of having deserved it. He was tied to the tail of a horse, and sent forward to the place of rendezvous, with an Archer for his guard, who was one of that tribe of booted missionaries who strove to make converts to his religion by oaths, threats and cruelties. He frightened his poor ignorant prisoner exceedingly, who, when he saw me, cried out : " Alas ! sir, are you also in the power of these cruel men ?"

To which I replied, " I feel it an honor to be esteemed worthy of suffering in such a cause."

Hearing that no more prisoners were likely to be brought in, we were ordered to proceed on our way. I had gained some favor with the Archers who had me in charge, by giving them money, and I was thus able to persuade them to indulge my companion, by lengthening his rope sufficiently for him to walk abreast with my horse. They also showed me personal consideration, for, as we were approaching the capital, they told me that they had received positive orders to tie my legs together under the horse, but that they would dispense with it, if I would let my cloak drop low enough to conceal my feet entirely.

We entered the town of Saintes at five o'clock in the afternoon of a day, near the end of April, 1684. We drew around us a crowd composed of two very different classes ; the one clapped their hands, jumped for joy, and cried out in loud tones, "Hang them! hang them!" The others felt for us deeply, they stood aloof and wept.

My companion was greatly alarmed; I tried to impart comfort by speaking kindly, and taking his hand and pressing it affectionately, which seemed to give him courage, but it made the papists very angry, for when they noticed it they redoubled their threats. We were taken straight to the prison, where many of the principal Protestants came that very evening to show their compassionate interest. They were without any minister at the time, both of theirs being in confinement at La Reolle.

I told the good people they would probably soon have an opportunity of showing the strength of their sympathy by action, but, in the mean time, I felt grateful for their kind words. I then told them that I felt assured it would not be long before my poor neighbors would be my companions in prison, and then I should look to them for contributions towards their support. After they had left me, I made a bargain with the jailer to pay him so much a day for a bed for myself, and for the use of his private apartment.

I could easily have avoided imprisonment, by flight, but I had resolved to stand my ground, for the benefit of the poor people to whom I had ministered. I thought that by sharing their confinement I might be able to prevent those who should be hereafter brought to prison from changing their religion. I determined, without loss of time, and before suspicion of my object could be aroused, to make the only arrangement by which I could hope to be useful to them, and *that* was, to obtain permission to pray aloud night and morning in the prison, an undertaking which hitherto, so far as I knew, no minister had dared to attempt.

After supper I entered into conversation with the jailer,
and told him that there was one thing I wished to mention to
him, namely, that it was my habit to pray aloud to God, night
and morning, and that it had become so necessary to me that
I had no peace of mind, if I were debarred from it, and he
would find me in such a case a most morose, unhappy, disagreeable inmate; but if I were allowed to follow my usual
practice he would find me a cheerful companion, and one who
would give him no trouble. I said to him that I wished to
show him all possible respect, and had not the least idea of
annoying him by praying in our joint apartment; therefore, if
he saw no objection to it, I would select as my altar the corner
of the common prison, behind the door that led to our room.

He was disposed to be facetious, and said, I should find
him, like the devil, not quite so black as he had been painted,
but that all my holy water would not make him drop the keys
out of his hand.

"Very well," said I, "I am glad to find that we agree so
well; you may retain possession of the key of the prison, and
I will endeavor to obtain that of eternal happiness."

I went directly to the corner I had named, knelt down and
began to pray aloud; I did not call any one to join me, but as
l had expected, my companion threw himself on his knees at
my side, and a poor Protestant who was imprisoned for debt
was glad to avail himself of the privilege and knelt also. My
prayer was chiefly composed of thanksgiving to Almighty
God, that amongst his many faithful followers, he had been
pleased to select me to suffer persecution for the truth of his
Gospel, and I implored his grace to enable me to do my duty
in this new sphere. I did not forget to make mention of the
choice of Moses, rather to suffer persecution with the people

of God than to sit upon the throne of Pharaoh. I also named, as an example, the zealous protestations of St. Paul, that neither death nor life, nor principalities nor powers, should be able to separate him from the love of God, which is in Christ Jesus our Lord. I also prayed for the king, that it might please God, in whose hand is the heart of the king, as the rivers of water, that he turneth it whithersoever he will, to incline his heart to examine for himself the pure faith against which he had issued so many edicts, and that he might be turned from its persecutor into its nurse and father.

I went on the following morning to pray aloud in the same corner, and continued regularly night and morning, by which means the poor ploughman became confirmed in his faith, and felt bold enough to disregard alike the promises and threats of the papists. The jailer and his wife had been accustomed to have haughty, turbulent spirits to deal with, and mine was so different, that they could only suppose I was disordered in my intellects, when they found that I considered it a privilege to be imprisoned.

CHAPTER V.

WHEN I had been in prison about ten days, the Provost and his Archers set out upon another circuit to look for those who had been at our meetings, and as I had foreseen, the country people would no longer flee. They had received timely warning, and the timid retreated to the woods, but the Provost was met by more than one hundred and fifty persons, who accosted him with the utmost intrepidity, saying: "We have all attended these holy meetings and prayed to God in the woods, and we are ready to justify our conduct."

The number who presented themselves was much greater than those against whom he held warrants, so he was obliged to make an examination, and he drew off to one side all those whose names did not appear upon his list. After this rejection, the number left was still too large to take to prisons already well filled with papists who had been committed for real crimes, so the Provost declared he would take only twenty. A holy strife then arose amongst these followers of the Lord as to who should be of the number.

The Archers were themselves struck at the scene they beheld. "What are you about?" said they. "Do you set no value upon life? What fury urges you to the gallows? Think for a moment of your wives and children! What will become of them?" They tried every expedient to intimidate them, and swore to them, by all that was sacred, that if once they were taken to prison they would only exchange it for the rack, the gibbet, or, at any rate, the galleys. They adduced numerous instances of such and such persons, who, for similar offences, had been hanged, broken on the wheel, &c., &c. It was all of no use, their words seemed to act like wind upon fire ; the more furious and violent were the Archers the more was the zeal of the people kindled.

At length, by a refinement of cruelty, the Provost determined to leave behind those who were most anxious to go, and he selected those to take with him who appeared the least eager. They were bound together two and two, as dogs are coupled for hunting, and tied to the tails of the horses. These poor countrymen betrayed not the least fear, they bade adieu to their wives and children with dry eyes. The wives also did their part to sustain their husbands, and they saw them led away without a murmur ; they had put their hands to the plough, and did not look back ; they placed full trust in Him, who has promised to be a husband to the widow and a father to the fatherless.

It was known in Saintes, where the Provost and Archers had gone, so the good Protestants were ready to minister to the temporal necessities of the prisoners who might be brought, and it was certainly not more than half an hour after their arrival at the prison, when ten beds with bedding complete were sent to them, and an abundant supper likewise. It deserves to be recorded that, to the honor of the Pro-

testants of Saintes, they continued to furnish the same
liberal supply during the whole time that the poor people
were imprisoned. Manna was not more abundant in the wil-
derness than food in the prison.

The beds were ranged along one side of the large common
room, apart from the papists. In the evening, when I went
to prayer as usual, they all knelt around me, and God, who
has promised a favorable answer to the prayer of faith,
answered ours by pouring into our hearts a holy joy and
peace which cannot be described. Those only can understand it who have tasted for themselves.

I soon found the advantage of the plan of praying aloud
which I had adopted; for when attempts would be made to
undermine the simple faith of these poor people, and they
would be puzzled with doctrinal arguments they were unable
to answer, they would speak amongst themselves of their
difficulties, and as I walked up and down the large room, I
listened to what they were saying, and when the hour for
prayer arrived, I availed myself of what I had overheard,
and I used to frame a petition in such a way as to furnish
them with an answer. I would pray that if the enemies of
the Lord should ask me such and such questions, and make
use of such and such arguments, I might receive the promised
aid of the Holy Spirit, and be ready to answer in such and
such a manner for the faith that was in me. I thus contrived to baffle all the arts of the Bishop's Chaplain, and to
prepare the people for his daily visits to them.

The Bishop himself and many other papists came to see
them, and were unceasing in their efforts to make some of
them fall, but thanks be to God, it was all in vain. This
went on for about three weeks, and then they began to think

they had discovered the secret of our strength, so they determined to remove me, and they hoped that when the poor countrymen were left to themselves, they might work upon their fears as successfully as they had done upon the mason. I had foreseen this step, and taken precautions accordingly. I showed them that prayer had proved the invincible armor of our faith, and I therefore recommended them, if I should be taken from them, to continue praying aloud, one for the rest; and if he-also should be removed, to let another take his place, and continue it so long as even two should be left together. For their farther encouragement, I told them that I did not think it at all improbable that by following this plan, we might all be placed in the same room again.

The King's Solicitor had made out an indictment for the offences of which I had been guilty in the prison; it contained three distinct charges :—

1st. I had taught in the prison, and thus I had prevented my companions changing their religion.

2d. I had given offence to the Roman Catholics who were in prison.

3d. I had interrupted the priest in his celebration of divine worship.

I have neglected to name that there was a small chapel attached to the prison, where the priest said mass every morning, and I had purposely selected the same time for our devotions, because the papists were then generally absent.

Two of the witnesses against me, whose ears had been offended by the holy name of God being pronounced within their hearing, were men who had waylaid a neighbor on the highway, murdered him and mangled his body, for which crime they were afterwards broken on the wheel. Oh! how infamous for a Huguenot to dare to pray to God in the presence of such worthy Catholics! and wound their delicate consciences with his fanatical discourse! Great God! what times!

Before removing me, I was brought into court for examination, and they began first with the offence for which I had been originally committed to prison.

On these occasions, in France, the accused is permitted to put as many questions as he pleases to the witnesses, in the presence of the Seneschal or President and the Register; and he has the right to have such answers as he considers favorable to himself committed to writing. This is called the "*confrontation.*"

The President, on behalf of the King, cross-examines both the accused and the witnesses, and has all the answers recorded that he considers sufficiently important. This is called "*recollement.*"

Upon this *confrontation* and *recollement* all the instructions for the prosecution turn. They are read by twelve or fifteen judges, who are called Counsellors, and are lawyers, as a matter of course. At the time of judging, the witnesses are not brought to the bar for examination, as is the practice in England, but the confrontation and recollement are produced as evidence. You are to understand that each witness has been separately examined, without knowing what any other has said; therefore it is an excellent plan for eliciting the truth. It is all important, you will perceive, for the accused to be on the alert, so that if there is any false statement made by a witness it may be discovered.

The only witness who could be produced against me, to give evidence as to the crime for which I had been brought

4

from home, was Agoust. He had made oath that he saw me on Easter Day among the poor people, returning from a religious meeting in the woods. I have already mentioned that he was a pettifogging attorney, and, consequently, he might be expected to be very well qualified for the task he had undertaken, of supporting a falsehood without contradicting himself.

In the end, we generally find truth triumphant, and so it was on this occasion, for I extracted from him at different times, and amidst a host of useless questions, the following replies :—

Firstly. That the time he saw me was in the dusk of the evening.

Secondly. That he was standing at his window when he saw me.

Thirdly. That I was in Mr. Mouillère's meadow.

Fourthly. That the distance was about a musket-shot from where he was standing.

Fifthly. That it was not in my way home from the woods.

You will readily believe, that I only obtained these answers at long intervals, putting many irrelevant questions to him in the mean time, in order to make him lose sight of the inconsistency of his present replies with those already recorded.

The President was out of all patience with me for consuming so much of his valuable time in asking foolish questions.

As Agoust had been brought up a Protestant, and had turned Papist to retain his office as attorney, I endeavored to rouse his conscience to some feeling of remorse. I put together the answers I have given above, and said to him :

" Miserable wretch that you are ; was it not enough that
you should deny your baptism, and renounce your religion
yourself, but you must also employ false testimony, to put
temptation in the way of those whom God has sustained by
his grace ? Now, look at your own statement, and give God
the glory.

" You say you were at your window in the dusk of the
evening, and that you recognized me at the distance of a
musket-shot. What sort of eyes do you pretend to have ?"

He was much confused at this, and said : " At any rate, I
thought it was you."

" Write down that," said I to the register.

The President, seeing his prey about to escape from the
snare, got into a violent passion, and accused me of abusing
the witness. " You have," said he, " perplexed and confused
him. I will not allow such proceedings."

" What," said I, " are you sorry that I have forced the
truth from his lips ? I looked up to you as my judge, but I
now see reason to fear you as my persecutor."

I spoke to the register several times, requesting him to
write down the last most decisive answer, but he looked to
the President for permission, and *he* shook his head. I would
not yield, and insisted upon it, that he should write down that
the witness no longer said he had seen me, but only that he
thought he had seen me.

The President wished to dictate it in modified terms, but
I said to him, " I declare to you, that if this last answer be
not written down, verbatim, as the witness spoke it, nothing
shall induce me to sign my confrontation." So I gained my
point, and it was written down. I scarcely believe I should
have succeeded, but from the fear he entertained of my enter-

ing a protest against his proceedings, which would have been
to his great dishonor.

I had parried the first blow successfully, and you shall
now hear how I replied to the dreadful accusation of having
prayed to my God in prison.

The two witnesses, already mentioned, who were afterwards broken on the wheel, were the first to be examined, in
order to obtain their evidence before it might be out of reach
from their execution.   One of them was of a Protestant family, and he could remember nothing more than that he had
heard me say, " Our Father, who art in heaven." The second
was unable to remember even as much as that.   The third
witness called up was the jailer, and he had made the accusation that I had prevented the recantation of the prisoners.

I said to him : " Did you ever hear me speak to the people on the subject of religion ?"

" No," said he.

" Did I even call them to prayers ?"

" No."

I put no further questions to him.

The fourth witness was his wife, and she was expected to
prove that I had interrupted the priest in his celebration of
mass.   She was possessed of some talent, and she was a great
bigot, therefore more dexterity was required in dealing with
her.

You must bear in mind that the chapel was separated
from the main building of the prison by a small court, and
also that it was on the ground-floor.   The common room of
the prison was in the second story, and I prayed in that corner of it which was the most remote from the chapel.   I had
my back towards it, and I always spoke in a subdued tone of

voice, only just loud enough to be audible to those around me. It would, indeed, have required lungs much stronger than mine to have made myself heard in the chapel. The President himself well knew that it was an impossibility; and had there been no other evidence of the falsity of the accusation, the non-appearance of the priest, who was said to have been interrupted, was sufficient. Had the complaint been true, he would certainly have been summoned as a witness.

When the wife of the jailer came forward, I complained to her of the injustice of preceding witnesses, and said that I was sure such a devout woman as she was could not have been shocked to see poor people, for whom punishment was in store, humbling themselves before God, and that, as all my expressions were drawn from the Holy Scriptures, they could not have given offence to a good Christian.

She replied, that my words had not given her offence.

That was written down.

"However," said I, "you had a much better opportunity of hearing me than any of the other witnesses. Do not you remember one morning, when I was praying, that you passed from one room to the other, and came quite close to my feet?"

"Yes; I remember it very well."

I had that written, almost in spite of the President, who considered the question so utterly useless. After a few unimportant queries, I asked her if she ever heard me call any one to prayer.

"No," said she; "but as soon as they see you kneeling down, they run like wild-fire."

"Did you ever hear me forbid any of the people to change their religion?"

"No," said she.

I then inquired whether she was able to remember a sermon she heard from one of the preachers of her own religion. She appeared piqued that I could entertain a doubt upon the subject, and answered, most unhesitatingly, that she could remember it. I did not require that to be written.

I then apologized for giving her the trouble, but humbly begged of her to oblige me by repeating to the President any passages she could remember of my prayers, because I felt assured he would find nothing to reprehend ; he would rather esteem me for them, than wish to bring punishment upon me.

She was abashed at having to acknowledge any deficiency in the memory, of which she had just now boasted, and she was therefore compelled to tell the truth, and to say that she could not oblige me, because I always spoke in so low a tone that she could not hear what I said.

That was written, and I was satisfied.

We both signed the confrontation, or, more properly, the refutation of the accusation. I then requested the President to set me at liberty, for I pointed out to him that every one of the witnesses had given contradictory evidence, and upon such, he could not think of sending me to the worse prison, with which I had been threatened.

The King's Advocate replied in an indignant tone, that I had been guilty of holding illegal assemblies within the prison.

I answered pleasantly enough to that accusation : " You are wrong to impute that crime to me. The Grand Provost and his Archers are to blame for it, and if you will order the prison doors to be opened, I will take upon myself to disperse the assembly, without loss of time."

"It is no jesting matter," said he, "you have prevented the conversion of these poor people."

I then spoke with more seriousness, and said to him: "You must perceive, by the confrontation, that you are mistaken in what you say; but, for the sake of argument, I will suppose it to be otherwise; but even then, the constancy of the prisoners could not be attributed to me. I look upon the conversion of the soul as exclusively the work of the Holy Spirit, and therefore, perseverance in our religion proceeds not from the influence of man, but from Him only who tries the heart and the reins, and strengthens whom he pleases. I am ashamed," said I, "to plead before Christians, as Christians formerly pleaded before Pagans. Now, just imagine yourself in the situation of one of us; what would you think of a religion which should impute it to you as a crime that you had prayed to God out of the deep gulf of your affliction? Would you be inclined to embrace such a religion?"

The King's Advocate appeared disposed to relent upon my making this appeal; but the President remained inflexible, and gave an order to have me taken to the dungeon of the tower of Pons.

I spoke once more to him with much warmth and indignation: "I feel persuaded you are convinced of my innocence, and therefore I think you are unmindful of your duty, when you are more inveterate against me than the King's Advocate, who, in virtue of his office, is my prosecutor. If you think you can prevent my calling upon my Creator by putting me in a dungeon, you are very much mistaken. The greater my affliction, the more importunate will be my prayers; and when I call upon God, I will not forget to pray for you, that you may repent, and that he will give you a better mind."

He replied, " I want neither your prayers nor your lectures."

He then called upon the sergeant to do his duty, and I was removed from the court.

I was placed, at eight o'clock in the morning, in a dark, miserable, filthy dungeon, in the Tower of Pons. It was already tenanted by one of the culprits, who was awaiting his trial for murder. We had not much conversation with each other. He asked me if I knew what was the general opinion entertained of him. I told him that he was believed to be guilty of the crime of which he was accused. He then asked me if I could tell him any thing of the mode of examining by torture. I said that if they were really guilty of the crime, it was more than probable that some one of them would confess it, under torture, and his confession would be sufficient to condemn the rest.

" What," said he, " if I go through the torture without confessing, and another accuses me falsely, shall I be broken on the wheel all the same?"

I said that all the particulars might be given with such circumstantial detail, that he would find it impossible to deny any longer.

He cried out in great distress, " Ah Jesu Maria !" His tone of voice removed from my mind any doubt I might have entertained of his guilt. I felt compassion for the poor, wretched man, and tried to turn his mind to the contemplation of a future state. I told him that if he would only repent truly of his sins, he might be forgiven. God's mercy, I said, was still open, if he would only apply for it through the Saviour who died for him.

He was curious to know what crime could have brought

me to be his companion in such a place; and when I told him, he said, "Alas! sir, why will you not change your religion? This is a sad place for one like you."

Poor fellow! I doubt not he would have acted up to the advice he gave me; and the probability is, that if he had been brought up a Protestant, he might now have saved his life by recantation.

On the following day he was put to the torture, ordinary and extraordinary; he uttered not a syllable; but one of his companions made a full confession, and all three were broken on the wheel.

Owing to the unceasing importunity of Mademoiselle de la Burgerie, afterwards wife of Colonel de Boisron, I was taken out of the stinking dungeon at nine o'clock the same night. She was well acquainted with the President, and she represented to him in the strongest language, the infamy of his proceedings, and gave him no peace until he signed an order for my removal, and gave it to her.

My next prison was just the opposite; instead of being under ground, it was very high, in a small tower at the top of the Town Hall of Pons, open to the town-clock, circular in its form, ten or twelve feet in diameter, and with two rather large grated windows. I procured a small bedstead, a table, and three chairs, and made myself as comfortable as I could. I was altogether dependent upon the caprice of the President, who would sometimes forbid all access to my apartment, and at other times, he would grant admission to any, and every body, who would pay the door-keeper a trifle for the trouble of taking them up stairs. During the three months I was in confinement there, I was visited by many worthy, excellent persons, through whose instrumentality I was enabled to send prayers, copied by unknown hands, which I prepared to

suit the wants of my fellow-sufferers in the prison at Saintes
I had the unspeakable satisfaction of learning that they persevered in their daily devotions, and that they remained a
united band of Christians, not one of whom could be persuaded by threat or bribe to recant.

It is worth mentioning, that during my solitary imprisonment I was never once disturbed by a visit from any bishop,
jesuit, priest, or monk, though a day never passed without
some of them visiting my companions. No one proposed to
me to change my religion, and I felt the truth of the saying,
that if you resist the devil he will flee from you.

The President gave out that I was kept in confinement
until there was time to prepare the process; but it was hinted
to me again and again, that I might let myself out with a silver key. I had only entered the prison for the benefit of my
poor neighbors, therefore I was determined not to come out
of it by means entirely out of their reach. I had also another reason, which alone would have been sufficient to make
me decline this plan, namely, that it would hold out an inducement to the avaricious President to treat other Protestants
with severity, in the hope of extorting money. My advocate,
Mr. Maureau, one day took out his purse, and showing me
the gold and silver, he said, " here is the key of your prison."
"I am fully aware of it," said I, "but I never will make use
of it."

He and some other kind friends would gladly have arranged the matter themselves, and not suffered me to pay a single farthing; but I received some intimation of what they
were about to do, and I told Mr. Maureau that I would scorn
such a proceeding, and that if he dared to take the step
without my consent, I would proclaim publicly that the President had taken money to enlarge me.

CHAPTER VI.

Trial before the Presidency—Digression—Defence—Angry discussion with the President—Query—Reply—Sentence.

THE month of August had come round by the time that the process was ready to be brought before the Presidency in the Hall of Justice.

In this court, the prisoner has to depend upon himself, he is not allowed the help of an advocate to plead for him. The door is locked, and guarded by Archers. The President sits in the centre, the Judges or Counsellors on each side; the Register remains in the lower part of the Hall, and the prisoner is usually seated near him, on a three-legged wooden stool, as a mark of disgrace.

There is a saying in France, "he has sat upon the stool," which is tantamount to the English phrase, "I have seen him hold up his hand at the bar."

The testimony recorded in the confrontation is read to the accused, and he is asked if it be correct, and if the signature attached to it be his. The judges then examine him more fully, and if it be a case which admits of appeal to Parliament, the answers are recorded. As soon as the examination is over, the accused is taken back to prison, and the sentence of the court, in writing, is sent to him by a sheriff's officer.

In preparing for my defence I thought much more of my poor neighbors than of myself, because I was really innocent of the charge in the indictment, they were not. Knowing that they would not be assisted by an advocate, I could not help feeling some apprehension for them, and I determined, if any opportunity offered itself, I would say something applicable to their case. I thought it possible that I might be able to soften the hearts or alarm the consciences of the judges; and I made it a subject of special prayer to God.

I will make a digression here, which you will presently perceive is not altogether irrelevant. My apartment in the tower of the Town Hall looked down into the court-yard of the residence of one of my judges. He was a very passionate man, much addicted to gambling and dissipation, but at the same time, he was said to be an able jurist. Two or three days before my trial, I was awakened out of sound sleep, about midnight, by this man swearing and cursing in a loud tone of voice. He had just returned home after losing a large sum of money at the gambling table; he was mad with vexation, and was venting his rage upon his innocent wife and children. I thought I heard blows, but of that I was not sure.

To proceed with the trial. When I entered the Hall of Justice, the Register civilly offered me the three-legged stool. I would not sit upon it, for I said I was not a criminal to deserve such disgrace. He attempted to force me upon it, which the Court perceiving ordered him to desist, and one of the judges smiling, said: "Mr. Fontaine is a young man, and he might lose a good match by being made to sit there."

I made him a profound bow.

I was asked whether I had not prayed to God in the woods on Easter Sunday?

I said, " No, and I can produce any number of witnesses to prove an alibi, if you will allow me to call them. I spent that day at Coses."

Very little was said about my crime in prison, because I acknowledged unhesitatingly that I had prayed there, but in a low tone of voice.

After some other questions, they asked me if I did not know that His Majesty had issued a declaration forbidding illegal assemblies.

I thought that God had now most assuredly opened the door for me to say something on behalf of my fellow-prisoners, and I replied : " Gentlemen, I am aware of it, and I have read the declaration over and over again, and I can find nothing in it which forbids people assembling to pray to God. I look upon it as the height of injustice to His Majesty to pretend that he calls such assemblies unlawful, and you, who are the interpreters of his declaration, ought to have more respect for him and for your own reputation as Christians, than to give it so bad an interpretation as to call assemblies illegal, to which no arms are carried but the Old and New Testament, and where no words are uttered but such as find an echo in those sacred volumes, and where prayers are offered up for the prosperity of the King and his kingdom, and for the conversion of those who persecute the Church of Christ."

A curious interruption occurred here. My advocate, Mr. Maureau, had been listening at the door, and he was afraid I should injure my cause by speaking so boldly, so he put his mouth to a crevice and cried, " Hist! hist! hist!" and ran away. The door was ordered to be opened, but the offender was not to be seen, so they contented themselves with guarding it more carefully. This incident roused the attention of

the judges, and they evidently hoped I should let fall some
unguarded expression they might use to my disadvantage, so
they encouraged me to proceed, which I did as follows : " Illegal assemblies, gentlemen, it appears to me, are assemblies
where something is done contrary to law, such as tumultu-
ously assembling in arms to conspire against the state ; and I
see none other to which it can be applied without losing sight
of the correct meaning of words.   If I were to extend its application, it is evident it should be to those meetings held in
summer on Sunday evenings, where they play, dance on the
green, quarrel with one another, and blaspheme their Maker
on his appointed day of rest.   Such assemblies might perhaps fall within the meaning of the declaration ; however, I
do not hear of any one being taken up for attending *them*,
while the prisons are filled with those whose only crime has
been praying to God.   In the name of all that is sacred, gentlemen, how dare you give such an interpretation to His Majesty's declaration without trembling to think of the wrath of
the King of kings?   You who assemble nightly at balls,
where they dance, speak evil of their neighbors, squander
their money, and perhaps lose in gambling that which is
wanted at home for the support of wives and children, to whom
they prove a burden and a curse, rather than the blessing
they ought to be.   You, I say, who are now sitting in judgment upon others, will one day stand before the just Judge of
all the world, and in that awful day, think you that He will
condemn those who have worshipped him in spirit and in
truth, or those who have frequented your assemblies?"

"Aha !" cried the President, "your rebellious spirit breaks
out at last.   You not only sermonize and reproach us, but
you say the King issues declarations, wherein he forbids as-

semblies where they pray to God, and permits those in which
the Divine Majesty is blasphemed." " Register, that is the
sense of his reply, write it down."

" It is not," said I.

He then rose up in great anger, and said, " I am void of
understanding if it mean any thing else."

Some of the judges were disposed to be more patient, and
proposed that they should listen to what I had to say.

This was good policy on their part, for an appeal to Parliament was open to me, and if I would not sign my name to
the answers recorded, they might get into trouble, because
they would then be required to verify upon oath every word
they had made the Register write as coming from me.

" Gentlemen," said I, " the sense of what I did say I take
to be this ; that the King, by his declaration of such a date,
never meant to prohibit assemblies where they pray to God,
but much rather balls, and Sunday evening assemblies for
dancing on the green, and more especially those wherein they
conspire against the state."

" No," said the President, " that is not it."

" Well, gentlemen," said I, " to put an end to the dispute
I am very willing to dictate, verbatim, to the Register all that
I have said ;" and I was about to begin.

" What !" cried the President, " you do not surely expect
us to listen to that long sermon over again, no ; that would
be rather beyond endurance."

At last, in order to save the trouble of the long reply,
they consented to take the following as the tenor of it :

" According to my judgment, the declaration of His Majesty of such a date does not forbid assemblies where they
only pray to God, and I think those who extend its application so far, depart from the intention of His Majesty."

This was written down, and I signed my name to it.

The President, by way of showing my stubborness, as he called it, to the Court, then said to me: " Mr. Fontaine, we have no more questions to put to you as an accused person, but merely as a matter of curiosity, I wish to have your opinion ; whether you think a private individual, we will say, a mechanic, for instance, can understand the Holy Scriptures as well as the learned doctors and councils ?"

I answered, " I must make some discrimination before I reply to your question. Suppose the individual in question should be blessed with the aid of the Holy Spirit, and the doctors and councils should not—which I think very possible —then I am of opinion the former would understand the sacred volume the best, because the same Spirit which dictated the Scriptures is necessary for their correct understanding. Our blessed Lord and his poor fishermen found themselves opposed by the Scribes and Pharisees at Jerusalem. To come nearer to our own days, I certainly think that Luther and Calvin understood the Scriptures better than all the popes, cardinals, and councils put together."

At these words they all arose, crying out, " Jesu Maria ! What infatuation !"

" Ere long, gentlemen," said I, " we shall all be summoned to leave this vain world, and we shall then see whose has been the infatuation."

I was then taken back to prison, and my poor neighbors succeeded me for trial in the Hall of Justice. I was well pleased that I had been able to put in a word for them. I had certainly shown the judges that, if they condemned me or these poor people, they might, in their turn, fear condemnation from Him whom they had forbidden us to worship.

The sermon, which it was reported I had preached to the

Court, made a great noise in the place, and became a topic of
conversation both among Protestants and Papists, each dressing it in his own fashion. The judges said I had put the rope
around my own neck. I received visits of condolence from the
principal Protestants in the town. Many letters were written
to me on the subject from various places. They seemed to
be unanimous in censuring me for my indiscretion, in speaking
so freely before my judges. However, when I told the whole
truth, and they understood how cautiously I had worded my
replies, and more especially when I told them what had actually been recorded, they no longer blamed, but were disposed to overwhelm me with commendation.

The next day I received my sentence from the hands of
the Serjeant, and I appealed to Parliament immediately.

My sentence was that I must pay a fine of a hundred
livres to the King, for having prayed in prison, and be declared for ever incapable of exercising any function of the
holy ministry.

My companions were condemned to make the " amende
honorable," to be banished from the province for six months,
pay all expenses, estimated at one hundred crowns in specie,
and a fine of six thousand francs was laid upon us all collec-
tively and individually. They had included me in the sentence of the people, though they had no proof against me,
because they intended to make sure of the money, and they
knew that I had some property, and my poor neighbors had
little or none.

I tendered the hundred livres imposed upon me individually, and then demanded my enlargement, or, at any rate,
the liberty of going in and out of the prison. This was refused me ; and, therefore, I was under the necessity of calling
upon my friends to present my appeal to Parliament.

CHAPTER VII.

Appeal to Parliament—Factum—President's remark — Sentence reversed—Registei refuses copy of decree—Apply for redress—Return home.

THE Parliament of Bourdeaux, or rather of Guienne, then held its sittings at La Reolle, and by its order we were removed to the prison of that town, which was so full that the jailer, contented with the payment of his entrance fee, allowed us to go and come on "parole" as we pleased. This promised to be a very advantageous arrangement for me, as I could thus have the opportunity of making personal application to Parliament, proving my own innocence, and exposing the injustice of the Presidency of Saintes in its true colors.

I had my Factum printed, of which the following is a true and faithful copy :

"FACTUM.

" JAMES FONTAINE is accused of two things. The one, of being found in the assemblies held in the wood of Chatelars, near Royan ; and the other, of having been heard praying to God, in the prison of Saintes. With regard to the first accusation, it is based upon the testimony of only one witness, named Agoust, who made affidavit to having seen him at the

distance of one hundred paces from his own house, and two
hundred paces from the place where the assemblies were said
to have been held. At the confrontation, this witness admitted that he only thought he had seen him, from a window,
and that, too, in the dusk of the evening, at the distance of
three or four hundred paces ; and upon the strength of sueh
testimony as this, the said Fontaine has been confined four
months in the prisons of Saintes, which are extremely rude in
their accommodations. The charge of praying to God rested
upon the evidence of four witnesses, who contradicted themselves upon cross-examination ; and it appeared that the said
Fontaine merely knelt down in a corner of the prison, and
spoke in so low a tone that the jailer's wife, after acknowledg-
ing that she passed within one pace of him when he was
kneeling down, was not able to repeat a single word of what
he had said. After the breviate of the case was completed,
the Seneschal, in the most extraordinary manner, refused to
judge, and the said Fontaine was obliged to take legal steps
in consequence ; and after four months' delay, the Attorney-
General's deputy, recognizing the injustice of the proceeding,
called for further inquiry, and the sentence resulting therefrom is the subject of the present appeal. The said Fontaine
has been declared guilty of contravening the King's Edict,
and has been condemned to pay a fine of a hundred livres,
and declared for ever incapable of exercising the functions of
candidate or minister. The said Fontaine appealed. He
tendered the sum of one hundred livres, the fine imposed
upon himself individually, and desired to be set at liberty.
This was refused ; but he has since obtained permission to go
in and out upon condition of returning to the prison.

" This is a brief statement of facts, and the said Fontaine

now proceeds to justify his appeal. In the first place, the
testimony of a single witness is not sufficient under any circumstances; and the witness in question merely testified to
seeing him on the highway, and not at the place of meeting,
and confessed afterwards that he only *thought* he had seen
him. A witness, to be depended upon, should speak with certainty, and not by *credit vel non credit* any more than by
hearsay. And, furthermore, it can be proved that the said
Fontaine was at Coses, distant three leagues, on the day and
at the hour named by the witness.

"As to the second accusation, could it, among Christians,
be considered a crime to pray to God, and that, too, in the
actual words dictated by our Blessed Lord to his disciples?
Surely the very situation of a prisoner would be likely to
make him, if a Christian, pray more fervently and frequently
than ever. He could appropriate the language of the Royal
Prophet and say, ' Out of the depths have I cried to thee, O
Lord,' and God, who is the judge of the quick and dead, will
not condemn him for it, whatever man may do. In order to
convict, there should be proof of words having been used that
could admit of evil construction; so far from it, all that has
appeared in evidence is, that he was seen on his knees in a
remote corner of the prison, and one witness heard him say,
' Our Father, who art in heaven.'

"The said Fontaine concludes with the prayer, that this,
his appeal for justice, may be favorably considered; the
former decision reversed, and he be released from confinement
and from all fines, costs, and damages.

" MONSIEUR DE LABOURIN, Reporter.

(Signèd)   " DUMAS, *Attorney.*

" Presented 6th August, 1684."

When I presented this Factum to the President of the Parliament, I said to him, " My Lord, I here present you with a true statement of facts, and if you find, upon examination, the slightest discrepancy or exaggeration when you come to compare it with the evidence which will be brought before you. I am willing not only to have the sentence of the Seneschal confirmed, but increased penalties added to it."

He read it over with attention, and then said to me, " I can scarcely imagine that this is correct. The Seneschal could have no inducement for acting thus."

" My Lord," said I, " his ruling passion is the spirit of avarice, which he hides under a specious display of false zeal; he only joined me with the poor people, in the sentence, to make sure of obtaining payment of the fine and costs. I can assure you his fees of office have been levied with an unsparing hand."

There are certain fees which are the perquisite of the reporter, who is the one, among the judges, to whom is confided the examination of the process. The fees vary in amount according to the importance of the cause. The Seneschal had an idea that our suit would be profitable, and he took care to have himself appointed reporter for it, and he made most exhorbitant charges.

The form of proceeding before Parliament is the same as before the Presidial Court.

When I entered the Hall of Justice, the Serjeant offered me the stool, as in the other Court ; but I cast a look towards the President, who did me the favor to exempt me from the opprobrium. I was treated most respectfully, no unnecessary questions were asked, and I received full justice. I obtained a final decision, reversing the sentence of the Presidency of

Saintes, and acquitting me entirely. My poor neighbors, for form's sake, were banished from the province for six months. The Seneschal of Saintes was ordered to return the hundred livres that I had deposited, and he was prohibited from receiving fees on this or any future occasion, where the King was the prosecutor. Two grievous blows for the Seneschal.

It was necessary that I should obtain a copy of the decree in order to regain my liberty, and then I must exhibit the copy to the Seneschal of Saintes, to compel him to pay me back my hundred livres.

The Register was, like some of the others with whom we had to deal, very fond of money. I applied to him for a copy of the decree, and offered him eight or ten pistoles for payment. He would not let me have a single copy unless I paid him for twenty-one, which, he said, would be required, one for each prisoner. I knew, as well as he did, that one would be sufficient, and that the jailer would set us all at liberty upon exhibiting one single copy.

I preferred a complaint to my reporter, who recommended me to go and make it in person to my Lord the President; which I did, and he told me I was to command the Register, in his name, to furnish me with a copy, paying only for that single one.

I went promptly and cheerfully with this order to the Chief Register, but he was a great man who interfered little with the business of his office, and he sent me to his deputy, one Cardon, who said it was none of his business. I returned to the Chief Register, for I did not begrudge my steps, and he told me to tell Cardon, from him, to speak to the President. For several days I was kept on the move, going from one to the other without any prospect of redress; and I then began to see the object of all this delay. I found that this day was the last upon which the Court would sit before the Christmas holidays, and the Register and his deputy knew that if Parliament had adjourned, and the Lords of Parliament were dispersed to their several homes, I should be completely in their power, I should have to pay their full demand for twenty-one copies, or remain a prisoner during the whole holidays.

I was almost in despair, Parliament had then met to move the adjournment until after the Christmas holidays, and I had neither solicitor nor advocate to help me. I determined to make a desperate effort; I wrote my grievance upon a slip of paper, and managed to get in to the hall when the doorkeeper was engaged elsewhere. I made a profound bow, said nothing, but held up my hands in an attitude of supplication towards the Lord President. Cardon was there, and called to the Serjeant to seize and expel the intruder : he hoped to have had me pushed out before I was recognized by the President ; but, most fortunately, he had observed my entrance as well as Cardon, and he called out to me, " Mr. Fontaine, have you not obtained your deed yet ?"

" No, indeed, my Lord ; what does it benefit me to have found favor in your eyes, and that you have done me justice, when it is in the power of Mr. Cardon to prevent my obtaining the necessary record of it ? Parliament once adjourned, he will leave me to rot in a dungeon. My despair has made me bold enough to enter this hall unbidden, and throw myself at the feet of your Lordship, as a petitioner for simple justice."

The President was extremely indignant, and he called out, " Mr. Cardon, how dare you disobey my orders ? What have you to say for yourself, that ought to save you from being punished as you deserve ?"

He began a shuffling sort of apology about not having received the instructions of the Chief Register.

I was on the point of contradicting him ; but my Reporter, Mr. Labourin, who wished well to my cause, put his finger on his lips, to show me that I ought to remain silent ; and I presently saw that it was the best policy, for the anger of the President was only increased by an apology that appeared to set at naught his own authority.

" And am I to understand, Mr. Cardon, that you consider an order from me a dead letter, unless it be confirmed by the Register ? If you know your duty no better than that, it is time that I should have done with you."

Cardon was in great dismay, and he begged pardon with all humility, and assured the Parliament that he would attend to the matter immediately.

The President then addressed himself to me, and said, " Sir, if you cannot get your deed to-day, come and tell me ; and when you have received it, let me know how much you have paid for it."

I made a low bow and withdrew, very well satisfied with the success of my bold attempt.

I waited patiently near the door, to be on the spot to waylay Mr. Cardon, as soon as the Parliament was adjourned. I asked him to give me my deed, and he replied he was going home to his dinner, and I should have it after he had dined. I determined not to lose sight of him, and followed to his mansion, which he observed, and told me I had better follow his example and go and get my dinner.

" No," said I, " I will neither eat nor drink until I am possessed of my deed."

I maintained my position outside of his door for about two hours; when, seeing neither him nor the deed, I knocked. A footman opened the door a very little way, and held it so that I could not possibly get in: he told me his master was out. I was not to be deceived in that way; I remained at my post, and saw several persons admitted. At last, two well-fed Franciscan friars came to the door, whom I followed in, unobserved, and keeping close in their rear, rather crouched down, I managed to get into the office; and there I waited in concealment until they had finished their business, and, as they retired, I rose to my full height, and stood like a spectre before Mr. Cardon.

" What devil placed you there?" said he.

I replied, " I entered under the auspices of the good fathers who are just gone."

He handed me the deed, and I gave him in gold the one-and-twentieth part of the sum he had demanded for furnishing the full number, and, much to my surprise, he returned to me five or six crowns.

" How is that? Are you satisfied?" said I.

" No," said he, with much bitterness, " nor shall I be until I see you with a halter round your neck."

" When people are hung for praying to God, I shall have reason to be afraid, and you will be able to sleep in peace."

Having given him this reply, I took the deed away with me, and presented it to the jailer, who released us from our " parol," and we were at full liberty.

I should not have dwelt upon this subject at so great length, but for the purpose of showing you the variety of difficulties we had to contend with. Every one seemed to

5

think he had a right to impose upon a poor Protestant, even
down to a register's clerk.

From this detail you may learn the necessity of standing
up for your rights with firmness, and the duty of using every
energy to overcome the obstacles in your path, instead of sitting down quietly as some indolent persons do, to complain
of fatigue and rebuffs, without making an effort. Remember,
God has promised his blessing to the diligent hand, as well
as the upright heart.

In the course of the day, I called to take leave of my
Lord the President, and to thank him for all his kindness. I
then turned my steps toward Saintes, quite victorious, with
the deed in my hand. I made the Seneschal refund the hundred livres already named, and once more I set foot within
my own dwelling. The expenses I had incurred during my
imprisonment amounted to two thousand livres.

Most of the poor people returned quietly to their own
homes, and were allowed to remain there without molestation.
They received contributions from charitably disposed Protestants to an amount that made ample amends for the loss of
time, and injury to their families, from deprivation of their
earnings, during their imprisonment.

The history of our persecution spread far and wide, and
I received many letters of congratulation upon the courage
and successful result of my appeal to Parliament. Amongst
others, the Marquis de Rouvigny, father of Lord Galway,
wrote me a complimentary letter. He had the management
of much of the business of our Reformed Churches.

Mr. Benoist gives an account of our trial and imprisonment in his "History of the Edict of Nantes." You will find
it in the third part of the third volume, pages 744 and 745.

CHAPTER VIII.

THE year 1685 opened with a bitter spirit of persecution far beyond all that had preceded it. There was no longer the slightest semblance of justice in the forms of proceeding, the dragoons ravaged and pillaged without mercy, resembling in their progress a lawless and victorious army taking possession of an enemy's country. In the history of the past we look in vain for any record of cruelties such as were inflicted upon the unoffending and unresisting Huguenots. They were not accountable to any one for their acts; each dragoon was a sovereign judge and an executioner; he who had ingenuity enough to invent any new species of torture was sure of applause, and even reward for his discovery. My blood boiled under the sense of injury, and I desired earnestly that the Protestants should take up arms in a body, and offer resistance, instead of waiting quietly to be slain like beasts at the shambles.

Early in the year I received an invitation to attend a meeting of ministers and elders at Coses, to hold a consultation as to what ought to be done in the present cruel crisis.

Twelve ministers and as many elders were present in answer to the summons. As I was only a candidate, and not a minister, I had no right to appear in such a meeting, and still less to give a vote, but my deportment in prison had gained me so much reputation, that young as I was, the ministers requested to have my opinion.

I pointed out to them what I considered the great error of which they had been guilty, namely, preaching the doctrine of non-resistance from their pulpits. I said it appeared to me that our quiet submission to all the grievous edicts and declarations of the king had encouraged him to go on. Our obedience to one edict only paved the way for another more intolerable to be issued, and I thought we might blame the timid policy of the day for much that we had endured. I dissented totally from the generally received doctrine that our lives and estates are the property of the king, and I thought such an admission reflected discredit upon our forefathers, who had obtained for us, sword in hand, the privileges which were now taken away from us. To make short of the matter, my opinion was that there was nothing left for us but to take up arms and leave the issue to the Lord of Hosts.

I was listened to thus far with impatience, and they then rebuked me sharply for the carnal spirit I had evinced in my remarks, which they said was the reverse of the patience and long-suffering taught in the Gospel, which at the utmost extremity permitted nothing but flight.

I replied that we were men as well as Christians, and that as men we had rights to maintain. If a compact entered into with our fathers, in virtue of which they laid down their arms, was broken, we were certainly called upon to enforce its fulfilment, and if necessary, even at the point of the sword. I entreated them to reflect that it was impossible for this immense Protestant population all to leave the country. I was interrupted by them again, they had not patience to hear me, but I entreated them to let me say one word more; and I made a solemn appeal to them, to the intent that they should well consider, before deciding against resistance, how many thousands of souls would probably be lost. The poor creatures unable to bear the sufferings inflicted by their cruel persecutors, would be almost sure to yield and abjure their faith, but if we could put arms in their hands, they would willingly shed their blood, and sacrifice their lives, in defence of the truth.

The meeting was not disposed to heed my counsel; I was rather considered to be an impetuous, headstrong youth, and we separated, without deciding upon any line of action.

When the dragoons made their appearance in our province, they were for a time kept away from the sea-coast. They had orders to overrun all the other districts first, and hence a rumor became current that sailors were to be spared.

The Intendant of Rochefort sent a letter to Royan, recommending the people to change without dragoons. A large meeting was held to deliberate upon the preparation of a suitable answer to this smooth letter. My voice was raised, as you may suppose, in favor of resistance. I said I was convinced that we could rally around us a party strong enough to possess ourselves of Rochefort and Brouage, in less than a week.

They would not listen to me; and I verily believe that nothing short of the feeling of regard for myself individually, and the respect for my family generally entertained throughout the neighborhood, would have prevented some who heard me from giving information, and handing me over to justice.

They concocted a reply to the letter, without my aid; the tenor of it was, that they would obey the King in all things consistent with their duty to God, but nothing would induce them to change their religion.

They told a very different story when the dragoons really came amongst them, for the principal men proved to be arrant cowards, and trod one upon another, trying who could get into the church first to make recantation. There was much more courageous and unshaken faith amongst the poor country people.

Before the dragoons appeared, a good many sailors embarked with their families, and crowds of persons followed them to the sea-shore, with the desire of going also, if room could be found in the vessels. It was on this occasion that a Mr. Certani, the Catholic Curé at Royan, a sensible, respectable man, went after them to the shore, and dissuaded many from embarking, by making them a promise that Royan should not be visited by dragoons. He said the King loved his brave seamen too well to allow them to be disturbed. He gave additional weight to his advice, by telling them, that if what he had said to them did not prove true, they should be at liberty to burn him alive in his house. Some were persuaded by him to change their plans and return home; others, less credulous, embarked, happily for themselves, while they had the opportunity.

I was from home on that day, and when I returned, and heard of the proceedings, I went to M. le Curé, and told him I was come to bid him farewell, for I was certain we should soon have the dragoons in our parish, and I did not mean to trust myself to their tender mercies, if I could help it.

He urged me to do as many others had done, appear to change, which would answer every purpose.

I answered, that I could not lull my conscience sufficiently to act in that way.

He then told me in confidence, that he was himself over-whelmed with grief at the state of things. He feared the just judgments of God would overtake the Catholics for forcing the Protestants to approach the altar without faith, and to partake of that Holy Sacrament which should only be received by the sincere in heart.

" I fear," said he, " War ! Famine ! and Pestilence !

" War !—What is more probable than that the princes with whom so many Huguenots have taken refuge, should be aroused to avenge them of their persecutors ?

" Famine ! For who will cultivate our fields ? There will remain to us only old men, women, and children ; all our young people are leaving us ; and what an army may be raised for our adversaries, out of the brave young men whom we are driving away !

" Pestilence ! Generally the last scourge, following upon the heels of famine. And who can say that we do not deserve such chastisement from the Almighty, for our profanation of his Holy Altar."

The Curé spoke with great force on the subject, and he really appeared to have the gift of prophecy, for what he anticipated all came literally to pass ; but he only lived to see the commencement.

The veteran army of France, formidable to the whole world, had been every where victorious until it made war upon the Saints ; and then it experienced the most gloomy reverses. The soldiers appeared shorn of their strength, and God took from them their ancient valor. We have seen this army of torturers and persecutors, fly from the face of an

enemy whom they formerly scorned, and seen them driven
from ther intrenchments, and forced to precipitate themselves into the water, like the swine of the Gadarenes, in the
fear of enemies who once dared not quit the shelter of their
fenced cities to encounter them. The glory of Louis, called
the Great, whose ambition aspired to universal monarchy, departed from him when he raised his hand against the people
of God, and he lived to reap his reward in seeing himself despised in his old age, as he deserved to be. Famine* and
poverty covered the face of the land. The gold and the silver disappeared, and their places were supplied by a species
of enchanted paper, which perished before it was consumed,
and still remains in portfolios, as a memento of what has
been lost. Pestilence also has marched over that doomed and
wretched land.

France! miserable France! my dear native country, wilt
thou never open thine eyes, and unstop thine ears, and understand the language in which God has spoken to thee? Shall
man say, I am stronger than my Maker; I have entirely destroyed the Reformation; I have disarmed the God who protected the Protestants; and I have caused a god of wafer to

---

* We have a more complete opportunity than our ancestors had of observing the consequences resulting from the cruel and impolitic conduct of
Louis, and we conscientiously believe that the French nation is still suffering from it. In reading the history of France, and her revolutions, we often
pause to think how different it might have been, if the descendants of the
expatriated Huguenots had been scattered through the length and breadth
of the land. They were generally of that middle class which constitutes the
strength of a nation. They were emphatically the courageous and sober-
minded; the moral, industrious, and the thinking portion of the community,
as well as the truly pious. The descendants of such men, inheriting even
in a moderate degree the traits of their fathers, might have had an influence of which we can form no idea in moderating the cruelty, the caprice,
and the frivolity which have of late years characterized the acts of the
French people.

be adored in his stead? No, no; God is not mocked, he will protect his faithful servants, and preserve his holy religion from destruction. Never canst thou, O France! enjoy thine ancient prosperity, whilst thou art the persecutor of God's elect. So long as his faithful servants were cherished in thy bosom, and the promises made to them in the Edict of Nantes carefully observed, His blessing was upon thee, as it was upon Abinadab, while the ark rested in his house. Thou hast driven them forth with cruelties unheard of, and thy prosperity has departed with them. The floods have gone over thee. Oh that thou wouldst return to the Almighty and confess thy sins, and cease to forbid his true and pure worship; and his blessing would return to thee, and thy days would be bright, and prosperity would appear again within thy borders.

Sympathy for my dear native land has carried me away from the object of my visit to M. Le Curé. To resume; I begged he would not persist in drawing upon himself the indignation and revenge of an infuriated community, which would assuredly follow the arrival of the dragoons.

"You deceive yourself," said I, "if you really believe that they will not be sent into our district. If they come, remember the penalty you will have to pay; you have given the people permission to burn you in your house, and I solemnly declare to you, that I this day heard a man, a stranger to me, swear by all that he held sacred, that if you had deceived the people, he would roast you alive, and carry the news to Holland." He turned pale at this, and said, that he had spoken to the people so strongly, in consequence of a letter he had received from the Intendant of Rochefort, which contained a positive promise, that the dragoons should not come. He took out the letter, and gave it to me for perusal.

5*

After I had read it, I said to him : " How could you think
of making yourself answerable for the intendant ? Suppose
he should not keep his word with you, think in what a dangerous position you will be placed. I beseech you, as you
value your life, go to the people before it is too late, take back
your promise to them, and let them see the letter, and then
they can judge for themselves as to the credit they are willing
to give to it."

He thanked me for my advice, and what is more to the
point, he followed it, and went down to the sea-shore to tell
the people the actual state of the case, so that they might decide for themselves.

During the three following days great numbers embarked,
and on the fourth the dragoons* made their appearance. All

---

* The Protestants lost most of their strong places during the reign of
Louis XIII., and the remainder in that of Louis XIV., so that they were
entirely at the mercy of the King, and he promised to secure to them liberty
of conscience, and he kept his word until his latter days, when he began to
think more upon religious subjects, and under the influence of Madame de
Maintenon, and his confessor, La Chaise, he determined to convert all the
Protestants in his dominions to Catholicism. Colbert, the Minister of
Finance, though a Catholic himself, estimated at its real value the superior
industry of the Huguenots, and he opposed violent measures successfully,
so long as he lived. After his death, in 1683, the monarch had no one to
restrain him, and the bigoted counsels of the confessor, and the chancellor,
Le Tellier, and his son, strengthened his own resolves. Almost all the
noblemen and courtiers recanted, and Louis thought he had only to say the
word, and their example would be followed throughout his dominions.
Missionaries were appointed, and furnished with large sums of money, to
make converts ; they gave in flattering reports of their success; but this
method was thought too expensive, and a cheaper plan was to be tried. All
Protestants were excluded from public office, children were allowed to recant at the age of seven years, and severe penalties were enacted against
relapse. This caused emigration, and those in power opened their eyes
wide enough to perceive that in the departure of seamen and artisans, they
were losing many of their most valuable subjects, and to put a stop to it,
they issued an edict prohibiting emigration on pain of death.

The Protestant churches were next ordered to be demolished, and no less

who were left, and did not intend to recant, fled for concealment to the woods.

I left the home of my childhood, never to return to it,
about midnight. I took with me about five hundred francs,
which was all the ready money I had, two good horses, upon
one of which I rode myself, and my valet was mounted upon
the other, with a portmanteau containing a few necessaries.
I was well armed, and I had resolved, if I should encounter
dragoons, to sell my life as dearly as possible.

My house was amply furnished, and I had removed nothing from it. It was taken possession of by eighteen dragoons in two hours after I quitted it; they lived there until
they had consumed or sold every thing they could lay their
hands upon, even to the bolts and locks of the doors.

I passed through Coses about three o'clock in the morning, and found dragoons were still there. They had made all

than seven hundred were destroyed even before the revocation of the Edict
of Nantes.

The last measure adopted was that which has been known by the name
of *dragooning;** and if we had not the most undoubted testimony on the
subject, it would be impossible to believe that such horrors could have been
perpetrated under the mask of the Christian religion.

A day was appointed for the conversion of a certain district, and the dragoons made their appearance accordingly; they took possession of the Protestants' houses, destroyed all that they could not consume or carry away,
turned the parlors into stables for their horses, treated the owners of the
houses with every species of cruelty, depriving them of food, beating them,
burning some alive, half-roasting others, and then letting them go, tying
mothers securely to posts, and leaving their sucking infants to perish at
their feet, hanging some upon hooks in the chimneys, and smoking them
with wisps of wet straw till they were suffocated; some they dipped in
wells; others they bound down, and poured wine into them through
funnels, until reason was destroyed; and many other tortures were inflicted,
some even more horrible than the above-named.

* We believe that the use of the word dragoon, as a verb, implying, to abandon to
the rage of the soldiery, is actually derived from the cruelties practised during these
persecutions.

the people abjure, except about five or six persons, so they were all quartered upon those. When any one announced his intention of changing his religion, he was at once relieved from the presence of the hated dragoons, who dispersed themselves amongst those who still held out.

I rode rapidly forward, choosing the by-ways, with which I was well acquainted in that part of the country. At break of day, I was near Jemosac, and was much startled by coming so suddenly upon a troop of soldiers, that I was seen by them before I had time to retire. They had been quartered at Jemosac, and had made the people who remained there perform the duty of the times, as they called recantation; and were hastening elsewhere to make more converts. I knew that if I were recognized, I should, in all probability, lose my life, but I concluded that my best chance was to ride fearlessly forward, and salute them as I passed. My horses were noble animals, worthy of carrying a general-officer and his aide-de-camp. I had scarlet housings with black fringe, and holsters for my pistols; and though I was dressed in black, I had taken the precaution of putting on a large periwig, and crape upon my hat, in order to evade the suspicion that might otherwise have attached to my dress. The officers, thanks be to God, took me for a country gentleman, and returned my salutation very civilly.

The first stoppage I made was at the house of my aunt Jagualt, my mother's sister. Her son had changed his religion to escape dragooning, but the old lady was unshaken, and I believe she remained so to the day of her death. I gave her all the spiritual instruction and consolation that I could during the day and night I spent with her.

I went next to Jonzac, where I had two married sisters

living, and, sad to relate, they had both recanted to escape the dragoons. I was extremely depressed, but continued my travels towards Meslars, to visit my dear sister Anne, and my heart was cheered to find this, my favorite sister, firm in her faith, even though her husband had abjured his religion. She gave him no peace until she persuaded him to take her out of France. After several days of sweet, delightful converse with her, I went to St. Mesme to see Mr. Forestier and my sister Mary, but I found they had fled.

Wherever I went, I tried to do some good, strengthening those who were firm, denouncing those who had fallen, and trying to persuade them to abjure their abjuration. It was distressing in the extreme to see the vast numbers who had made shipwreck of their faith.

Many individuals there were who had borne umoved the bitter tortures of persecution, and who had been stripped of their property without yielding to temptation, and yet at last gave way under the influence of specious arguments from false friends, who represented to them, that as it was a commandment of God to honor and obey the King, they failed in duty to Him when they refused obedience to the monstrous decrees of the King. They thus became idolatrous renegades, and gave adoration to that which they knew to be nothing more than a morsel of bread.

In travelling about the country I discovered an extent of defection that was most lamentable, and I was so afflicted and depressed by it that I became sick; I lost my strength and spirits, and suffered much from bilious vomitings.

I often encountered parties of soldiers, and I had become so low-spirited that I used to think I should not be sorry if they took away my life. Indeed, at that time, I would have

parted with it willingly, if, in the combat, I could have destroyed any of the leaders of these troops who were doing the
Devil's work throughout the land.

You must know, that though I was a poor soldier on foot from
my lameness, I was by no means a contemptible opponent when
mounted. I was an excellent horseman, and so good a shot
that I could hit a mark at twelve or fifteen paces with my
horse at full gallop. One of my horses was an Arabian, remarkably fleet ; if I gave him the bridle he would move with
the swiftness of a race horse, stretching out his legs, and then
doubling them under him, so as to bring his body very near
the ground. The eyes of the rider were dazzled by the rapidity with which he passed over the ground, but there was no
uneasinsss from the motion. I knew that none of the dragoons could overtake me when mounted on him, and I determined, if they should pursue me, to fight like the Parthians,
wait for any one of them who should distance the rest by the
fleetness of his horse, shoot him, gallop off, and load my pistol
to be ready for another. I scarcely feared a whole company
when I was riding my Arabian, for they could not approach
me in a body, and one by one, I was sure I could dispose of
several of them. In addition to this, I was very well acquainted with that part of the country, which gave me a great advantage over them, and in extremity I could have availed
myself of windings and thickets among the woods where they
would not dare to follow. I made every preparation that I
could for self-defence, but my reliance was not so much upon
that as upon the protection of my Father in Heaven, whom
I tried to serve to the best of my power, and who, in his infinite mercy, has upheld me through many and great dangers
as well then as at other periods of my life.

I was much aided by some of the enemies of the Gospel during my wanderings. My little stock of money was dwindling rapidly away, and I had no prospect of obtaining any more, so I had to think how I could make my present supply hold out the longest. I dismissed my valet as an unnecessary expense, and, at the same time, hit upon a plan for recruiting one of my horses, while I was travelling about on the other. Between Jonzac and Jemosac, there stood an old castle belonging to the Count of Jonzac, who lived much at court, and followed the fashion of the day among the courtiers, in being a great persecutor of the Protestants. I had taken rest occasionally at a small tavern on his estate, where I felt myself very safe, for I was personally unknown to the people, and as they were all Papists there was no fear of any dragoons making their appearance. Mine host was a humane, simple peasant, who always received me with kindness. I told him I had some business to transact which kept me from home, and obliged me to ride through the country a great deal, and I should esteem it a favor if he would take care of one of my horses while I was making use of the other. I said that I expected to pay for it as a matter of course. He sent for a groom from the castle who had charge of the horses belonging to the Count, who, finding he could make a little money, very readily consented to put my horse in the meadow, and attend to it. I used to return there every week, or two, or three, as might be convenient to me, and change my horse, leaving the jaded animal to recruit in the meadow. I pursued this plan regularly for at least three months, and I found the people uniformly kind and faithful to me during the whole time.

It was by no means uncommon for me to be six or seven

days without being able to undress myself, or even so much
as draw off my boots, afraid to venture abroad in the day-
time ; I generally rode from place to place in the night.

My troubles were increased by the great anxiety I felt
lest any evil should befall that worthy and pious woman,
whom God gave to me afterwards for my beloved partner and
help-mate, and my greatest earthly comfort—your dear mother. She was concealed in the house of a Mr. Mechinet,
where I feared she might not be safe from persecution, and
therefore I was on the look-out for a better place of refuge,
and I found it for her under the roof of a Mr. Brejon, an advocate, who had changed his religion. There was no fear of
his being visited by dragoons, besides he lived at Pisauyau
Castle, the seat of the Duke of Montausier, of whose estates
he had the management. I felt that no asylum could be found
that offered greater security.

CHAPTER IX.

Revocation of the Edict of Nantes—Preparations for flight—Difficulties and dangers of embarkation—Land in England—Cheapness of bread—Speculation in grain—Cruelty of a captain of a vessel.

In the month of October, 1685, the edict of Nantes was actually revoked* by that great persecutor, Louis the 14th. Of course no choice was now left for Protestants; flight was the only alternative.

I went to Marennes to make preparations in good earnest, and I was so fortunate as to find an English captain of a

---

* Surely this act has been incorrectly termed the Revocation of the Edict of Nantes. All its provisions had been repealed long ago by royal edicts and ordinances, except the bare toleration of Protestantism in some few towns and districts. The edict of the 22d October, 1685, forbade all exercise of the reformed religion, ordered the clergy to expatriate themselves within a fortnight, unless they would recant, and in.that case their incomes were to be increased one-third, and continued to their wives. All infants were required to receive popish baptism, and every one caught in the attempt to escape (unless he was a minister) was condemned to the galleys for life. In 1686, the enactments were still more severe. A Protestant taken in the act of public worship was punished with death, and all Protestant clergymen, whether natives or foreigners, were to be executed. To increase the vigilance of the soldiery, a reward of three or four pistoles was given for every Protestant that was taken up.

In spite of the care with which the coast and frontiers were guarded, it is believed that not less than 50,000 families made their escape, and they enriched every land that received them, carrying arts and manufactures and industry in their train; and it has been remarked by close observers that their descendants, up to this day, continue to be distinguished for virtue and respectability.

vessel, with whom I was able to make a bargain. He agreed
to take me, and four or five persons with me, to England, at
the rate of ten pistoles each, and it was arranged that we
should assemble at Tremblade for embarkation. I went immediately to fetch your dear mother, Anne Elizabeth Boursiquot, and her sister Elizabeth, and my niece Janette Forestier; the latter was my god-daughter, and I felt it incumbent
upon me to provide for her safety.

I mentioned the plan to some few persons, and I expected they would have rejoiced at the prospect of getting away,
but their fears were stronger than their hopes, and they
dared not venture to encounter so many dangers. The coast
was carefully guarded both by sea and land to prevent emigration.

We went to Tremblade to be ready, and took up our
abode in the house of a man who was to act as our pilot because he could speak English. He was a very imprudent
as well as a drunken man, which made our situation very
dangerous while under his roof.

After several days of cruel suspense, the Captain sent us
word that he should be ready to sail the next day, and he
wished us to be in readiness also. He said that he should
pass between the Isle of Oleron and the main-land, and that
if we would be on the sands near the Forest of Arvert, he
would send a boat ashore for us.

We set off during the night, and had two horses to carry
the few little possessions we were able to take with us. In
the course of the following day, upwards of fifty persons assembled on the sands, with the hope that they might be
taken on board the vessel, and make their escape with us.
Most of them were very young, and they had not taken due

precaution to conceal their intentions, so the Papists became aware of what was going on, and they gave information of it, upon which the Custom House detained the vessel. We waited anxiously all day, in utter ignorance of the cause of delay, and while we were in this painful state of suspense, I called the people around me and addressed them; then we all knelt upon the shore, and I offered up a prayer suited to our distressing condition. You will find a copy among my papers, and I am sure when you read it you will be convinced that it was a prayer of the heart as well as the lips.

The Curé of Tremblade had heard that a number of persons were collected on the shore, and he had the curiosity to come down and see for himself. He brought with him a man who had formerly been a sort of juggler. They were once so near to us that we actually saw their little dog, which was rather in advance of them, when they were providentially met by two fishermen, who had seen us, and whose sympathies were enlisted in our favor, and they purposely misled them. They enlarged to them also upon the great danger they were in of losing themselves amongst the sand hills, and they offered to act as guides, and led them to a path by which they would be sure not to stumble upon us.

At night some of our friends sent horses down for us to return to Tremblade. Fifteen or twenty of us were taken in by a man who had changed his religion. He did it unwillingly and was in a dreadful fright all the time, for there was a fine of 1000 crowns laid upon any one who was discovered to have harbored a Protestant: and houses were liable to be searched at any moment upon the slightest suspicion. After concealing us during the whole day, his fear

got the better of his humanity, and towards night he turned
us all out of his house, saying to us : " I have damned my own
soul to save my property, and I am not going to run the risk
of losing it for you. Take your chance elsewhere, or do as
I have done." We were much depressed by this unkind
treatment, but we knew not what was best for us, and it
turned out that we had great reason to thank God that we
were not allowed to spend the night where we had passed the
day. Some one had given information that led the magistrate to suspect the place of our concealment, and we had
not quitted the house more than half an hour, before a Justice of the Peace and some soldiers went to it. and examined every part most carefully in search of secreted Protestants, but found none.

Tremblade is a very populous place, and before it was
visited by the dragoons it did not contain more than twenty
Papists, but all the Protestants had recanted who remained
there. We did the best we could amongst them, one finding
shelter here, another there, and I must acknowledge that we
experienced much more of humanity and Christian hospitality amongst the wives of the poor fishermen than we did
with the comparatively affluent. We passed the next four or
five days in the cottages of the former.

At last the Captain of the English vessel came to La
Tremblade, to tell me that he was afraid he should not be
able to take us on board. However, he said he meant to go
to sea the next day, and he should pass between the islands
of Ré and Oleron, and if we were disposed to run the risk of
going out there in small boats, he might receive us on board
after he had got rid of all visitors, custom-house officers
and others, and that he could not possibly assist us in any

other way. That very evening, the 30th November, 1685
(French or new style), we embarked in a little shallop as soon
as it was dusk. Our party consisted of your dear mother,
your aunt Elizabeth, Janette Forestier, myself, two young
men from Bourdeaux, and six young women from Marennes,
twelve in all, in place of the fifty who were ready to embark
a few days before. Under cover of the night we passed, without being observed, all the pinnaces that were keeping guard,
as well as the Fort of Oleron. At ten o'clock next morning
we dropped our anchor to wait for the ship. We had in
structed our boatmen that in case of being pursued, they were
immediately to run the boat ashore, abandon her, and then
"sauve qui peut."

I was as usual well armed to meet any emergency, and I
had resolved to defend myself to the last gasp, and never to
be taken alive. Thanks be to God, our merciful guide and
preserver, I was not put to the trial, for he watched over us
and blinded the eyes of our enemies.

We had agreed with the English captain that when we
saw him, we should make ourselves known by hoisting a sail
and letting it fall three times. About three o'clock in the
afternoon we first espied the vessel, but she had the official
visitors and pilot still on board. We watched her movements
with intense anxiety, and we saw her cast anchor when she
reached the extreme point of the Isle of Oleron, then she
put out the visitors and pilot, took her boat on board again,
got under way and sailed towards us. It was a joyful sight;
we felt confident that we had surmounted every difficulty,
and we expected in a very few minutes to be under full sail
for England. Our joy was of short duration, for at that moment one of the King's frigates hove in sight and gradually

approached us. She was one of the vessels constantly employed on the coast to prevent Protestants leaving the kingdom ; and all who were found were seized, and the men sent
to the galleys, the women to convents. No language can describe our consternation at this sudden change in our prospects ; a moment before the cup of happiness was at our lips
and now dashed to the ground.

We were at the distance of a cannon-shot from the frigate,
and what would she think of us ? We were in a little bit of
a boat, at anchor, in a place which did not afford safe anchor-
age even for large shipping. She cast anchor, ordered the
English vessel to do the like, boarded her, and searched every
nook and corner, without finding any French Protestants on
board except Mr. Mausy, the minister, whose departure was
authorized by law, and his family, who were with him, and had
passports. What a blessing that we were not on board at this
time ! Had the frigate been only one hour later in appearing,
we should all have been lost. After the search, the Englishman was ordered to sail instantly. The wind was favorable,
so he could make no excuse, and we had the misery of seeing
him leave us behind. He could not even see us, for the frigate
was between him and our boat.

Our situation was deplorable, we were in a state of perfect
despair and knew not what to do, for danger stared us in the face
alike in every direction. If we remained where we were, we
should certainly excite suspicion, and the frigate would send
to overhaul us. If we attempted to return to Tremblade, the
chances were a hundred to one against our succeeding. To
add to our dismay, our poor boatman seemed incapable of exertion, he did nothing but cry and lament over his infatuation,
that he should have allowed himself to be persuaded to take

us on board. He and his son, who was also with us, had been
Protestants, and they had abjured under compulsion. He
knew well that nothing short of a halter awaited them, if
caught in the act of aiding Protestants to make their escape.

I may truly say, that prayer has been my resource in all
difficulties through the whole course of my life. I betook myself to it on this occasion, and I felt a strong persuasion that
God would not suffer us to fall into the hands of his enemies
and ours, but open a way for our escape.

All at once I thought of a feint which, thank God, proved
successful, and effected our deliverance. Having considered
that the wind was fair to Rochelle and contrary to Tremblade, I said to the boatman, " Cover us all up, in the bottom
of the boat, with an old sail, then hoist your sail and go right
towards the frigate, pretending to endeavor to gain Tremblade ; and if they should hail you from the frigate, you must
say, you are from Rochelle, and going to Tremblade. If they
ask what you have on board, say nothing but ballast ; and it
would be well for you and your son to counterfeit drunken-
ness, tumbling about in the boat, and then you can, as if by
accident, let the sail fall three times, and so inform the English captain who we are."

He determined to abide by my counsel, and he immediately covered us all up with a sail, and actually went within pis-
tol-shot of the frigate. As I had expected, she hailed him,
asked whence he came, whither he was going, and what he
had on board.

To all which he replied as I had instructed him.

" But what made you cast anchor ?" said they.

" I was in hopes," he said, " that the wind would change,
and I might make Tremblade, but it is still too strong for me."

At that moment the son fell down in the boat and dropped the sail, his father left the helm, and, instead of hoisting the sail at once, took a rope's-end and pretended to chastise him, the hard blows falling on the wood and making a great noise. The son cried out lustily, and the people in the frigate threatened that if the father had not more patience with his son, they would be with him directly, and treat him in the same way. He made excuses for himself by saying, that his son was as drunk as a hog. He then ordered him to hoist the sail again, and he resumed his station at the helm. The son let it fall a second time, almost as soon as he had raised it, and repeated the same manœuvre a third time, and thus we managed to give the English captain information of who we were, without exciting the suspicions of the officers in the frigate. They were so fearful of some accident happening, that they called out to our boatman not to think of making Tremblade, for night was fast approaching, the wind contrary, and he would inevitably be lost. They advised him to return to Rochelle with the fair wind, which was exactly the advice we wished to receive from the frigate. Our course was instantly altered, the boat was put before the wind, and we bade them adieu very cordially in our hearts, but we still remained closely covered at the bottom of the boat.

In the mean time, the English vessel had answered our signal, but she was getting fairly out to sea, and we dared not follow her for fear of the frigate, which still remained at anchor. About twilight the boatman said we must make the attempt while it was yet not quite dark, or we should be swallowed up by the waves. We had no sooner altered our course, than we observed the frigate take up her an-

chor and set her sails. We naturally thought that she had
noticed us and was preparing to pursue us, and we again
turned towards Rochelle, in great agony of mind. We should
all have preferred instant death to capture, for we were aware of
our own weakness and frailty, and we feared persecution might
destroy our constancy. A few minutes put an end to our
anxiety, for we saw the frigate steering towards Rochefort, and
we again changed our course and made for the English vessel,
which slackened her rate to allow us to overtake her. We
went on board with the frigate still in sight. A blessed and
ever-memorable day for us, who then effected our escape from
our cruel enemies, who were not so much to be feared because they had power to kill the body, but the rather from
the pains they took to destroy the souls of their victims.

I bless God for the multitude of his mercies in earthly
enjoyments also. He allowed me to bring to England
the dear one whom I loved better than myself, and she willingly gave up relations, friends and wealth to be the sharer
of my poverty in a strange land, where we could worship
God according to the dictates of conscience. I here testify
that we have fully experienced the truth of that promise of our Blessed Saviour, to give an hundred fold more,
even in this present life, to those who leave all and follow
him. We have never wanted for any thing, we have not only
been supplied with necessaries, but comforts, and oftentimes
luxuries also. Certain it is, that a man's life consisteth not
in the abundance of the things that he possesseth, but in the
enjoyment he has of them, and it is in this sense that I would
be understood, when I say that we have received the hundred
fold promised in the Gospel ; for we have had infinitely more
joy and satisfaction in having abandoned our property for

6

the glory of God, than they can have had who took possession of it.

We had contrary winds, and were eleven days on the
voyage. We suffered a little from shortness of provisions,
especially water, but we could not venture into any French
port for a supply.

We landed on the first day of December 1685,—English
or old style—at Appledore, a small town in the British Channel, below the river Taw, which goes up to Barnstaple.
After paying passage money for the party I had only twenty
gold pistoles left. God had not conducted us in safety to a
haven there to leave us to perish with hunger. The good
people of Barnstaple were full of compassion, they took us
into their houses and treated us with the greatest kindness;
thus God raised up for us fathers and mothers, and brothers
and sisters in a strange land.

The first thing that struck me on my arrival in England
was the extreme cheapness of bread. What with sea-sick-
ness, and shortness of provisions on board ship, we had suffered a good deal, and we were very anxious for something
to eat as soon as we landed

The first act after getting out of the vessel, was to return
thanks to God for his merciful goodness in having brought
us safely to the shores of England; the second was to ask
for bread. We were supplied with very large biscuits,
such as in France would have cost twopence each, and to my
surprise I was told that here they only cost one half-penny.
I was doubtful of the fact, thinking I might be misled by
my ignorance of the English language, so I gave a penny
to a little girl and asked her to buy me some bread. She
went to a baker, and sure enough, she brought me back two

of these large biscuits. It instantly occurred to me that any one who could buy grain here, and ship it to France, must realize a large profit, but alas! I had no money. I knew that there were some French Protestant refugees living at Plymouth, who had brought considerable property over with them, and perhaps if I were to suggest this plan to them, they might be willing to lend me some money to join them in an adventure. But I wished to be perfectly well informed on the subject before speaking to them; so having learnt that a corn market would be held next day at Biddeford, I walked over there and took a man, understanding both French and English, to act as interpreter. I found that the finest description of wheat could be bought at the rate of two shillings and sixpence, or three shillings at the outside, for such a sack as in France would cost two crowns.

I then made inquiries about export duties upon grain, and I ascertained, that, on the contrary, a drawback was allowed at the Custom House on the exportation of grain, when the price was as low as it was at this time.

In four or five days after our landing I was taken into the house of a most kind and charitable gentleman, a Mr. Downe. I requested him to lend me a horse to ride over to Plymouth, to confer with my friends and fellow-countrymen there. I found upon opening my plans to them that they ` ' like me, been struck with the low price of grain, and had invested all their money in it already to ship to France, so I had my trouble for nothing, and I returned to Barnstaple in rather a pensive mood.

After revolving the matter in my mind during a sleepless night, I decided that it would be right to let my host have the benefit of my knowledge, as a small return for his hospitality, for it was possible he might be disposed to send some corn to France. He entered into my plan very readily, the more so from having been engaged in trade in his youth. He had been to Spain as supercargo of a vessel on one occasion, so my project was quite in his way. He said he would willingly risk as much as £300 or £400 upon it, and he most generously offered to give me half the profit. I hesitated about the propriety of accepting it, because loss was possible, though profit was probable, and if it should be loss, how could I pay my share of it? Upon further consideration I made up my mind to accept his offer, but to provide against loss by effecting an insurance upon my half, for which I paid a premium of two and a half per cent. to insure me against loss both in going and returning.

The whole of my personal property consisted of twenty pistoles in gold, six silver spoons, one of them a very handsome silver gilt, with the initials I. D. L. F. engraved upon it. I had great value for that spoon, it having been used by my father when he was upon his travels before he was married, and my mother gave it to me in the same case he had carried it in. I had also a silver watch, and a rose diamond worth ten or twelve pistoles. My intended wife had a gold chain for the neck, a pearl necklace, an emerald, and a diamond worth five pistoles. If any loss occurred which was not covered by the insurance, I thought that we could pay for it by the sale of our possessions, enumerated above. You observe I have put your mother's articles in the list, for though not yet united by marriage, we felt our interests were one and the same from our mutual vows, our affection and our confidence.

Mr. Downe chartered a vessel of about 50 tons burthen.

loaded her without delay, and consigned her to Mr. Boursiquot, a brother of your mother, and to Peter Robin, a distant
cousin of mine. You may guess their astonishment at receiving such a consignment from their relation, whom they
had pronounced to be a madman, to abandon his country, forfeit his property and go to a foreign land, as they predicted
to die of hunger. They would scarcely have lent him five
sous, and in less than five weeks after his departure from
home, he sends to them a vessel laden with corn of the
value of 6 or 7000 livres. It appeared absolutely incredible.

The profit would have been very great if it could have
been sold instantly, but the king had sent for corn from
foreign countries, which arrived about the same time mine
did, and that which belonged to the Royal speculator was
ordered to be all sold before the cargoes of private individuals could be touched. Nevertheless, the profit was considerable, and the return cargo, nine tons and three hogsheads
of Bourdeaux wine, some chestnuts, and salt also sold to advantage.

Mr. Downe prepared to make a second shipment, and he
was persuaded by some friends that the first cargo would
have done better had it been consigned to a regular merchant—the English seldom know when they are well off—
and I, from a foolish diffidence, did not stand up for my
cousin as I ought to have done. The vessel was therefore,
much to my sorrow and to our great loss, sent to a merchant
at Marennes, who understood merchandise rather too well for
us. He swallowed all the profits in his enormous charges,
and then instead of returning, as we had instructed him to
do, the best Bourdeaux wines, he shipped the " Vin du
Pays" which he had received in the way of trade from the

peasants, and he invoiced it to us at the price of real good
wine.

We made still another adventure, and ordered the return
cargo to be in salt. I lost by this more than all I had
gained, and I was saddled with debts besides. I will give
the particulars.

After the Captain had taken in his cargo, he was applied
to by several Protestants to give them a passage to England,
which he agreed to do most cheerfully. They were some of
a numerous class, those who had made abjuration in the
hope of being free from disturbance, and gaining time to
turn all their property into cash, and then to watch an opportunity for escaping withit. In this case they placed mistaken
confidence in the integrity of the Captain, and put their
money into his hands for safe keeping. The sight of the
treasure was a temptation beyond his powers of resistance,
and he determined in some way or other to make it his own.
He let one or two of the sailors into his confidence, and arranged with them to take the vessel to Spain. The Captain
told the passengers that the wind was contrary, and they
might require to shelter the vessel in some port, and as
they would run great risk by going into a French port, he
intended to stretch over to the coast of Spain. When between Bilboa and St. Sebastian, with every sail set, the wind
and tide favoring their wicked purposes, they ran the vessel
upon the beach and she was a complete wreck. Here was an
end of our cargo of salt; it returned to the sea whence it
came.

The most horrible part of the story is yet to come. The
Captain and crew jumped into the boat with the treasure, and
left the passengers to be drowned, for every wave washed com-

pletely over the wreck. One of their number, a lady of quality, who owned the largest part of the treasure, wore a thick quilted petticoat, which buoyed her up so entirely that she might have floated ashore, had not the Captain espied her and prevented it. He put off towards her in his boat, as though he were going to assist her, but when he got within reach, he plunged her under the water with a boat-hook, and held her down for so long a time that the petticoat which had in the first instance resisted the water, becoming saturated, prevented her rising. *Auri sacra fames pectora cogis.*

After having thus barbarously drowned those who had placed unlimited confidence in him, he went to Cadiz with his ill-gotten wealth, bought a share in a Spanish privateer, of which he took command, and that is the last I ever heard of him.

My losses were so heavy that I was obliged to dispose of my watch, gold chain, and silver spoons, and still something remained unpaid. These various transactions occupied several months, but as the commencement occurred immediately after my arrival, I have thought it best to continue the account to its winding up, so as not to break the thread of the history.

CHAPTER X.

I HAVE already mentioned that I had been hospitably received into the house of a Mr. Downe at Barnstaple. This gentleman was a bachelor of some forty years of age, and he had an unmarried sister living with him, who was about thirty-three or thirty-four years old. They were kindness itself, and I was as completely domesticated with them as if I had been a brother. They were in easy circumstances. Miss Downe was worth about £3000, and her brother had an estate near Minehead, worth £10,000.

The poor lady most unfortunately took a great fancy to me, and she persuaded herself that it would be greatly for the benefit of all concerned if she were to be married to me, and her brother to my intended. I should have supposed it an easy matter for any one to have fallen in love with your dear mother in those days, for she was very beautiful, her skin was delicately fair, she had a brilliant color in her cheeks, a high forehead, a remarkably intellectual expression of countenance; her bust was fine, rather inclined to embonpoint, and she had a very dignified carriage, which some persons condemned as haughty, but I always thought it peculiarly becoming to one

of her beauty. The charms of her mind and disposition were
no way inferior to those of her person, so that altogether she
seemed formed to captivate the most indifferent, yet I am
almost sure that Mr. Downe only yielded to the solicitations
of his sister, and had really no love in his heart.

Miss Downe opened her project to me one day by observing that she thought we must be two fools, to think of being
married to each other, when our only portion would be beg-
gary. I did not at first comprehend her, but she persevered
in her attacks upon me at every opportunity, and began to
give me broad hints that if I would only open my eyes, I
might plainly see where I could do much better for myself.
I then discovered her meaning, but I was determined not to
appear to understand it, and our languages being different,
made it very easy for me to appear as ignorant as I pleased.
However, it so happened that her brother entered the room
one day when she was trying to drive it into me, that a more
suitable match was within my power than the one I was in-
tending to make. She turned to him and begged he would
make the explanation for her, which, from our mutual knowledge of Latin, and his slight acquaintance with the French
language, he was well able to do. The request his sister had
made evidently embarrassed him a good deal; he was not
nearly so much taken with your dear mother as Miss Downe
was with me, which seemed most strange, for I am sure he
had much more reason to be smitten than she had. After a
little hesitation and clearing of his.throat, he told me that the
plain truth of the matter was this : " My sister wishes to
marry you, and if you will agree to it, I have promised to
help to remove the difficulty, we see in the way, by taking for
my wife, your intended lady, whom you brought with you

6*

from France." I should mention that there was nothing attractive, but rather the reverse, in the personal appearance of
Miss Downe; she was short, thin, sallow, and marked with the
small-pox. Mr. Downe was by no means handsome, but he
was much better looking for a man than his sister for a woman. In answer to the above most singular offer, I said not
a word, but drew from my pocket a paper which I gave him
to read. It contained a solemn promise of mutual constancy,
and your mother and I had each signed it. We had executed
two such documents, and each kept one. After Mr. Downe
had read it, I said to him : " My love is so strong and so sincere that, even now, if I thought the dear object of my devoted attachment would be more happy in being the wife of a
rich man, I feel that I am equal to making the sacrifice of my
own happiness and releasing her from every promise ; but if I
may judge of her feelings by mine, I think she would not give
me up to become the possessor of untold wealth. I will give
you this strong proof of the sincerity of my assertion, I will
promise to deliver your message faithfully to her."

Accordingly I went that very evening to the house of Mr.
Fraine where she was staying, and I executed the delicate
commission with which I had been charged. To tell the
truth, I was not altogether sorry that so good an opportunity
should offer itself for discovering whether her love was equal
to mine. As soon as she had heard the message, she burst
into tears ; she evidently thought I was attracted by the fortune of Miss Downe, and wished to break off my engagement
with her. She continued to weep in silence, so I repeated the
offer over again, and added that she would have altogether the
best of the bargain, because the fortune of Mr. Downe was
three times as large as that of his sister. She then made a

great effort to speak with composure, and scarcely raising her eyes, she said, slowly and distinctly, "You are free, I release you absolutely and entirely from every promise that you have ever made to me. I feel deeply sensible of the great weight of my obligation to you for having rescued me from persecution and brought me to this country. I shall be for ever grateful to you for it; and I will not make you such an unkind return for those favors as holding you to your contract would be, and thus condemning you to poverty for life. Think no more of me; I am contented to remain as I am; only be so good as convey to Mr. Downe a request not to repeat to me himself that which I have heard from you, for I never will be his wife."

This answer was quite too much for me; it was now my turn to weep, and our tears flowed together. When I had somewhat recovered from the effect of her words, I spoke to her with much solemnity: "Think you, dearest, that you could live contentedly with me? Could you resolve to help me to labor for our living, and for the support of those whom God might give us? Remember! poverty is a hard, grinding mistress, and one under whom we shall probably be obliged to work all the days of our lives. For my part, I have a strong confidence that God will not suffer us to know actual want, and I am ready to encounter the difficulties and hardships that may stand in the way with you for my partner through them all. If you dare venture to run the risk, say so; and I assure you I shall think myself infinitely happier with the prospect of laboring with my hands, earning bread for you to eat, with the sweat of my brow, than if I were going to wed the wealthiest of women. I can live single; but I will be the husband of none but you on the face of the earth."

She replied to this with much animation of countenance, and said, " Every word you say finds its answering echo in my breast."

That evening, which had begun with tears, ended most joyfully. We had thought, until then, that we would defer our marriage until we had some visible means of maintaining ourselves; but now, prudential considerations were laid aside, and we resolved to become one by the laws of God and man, as we already were in heart, without delay, and thus prevent any future attempt to separate us.

I returned with a light heart to my host and hostess, and gave such an answer as might have been expected under the circumstances. I endeavored to make them comprehend the strength of our affection, and how impossible it would be to break off an engagement of such long standing as ours, and cemented by so much joint anxiety and suffering. Our mutual vows were to be binding until death, under all imaginable change of circumstances, with the exception only of apostasy on either side, of which now, thanks be to God, there was no longer any danger.

Mr. Downe was a man of good sense and kind feelings, and I verily believe he was relieved by the issue of the negotiation. It was otherwise with his sister; she was displeased and aggrieved, and made no secret that she was so.

We were married on the 8th February, 1686, at the Parish Church of Barnstaple, by Mr. Wood, the Rector.

My wife had lived at the house of Mr. Fraine, since the day after our landing, and he took upon himself the furnishing of a wedding-feast for us, to which he invited almost all the French Refugees in the neighborhood.

Mr. Downe invited the same party to a similar entertainment at his house the day following.

Our funds were as low as they well could be, for I had paid £5 for the insurance of my merchandise, and I had been obliged to pay £3 for the purchase of a wedding-ring, and procuring the license for our marriage. You may judge of our mutual affection, by our having refused to marry persons of wealth. You should also observe the strong confidence we had in the good Providence of God; and blessed be his name! we have never had reason to repent.

We lived for a month or two in a furnished room; then I received from France a feather-bed, and several coverlets, which my former valet, Manseau, had contrived to save from my house. My sister Forestier sent me some household linen from London, and with these grand additions to our possessions, we ventured upon hiring a small house in a back street. The French Refugees had talked about our marriage, and our poverty, which caused some of the inhabitants of the town to come and see us; and they added to our stock all the articles of furniture that were necessary to the comfort of a small family; so we were furnished with all we could desire, without having spent one farthing upon it from our own very small purse. The liberality shown to us did not stop there, for every market day meat, poultry, and grain poured upon us in such abundance, that during the six or eight months we lived there, I only bought one bushel of wheat; and we had two bushels left when we removed. All this was done in the true spirit of Christian charity; we never knew from whom any of these things came.

Our good cheer costing us little or nothing, we were glad to share it with our fellow Refugees, who did not meet with the same generous kindness. Many of them, too, had a distaste for English cookery, and they liked exceedingly to partake of my soup and bread. They came to assist in the cooking first, and then in eating the food.

This mode of living might be very agreeable to some persons, but it did not suit my wife or me. Each gift reminded us of our painful dependence; and we looked eagerly around, hoping to discover some mode by which we could maintain ourselves without charity.

I had occasion to go to Bridgewater, on some business connected with the second cargo that was sent to France; and while I was there, Mr. Hoare, an alderman of the borough, and a very upright, worthy man, introduced me to Sir Halsewell Tynte, who lived about two miles from Bridgewater, which led to my making an arrangement to live in his family, and render certain services, for which I was to receive £20 per annum; and as I was to live at his table, I thought the sum would be sufficient for the support of my wife. It was on the 18th September, that I went to live at a distance from her, in the hope of supporting her independently, but I found the separation so grievous, that I determined to fetch her to Bridgewater, where I took a small house. Early in the year 1687 I went for her, and brought also my sister-in-law, Elizabeth Boursiquot, who had fled from France with us, and our infant son, who had been born during my absence, and been baptized by Mr. Mausy, the French minister, and presented for that sacrament by Mr. Fraine, Mr. Juliot, and his aunt Elizabeth.

Even after I had brought your mother so near to me that I could visit her frequently, I found it a great trial not to be with her constantly, and she also felt the privation so painfully, that I determined to give up my employment and return to her. I preferred the coarsest food with her for my companion to the continual feasts of which I partook at Sir Halsewell's.

Poverty stared us in the face, and exertion of some kind was absolutely necessary. We tried to keep a small shop in Bridgewater, but our efforts were not crowned with success

You may be surprised that in my difficulties I received no assistance from the fund, collected for distribution among the suffering French Refugees, so I will tell you how it happened. I must begin the story at a period dating about the time of my arrival in England. As soon as my friends in London heard of my being in the country, they brought my case, unknown to me, before the committee for dispensing the fund. Mr. Maureau, my advocate at Saintes, drew such a picture of my zeal and constancy that there was no opposition made to placing my name on the list of ministers, although I was only a candidate, and I was to receive £30 per annum. The first I knew of what was done was by the receipt of a letter from Mr. Maureau, congratulating me on my escape, and enclosing to me the sum of £7 10s. as the first quarter of a pension that the committee had granted me. He further requested me to send him a certificate of my having received the Communion according to the rites of the Church of England, which it would be necessary to produce to the committee before I could receive the second quarter.

I, who had but just escaped from the Tempter, felt alarmed at this mode of entitling myself to receive charity. Before this communication reached me I had communed most cordially with the English, after the manner of the Established Church, without the least scruple of conscience, but when it became the condition upon which I was to receive the chari-

ties of the Kingdom, the case was altered. I looked upon
the Communion as one of the most sacred mysteries of our
holy religion, one which it was unlawful to approach with any
other view than to receive thereby the benefits of the sacrifice of
the death of Christ. When I saw it imposed upon me to
gain pecuniary advantages, I doubted very much whether any
spiritual benefit could be derived from a communion received
for the express purpose of procuring a pension. It seemed
to me a very papistical sort of proceeding, much like what I
had seen in France, " Come to mass and you shall be exempt-
ed from dragoons."

I had hitherto found nothing whatever to offend me in
the service of the Church of England. I then studied it very
carefully, and I heartily embraced all its doctrines as set forth
in the thirty-nine articles; but the Church Government, especially the point so much insisted upon of Episcopacy by divine
right, seemed to me to bear too strong a resemblance to Popery.

I might have gotten over these objections, perhaps, if I
had not learnt their cruel persecution of their brother Protestants, the Calvinists, only for differing on the subject of Episcopacy,* and some ceremonies which were, in themselves, of
no great importance. I found that the poor Presbyterians
had been imprisoned, fined, and deprived of their employments,
because they would not consent to receive Episcopal ordination, in conformity with the laws passed in the reign of Charles
II., and furthermore, I was told by the Presbyterians, that
the unfortunate people who had been executed after the Duke

* It is not surprising that a foreigner should confound the conscientious
members of the Church of England with the disguised Papists who were so
numerous in the days of Charles II. and James II., by whom the Calvinists
were persecuted.

of Monmouth's rebellion, a few days before our arrival, and whose heads and quarters I saw exposed on all the towers, gates and cross-roads, looking absolutely like butchers' shambles, had many of them been guilty of no crime but that of being Presbyterians.*

I confess that all these circumstances combined to give me a prejudice against the Established Church, and the use, which it was proposed to me to make of the Holy Sacrament, went so much against my conscience, that I have never yet sent the certificate to qualify me for receiving the second quarter of my pension.

The committee, appointed for distributing the money, were guilty of a flagrant error in my judgment. The money placed under their control arose from the voluntary contributions of the whole English nation, and I honestly believe, that the Nonconformists had been as liberal as the Episcopalians, and yet from this fund no relief was given to any one who did not hand in a certificate of his being a member of the Church of England, and surely this was unjust.

I was at one time so ground down by poverty, and my spirit was so humbled, that I actually made a journey to London for the purpose of making personal application to this committee. My friends told me that the best plan would be for me to call upon certain Deans and other high dignitaries, the most influential members of the committee. I followed their advice, but my garments were old and shabby, and I found it very difficult to obtain an entrance at any of the great houses. The usual ordeal through which I passed was

* This has evidently been a party statement, and according to history must have been untrue, for Monmouth's rebellion was an effort to subvert the government, without religious object.

that the footman who opened the door would leave me to wait a long time in the hall, as though I were a common beggar, and, at last, return to tell me that his Reverence was not at leisure to speak to me. I called again and again, until the servant was so weary of opening the door, that to avoid further importunity, he would obtain for me the desired audience. He would accompany me through divers richly furnished apartments, watching me the while to see that I did not steal any of the plate, piled up on the sideboards, and finally usher me into the private apartment where the Dean was sitting. He would inquire my business without so much as offering the poor beggar a seat. In as few words as possible, I would tell him of my situation and sufferings, and be proceeding to open my papers that he might judge for himself. I was stopped at once, "No, no, I have no time to read any testimonials, fold them up again. I shall hear all about it when your case comes before the committee."

The urgent necessities of those who were dearer to me than life itself, had so subdued my pride, that I made, not one or two only, but a round of such visits as these. It was all to no purpose, the money was for Episcopalians only.

My friend, Mr. Maureau, held the office of Secretary to the Committee; he took up my cause with much warmth, and said, " You will not, I trust, suffer so worthy a man to be reduced to extreme want, without affording him any assistance; a man who has shown that he counted his life as nothing when the glory of God was in question, and who voluntarily and generously exposed himself to uphold the faith of a number of poor country people. Perhaps there are not four ministers who have received the charity of the committee, who have done so much for the cause of true religion as he has done."

He could say nothing that would help my cause with this committee, so long as the fact remained without contradiction, that I was a Presbyterian.

Some of them said, " He is a young man, let him get a situation as a servant ; his wife can do the same ; and they may send their two children to us, and we will have them taken care of in the house we have provided for the purpose."

After the meeting, I was directed to go to the Grand Almoner, to receive the answer, which was couched in much the same language as that given above. My eyes filled with tears, and I felt so indignant that I spoke hastily, and said : " You ought to follow the directions in the New Testament, and put yourself in my place, before giving such cruel advice." His wife was present at the time, and turning to her, I said : " Madam, I pity you most sincerely, for being united to a man who can speak with so much indifference of the separation of husband and wife." I knew that they had no children, and I went on : " I adore the wisdom of God, who has not thought fit to bestow the blessing of children upon one, who feels it so trifling a matter for a parent to part with them. Before I would place mine under your guardianship, or give up the spouse whom I consider as one of the choicest blessings God has bestowed upon me, I would dig the ground all day as a common laborer, in order to share with my wife and children, at night, the bread I had earned by the sweat of my brow."

The committee bestowed upon me the sum of three pounds, which I was told was all that I should ever receive from that source. I returned home very much cast down by the result of my humiliating application, for I had expended between seven and eight pounds upon travelling and its necessary accompaniments.

Some charitable Presbyterians heard of my distress, and of the refusal of any aid from the fund collected for the relief of suffering French Protestant Refugees, and they kindly volunteered to make a collection for me in their congregation, which was a most seasonable help in my need.

You may suppose my feelings were still more soured towards Episcopalians by their treatment of me. I now realized, by bitter experience, that opposition and unkindness, for difference of opinion, have a much greater tendency to widen the breach than to bring opponents to one way of thinking.

At a time when I was greatly in want of money, I found by accident, among my papers which I had brought from France, half a sheet of stamped paper, entirely blank. It occurred to me instantly, that it might be the means of recovering for me something, from the sale of the property I had left in France. My cousin, Peter Robin, had acted the part of a faithful agent in his management of the cargo of wheat which Mr. Downe and I had consigned to him, and he was therefore the person whom I fixed upon to act for me now. I signed my name at the foot of the sheet, and sent it to him. I told him I wished him to make use of it, so as to obtain money for me for the sale or lease of my estate. I desired him to take care that he affixed, to the deed he executed, a date previous to that of my leaving France. The latter precaution was necessary to prevent the King seizing the property. I never had a word from him in reply; but I have reason to know that he, the said Peter Robin, went to live at my house after he received my letter, and from that day he considered it was his own. He took advantage of the confidence I placed in him when I put my name to the stamped paper and sent it to him. He has cheated me and my heirs after me, for no claim could now be made, because he would at once defeat it, by producing a deed of sale, signed by my own hand.

I would have you look upon the moral furnished by this proceeding. I was miserable enough to desire that he should execute a false deed for me, in order that I might obtain something from the property I had left in France. He did execute the false deed, in the way I had pointed out, but he did it for his own advantage, not for mine! I recognise in this, as in all other things, the justice and the mercy of the just Judge of the universe. I was punished, as I deserved to be; God directs all things for the good of those who love him, and who serve him with faith and humility, and mingles mercies with the punishment of his children; and in this case, I think I see plainly the great benefit to my family that he has extracted from my sin. It has removed all temptation out of the way of my descendants, that might have seduced them into returning to the Babylon whence he had withdrawn me, in the hope of recovering my estate. The children of some Huguenot Refugees, unworthy of their parents, have returned to France from similar inducements. My children can never do so; the property is irrecoverably lost. When I rejoice that the temptation is removed, you are not to suppose that I imagine any of my children would ever have been seduced into returning to idolatry for the sake of money. I think better things of you; and I have a strong confidence that you also will so instruct your children, that the love of God and of his true religion may be perpetuated in our family to the remotest generation.

CHAPTER XI.

I WENT over to Taunton, to look about me, for any prospect of improving my circumstances, and I was so far successful that I obtained a few pupils to instruct in the French language. At first I went there only for the day, three times a week, to give lessons, but after a while, I decided that it would be the most advantageous plan to remove my family there entirely, and keep a shop as we had done in Bridgewater, and I hoped that the addition of the profits, from teaching, to those from the shop, would maintain us all.

I had been in the habit not only of having family worship, but of preaching to the circle of relatives who clustered around us. When I removed to Taunton, three or four French families wished to join us, and so form a small congregation. I then thought that I ought to receive that authority from man which I had already received from God.

I was aware that the Episcopalians possessed all the Church Benefices, and filled all the offices of trust throughout the kingdom, but I was not dazzled by their splendor. I preferred the simplicity of Divine worship, to which I had been accustomed from my childhood, to the grandeur and wealth of the Episcopalians.

Some of the Presbyterians, with whom I had become acquainted, actually hated the Episcopalians, and they made me believe that the Church of England was a kind of Romanism. I held in abhorrence all the practices of the Papists, so I determined to have nothing to do with the skin of the beast, even though the beast itself had been rejected. I was attached to the leaves of the tree of life as well as to the trunk, branches and fruit ; and in my exile I determined to join myself to that company of believers, who most nearly resembled those with whom I had suffered in my own country. I resolved rather to labor with my hands while I preached the pure doctrines of the Gospel, and admitted only the simplest ceremonies, than to wound my conscience by entering the Church which was upheld by the State.

I presented myself before the Protestant Synod assembled at Taunton. I produced the testimonials of my education, manner of life and sufferings, which I had brought with me from France. I then underwent an examination, and received Holy Orders from their hands on the 10th June, 1688, having an earnest desire to exercise the functions with all the Christian humility, zeal and affection of which I was capable.

After leaving Barnstaple I was never again so poor as to require charity. Mr. Travernier of Plymouth sent his son to be under my care for two years, and he lent me £100, without interest, for that length of time. I found the wholesale dealers in Bristol and Exeter very accommodating to me in granting credit. I paid for the goods as fast as I sold them, and I was then allowed to take a fresh supply on credit. In this way we gradually increased in our dealings until we had a stock of one thing or other to the amount of £400.

When I lived in Bridgewater two Frenchmen had applied

to me for assistance, which I could not furnish myself, but I
had obtained it from others, and when I gave them the money
I said, " If you will follow my advice, and learn a trade at
once, you will never be obliged to ask for charity again, but
will become independent. There are in Bristol French manufacturers of light stuffs, to whom I would recommend you to
bind yourselves." They followed my advice, and soon after I
had established myself at Taunton, they called on me for the
express purpose of returning their thanks. I did not recognise them in the least ; the rags and tatters in which they had
formerly appeared had given place to decent and respectable
clothing. They were obliged to tell me that they were the persons whom I had formerly assisted, and recommended to learn
a trade, and that they had done so, and now, all they wanted,
was a small advance of money from some one, and they would
work for half the profits. They urged me to undertake it,
and they said £20 would be amply sufficient to buy worsted,
yarn and dyes, and that they themselves had wherewithal to
buy tools. They said if I would make the necessary purchases
for them they would work two years for me, and be contented
with half the profit on the work. I consented to it, and as I was
unwilling to cramp the business of the shop by taking money
from it, I borrowed the £20 from Mrs. White, a widow, who
dealt in tobacco, at Bridgewater.

Behold me now, not only a French teacher and a shop-
keeper, but a manufacturer also. The sea had been too cruel
for me to think of being a merchant again.

One of these Frenchmen whom I took, as it were, into
partnership with me, had formerly been a pickpocket in London, and had only given up the employment from fear of the
consequences. He was a very skilful workman, he would

accomplish more in a given time than any two others, and his
work was always well finished. I knew nothing of his former
habits of life, and he commended himself so much to me by
his cleverness, that I made him the chief manager, and I used
to send him to Exeter to make the purchases, and he was as
skilful in making bargains as in working. I frequently trusted
him with as much as £20 or £25 at once, for this purpose, and
he was uniformly honest and correct in all his dealings with
me. He told one of his fellow workmen that he often had
been strongly tempted to run away with the money, and then he
would say to himself, " What ! steal from a man who has been
so invariably kind to me ! and who places such perfect confidence in me ! No; I cannot do it."

When he left me, I have understood that he returned to
London, met with his old associates and fell into bad habits
again.

At the end of three months I knew much more than the
workmen did. I invented new patterns for the stuffs, which
I showed them how to execute. The employment proved profitable, and I had insensibly put more and more capital into
it, until at the end of a year I had £80 embarked in the manufactory, in place of the original £20 which was the estimate
of the men. They quarrelled amongst themselves about the
division of their share of the profits, and finally came to me
to propose that I should pay them fixed wages, and carry on
the business altogether on my own account.

Every thing now seemed to prosper with me. I hired the
handsomest shop in Taunton, opposite the cross in the Market
Place. I was able to furnish it with so great a variety that
it was always full of customers. My wife was kept very
busy, though she had two boys, Travernier and Garaché, to

7

help her. I manufactured stuffs in the upper part of the
house which she sold, at a profit, in the lower part. I went to
Bristol and Exeter, once a quarter, to lay in a fresh supply of
groceries and pay off the old debt. I procured direct from Holland linens of various qualities, galloons, thread, needles, and
tin and copper ware, manufactured there by French refugees.
These articles cost me much less than if I had bought them
in England. I was supplied with beaver hats from Exeter,
where they were made by Frenchmen, who furnished them to
no one in Taunton but myself. I sold French brandy, pure
and unadulterated, whereas the Englishmen generally played
tricks with theirs. I drew custom by selling Malaga and
Alicant raisins, at the price retail that I paid for them by
wholesale. I sold needles on the same terms. Every one
knew the value of these articles, and the sale of them did not
amount to any great sum. One would say to another, " You
can buy beautiful raisins from the Frenchman at such a price,"
and then they would come to see for themselves, buy some
raisins, and probably ten or twelve shillings worth of other
articles, upon which we made a profit, so we found our account
in selling cheap raisins.

The other shopkeepers were very angry, and said I should
most certainly be bankrupt soon, for I sold the raisins at the
same price they paid in Bristol, without reckoning the cost of
transportation and loss of weight. Their mode of talking
about me only increased my sales, for the people came to get
all they wanted before I was ruined. When my friends asked
me privately why I sold so cheap, I told them that I found it to
answer very well, and I repeated the common proverb, " Light
gains make a heavy purse."

Stranger, as I was, I had more custom than any other shop

in the town. My competitors looked on patiently, expecting that it could not last much longer, and their day would come, when I had to put the key under the door. Instead of that, I became only more prosperous. I appeared to succeed in every thing I undertook.

I had just begun to breathe freely, after all my trials, and to feel myself comfortable, when a prosecution was commenced, and I was summoned to appear before the Mayor and Court of Aldermen.

The Mayor was a wool-comber, who came to the town originally possessed of one single groat. He worked a long time as a boy comber; he then married one of his master's servants, scraped together a little money, and began business on his own account. At the age of thirty-six or thirty-seven years he learnt to read, and to write a little. In course of time he accumulated as much as £7000 or £8000, and thereby obtained the honors of the town, for this was the third time he had filled the office of Mayor.

The Aldermen were generally persons of the same class, men who had risen in the world, but who had received very little education. Some were woollen manufacturers, others were shopkeepers, and they all seemed to think that I had interfered with them, so they could scarcely be impartial judges in the case. I certainly had entered into competition with most of them, for I employed men to work for me in my little manufactory, and I sold in my shop most of the articles which they dealt in.

There was but one man in all this body, who had received a good education—the Recorder. He had consequently great influence over the others, and could govern the cohort very much as he pleased. I had every reason to believe that he regarded me with esteem, for I had frequently been in his company, and had had many interesting conversations with him upon philosophical and theological subjects.

When I appeared in answer to the summons I had received, I found the accusations were of a very multifarious character. They said I was a sharper, a Jack-of-all-trades. The manufacturers complained that I had the wool combed. I dyed it myself, had it spun and woven in my own house, and then I retailed it myself in my shop. The grocers brought forward their grievance, which was that I sold a better article retail than they could buy wholesale at the same price; and that I sold all sorts of things except apothecaries' drugs. The dealers in tin and copper ware said I injured their trade so much, that they would have to give up, and go to the parish, if I did not soon shut up my shop. Those who dealt in brandy and vinegar, complained that they were left to sit quietly with their arms crossed all day long, while customers thronged my shop, so that the liquor could hardly be measured out as rapidly as it was inquired for. The hatters said their trade was broken up by the French beaver hats of various kinds, which I furnished at a lower price than it cost them to import them from France. The hosiers felt themselves injured by the stockings of St. Maixant, which I sold. The drapers were neglected by their old customers since I had introduced chamois leather, dyed of all colors, for making breeches—one pair of which outlasted three of cloth, and looked better. Added to all this, the stranger, who was pocketing the profits they thought they ought to have, was not liable to assessment for government taxes and town rates, as they were. He was also, they said, a Jesuit in disguise, who said mass in his own house every Sunday. One word would describe him as well as a thousand; he was a French dog, taking the bread out of the mouths of the English.

Any one who had heard their accusation, would have supposed I was as rich as a Jew. I attended, to make my own defence, without the assistance of an attorney, and I had no fear for the result.

Mr. Mayor came to the point at once, and said to me, "Have you served an apprenticeship to all these trades?"

This question was quite to the purpose; for by law no man can carry on a trade to which he has not served an apprenticeship.

I rose without embarrassment to reply, and spoke in a tone loud enough to be heard throughout the court: "Gentlemen, in France a man is esteemed according to his qualifications; and men of letters and study are especially honored by every body, if they conduct themselves with propriety, even though they should not be worth a penny. All the nobility of the land, the lords, the marquises, and dukes take pleasure in the society of such persons. In fact, there, a man is thought fit for any honorable employment, if he be but learned; therefore, my father, who was a worthy minister of the Gospel, brought up four boys, of whom I was the youngest, in good manners and the liberal arts, hoping that wherever fortune might transport us, our education would serve instead of riches, and gain us honor among persons of honor. All the apprenticeship I have ever served, from the age of four years, has been to turn over the leaves of a book. I took the degree of Master of Arts at the age of twenty-two, and then devoted myself to the study of the Holy Scriptures. Hitherto, I had been thought worthy of the best company

wherever I had been; but when I came to this town, I found
that science without riches, was regarded as a cloud without
water, or a tree without fruit; in a word, a thing worthy of
supreme contempt; so much so, that if a poor ignorant wool-
comber, or a hawker, amassed money, he was honored by all,
and looked up to as the first in the place. I have, therefore,
gentlemen, renounced all speculative science; I have become
a wool-comber, a dealer in pins and laces, hoping that I may
one day attain wealth, and be also one of the first men in
the town."

When I ceased speaking, there was a general laugh
throughout the assembly. The Mayor and some few of the
Aldermen were exceptions. The Recorder himself lost his
gravity for a few moments, and joined in the mirth. He recovered himself presently, and rose with a dignity that reminded me of the Town Clerk of Ephesus; there was a profound silence as soon as he stretched out his hand.

"Gentlemen," said he, "King Charles II., of blessed
memory, issued a declaration, of such a date, whereby he invited the poor Protestants who were persecuted in France for
the cause of the Gospel, to take refuge in this kingdom, not,
most assuredly, with the intention of suffering them to die of
hunger, but rather that they might live in comfort amongst
his subjects. Thus you see they are fully entitled to every
privilege that we enjoy. Suppose Mr. Fontaine and his
family had not the means of gaining a livelihood, and they
were famishing in the midst of us, we should in that case be
obliged to feed them. By law, the parish would be burdened
with their maintenance; for you know you could not send him
to his birth-place, therefore you must treat him as if he had
been born in the place where he resides.

"Although Mr. Fontaine was brought up to nothing but study, yet in the desire he has to live independently, without being burdensome to any one, he humbles himself so far as to become a mechanic, a thing very rarely seen among learned men, such as I know him to be from my own conversations with him. Do not you think our parish is obliged to him for every morsel of bread he earns for his family? It would be perfect barbarity to pretend to put any obstacle in the way of his earning a livelihood. Are you, his accusers, disposed to raise a fund, and settle an annuity upon him and his family for life? Strangers are as much entitled to justice at our hands as our neighbors are. I will answer for Mr. Fontaine, that if you will secure to him a moderate income, he will leave mechanical occupations, and gladly return to intellectual labor."

He paused awhile and looked around the Court-room, but no one broke the silence, so he resumed :—" Is nobody disposed to come forward? It is a strange thing, gentlemen, you are not willing to let him earn his own bread, and yet none of you offer to give it to him. Shall it be said of us, that there are only one or two families of poor Refugees settled in our town, who have abandoned country, friends, property, and every thing sweet and agreeable in this life for their religion and the glory of the Gospel, and instead of cherishing these people, and treating them as the suffering members of our Saviour Jesus Christ, and providing for them tenderly and abundantly by our charities, we would even hinder them from gaining a living by their labor? There is not a Turk in Turkey so barbarous."

He then turned around and addressed himself to me. "You may go away, there is no law that can disturb you, I

will answer for it. We return you our thanks for the bread
you earn. God bless you and your labor!"

I said, "May the Lord bless you also!"

The Court resounded with thousands "God bless you, Mr.
Fontaine!"

This was the end of the law proceedings, but not of the
malicious feeling that had caused the prosecution. The
Mayor and his party hated me all the more for having con-
temned them in the face of the whole town. They continued
to annoy me in every possible way. They exaggerated my
profits very much, they magnified them to guineas when my
gain was but in pennies, and consequently I was taxed to
the utmost.

CHAPTER XII.

Revolution of 1688—Landing of the Dutch—Unexpected visitor—Soldiers billeted on me—Retirement from business—Calimanco—Profitable manufacture—Crippled Weaver—Secret discovered—Visit Dublin and Cork—Send sons to Holland—Increase of family.

A SHORT time after the prosecution related in the last chapter the glorious Revolution of 1688 commenced. I felt very anxious about the effect it might have upon the welfare of me and mine. I had a vivid recollection of the end of the Monmouth rebellion, for they were still busy hanging and quartering when I landed in England.

The Prince of Orange marched with his army to Exeter, where he was welcomed by the same party that had declared for Monmouth. Three sorry-looking Dutchmen were sent to Taunton, and they were suffered to take possession of the place without the slightest show of resistance from any quarter. The common people hailed their arrival as a joyous event.

The Mayor and Aldermen were most decided Jacobites; they stood aloof to watch the course of events, and contented themselves, meanwhile, with noting down the names of all persons who appeared to favor the Dutch, in the expectation of having them hanged after a while, as those had been who joined the Duke of Monmouth. I felt very certain that which-

7*

ever side I might espouse, my name would have a prominent
place in the list of culprits, and I was the more convinced
of this from the story that was told about me.

On the arrival of a company of soldiers at Taunton, they
were informed that there was a French Jesuit in the place
who said Mass in his house every Sunday. It happened fortunately for me, that the Captain of this company was a
French Protestant, who had taken refuge in Holland, and entered the army of the Prince of Orange. He was pleased
with the idea of attacking a French Jesuit, and was determined to be the first to seize him, so he obtained a direction
to his abode, and was posted opposite to the door of my house
with a guard of soldiers, before any of the family were stirring, except a female domestic who was a French woman. The
Captain asked her who lived in that house.

She replied, " Mr. Fontaine, a minister from Royan in
France, lives here."

The Captain immediately desired her to go up to my
room and tell me that Captain Rabainières was below, anxious to embrace me. I only waited long enough to get on
my dressing-gown, and went down to welcome a dear friend;
for you must know, we had been intimately acquainted with
each other in France, and our residences were only four or
five miles apart. We embraced one another with the warmth
of fraternal affection. I was then introduced to the rest of
the officers, who were most kind in their offers of friendship.
I cannot pass on without calling your attention to this fresh
instance of the goodness of God, whose providence watched
over and shielded me from threatened danger.

The street was crowded with people who had followed the
soldiers, and some had even forced their way into my house

after the Captain, to make sure of being near enough to enjoy
the sport of seeing the Jesuit hung. When these witnessed
the warmth of our salutations, they knew not what to make
of it, and cried out that they were lost and ruined. " Those,"
said they, " whom we hailed as our liberators must themselves
be Papists."

I had never attended the Parish Church in Taunton,
which led many into the belief that I really was a Jesuit, and
those who knew better studiously kept up the false impression, in order to injure me with the community at large.

The officers went to the door to disperse the crowd, which
was not an easy matter, under the disappointment they felt
at not seeing the Jesuit punished. They told them that their
Captain knew Mr. Fontaine to be a good Protestant, better
than they were in all probability. They manifested a bitterness of feeling that made my friend decide upon leaving a
few soldiers at my door, as a precautionary measure, in case
of violence.

When several more regiments belonging to King William's
army were quartered in Taunton, you may rest assured I was
not forgotten in the billeting of them upon the inhabitants.

I went to complain to the Mayor and Sheriff because two
soldiers had been billeted upon me, and it was not customary to
quarter them on a minister. They heard me patiently, but I
had scarcely reached home before two more soldiers presented
themselves with a billet for me.

I complained a second time, and I was answered by an
assurance, that I should receive full justice, and directly I
got home, four more came upon me. I made no further complaint, lest I should draw upon myself sixteen instead of
eight. I had to support them for three whole weeks, during

which time I treated them as well as I could ; and I explained
my circumstances to them. The times were so ticklish, and
the town magistrates showed so decided an inclination to put
difficulties in my way, that I thought I had better examine
into my affairs, pay my debts, and withdraw from all large
transactions for the present. I was occupied during the day
teaching French and Latin, so that I was obliged to steal
many hours of the night from sleep, to find time to make an
exact inventory of all that I possessed. I put down every
thing at a low valuation, and I was pleased to find that there
was enough to pay all that I owed, and a little to spare. I
sent some of the stuffs of my own making to the wholesale
dealers, from whom I had made purchases on credit, and
I begged they would sell them as opportunity offered, repay
themselves with the proceeds first, and then return to me any
balance that should remain. This arrangement was equally
satisfactory to both parties ; I was able to pay my debts by
it, and those from whom I had bought on credit, were very
glad, in these hard times, to find themselves secured against
possible loss.

As soon as it became known that I wished to dispose of
my shop, and stock in trade, a young man came forward to be
the purchaser, who expected to do wonders ; he had heard
such exaggerated accounts of the money I had made by the
business. He took every thing as it stood, paying me the
actual cost, as appeared from the entries in my books. The
whole amounted to four hundred pounds, which sum he paid to
me in cash, and I made use of it at once to pay the wholesale
dealers ; so that, after the sale of my manufactured stuffs,
which I had already sent to them, they found themselves indebted to me. I requested them to keep the money in their

hands for me at present, in order that I might have it as a little leaven, to begin again with renewed vigor, whenever the political troubles should be at an end.

When I looked upon the result of this winding up of my business, I could not but feel very grateful to my Maker for the blessing upon my labors, which had enabled me to pay every thing I owed, including the debt left after that last disastrous voyage, which had hung most heavily upon me ever since. Though I had not been pressed for payment by those who had lent me the money in my extremity, yet I now felt it a vast relief to be able to clear it all off, principal and interest. After all this, I was sole owner of the tools and utensils required in manufacturing the stuffs, I was the proprietor of good, comfortable household furniture, and had fourteen pounds in cash. Your mother and I had undergone much labor and fatigue of body, and considerable anxiety of mind, in accomplishing these great things, but it was for the sake of our dear children, and what will not parents do for their offspring! How much better was it for us all thus to struggle through difficulties together, than to have weakly followed the advice of the committee in London, and given up my children to be educated in their Institution! We always find that God assists those who put their trust in Him.

On the 12th April, 1690, my wife gave birth to a daughter, whom she and I presented for baptism the next day; and I baptized her myself, naming her Mary Anne: Mary, after my mother, and Anne, from the second name of my wife.

For several months I followed only the one employment of keeping a school, by which I did not make quite enough to maintain my family. I found it, too, a very ungrateful employment, and I became tired of it.

When James II. had taken refuge in France, and William and Mary been received as King and Queen of England, things began to assume a settled aspect, and I thought I might venture to begin some sort of business again.

There was a sort of stuff, manufactured at Norwich at that time, called Calimanco, which was very substantial, and also fashionable, and I determined upon making the attempt to imitate it. I had never, you know, served any apprenticeship, so it was all the same to me what I undertook to make, I must call upon the ingenuity of my own brain to aid me. I therefore thought it would be better, when I began again, to try something new instead of going on in the old beaten track. The stuff called serge, which we had made before, was now out of fashion, and those who manufactured it scarcely earned salt to their porridge; but then, they had served an apprenticeship to it, and as they worked altogether mechanically, and not with the understanding, they were really incapable of putting their hands to any thing else. I was possessed of a large share of that sort of perseverance which some people call obstinacy, and without which I certainly could not have overcome the almost insurmountable difficulty which met me at the outset.

The Norwich stuff was made of extremely fine worsted, double twisted. Now, there was not in Taunton a spinner who could spin so fine, nor a weaver who knew how to weave it; no machinery suitable for the manufacture, nor a person who knew how to construct it. I had never seen the machinery, but I saw that if money was to be gained by manufacturing, this was the stuff that ought to be produced. As I could not get the worsted spun fine enough to allow of re-twisting and doubling it, I must try what could be done with a single thread.

I engaged a weaver for my experimental attempt, who was out of employment, and was apparently very docile; I made all the machinery, I put it up with my own hands, and spent a couple of hours every day trying to instruct him. This went on for three months, altering the threads and machinery for new trials about once a fortnight, and still not an inch of the desired fabric was produced; and I was paying the weaver his full wages all the time.

Some little time after this, a young man came to solicit charity from me; he was in extreme distress, absolutely penniless, and his wife in hourly expectation of her confinement. He entreated me to give him some employment, and said that he would spare no pains to give me satisfaction; and he was sure that I never should see cause to repent of it, for his urgent need would be a spur to his assiduity in laboring for one who should help him at this pinch. I took him and his wife into my house, I fed the two, and soon three of them. I fitted up a loom for him, to try what he could do; and he kept his word, for he worked day and night, entering into all my plans, and never appearing wearied of making efforts. He was very grateful to me for maintaining him and his wife, and he tried to give proof of it by faithful industry. He also knew, that if he was successful, he would certainly be able to earn a comfortable subsistence. He tried seven or eight different plans during a fortnight, and at the end of it produced one yard of Calimanco, which looked very well; but being of single thread, it had no more substance than serge. I was obliged to set my wits to work once more, to try whether I could not discover some mode, by which a substantial fabric could be made out of the materials I had at command. I contrived it, at last, by the following process: I made the warp, which appeared all on the right side, of fine wool coarsely spun ; and the weft, of very coarse wool, combed like fine wool, and spun in a thick, compact thread. The second piece was begun, upon this new and successful plan, just two months after I received the family into my house. The one piece of twenty yards, which was all that we had to show for our labor, sold for threepence a yard, but we did not tell any one how long we had been employed in making it.

I kept an exact account of all that I had expended in these fruitless attempts and the small proceeds resulting from the sale of the first piece made my inmate very discreet and considerate in his expenses. He never asked me for any money that he could possibly do without.

By degrees he became more expert in the work. He was soon able to make half-a-yard a-day, then a yard, and after more practice several yards. When the second piece was taken out of the frame it appeared really handsome, and was as strong and substantial as the Norwich Calimanco ; but there was great disappointment when it came home from the mill where it had been pressed, it looked no better than a coarse coverlet, for it had great strong hairs sticking out in all directions. I recollected that when I was at school I had often gone to warm myself in a hatter's shop opposite to the school, and I used to watch the process of burning off the long hairs from the hats with a wisp of straw, so I thought that a similar plan might be adopted for remedying the defect in my Calimanco.

A hat can easily be turned round in the hand to apply the flame to all sides, not so a long piece of stuff. A machine would be required to apply it with certainty and regularity. I was too impatient to wait for the production of a machine,

and determined to singe this first piece as well as I could
by hand.   I had to call in the aid of my wife and her sister
Jane Boursiquot, who laughed so much at my dilemma that
I almost felt discouraged.   I made the stuff damp all over so
that I might not burn it as well as the hairs, and they held
it, one on each side, while I passed the blazing wisp of straw
over it.   At last the work was finished, and then I had the
right to laugh, for, when washed and pressed, it looked really
beautiful.   I sent it to a draper at Exeter, who allowed me
two shillings and sixpence a yard for it.   I found I could
make it for just half the sum, so I gained an ample reward
for all my expenditure of time, labor and money.

My workman improved rapidly, he made it better and
better every day, and he gained such facility by practice that
at last he was able to turn out ten or twelve yards in a day.
I had hitherto merely supplied him with what was absolutely
necessary for himself and his wife, but I now promised to pay
him four pence half-penny for every yard he made in future.
I also took into my employ again the first weaver who had
labored so long unsuccessfully, and he too acquired the art
after a while.

I now hired a shop for the sale of my Calimanco ; I took
from my old tradesmen all the articles I wanted, and paid
them with my own goods.   I employed more workmen, and I
bound each one, under a penalty of £10, not to work for any
one else, or to teach the art to other workmen.   They were
all willing to make such terms, because they could earn three
times as much by working for me as by making serge.

When I had planned a machine to singe off the hairs, I
employed a different mechanic to make each part, so that not
one of them knew the use of that which he was making, and

when I had got the various parts ready I put the machine together myself. It consisted of two large rollers, and the
piece was wound gently, off the one, and upon the other, and
fire applied during its passage ; when both sides were singed
it was washed in the river, then pressed, and it really had
much the appearance of the true Calimanco ; the strength of
the coarse worsted gave it substance, and the fineness of the
warp gave it lustre. I now gave up teaching entirely, and
confined myself to my manufactory, which proved very great
slavery, for it was absolutely necessary to keep secret the
mode by which we removed the coarse hairs, and therefore I
was obliged to do that part of the work myself. My wife or
my sister-in-law turned the spit while I roasted the joint.

I succeeded so well, that in the course of seven or eight
months I was able to keep from twelve to fifteen looms constantly going. I had not been long at work before the profitable nature of my new trade became known, and the old-fashioned manufacturers of serge were envious of it. Their astonishment at my inventive genius was very great, they almost
looked upon it as sorcery ; and it was increased by an incident which I will relate. I heard accidentally of a poor weaver who had lost a leg, and in consequence of it, he was, according to the general opinion, incapable of ever working
again at his trade of weaving serge, because they and their fathers before them had made use of two feet to work the loom,
they did not imagine it possible that anybody could weave
with only one leg. The poor man had been supported by the
parish for three years. I thought much about his distressed
condition, and wondered within myself whether it would not
be possible to devise some plan, whereby he could work at his
old trade. I made many experiments, and at last I hit upon

the right thing; I went without loss of time to see the poor fellow, who lived in the house of his brother. I asked him if he would not like to be able to weave once more.

"Alas!" said he, weeping, "God has been pleased to deprive me of my leg and it is impossible for me to weave."

His brother was then working in a loom by his side; I turned to him, and asked him to get out of the frame and let me make some alterations in the treads. He allowed me to do so, and I then detached all the cords from the treads, and arranged them differently, and asked the cripple to enter the frame. I then showed him how his remaining leg was competent to all the work, directing him to put his foot first on the one tread and then on the other. In the course of an hour he made a quarter of a yard of serge, equal in every respect to the rest of the piece which had been woven by his brother who possessed two legs.

I then explained to him most particularly the manner in which he must make the preparation for weaving with one foot, so as not to run any risk of getting his work in confusion. I then left him in the act of calling upon God for blessings to be showered upon me and mine, in return for the benefit I had conferred upon him and his family, by enabling him to earn a livelihood by his labor. For several days afterwards the house was thronged with weavers who went to witness the extraordinary sight of a man weaving with but one leg.

The son of the Mayor, before whom I was formerly cited to appear, had a great desire to make Calimanco like mine, so he bribed one of my workmen to teach him how to do it, and guaranteed to him the £10 which he was bound to forfeit to me if he worked for any one else. I did not sue him for it, I thought the trouble would be more than it was worth.

The young man had not possessed himself of my whole secret by his underhand proceeding. The workman made the Calimanco for him as he had done for me, but he knew nothing of the mode by which I got rid of the long hairs that had perplexed me at the outset. When several pieces had been made and pressed, they proved utterly unsaleable, from the hairs upon them ; so I stepped forward and made an offer of fifteen pence a yard, which was gladly accepted. I burnt off the hairs, and then resold them at two shillings and sixpence a yard. The treacherous weaver was now thrown completely out of employment. He dared not show himself to me, and as he could not produce a profitable article for the man who had tempted him to betray my secret, he would not employ him any more, for he was not disposed to make stuff merely to sell it in an unfinished state to me. The wretched workman went off one morning with whatever he could lay hands on belonging to his late employer, and among other things, a handsome overcoat with very large silver gilt buttons upon it. He went to London, and I have heard he became a regular thief, and was eventually hanged.

The attempt to supplant me had proved so unfortunate to both master and workman, that a long time was allowed to elapse before any further effort of that kind was made, From the end of the year 1690 until the year 1693, I worked in peace, and retained for my own benefit the profit of my invention. During this interval the demand for serge gradually decreased, and trade became so bad that actual want seemed to sharpen the faculties of the serge manufacturers, and they determined to do their best to imitate my Calimanco. My secret was at length discovered by some pieces having inadvertently been sent to be pressed without having been sufficiently washed in the river first, and the smell of burning disclosed the mystery. Then it was recollected how many trusses of straw I had been in the habit of buying, and laying the two circumstances together, they could have no longer any doubt as to my plan of removing the hairs by fire. After a good deal of trouble they got rollers at work like mine, and every one left off making serge.

The coarse worsted had been despised before, and I purchased it at the rate of a penny half-penny a pound; the increased demand raised the price to fourpence a pound. The market became overstocked with Calimancos, and the price fell to two shillings, then to eighteen pence, and at last to fifteen pence a yard.

I made mine spotted with a different color from the ground, and obtained a preference over theirs, but they soon imitated me. I then contrived fresh variations in the patterns, and made a kind of spotted serge, which sold at three times the price of the old-fashioned kind. I spent the whole of the year 1694 in this most vexatious occupation; all the time racking my brains to invent something new, and as soon as I had succeeded, I had the mortification of finding myself imitated and undersold. I became weary of the business, and seeing that I had now made £1000 in the course of three years, I thought I would leave the place and try whether I could not find a French Church in want of a minister. I knew that there were many French Protestant Refugees in Ireland, so I went to Dublin to make inquiries. I was there recommended to go to Cork, and I accordingly proceeded thither, and found that several French families were settled there, who were very desirous to have a minister, but they had hitherto hardly dared to make the attempt, because their means would not allow them to offer a sufficient stipend.

God had vouchsafed to bless my labors, and I felt myself independent, therefore this opportunity, of preaching the Gospel without remuneration, was most pleasing to me, and I agreed to return. to Cork and take charge of the Church, as soon as I could wind up my affairs in Taunton and remove my family.

I met with two very poor French families in Cork, who were almost in a state of starvation from want of employment; they were weavers by trade. .My sympathy was much excited by their condition, and I was anxious to help them, and as the most feasible plan for doing so appeared to me to give them work in their own trades, I bought worsted and dyes for their use, and deposited £25 with Mr. Abelin, an Elder of our Church, and I directed him to expend it in whatever appeared requisite to enable them to manufacture such stuffs as they had been accustomed to make in France.   He kept a shop, and I requested he would receive their work and sell it for them as fast as it was finished, and out of the proceeds furnish them with fresh materials, and at the same time keep a sort of general supervision over their families until my return. He attended to my wishes, and I had the satisfaction of finding, when I returned to Cork, that they had been comfortably supported, out of the profits upon their labor, during my absence, and the little capital I had deposited with Mr. Abelin was undiminished.

On my return to Taunton we set to work most vigorously to prepare for removing to Ireland, and the packing up our goods, and closing my manufacturing concerns, occupied about six weeks. We took twelve horse loads of furniture and baggage to Bristol, whence we intended to embark for Ireland. I purchased there a variety of drugs for dyeing, and large coppers for the same purpose, and screws, such as might be required for putting up presses, and, in short, every thing that I thought would be of use in the manufactory which I proposed establishing at Cork. I knew that it would be absolutely necessary for me to do something for the support of my family, or I should soon see the end of my thousand pounds, as the congregation for whom I was called to officiate were unable to pay me any stipend.

Before I embarked for Ireland I took my two oldest sons, James and Aaron, to London, and sent them thence to Amsterdam to be under the care of a relation settled there. My chief reason for this step was to avoid a sweeping catastrophe, like that which cut off the whole family of my brother-in-law Sautreau, which I have already mentioned. By separating my family I hoped that some of them might be spared, in case of shipwreck.

I ought not to take leave of Taunton, without naming that, during our residence there, my wife had not been less fruitful than my brain; we were now the parents of six children; James, Aaron, Mary Anne, Peter, John and Moses.

CHAPTER XIII.

WE landed in safety at Cork on the 24th December, 1694, and the agreement I had already entered into with the congregation was solemnly renewed. You can see the particulars in the Act of the Consistory of Cork, dated 19th January, 1695, on which day I commenced the discharge of my pastoral duties.

At first I preached in Christ Church, the use of it being granted to us after the English had finished the services of the day. We then assembled in the County Court-room for our worship; and finally, I gave up, for the use of the Church, a spacious apartment on the lower floor of my house, which we had regularly fitted up for the purpose with pulpit, benches, and every thing necessary.

My manufactory here was altogether different from that which I had carried on at Taunton. I considered it most for my advantage to make something for which there would be a demand near home. The great article of manufacture in Cork at that time was a sort of coarse baize, two yards wide. I thought I would try to make something better than that, and I soon succeeded in making good broadcloth, for which it was only necessary to use finer wool than for baize and to weave it more closely and compactly.

I took a large house, a little out of town, in which I established my manufactory. I gave out the spinning and weaving. I put up a hot-press and a cold-press in my house, and the latter was so contrived as to compress the bales of goods. I had all the tools and machinery required for teasing and dressing the cloth, and for combing and carding the wool. I built my dye-house near the river for the convenience of pumping up the water. A dyer in the city applied to me for permission to make use of my apparatus, which I granted on condition that he should dye all my worsted and cloth without charge, and make me a certain allowance out of his profits in dyeing for other people, and I well remember that in fifteen months he gained enough to pay me nearly £50 for my share. My knowledge and experience were of great service to him, because I had always written down the exact proportion of each drug that we used at Taunton, and attached to the memorandum a pattern of the article dyed. When he received any order he invariably came to consult with me, and by referring to my books and comparing his pattern with those I had preserved, I was able to tell him at once the exact quantity he would require of each drug, and my instruction never failed to prove correct.

I was now at the height of my ambition. I was beloved by my flock, to whom I preached gratuitously, and thereby had the heartfelt satisfaction of serving the God who had blessed me without deriving any pecuniary advantage from it. My dear wife gained from our manufactory an ample support for the family. We were able to furnish a number of French

8

Refugees with employment, by which they earned enough to
maintain their families respectably. The Church increased
daily; Refugees came from various parts to settle in Cork
when they heard that a French Church was established there.
After a while those members of the congregation who were
in easy circumstances became ashamed of allowing me to
preach without compensation, and they proposed to raise something by voluntary contribution, if it were only to show that
they were grateful for my services. When it came to my
knowledge, I thanked them much for their kind intentions;
but I told them that as they could not possibly raise enough
to support my family without exertion on my part, I would
greatly prefer that whatever sum they were able to collect
should be appropriated to the relief of the poor, of whom
there were many in the congregation. I said that it was a very
great pleasure to me to imitate St. Paul, preaching the Gospel
and at the same time earning my living by the labor of my
hands. They were well satisfied with the view I took, for
they could not raise more than £10, or at the very utmost
£15, which would have been a mere trifle towards the support
of my large family.

On the 16th September, 1697, my wife gave birth to another boy, whom we presented to the Holy Sacrament of Baptism, and I baptized him myself, after our service was over,
on the 19th of the same month. We gave him the name of
Francis. I was the godfather, for I had a great dislike to
make people solemnly promise that which they had no intention of performing. On the day of his baptism I made a
great supper, as though I intended to feast the wealthiest of
the French Refugees in Cork, but instead of that I invited
about a dozen of the poor of my flock, and after they had

eaten and drank abundantly of the best, I gave each one a shilling to take home.

I have already said that the French had received me with much kindness, and I may say the same of the people generally. The Corporation of Cork, as a mark of their esteem, presented me with the freedom of the City.*

This state of things was altogether too good to last; my cup of happiness was now full to overflowing, and like all the enjoyments of this world, it proved very transitory.

Great numbers of zealous, pious, and upright persons had joined our communion; but it could not be expected that all should be of this class. Unfortunately, there were some in the flock whose conduct was not regulated by the principles of our holy religion.

A man named Isaac de la Croix, originally a merchant in Calais, had caused dissension in the Church there before its condemnation, and had then settled in Dover, where he also made dissension in the Church. It must have been to punish us for our sins, that he came from there to join our Church, and he had not been with us more than eighteen months, when he was the occasion of discord amongst us also. The history of it is as follows: he had a son of about twenty-five years of age, who was in the habit of doing business on his own account. This young man chartered a vessel of about thirty tons, for Ostend, which he loaded with butter and tallow, promising payment in ready money. On a certain Saturday afternoon, he weighed anchor and dropped down to Cove,

---

* It is a remarkable coincidence that my father, James Maury, the great-grandson of James Fontaine, was also settled in a foreign land, and was so highly esteemed by the community amongst whom he lived, that the Corporation of Liverpool did by him, as that of Cork by his ancestor, voted to him the freedom of the Borough.

at the mouth of the harbor, expecting to sail early in the morning, and being Sunday, he hoped to steal away unobserved, and get off to sea without paying for his cargo. Amongst the tradespeople to whom he had given a written promise of payment, was a butcher, who had some doubt of the young man's integrity, and therefore took the precaution of going to the father to ask him to put his name to his son's promissory note. The father refused to do so, saying he had nothing whatever to do with the business. He imagined his son had by that time placed himself beyond pursuit; but it was not so, for the butcher hired a boat immediately, took bailiffs with him, and followed the vessel to Cove, and before sunset he put a stop to her sailing, unless the bills were paid first. The dishonest intentions of both father and son became apparent, and were frustrated.

I solemnly declare that I had not heard a whisper of the transaction when I mounted the pulpit next day. It so happened, strangely enough, that I had been for some weeks engaged in delivering a series of sermons upon the Ten Commandments; and on that day I had arrived at the Eighth Commandment, in regular course. In explaining to the best of my ability, the various ways in which the command of God, " Thou shalt not steal," may be broken by violating the spirit of it, I very naturally mentioned the tricks and evasions sometimes practised in commercial dealings. I pointed to acts so similar to the recent fraudulent attempt, that Isaac de la Croix was sure I meant it for him ; others of the congregation thought so likewise. It was concluded I could not have sketched his character so true to the life, without knowing his history. He was extremely displeased, and uttered most blasphemous oaths as he left the church, and ended with exclaiming, " Thou shalt pay me for this."

After the service was concluded, some of the elders of the Church came and spoke to me on the subject. I protested to them that it was the first I had heard of it, and therefore they must ascribe the singular coincidence to the Providence of God alone. Mr. de la Croix would never believe it, and he continued his threats of vengeance; and in the end, he made his words good, for he was the cause of much anxiety and distress to me.

On Monday morning it was ascertained that father and son were alike unable to pay for the cargo. The son absconded, and I never heard more of him. The creditors took possession of the articles, and each tradesman, as far as possible, took back his own property, and the vessel was soon emptied. The captain was the chief loser, for he had to seek a fresh freight.

Mr. de la Croix kept his promise, and lost no opportunity by which he could revenge himself upon me for the injury he imagined I had inflicted upon him. His plan was to try to poison the minds of my flock, and make them dissatisfied with me. He began first with persons whom he knew to be weak and vain; he told them they need not expect to rise to consideration in the city while they had a Presbyterian for their pastor. In this way he made an impression on the minds of some who aspired to the office of Mayor or Sheriff; they in turn talked over the matter with others, and by degrees a spirit of opposition was infused into the minds of a number of my hearers, and they waited upon me to request that I would receive ordination from the Bishop. I was not at all disposed to accede to their request, on the contrary, I used every argument to prevent them from deserting us, and going over to the Established Church. In the course of the discussion I became warm, and in the heat of dispute, I said that which I must acknowledge it would have been much better to have left unsaid, even though true. My opponents went to the Bishop to make a complaint of me, and they told him all that I had said, much that I had not said, and most assuredly had not even so much as thought. They effected what they wished, and exasperated the Bishop so much against me, that he made a formal complaint to Lord Galway, then in a high office in Ireland, who was disposed to sacrifice me to please the Bishop of Cork. We had a long correspondence on the occasion, of which you will find copies amongst my papers. Mr. de la Croix declared that I was not a minister at all, and he went about in the congregation, and visited amongst them from house to house, and told them all, that I was not an authorized minister. His misrepresentations were so far credited, that I was obliged to write for vouchers to the gentlemen of the Walloon Church, in Threadneedle-street, London. All this was most distressing to me, and, finally, for the peace of the church, I felt it my duty to request the Consistory of Cork to receive my resignation. I annex a copy of their reply to me.

(C O P Y.)

Mr. James Fontaine, our Minister, having written to this congregation to request to be released from the service of the church, for reasons assigned in his letter of 30th May last, this congregation, distressed at the prospect of separation, and the causes which have led him to request it, deem it expedient, nevertheless, to give a reluctant and sorrowful con-

sent to his desire ; thanking him most humbly for the services
he has rendered to this church during two years and a half,
without receiving any stipend or equivalent whatever for his
unceasing exertions. We feel bound to testify, that, though
he has been obliged to use his own industry for the support
of his family, yet it has never occasioned him to neglect any
duty of the Holy Ministry. We have been extremely edified
by his preaching, which has always been in strict accordance
with the pure word of God. He has imparted consolation to
the sick and afflicted, and set a bright example to the flock of
the most exemplary piety and good conduct. We pray God
to bless him and his family, and to grant him the consolation of
exercising elsewhere, with more comfort to himself, those gifts
which God has given him for the holy ministry to which he
has been called.

In testimony whereof we have given to him this present
certificate at Cork, 5th June, 1698.

Signed,   P. RENUE,
                  P. CESTEAU,
                  M. ARDOUIN,   *Elders.*
                  CAILLON,
                  JOHN HANNETON,

Thus you see how much injury may be done by one quarrel-
some, malicious individual in a church. The poor minister is
under the necessity of sacrificing his own comfort for the peace
of the Church. I was certain that if I did not resign, a
schism would be created, and did my best to prevent it. I
wrote to Lord Galway and told him that if any change should
be made in the mode of worship I had adopted, by the appointment of an English clergymen, I should feel myself bound, in
spite of my resignation, to officiate for that portion of the

flock who preferred the French usage. I believe this threat was not without its effect in causing Lord Galway to recommend Mr. Marcomb for my successor, which was most satisfactory to me, for he continued to carry on every thing in the way I had commenced, and the Church service has ever since been conducted in the French mode.

I sometimes felt regret that I had been so humble as to request my discharge, for you will find in the sequel that I lost at Bear Haven all the property I had acquired. Nevertheless God, who only sends afflictions to try our faith, and not to bring us to ruin, has, in his infinite wisdom, turned all my misfortunes, losses and mortifications to my ultimate advantage, even in this life, and he has, in a manner almost miraculous, provided for all my wants, and enabled me to give my children the good education I desired.

In the month of July, 1698, my property began to diminish. A merchant in France who had heard that I lived in Cork, and could be depended on for honesty, consigned a vessel to my address. I knew nothing whatever of the man, but I received from him a very complimentary letter. I was simple enough to accept the consignment, and pay the freight and duties. The cargo consisted chiefly of salt and red wine from the Isle of Ré. When the wine came to be tried, it was found of such inferior quality that the dealers only offered £1 per hogshead for that on which I had paid a duty of £3 the hogshead. This vessel was no sooner discharged than another followed with similar lading, except that there was white wine also. I was obliged to pay the freight, but I had gained experience enough by the first cargo not to pay the duty. By the representations which were made, part of the duty was remitted on the second cargo. After all was sold I was left a loser by the payment of the duty on the first cargo. I drew upon the merchant for the deficiency, but he allowed the bill to be protested and never paid me the balance.

Before proceeding, I must relate a very extraordinary event. I have already mentioned sending my two older boys, James and Aaron, to Amsterdam at the time I left Taunton. They remained there two whole years, and when I wished them to return, a captain of a vessel, who was named De Coudre, was going from Cork to Ostend, and I made an arrangement with him to bring them back on his return voyage. We were quite ignorant of the character of De Coudre, we only knew that he had relations living in that part of France from which my wife came, but the opportunity seemed most favorable for the return of our boys, and we had no reason to mistrust the man. I shipped £40 worth of my manufactures on board his vessel. I wrote by him and desired the boys to join him at Ostend, which they did. The vessel was not to come direct to Cork, but to stop first and discharge part of the cargo in London. The Captain was instructed to take the boys immediately on arrival to my brother Peter, at the Pest House. I had a letter announcing their safety at my brother's house, where they were to stay until the merchandise was discharged and the vessel ready for sea. The night after I received this letter I was disturbed by the most distressing dream that could be imagined. I saw my poor boys struggling in the water, without any possibility of receiving help, they must inevitably be drowned. I awoke in perfect agony, and only closed my eyes to be distressed again by a recurrence of the same dreadful vision. In the morning I wrote a letter to my brother; I told him I had altered my plan, and did not like to trust the boys at sea any more, so he must

8*

send them by land to Chester, and from Chester they could cross the Channel to Dublin, and proceed thence by land to Cork. The letter was sent, and it might have been supposed that the weight would have been taken from my mind, and my fears have been dissipated, but it was no such thing; the same dreadful sight appeared before me again, in my dreams, each succeeding night, and the impression made upon my mind was so powerful that I was really sick with anxiety and distress; On the next post day I wrote a second letter to my brother, I gave him the particulars of the repeated dreams which had affected me so much. I told him I could not look upon them in any light but that of a warning from God, and that if my children should still be with him, I charged him not to let them go to sea. I said that if he should do so, after my telling him of the warning I had received, and the calamity I feared were to befall them, I should for ever lay the blame at his door. I made use of the most solemn and impressive language in this letter, which he had but just received when De Coudre, being ready for sea, called upon my brother to take the boys from his house to the vessel. He put the letter into his hand that he might read it for himself. He was greatly infuriated and tried to take the boys by force. When he found he could not get them, he went off, and refused to let them have any of their effects from the vessel.

They returned by land, according to my directions; thanks be to my Heavenly Father for his providential warning! De Coudre put to sea without them; and neither he nor any of his crew have ever since been heard of.

The boys told me, when they reached home, that this man was the most horrid blasphemer they had ever heard; they said they had trembled with fright at hearing him vomit forth his imprecations, even against Heaven itself. On one occasion, when they had stormy weather, he had stamped upon the deck like a madman, roaring out to the devil to come and do his work. Who knows but that God, at that moment, would have punished this impious blasphemer, and precipitated his body to the bottom of the sea, and his soul into the gulf of hell, if it had not been for those two innocent children, in favor of whom he deferred his vengeance, and warned me in a dream what I should do.

James will confirm to you the truth of this most extraordinary incident. I am sure he can never forget his wonderful preservation. I would say to him, that I trust the grateful recollection of it may be of service to him through the whole course of his life. When he is tempted to sin against God, I would have him pause, and ask himself the question, whether it was to commit this sin, that God withdrew him so miraculously from the waves of the sea.

I now resume the thread of my story. About the time that I was deprived of the very great comfort of preaching the word of God to my countrymen in Cork, there was an Act passed by the Parliament of Great Britain, forbidding the exportation of any manufactured woollen goods from Ireland. This law broke up my manufactury entirely; for the broadcloth I made was much better suited for exportation than for home use. Cork had ceased to be an agreeable residence to me after the disputes in the Church; and though I remained there for some months, and I preached in English in a Presbyterian Church every Sunday, yet I had an unsettled feeling, and was all the time on the look-out for any thing that might turn up to suit me better.

I sometimes thought of buying a farm to live upon with

the money I had realized. While I was in this state, looking on all sides for something advantageous, I accidentally met with a merchant from Kinsale, who told me of his having purchased fish at Bantry, for shipment to Spain, upon which he had made a large profit, and that the fisherman from whom he made the purchase, had also made a profit. I thought I should like such an employment very much, being one so immediately dependent upon the good Providence of God for guiding the nets, and giving success according to his pleasure. It seemed to me one of the most innocent of all occupations; so, contrary to the course of the Apostles, who, from fishermen became preachers, I, who had been a preacher, thought of becoming a fisherman.

I sold all my manufacturing implements and utensils, gave up the employment, and leaving my family in Cork, I set out upon a tour of observation through the fishing region. At Baltimore I made acquaintance with Colonel Beecher, who had very extensive fisheries, and at Castle Haven with Colonel Townsend; I purchased from the latter gentleman some very good second-hand tackle and boats, all complete. I ascertained that it was impossible to carry on fishing with success unless you had a large farm, with many tenants upon it, bound to fish only for you. I went to Bear Haven, and there hired a considerable farm from Mr. Boyd, at £100 per annum, another from Mr. Davis, at £31, 10s, and a third at £18.

Behold me now in the midst of great preparations for being both a farmer and a fisherman. I purchased a cargo of salt to be in readiness; I put part of it in a cellar at Bantry, and part at Bear Haven. I did nothing but spend money this season; it was too late for fishing when I began, but I was full of sanguine expectations for the next year.

Whilst I was making these preparations at Bear Haven, in the year 1699, it pleased God to withdraw my second son, Aaron, from this world. This event was the most afflictive that I had ever yet experienced during the whole course of my life. The loss of property had never weighed heavily upon me, but the loss of this dear child afflicted me extremely. He had been long an invalid; his complaint was consumption, and his sufferings were very great at times, from violent pain in his chest. He evinced the most entire resignation to the will of God, and with a firmness beyond his years tried to console his mother, who was shedding tears at his bedside. He assured her of the fulness of his hope, that through the merits of his Saviour he was going to be received into a state of everlasting happiness.

This grievous dispensation made Cork still more unpleasant to us, and we determined to remove to Bear Haven, where I had rented the farms for the fishery. I sold the lease of my house at Cork, with the improvements I had made in it, for £100.

In this new undertaking I went into partnership with my cousin, John Arnauld, and Messrs. Renue, Thomas and Gourbould, all merchants in London. They were to have one half and I the other. I put down to their share, at cost price, half of the Robert, a ketch of about 40 tons burthen, that I already owned, and half the price of the tackle, boats, and salt, that I had purchased. They bought in London, on joint account with me, two other vessels, of about 50 tons each, the Goodwill and the Judith. They sent the Goodwill to me with nets, cordage, and every thing necessary to make two more tackles, and the Judith was sent to France for another cargo of salt. As we intended to salt the fish ourselves, I built a house for the purpose, with stone walls and a slated roof, and shelves suitable for the purpose required, cellars to store the salt in, and presses in which to press the fish. I also built more boats, and got the tackle all ready; and so now, in the year 1700, we were only waiting for God to send us the fish; we were fully prepared to catch them, and turn them to the best advantage.

At first I had only James, my eldest son, with me. As soon as I had completed my preparations, and had every thing ready for the comfort of the family, I sent James to Cork for his mother and the children. They came round by sea in the Robert to Bantry, and thence to Bear Haven.

The first year and a half we lived in a mere cottage, thatched with straw; and we owe it to the good Providence of God, that, while we were so much exposed, we never suffered from the tories,* or robbers, of whom there were great numbers in these parts.

Having no immediate use for the Robert, we chartered her to a merchant in Cork to go to Spain. The captain was an Irishman, named James Joy, and he was instructed to receive the money for the freight, and to employ it immediately in purchasing salt, oranges and lemons. He obeyed his instructions thus far, but instead of bringing the cargo to Cork,

---

* The word tory having been long known as a cant term applied to a particular party, it may not be amiss to remark that it is here used according to its original signification. It is derived from the Irish word *toruighim*, to pursue for purposes of violence, and in the days of Queen Elizabeth we discover it first used to signify the lawless banditti who were so troublesome in Ireland during her reign. In England we find it applied for the first time, by the opponents of Charles I., to the followers of that unfortunate prince, under an idea that he favored the Irish rebels; and by an easy transition it became the distinctive appellation of that party who wished for the greatest extension of the royal prerogative.

he ran the vessel ashore on the coast of France, scuttled her, and sold the wreck with whatever was recovered from it to a French merchant, and he remained in France to enjoy his ill-gotten wealth. This was the unfortunate end of the ketch Robert, so far as we were concerned, but I have heard that the person who purchased her, as a wreck, was able to have her repaired, at a cost of little more than a crown, and that she has since been making trading voyages on the French coast.

In the month of May, 1700, we first commenced fishing for cod, off the Island of Durzey, but the weather was unfavorable, high winds and rough sea, which obliged us to return with scarcely any fish, and we had been at great expense. We next attempted to take salmon ; our expenses were but small, our gains smaller still.

In July we mustered our whole force to take herrings, three tackles, six boats, and forty-five men, at an incredible expense. Had the fish been as abundant as usual at this season of the year, our profits would have been considerable, even though the expenses were so heavy. Very few fish appeared, but we were obliged to keep up the expensive establishment, for perhaps the fish might come, on the very day when we, for the sake of economy, had disbanded our force and given up waiting for them. One single draught in a large shoal of herring might pay all the expenses of one, two, or even three years. We were paying the same wages to the men all the time they were waiting, whether they caught any fish or not.

This season passing away with so little result, we thought it needless to keep both our vessels waiting for fish ; so we sent the Judith on a trading voyage to Spain. With the pro-

bability before us of some day sending the Goodwill to Virginia, we added another deck for the purpose of keeping tobacco dry if she should have a cargo of it. This was an expense of £80, and made the vessel look clumsy, but she still
sailed well. Finding that I had not fish enough to give her a
full cargo, I proceeded by the directions of my partners in London to fill her up with beef, butter, cheese and candles, which
were of the value, including the fish, of £450. They recommended that she should be sent to Madeira first to dispose of
her cargo, that she should there invest the proceeds in wine,
then go to Barbadoes to sell the wine, and purchase with the
proceeds sugar, rum and molasses, and proceed with these to
Virginia, and after disposing of this third cargo, take in
tobacco to bring home.

She accordingly went to Madeira, where she found so many
vessels had already arrived laden with provisions, that every
thing had to be sold under its cost. The same bad fortune
attended them at Barbadoes, many vessels had brought wine,
and the price was low. It had been agreed that the seamen
should receive their wages at the second port, and this swallowed up so much money, in addition to the losses sustained
by each cargo, that only £130 was left to invest in sugar,
&c. With this small cargo they went on to Virginia, where
the cry was still the same, so many vessels were there already,
that the foreign produce was at a low price, and tobacco was
so much in demand to fill the vessels, that it was high. The
Pilot, who had come on board the vessel, saw how unpleasantly
the Captain was situated, and he suggested to him that it
would be for his advantage to take his cargo more into the interior, and he offered to conduct the vessel to a river he told
him of that ran eighty leagues up the country, named, I think,

Patuxent. The Captain decided to follow his advice, for he thought he might almost as well return without a vessel as without a cargo. When they reached the port, the Captain had every thing his own way, for no vessel had been there for more than six months, and they had not a pound of sugar, or a drop of rum or molasses in the place. He did so well with his half cargo, that he got in exchange a full cargo of tobacco. Every part of the vessel was crammed, even to the cabin and the sailors' beds. She arrived at Bear Haven in August, 1701, and I had been so perfectly successful with the fishery, that I had a cargo ready for her to take in ; but the tobacco was obliged to be first taken to London to be discharged. I wrote to my partners most urgently to use all possible dispatch and send her back to me for the fish.

On the 3d day of August, 1701, my wife was brought to bed of our youngest child Elizabeth. On that day we had most remarkable success in fishing. Our new slated house was not yet quite finished, and we were living in one end of the herring house, which was so full with the immense quantity taken, that every place was piled up with them, even to the very door of the chamber in which my wife was confined.

We cured this season more than two hundred thousand herrings ; we pressed enough to fill two hundred hogsheads, and we also put up two hundred barrels of pickled herrings. Besides this, we had twelve tierces of salmon, seven or eight hundred dried codfish, and two thousand dried flukes, altogether worth about £1200. I was in daily and hourly expectation of the arrival of the Goodwill. I wrote and wrote again to my partners to make haste and send her, in order that she might take the first cargo of the season to Leghorn, and being first in the market would give us a large profit.

While I was in this state of suspense, I sent a small quantity by a vessel loading at Bear Haven for Leghorn, a few of each kind, and valuing the whole stock at the price I obtained for these, we should have received £1500 for them, if the Goodwill had only returned to take them.

It turned out that my partners owned a large quantity of wine in Spain, and they were alarmed by rumors of war. In such an event they would have lost all their wine if it had remained in Spain ; and, on the other hand, if brought to England the prospect of war would be sure to increase its value. This was a large concern, and the fishery a small one to them, though a very large one to me. They thought nothing of the non-shipment of the fish, and kept the Goodwill running to and fro as fast as possible, hoping to secure all their wine for them before the declaration of war.

At last they wrote to me to sell the fish at Cork, as they really could not send the Goodwill. I went there, and found no purchaser. I wrote again, and begged them to send me another vessel if they could not let me have the Goodwill, for time was flying rapidly, and the fish, which ought to have been shipped long ago, were still on hand deteriorating in value. A man named Carré, in Cork, wrote to my partners, and told them he was expecting a ship, and that if it came he would give a certain price for the fish, about £600 for the whole. Instead of sending me another vessel in place of the Goodwill, they said I had better by all means let Carré have the fish at his price. I went to conclude the bargain with him early in December, for it was better to sell at half price than lose them altogether by keeping too long. Mr. Carré said he took them only on condition that a vessel he was expecting, I know not whence, perhaps from the kingdom of the Moon, should arrive in the course of the month of December. I wrote again to my partners, I complained excessively of their neglect of my interests. I told them that Carré had not the character of being a man of integrity, and it was absurd to depend upon him. As I had anticipated, his ship came not, and I doubt whether he had ever expected any. Wearied by my importunities, they at last bought an old vessel from Mr. Renue, which was delayed for repairs, and did not reach Bear Haven till the end of January, 1702. I loaded her with all possible dispatch, and on the 5th February she cleared out, and went as far as the mouth of the harbor, where she sprung a leak, and most of the sailors ran away, only three or four remaining with the master to work the pumps. I hired some Irishmen to pursue the sailors and bring them back. By much entreaty and many smooth words I persuaded them to go on board, help to stop the leak, and continue the voyage. They sailed for Leghorn and there sold the fish, from which I never received one single farthing. I was informed that the fish were so bad, that nothing more than was sufficient for paying the charges of all kinds had been received for them. I did not expect much, for Lent was over before the vessel reached Leghorn, and some of the fish would probably be injured by the leak ; but I could not suppose there would be no return whatever, unless there was dishonesty.

Thus God, to whose blessed will we must submit, in his infinite and unsearchable wisdom, saw fit to deprive us of all the advantages we had anticipated from this most abundant season. We had stretched out our hands to receive the gift, but we could only see it, we were not allowed to grasp it. All! all was lost! Thus had God willed it. We were not worthy of it.

My London partners had sustained so much loss by the
fishery, never considering that they alone were to blame for it,
that they wrote to me saying they would have nothing
more to do with such a losing concern. It was in vain
I wrote to them that their agreement was for three years,
and that I had made all my engagements for that length of
time, and this was only the second year. And I had hired
fishermen for the next year, and it would be impossible for
me to draw back without forfeiting at least £100. I made
a full representation of all these circumstances; I pointed out
to them how hard it was upon me, when they had occasioned
the loss by detaining the Goodwill for their own purposes. I
could not induce them to continue, and therefore I was obliged
to go on for another year on my own account. The Goodwill was sold in London for a trifle compared with her cost.
The expenses attendant upon building the cellars, herring-
house and presses, as well as the cost of the boats and tackle,
were all charged to my account. They allowed me something for their share of the use of them during the two past
years. They made it out that I owed them £600 when all
was wound up. Thus I was totally and entirely ruined, but
it was the will of God, and blessed be his name for the support of his grace, which enabled my dear wife as well as myself to submit to the chastisement without murmuring. We
were able to say from the heart, "Thy will be done!"

Amongst other expenses necessarily entailed upon me,
was the building of a house for our residence, with substantial stone walls, slated roof and towers ; in fact, a sort of little
fortification, for defence, in case of need, from the French
Corsairs who sometimes made attacks upon unprotected parts
of the coast. This cost me a great deal of money, but you

will find in the sequel it was not thrown away. The good providence of God made it the human means of procuring for me great advantages hereafter.

My Irish neighbors were in the habit of pillaging and cheating me in a thousand indirect ways. I had brought thirteen destitute Frenchmen into the neighborhood, who had served in the army under King William, and had been discharged, the war being over, and they knew not where to lay their heads.

I gave them land to cultivate, but whether it was owing to their ignorance of agriculture, their habits of indolence engendered by a military life, or the perpetual injuries they received at the hands of the Irish, I know not ; but certain it is, they became discouraged, and most of them left me before the end of the three years. I lost £80 by them, having advanced so much for their use.

When God vouchsafes his blessing, every thing prospers, but let him withdraw the light of his countenance, and the best laid plans and most energetic labors result in nothing but failure. Every thing now went wrong with us. There was a Court held for the Barony at Bear Haven which was competent to decide in all causes under forty shillings. I do not believe that there were more than a half a dozen Protestants in the adjacent country besides my own family, and those I had brought with me, so that when I or any of my Protestants demanded what was due to us, the matter was referred to a jury of Papists, who invariably decided against us. Protestants were never by any chance summoned to sit as jurors, and the consequences were most vexatious, for we not only lost our lawful dues, but were condemned to pay costs likewise. On the other hand, if the Irish took it into their heads to make any claim upon us, how unfounded soever it might be, they were sure to recover. Boyd was the judge for the Barony; he was a great rogue; Dwyer was the attorney, and he was no better. After some little experience, I put a stop to this system of cheatery and false swearing by appealing from the decision of the Barony to the County Assizes. I may say with truth, that I was the only person in the whole Barony who could be said to be really and truly in the Protestant interest, for the very few Protestants who had lived there any length of time appeared to have caught the infection, and become as bad as the Irish Papists themselves.

I was a Justice of the Peace, and in that capacity I exerted myself to the utmost to break up the intercourse subsisting between the Irish robbers and the French privateersmen, who were the best of friends, mutually aiding each other on all occasions, for the Irish seemed to look upon it as a settled point, that the enemies of the English must be their greatest friends. It was quite natural that my steady course of opposition to their evil practices should draw upon me the hatred of these people, and I soon had the evidence of its being so; for I received a message from one Skelton, a captain of an organized band of robbers in the woods, threatening me with an attack, saying that I might keep what guard I pleased, but they would manage to surprise me some day or other, and they would be with me before I had time to turn round. I caused Skelton to be informed that if he declared foxes' war I should do the same; so he and his comrades had better be upon their guard, lest I should be beforehand and seize upon some of them first. It so happened, about four or five months afterwards, I received information that a notorious robber was concealed in the cleft of a rock, close to the sea-shore, upon my farm. I armed myself, and took some of my Protestant servants, upon whom I could depend, and went down to the rock, which we surrounded, and finding him there, we took him prisoner and sent him to Cork, where he was tried at the next Assizes, condemned and executed. I received the thanks of the magistrates and the Government for the service I had rendered to the country by taking up this man. The others were rather afraid of me afterwards, and kept aloof. In the course of twelve months this whole troop of brigands was dispersed. They had quarrels amongst themselves, and betrayed one another. I notice this as one more instance of the superintending providence of God, which most mercifully turned aside a threatened blow.

The animosity against me still continued, nay, it rather gained strength, for I was determined to do my duty as a Justice of the Peace, and I persevered in sending to Cork for trial all persons who were found to be in the habit of holding communications with French privateers, and trading with smugglers. The number was commonly eight or ten every Assizes. The privateers sustained a heavy loss by this, or rather I should say, lost the opportunity of making their usual gains, by being deprived of the means of obtaining the information they were in the habit of receiving, as to what vessels were in the neighboring ports, where they were going the value of their cargoes, &c., &c., which had enabled them to make many rich prizes. The Irish were rewarded for their treachery on such occasions by a considerable share of the booty, and they were of course very much enraged at me for putting a stop to their trade. All efforts to injure me had hitherto been unsuccessful, but they felt that they must make a desperate effort to drive me away from the neighborhood, or their occupation was gone ; but once rid of me, they knew they could have it all their own way again. So it proved ; for after I left the neighborhood the privateers hovered on the coast, and received information, took prizes, and bestowed rewards as heretofore, and one by one, all the respectable Protestants moved away.

CHAPTER XIV.

AFTER having well deliberated, a force was brought to bear against me that, to all human appearance, would be amply sufficient to accomplish the purposes of my enemies. Early in the morning of the first day of June, in the year 1704, a French privateer hove in sight; she floated gently towards my house, in a perfect calm. She had a force of eighty men on board, besides four of my Irish neighbors who acted as guides. She mounted ten guns. I watched her progress, and thought their object was to bring her to the south of my house, where at high water the guns would have full scope and bear directly upon the front. I would prevent that, if it were possible, and therefore I mustered all the men I could find, exactly twenty in number. I furnished all the Protestants with muskets, and the Papists with clubs to carry on their shoulders, which made them look like armed men when seen from a distance. I gave directions that all should follow me and do as I did. We went round the little cove, stooping very low, as if we wished to hide ourselves, though in reality I made choice of the highest ground in order that we might the more certainly be seen from the privateer. I then

9

ordered all the men to go behind a large rock near the shore,
while I stood alone on the top of it, within sight of the vessel.
I told them all to appear on one side of the rock, as if they
were peeping out of curiosity, while I was looking the other
way; then I turned round and made angry gesticulations, as
if I were finding fault and striking some of them, and at the
same time I directed them all to show their heads on the other
side of the rock; I turned again, and appeared as if I were
anxious that they should be concealed. The enemy having
seen, as they thought, forty men behind the rock, did not
deem it expedient to effect their landing at a point so well
guarded. They turned about towards the mouth of the creek
upon which my house stood, and there they were opposite to
one corner of the house, from which point their fire would be
comparatively without effect. Thus, my manœuvre produced
exactly the change in their purpose which I had intended it
should. They dared not venture up the creek for fear of getting aground at low water.

When I saw that they had decided upon their position I
took my men back by a low path, and this time I really made
them hide themselves, so that the men on board the vessel
could not see one of us on our way back to the house. I
took all the Protestants in with me to assist in the defence,
and sent the Papists away. The privateer cast anchor about
a long musket-shot distant from the house, and presently the
lieutenant landed with twenty men, and made haste, apparently
with the intention of reaching the house before he thought I
could have had time to return from the rock. I had seven
men with me in addition to my wife and children; four or
five of these were of very little use to me. I placed them all
at different windows, I posted myself in one of the towers

over the door, and as the lieutenant was advancing with every
appearance of confidence in his mien, I fired at him with a
blunderbuss loaded with large shot, some of which entered his
neck above the shoulder-blade, and the rest his side. He was
taking aim at me as he fell, which made the fire go too high.
I ran for another loaded piece which was in the next room,
and during my short absence his men took him up, crossed
the ditch and carried him back to the vessel.

The Commander was furious at such unexpected resistance from a Minister, and sent another officer on shore, with
twenty more men and two small cannon. They placed these
under cover of the rocks and hedges, and cannonaded the
north side of the house, while the guns of the vessel bore upon the south-east. Being altogether unaccustomed to this
kind of music, I must acknowledge that when the first cannon
ball struck the house, I felt some tremors of fear. I instantly
humbled myself internally, before my Maker, and having
committed myself, both soul and body, to his keeping, my
heart revived within me. I regained my courage, and suffered
no more from fear. I popped my head out of the window to
see what effect the ball had produced on our stone wall; and
when I perceived that it had only made a slight scratch, I
cried out joyfully, " Be of good courage, my children, their
cannon-balls make nó more impression on óur stone walls,
than if they were so many apples !"

I had an officer staying with me, with whom I had been
conversing the night before this attack, as to the probable
chance of my being able to offer successful resistance upon
such an occasion as the present. His reply had been very
discouraging ; he thought a cannon would make as short work
with us as if our habitation had been a castle of cards. I be-

lieve that it was the impression he had given me of our weakness, which occasioned the apprehension I felt when the ball
struck the house, but which was perceptible to no one but
myself and my Heavenly Father, who, in answer to my petition, had dissipated my fears.

John McLiney, a brave Scotchman, was stationed at a
window which overlooked the cannon upon the shore. He
had fired repeatedly, without effect ; so at last he put a double charge of powder into his musket, fired again, and killed
the man who was pointing the cannon. After this, they removed their battery to a more sheltered position ; they placed
themselves behind a rock, about thirty paces distant from the
north-east corner of the house, where every one could be protected from our fire, except at the time of reloading the cannons, when we could take aim at the men so employed. The
change of place was much more favorable for us, because, being at a corner of the house, the walls could not be injured
by their fire ; they could only strike the slates on the roof. During the whole time, there were two or three hundred Irishmen collected on a neighboring height, watching the conflict,
rejoicing in the anticipation of our defeat, and waiting impatiently for the moment when they might come down and par-
ticipate in the plunder.

A Frenchman, named Paul Roussier, a very brave man,
and a skilful soldier, was posted in the garret, opposite to the
battery of our enemy. He constructed a sort of rampart,
with sheeps' fleeces, that we had stored away there, and he
then made an opening in the roof, through which he kept up
an incessant fire. He was constantly supplied with arms
ready loaded. As soon as he had fired, he handed his piece
to one of the children, who gave him another in exchange, all

ready to be fired. He killed one of the assailants. They on their part displayed equal activity, keeping up a constant fire with their cannons. The pirates on board the vessel fired against the windows with small arms. We did our best to barricade them with mattresses and large books.

At the commencement of the action, some of our muskets were a little out of order. The officer who was loading for Paul Roussier, was in such a state of confusion, that he had actually put in the ball before the powder. My wife was here, and there, and everywhere, carrying ammunition, and giving encouragement to all, as well by what she said, as by her own calm deportment. When she came into the room where the officer had just made the mistake I have mentioned, he went up to her and took her by the hand, and said, "Alas ! my dear lady, what must be done ? we are ruined. It is the height of folly to attempt to resist any longer, for our arms are in bad order ; here are no less than three useless muskets."

I would observe to you that we had not less than eighteen muskets in the house, besides two blunderbusses and several pistols.

My wife replied to him with her usual composure, "We are in the hands of the Almighty, and nothing can happen to us without his permission. I trust he will not suffer us to fall into the hands of these wicked men ; but we must not lose our courage ; rather let us try if we cannot mend any thing that is out of repair."

She then came to me, and begged I would leave my post, and go into the parlor, to encourage the men, and do away with the alarm engendered by the fears this faint-hearted gentleman had expressed. I went immediately, and upon examining the useless muskets, I found that one of them wanted a flint, another had some dirt in the touch-hole, and the third had two cartridges in it, one on the top of the other, and a ball below both, next to the touch-hole. I laughed at him when I showed him how promptly the muskets were put in order, and there were no more complaints on that score. My wife was perfectly fearless. I wanted a needle to broach the muskets, which she went to fetch for me from a place where the balls were coming in at the window like hail, and she did not think of stooping to avoid them until I called out to her to do so.

The children were naturally very much frightened by the noise made, when the roof was struck, and slates were shivered by the balls, which she observed, and she said to them, " Take courage, my children, do not forget that we are in the hands of God. It is not our fear that will give us safety, on the contrary, God will bless our courage. If you are not able to fire upon the enemy yourselves, you can at least load the muskets for your father, and for others who are older and stronger than you are. Drive away fear from your hearts as much as possible, and leave the care of your persons to God."

This address to the children was of much use to the older persons who were present; it appeared to inspire them with fresh confidence and courage. Ere long, however, we had a serious cause for anxiety; our powder was becoming so scarce, that we felt as if we ought to begin to use it more sparingly. We were in a state of great perplexity. If we did not continue the same fire, we thought the enemy would perceive the difference, and attack us with fresh vigor; and if we went on at the rate we had hitherto done, we should not have more than enough to last three hours. The whole stock, at the out-set, was but twelve pounds. "Great God! it was then, in our moment of need, that thou didst discourage our enemies, and make them to turn their backs upon us in flight."

Claude Bonnet, a French soldier, discovered that one of them was running away, so he went forward to fire upon him, and at that very moment a ball from the enemy struck against the house, rebounded, and entered the fleshy part of his arm, without touching the bone. This showed us that we were not invulnerable, and that if we had been spared, it was to God that we owed our preservation, and to Him we ought to return thanks.

My dear wife was the surgeon; she had him laid upon a bed without any noise, and applied the first dressing to his wound with her own hands. The engagement lasted from eight o'clock in the morning till four in the afternoon, and during the whole time there had never been the least cessation in the firing, except for a very few minutes after the first man was killed. We had no one wounded but Claude Bonnet, with the exception of a slight hurt one of the children received from a piece of slate striking against his thumb. The loss sustained by the enemy was three killed and seven wound-ed, as we afterwards ascertained from the Irishmen who were on board. When the assailants had returned to their vessel, we inspected the stations they had occupied on shore, and we found a quantity of blood which they had evidently tried to hide by treading earth and leaves into it.

The privateer remained at anchor for some time, and we feared they might be preparing for a second attack, for which we were in very poor condition, being so near the end of our powder. We determined, however, that if they should land

again, we would not waste the little powder we had left, but
only fire when we could take aim. While we were waiting
the development of their plans, we all took some nourishment,
which we stood in much need of after our fatigue.

When we returned from the rock, first thing in the morning, I had given to each man one large glass of Sherry, and
after that, during the whole action, I did not permit any one
to taste a single drop of wine, spirit, or strong beer.

In a short time we had the satisfaction of seeing the vessel
draw up her anchor, and sail away; and we then returned
most hearty thanks to God for our glorious deliverance.

I wrote immediately to Lord Cox, then Lord Chancellor
of Ireland, and to the Duke of Ormond, the Lord Lieutenant.
I gave them a full account of the whole affair. Before I mention the opening paragraph of my letter to the Duke, I should
name, that about nine months previous to the attack, he had
made a tour through a great part of Ireland, in company with
the Chancellor. When they were at Kinsale, Mr. Davis, one
of my landlords, and I, went there to pay our respects to
them. Before the interview, it had been agreed between Mr.
Davis, the Chancellor, and myself, that if there should be any
opening for it, I should contrive to say something in favor of
erecting a fort in our neighborhood, and they would support
me in it; for they were fully as anxious to have one as I was.

The Chancellor introduced us both to the Duke as Justices
of the Peace, who did our duty. His Grace conversed with
Mr. Davis for a few minutes ; but when he found that I was
a French Refugee, he addressed himself more particularly to
me, and he carried on the conversation in the French language. He asked me how long I had resided in this barbarous part of the country, what flock I had, &c., to all which I

replied. He then inquired about the produce of the country, and how we managed to transact our business in this quarter. I told him what a fine harbor we had, and mentioned its particular advantages, and thinking the opportunity a good one for introducing the subject, I mentioned the danger to which we were exposed from the iniquitous practices of French privateers. I then said, " If the Government could only be induced to build a fort there for our protection, I am sure it would become a favorite place for the settlement of French Refugees; and I have no doubt it would also prove a safeguard to the commerce of the whole kingdom."

According to our previous arrangement, the other gentlemen were ready to support what I had recommended with various arguments; but the Duke rather wittily cut short our discourse by saying: " Pray to God for us, and we will take care to defend you in return."

This reply was so much to the purpose, that we were silenced; we had not another word to say. I felt a little confused, and the tittering of some of the Duke's friends was annoying.

God having now given us this remarkable deliverance, I thought the time had arrived when I should be justified in reproaching his Grace with breach of promise. Immediately after the battle, before the sun had set, on that very evening, I wrote him a letter, beginning as follows:—

" Since I had the honor of paying my respects to your Grace at Kinsale, I have not failed to pray for you daily, in conformity with the request you then made ; but you must allow me to complain, that your Grace has not been equally true to the promise you then made of defending me, for without your assistance I have had to defend myself from the

9*

attack of a French corsair, who," &c., &c.   I then went on to
give him the particulars of the engagement, and of our glorious victory.

I inclosed this letter, unsealed, to my cousin, Arnauld, in
London, and I begged him, after he had read it, to seal and
deliver it.   He had some hesitation about the expediency of
delivering it; he thought it was too bold.   Nevertheless, he
complied with my request, sealed it, and then went with it to
the door of the Duke's hotel, and gave it to the first servant
he saw, without waiting for any answer, or even ascertaining
that it had reached its destination.

The good and generous Duke was delighted, seeing that
the boldness of it was justified by the defence we had made.
He inquired immediately for the person who had brought it,
and as he was not forthcoming, he requested Colonel Boisron,
who happened to be with him, to write an answer, telling me
how much he was charmed with my conduct, as well as with
my manner of relating it to him ; and that, if it should ever
be in his power to serve me, I might be assured he would take
great pleasure in doing so.

In the mean time my name, and that of my wife also, became known throughout Europe, by means of the newspapers
giving the history of our defence.   I received a letter from
Government, dated 10th June, 1764, complimenting me on
my conduct, congratulating me on the happy result of the
conflict, and adding, they would take care I should be better
provided for defence in case of another attack.   A warrant
was inclosed in the letter, directing the keeper of the magazine at Kinsale to deliver to me one barrel of gunpowder and
two barrels of musket-balls.   I had not asked any such
supply.

The four Irishmen who had acted as guides to the French were very much alarmed; they feared that if I discovered them I should hand them over to justice; so they prudently determined to be beforehand, and they came voluntarily before me, and made oath that the French had taken them by main force. They furnished us with the information I have given already of the extent of the loss sustained by the French. They told us that the lieutenant, whom we had slain, was a near relation of the Captain, who was so furious at his death, that he swore if he took me he would roast me alive and salt me.

After this I determined to build a kind of fortification at the back of my house, to answer the double purpose of protecting the lower floor from the guns of ships, and defending the mouth of the creek. I bought several six-pounders which had been fished up from a vessel lost on the coast. I had three carriages made for them, and I raised a fortification of turf, whose parapet was eighteen feet in thickness, and so situated as to command the entrance of the creek, and cover the lower story of my house entirely, on the side next the creek.

My Irish neighbors were much chagrined at the unexpected issue of the attack, which they had felt certain was to rid the country of me for ever. They were more and more annoyed as they saw the progress of my preparations for future defence. They tried to alarm me; they said to me that perhaps I was not aware there was an Act of Parliament which forbade any person to erect a fortification, or mount guns without the special permission of Government. I replied to them that I knew all about the Act of Parliament quite as well as they did, but I had no fear of disturbance in my work, after the decided evidences I had received of the friendship and esteem of the Government. "Were it otherwise," said I, "I would much rather fall into the hands of an English jury than those of French pirates."

I made an application to the Government for ammunition when I had completed my fort. I was promptly furnished with five hundred cannon balls, four barrels of gunpowder, and the greatest abundance of matches. I required no stronger proof of approbation.

By the month of November I had completed every thing, and finding that the Lord Lieutenant had returned to Dublin, I thought it would be right that I should go and wait upon him, and present a full report of what I had done. During my residence at Bear Haven, I had from time to time been able to render material assistance to merchant vessels, and more than once to ships of war, in distress. I took with me certificates of these facts.

Upon my arrival in Dublin I was received by the Council with the utmost kindness. They voted the sum of £50 to me at once, as a temporary assistance until something better could be done for me, and they recommended me most strongly to claim a pension for my services, and they themselves brought my case officially before the Lord Lieutenant. After a while he issued an order to the Secretary of State for Ireland, to give me a letter addressed to the Secretary of Lord Godolphin, then Lord High Treasurer of England.

I went to England with my documents in the month of April, 1705, and while I was still in London, urging my claims, the Duke of Ormond, the Lord Lieutenant, came there, and was of essential service to me in gaining my pension. He treated me at all times with every possible kindness.

The warrant for my pension was presented to me on the 17th October, 1705, and here follows a copy of the document.

(COPY.)

To our right trusty, and right entirely beloved Cousin and Councillor, James, Duke of Ormond, our Lieutenant-General and General Governor of our Kingdom of Ireland, and to our Lieutenant Deputy, or other chief governor or governors of that, our kingdom for the time being.

ANNE R.

"Right trusty, and right entirely beloved Cousin and Councillor, we greet you well. Whereas James Fontaine, Clerk, did by his humble petition to us, pray that we would be graciously pleased to bestow on him a pension of five shillings a day on our establishment of our kingdom of Ireland, in consideration of his good services in his defence against a French Privateer, and the great charge he is at in securing the remote port he lives in against the insults of the French, and whereas our High Treasurer of England hath laid before us a report made by you upon said petition, wherein you testify that the petitioner is settled in a very remote port, in Bear Haven, in our said kingdom, which place is very much infested with the privateers, that he hath built a very strong house with a small sort of sod fort, on which he hath the permission of our said government to mount five guns; that he hath often been in danger of being attacked by the Privateers, and that, by the continuance of the said fort, he hath protected several merchant ships; that there hath been produced to you several very ample certificates from the merchants of Dublin and of Cork, of the commodiousness of that place for securing mer-

chant ships, as also from the Captains of our ships, the Arundel
and the Bridgewater, and that, upon the whole, you are of
opinion that the said James Fontaine very well deserves our
favor and encouragement, in consideration of his said services
and expenses, and in regard he is a French Refugee, you propose that a pension of five shillings a day may be inserted for
him on the establishment, under the head of French Pen-
sioner, to commence from Michaelmas, 1705.   Now, we having taken the premises into our Royal consideration, are graciously pleased to consent thereunto, and accordingly, our will
and pleasure is, and we do hereby direct, authorize and command, that you cause the said pension or allowance of five
shillings a day to be paid to him, the said James Fontaine, or
his assignees from Michaelmas last, 1705, as aforesaid, for
maintaining the said fort for the better preservation of our
subjects of our said Kingdom against the insults of French
Privateers, the same to continue during our pleasure, and to
be placed for him in the list of French Pensioners on the
establishment of our expenses in our said Kingdom, and paid
in like manner as others, the pensions within the said list are,
or shall be payable.   And this shall be as well to you for so
doing, as to our Lieutenant Deputy, or other chief governor
or governors of our said Kingdom for the time being, and to
our Receiver General, and all others concerned in making the
said payments, and allowing thereof, upon account, a sufficient
warrant, and so bid you very heartily farewell.

"Given at our Court at St. James's, the twelfth day of
October, 1705, in the fourth year of our reign.

"By Her Majesty's command,

"GODOLPHIN.

"Entered at the Signet Office, on the 17th } "GEO. WOODDESON, *Dep.*"
day of October, 1705.

My inventive genius had now entirely forsaken me, but the providence of God had not. The same God who at first called light out of darkness, had now shown his power in frustrating the designs of our enemies, and turning to our honor and advantage the very enterprise by which they had hoped and expected to seal our ruin. If it had not been for their cruel attack, we should never have become known to persons who have proved most kind friends to us. Let us never forget that we are indebted to our Heavenly Father for inclining towards us the heart of a kind and charitable earthly sovereign. The signal failure of our adversaries' schemes reminded me of the enigma of Samson in the Bible; "Out of the eater came forth meat, and out of the strong came forth sweetness."

I must not omit to mention the kindness and hospitality of my cousin, John Arnauld. I was his guest during the whole time I was in London, and he not only declined accepting any compensation for my board, but he lent me nearly £30 to further my views in applying for a pension, and at a time, too, when he saw little chance of my ever being in a situation to repay him. Thanks be to God, I have since that time so far prospered in my school as to be able to return him this money.

During my absence from home, privateers had been occasionally seen hovering about the mouth of the harbor. One of them had approached the house, and appeared to be taking the same course that had been followed by the vessel that attacked us. My wife was on the alert, she had all the cannons loaded, and one of them fired off, to show that all was in readiness for defence, and when they saw this, they veered about, landed on Great Island, stole some cattle, and sailed away.

After my return we had occasional alarms, vessels would approach now and then and seem to threaten a descent; but it ended in nothing but giving us a little fright, and making us brush up our arms, for when they saw that we were in a state of preparation they went off, contented with stealing whatever they could lay their hands upon.

CHAPTER XV.

WITH a constant apprehension of attack before us, we lived
on the " qui vive " from the first day of June, 1704, until the
eighth day of October, 1708, when, with all our precautions,
we were actually taken by surprise.

A company of soldiers was quartered among the Irish in
the Half Barony, and the Captain, who commanded them,
lodged and boarded at my house, but unfortunately, both he
and the Lieutenant happened to be absent at that time, they
had gone to Bantry, and the Ensign was left in command of
the company. He was an imprudent inexperienced youth,
without any sort of judgment.

A French privateer entered the harbor during the night,
and anchored off Bear Haven, about five miles from my house,
and entirely out of our sight. She hoisted English colors by
way of deception, and she succeeded to her wish, for the Ensign no sooner discovered her, than, concluding she was a vessel just arrived from America, he went down with two or three
soldiers of his company, in great haste to be the first to board
her, in order to regale himself with rum punch, a beverage of
which he was unhappily much too fond. He was made a

prisoner the instant his foot touched the deck of the vessel, but the Captain and the officers behaved towards him with the greatest civility. He was a little shocked at first, but they made him so very welcome, treating him to the best of wine and brandy, that he soon lost the remembrance of his situation, and gave the Captain all the information he wanted, and it was of a nature to encourage him to proceed. He told him that the soldiers were dispersed throughout the Barony, without any commander, for the Captain and Lieutenant were both absent, as well as himself, and that he was sure it would be very easy to surprise my house, for I had no one near enough to help me but my own family. Upon the strength of this information, the Captain had the boats prepared for going ashore. He sent eighty men in three boats, commanded by two Lieutenants, who were both Irishmen, natives of the Barony.

A great portion of the crew were Irishmen, and amongst them was a man named Sullivan, whose life I had formerly been the means of saving, when he was proclaimed as a tory and a robber. He fled to France, and I had so much compassionate feeling for his wife, whom he had left behind with seven or eight children to maintain, that I allowed her to live rent-free on my farm, and fearing the family might perish with hunger, I returned to her a milch cow and ten or twelve sheep, which Sullivan had made over to me for rent due before he went away. This was the man who came to reward me for my kindness to him and his, by acting as a guide to the party. No one knew better than he the exact situation of my house, and every thing belonging to it.

They quitted the ship at midnight, landed before it was light, and commenced their march about daybreak, in perfect

silence, and stooping very low, in order that they might be
neither seen nor heard. An Irish servant who was fetching
home the cows was the first person to discover them, marching in good order, and only the distance of a long musket
shot from the house. He ran home as fast as he could, and
cried out that we were all lost, for a number of armed men
were in sight. We got up directly, and I ordered every door
to be shut, but there was so much confusion that the gates of
the large court in front, and even the house door below the
tower were forgotten and left open for some time. This was
perceived by the enemy as we afterwards learned, but it was
supposed to have been done on purpose as a feint, and that
we must have a loaded cannon within ready to fire if any one
approached. When the men were near enough to hear me, I
hailed them through a speaking-trumpet, and told them if they
were friends to stop, and let us know who they were, and if
enemies, to come forward, and we would receive them with
vigor.

In the mean time my children were busily engaged loading our arms and putting them in order. The men continued
to advance ; so I ordered my son James to fire upon them
from a garret window with our largest gun, which was six feet
long. This made them lower their heads ; they then separated into six detachments and took various posts, and some of
them, under cover of hedges and ditches, contrived to get
round to the back of the house. They had determined to
root us out this time, for their first act was to set fire to the
malt-house, which was towards the east, then to the stacks of
hay, straw and grain which were at the north and east, and
after that to the cow-house, stable, and long fish-press which
were at the west of my house. These were all very combus-

tible, and in less than half an hour we were encompassed with flames on every side but one, and by reason of the fire and smoke between them and us we were unable to see our enemies, and we suffered much from the smoke, which found its way to us through every crevice.

I ordered the servants to put water in every tub and bucket that could be found, and then immerse sheep-skins with wool upon them, and ox-skins, of both which we had many in the house. When these were thoroughly saturated I had them placed in the windows, as being the most exposed parts of the house. My dear wife superintended these arrangements. The roof was slated, so there appeared but little danger of fire being communicated to us through that channel.

The whole garrison consisted of my wife and myself, our children and four servants; two of the latter were mere cowboys, and the other two had never seen a battle. We fired hap-hazard, as fast as we could load; we did so, because we could actually see nothing but fire and smoke, and therefore could not aim at our enemies. My chief apprehension arose from the fear that they might possess themselves of our cannon and turn them against ourselves, and therefore I thought that while unable to see what our assailants were doing, I could not employ myself better than in firing my large blunderbuss every few minutes in the direction of the cannon. Once after I had fired, I thought I discovered that they had been making the attempt, for there was much noise and confusion, and it was evident they were carrying off a wounded man. I could hear them very distinctly, but I could see nothing; I was encouraged, however, by what I heard, to fire from time to time in the same direction.

It was not until all that I have related had been done,
that I became aware of the doors being open of which I have
already spoken, and I sent some one to shut them.

While I was firing at random, I had a glimpse of a man
setting fire to the covering of the fish-press; I took deliberate
aim at him with my blunderbuss, loaded as usual with swan-
shot. and wounded him in several places, but not seriously.

While we were blinded and suffocated by the smoke from
the burning stacks, our adversaries raised a small mound of
turf and wood, behind which they intrenched themselves, and
set to work with long poles to detach the slates from the roof
of the north-east tower. At soon as they uncovered a portion, they applied fire to it, by means of burning straw at
the end of their poles, and in this way the roof was on fire
three times, and we as often extinguished it from within.

About two o'clock in the afternoon, they accomplished
making a breach in the wall of this same north-east tower.
We could see them at work with iron bars, and while they
were so engaged my children fired upon them; they formed a
sort of rampart with a mattress on the top of a large basket,
such as is used in the country for carrying peat. They knelt
behind this rampart, and fired as fast as they could one after
the other, without daring to show their noses.

The enemy still continued at work with their long poles
and firebrands endeavoring to set the roof on fire. When
the smoke had subsided a little, I hit upon a position from
which I could see to take aim at their hands, as they raised
them above their intrenchment to guide the poles. I fired,
and I thought I hit them, but as they still persevered in
their work, I began to think it probable that I had not put a
sufficient charge in the piece, so when I loaded again I put in

a double quantity of powder. I had no sooner loaded than I had the opportunity of aiming at a hand I saw raised; I fired, but my piece was overloaded, and it burst, by which unfortunate accident I was thrown down with much violence, three of my ribs and my right collar-bone were broken, and the flesh of my right hand was much torn. I was so completely stunned that I had no power to move, or even to breathe for some seconds. My wife saw me fall, and she naturally concluded I had been struck by a ball from the enemy. She ran to my assistance, and raised me up without making any noise whatever. As soon as I was able to articulate, I told her how it had happened. I was now completely "hors de combat," but I had already done much work, for I had fired five pounds of swan shot from my now disabled piece, during the morning. After I was prostrated, my dearest wife assumed the command; she had an eye to every thing; she went round to furnish ammunition as it was required, and she gave courage as well by her exhortations as by her example.

In the mean time the enemy had been engaged upon the breach, which they had increased to four or five feet square: nevertheless, they derived no benefit from it; my sons defended it by an incessant fire from behind their mattress rampart. At last, a grenade was thrown in at the breach, which ran under the basket, and overturned the whole affair, but without doing any harm, thanks be to God, except giving the boys a fright which made them abandon their post; but only for a very short time. One of them ran to me, in great dismay, to tell me that the hole was as large as any door, and that the enemy were entering by it; the other boys were still firing from the dormar windows.

I immediately rose from my bed, and asked them to give me a pistol ready cocked and loaded, which I took in my left hand, the right being useless. I called my family around me, and I said to them, "I see, my dear children, that we must be overpowered by the great number of those who are attack· ing us; it is inevitable; but we will not stand quietly to be killed like dogs; let us rather sell our lives dearly, and die like lions." I was advancing towards the breach while I said these words.

As soon as I had done speaking, my poor boys re-entered the room, and took up their old position without a word or a gesture indicative of fear; they replaced their basket and mat· tress, exposed to the fire of more than ten muskets. It was, indeed, a melancholy sight! but, at the same time, I was gratified with their display of unflinching courage. Blessed be thou, O my God! who preserved them from injury amid such a shower of balls.

When they resumed the fire, the enemy retreated from the breach, and did not dare to show their heads, or even their hands, which caused all their fire to be thrown away; for, by not raising the butt-end of their muskets, they carried too high, and the shot went far above us every time. Seeing that we did not give way in the least, they began to tire of our obstinate resistance. They might possibly have heard me speak to the children, and it is very certain they overrated our force extremely; for, from the constant fire in all directions, as well as upon the main point of attack, they concluded that we must have at least twenty men. They called out to us to surrender, and they would give us good quarter.

I held a conversation with my wife and children, and we determined, at any rate, to hear what terms they offered

The firing was stopped on both sides, and I advanced to the breach to hold a parley with them. One of the Irish lieutenants came forward and took aim at me; my second son, Peter, saw what he was about, before I observed him, and he immediately caught hold of me and drew me one side, barely in time to save me from being the victim of their treachery, for the ball passed within two or three inches of my stomach.

I was extremely indignant, and said, " Ah! you traitors! was it then merely with the view of surprising me, that you proposed a parley? Fire upon these traitors, my sons; fire, I say." The boys obeyed me without loss of time, and fired upon the deceitful miscreants.

I had foolishly exposed myself to a very great danger, by placing confidence in the good faith of an enemy whom I might have known was destitute of all honorable feeling. The ever watchful providence of God again interposed for my deliverance.

We kept up an incessant fire for another quarter of an hour, when the enemy called out to us again, and made a second offer of good quarter. I reproached them with their recent perfidy, and told them I could not trust persons who had already attempted to betray the confidence I had reposed in them.

They then threatened that, if we refused to surrender, they would throw a barrel of powder in the breach, and blow us all up.

" I have three or four at your service here," said I, " and I intend to scatter their contents over this floor and the inner hall, and whenever you are pleased to enter, I will throw a lighted turf upon it, and make you dance. You may depend upon it, I will not perish without you."

The desperate tone of this reply made them repeat once more their offer of good quarter.

I said, " I do not know what you mean by *good quarter*; but this I know, I am resolved not to surrender unconditionally. I would rather perish with my whole family."

They left off firing, and begged I would order my people to do the same, that we might speak about terms; so we had a cessation of hostilities on both sides. Their proposition was, that they should have the plunder, to which I assented; for, with our lives, we should most certainly have lost our goods. I demanded life and liberty for myself and all who were with me. They spoke to me in English; and I said I would have nothing to do with Englishmen or Irishmen in making the treaty.

" I consider myself a British subject, and as such, I will only treat with the French, who are at war with England, and I request the French commander to come forward, and put his head to the breach; I assure him that he may do so with perfect safety. We have no traitors in our ranks."

One of the rascally Irish lieutenants then presented himself as the commander of the party. He went by the name of Carty in Ireland, and La Touche in France; he could speak French as well as I could. I told him, that as an Irishman, I had not the slightest reliance upon him, but it was as the authorized agent of the French commander, that I was willing to treat with him. I then repeated to him the terms of capitulation, speaking French all the time. He was to guarantee life and liberty to all of us, and to promise on their part the most strictly honorable deportment while in possession, and they were to have the plunder.

They swore to the observance of these terms as French-

10

men and men of honor. After which I had one thing more
to say : " I am now going to open the door for your admittance, and I give you warning beforehand, that I will not suffer any one to enter but through the door. Whoever attempts
to come in by the breach, will be shot down directly."

This was agreed to likewise, and I then had the doors
opened, and I ranged myself, my wife, my sons and four servants in regular order, to surrender our arms to the Commander, as he entered.

Oh, God ! our Preserver ! thou knowest, and none else
can know the state of my feelings at that moment, to see my
beloved wife and dear children, at the mercy of enemies, fourteen of whom we had wounded. Oh ! what everlasting
praises do we owe to thee for our preservation. It was thou
who restrained our blood-thirsty enemies from executing the
vengeance which they had sworn against us. Oh, my God !
I beseech thee to sanctify the lives which thou hast so miraculously preserved, and assist us to devote them to thy
service.

The Commander, and a good many of the men came in,
and seeing only five youths, and four cowherds, they looked
anxiously around, and asked me where all my men were, evidently fearing an ambuscade.

" You need not fear any thing dishonorable from me,"
said I, " you now see our whole garrison." " Impossible,"
said he, " these children could never have kept up all the
firing."

My wife then spoke to him, and said, " I am in hopes, sir,
that the fact of so few persons having made this gallant defence, will be an inducement to you—whom I trust we shall
find a man of honor—to treat us with the more considera-

tion." She then said, " Are you the Commander of this party ?"

" I am, Madam."

" Wait a moment," said she, " and I will give you my keys." As she handed them to him, she begged he would restrain his followers within the bounds of propriety. He promised to do so.

" In making terms with you, I forgot to name my library," said I. " I hope that you will not take advantage of my omission, but allow me to retain my books, which are of great value to me, and can be of no use to you or your followers."

He promised that they should be spared, and he placed a guard at the door of my study; but very soon the men forced their way there, as elsewhere, and took possession of all my handsomest books, leaving behind but few, and those the shabbiest in external appearance.

My house was well furnished; and as we had not thought of a surrender until it actually took place, we had not had time or opportunity for secreting any thing. We were stripped of every thing, furniture, linen, clothing, even to our very coats, which, in the heat of action we had taken off to give more freedom in the movement of our arms.

They filled their own three boats quite full, and then they took three of mine, and filled them also with their booty. When they were ready to return with their rich prize to the vessel, they took me, my sons James and Peter, and two of the servants, prisoners. It was all to no purpose that I reminded the Commander of the terms upon which we had surrendered, and that it was a decided infraction of the treaty which he had sworn to observe. He replied that my name had become so notorious amongst the privateers of St. Ma-

loes, that he dared not return to the vessel without me; the
Captain's order was most peremptory, not to think of coming
back to the vessel unless he had me with him, dead or alive.
He promised again, in the most faithful manner, that I should
not be retained as a prisoner: he said that as soon as the
Captain had seen me, I should be set at liberty.

Remonstrances were of no avail; I was obliged to go
with them, and by the time I reached the vessel, my wounds
and fractured bones had become so painful, that I lost all
power of helping myself, and was obliged to be hoisted up
like a log.

When the crew first saw me on the deck, they shouted
with one accord, " Vive le Roi," and repeated it three times
in grand chorus.

This roused me from my pain and depression: and when
their shouting ceased, I raised my voice to its highest pitch,
and said, " Gentlemen, how long is it since victories have
been so rare in France that you are glad to avail yourselves
of such an occasion as this, to sing in triumph? I am ashamed,
positively ashamed of my native country, to hear rejoicings
over such a victory. A glorious achievement truly! Eighty
men, accustomed to warfare, have actually been so successful
as to compel one poor minister, four cowherds, and five children, to surrender upon *terms!* Furthermore, gentlemen, I
would have you to know that though I do appear before you
as a prisoner, it is in direct violation of the treaty made with
your commanding officer, and sworn to by him previous to
our surrender. He cannot deny that he has broken his faith,
and committed a flagrant offence against the established law
of nations."

I was then carried to the Captain's cabin, and I renewed

my complaint. I told him the agreement which his authorized agent had sworn to, and I added, " Sir, I can assure you that if I had had the least idea of being carried off as a prisoner, so far from surrendering, I would have resisted as long as I had had any breath left in my body. I trust, under these circumstances, you will see the justice of restoring me to liberty immediately."

He replied to me with much suavity and courtesy of manner, " I cannot tell you how much I am delighted to have you on board my vessel, a man of such undaunted courage, and whose name has made so much noise."

" You may, perhaps, sir," said I, " find to your cost, that my name is pretty well known in England and Ireland. I have received so many proofs of friendship from the Lords in Council, at the Irish seat of Government, that I feel certain, as soon as they become aware of my situation, and especially that my being a prisoner at all is contrary to the sworn terms of a treaty, they will send instructions to Kinsale to retaliate upon the French prisoners there, which may probably bring you into trouble."

" What is it you say ? Do you dare to make use of threats to me ?"

" No, no," said I, " I only give you fair warning of that which will most assuredly come to pass. This unjustifiable conduct will be the occasion of many an honest man suffering hardships, to which the mere circumstance of his being a captive would not subject him ; probably friends of your own among the number, and nobody will give you any thanks for what you are doing."

" Never mind, let us drink a glass of wine together now, and discuss these matters in the morning."

"I want no wine," said I, "but I stand in great need of
the assistance of some one to dress my wounds."

The surgeon was therefore summoned, and he applied
some linen dipped in brandy. Notwithstanding the number
of good beds they had brought from my house, I had great
difficulty in obtaining a very poor one to lie down upon, and a
coarse sheet and coverlet to throw over me. I was placed between decks, with the bed resting on some cordage. This was
Saturday night, the 8th October, 1708.

Our noble Ensign, who ought to have been our protector
from the enemy, was still on board as drunk as a hog. He
was in excellent spirits, on the best of terms with the Captain
and crew, to whom he was infinitely obliged for having indulged him in his vicious propensity. The next day was Sunday; he was sent ashore early in the morning, without having
received the least injury or having been deprived of any thing
whatever. My two sons and the servants were sent away at
the same time, and I alone was detained. As soon as the
boat was taken on board after landing them, the Captain gave
orders to raise the anchor and make sail.

My wife did not sit down quietly to bemoan and lament
over her misfortunes, as many would have done in her situation, but was in action at once to endeavor to find a remedy.
She went, early in the morning to the place where the Papists
said mass, to see the priest, whom she hoped to persuade to
follow the vessel, and use his influence to obtain my discharge. He positively refused. She dwelt upon the many
obligations under which I had laid his people from time to
time, and reminded him of those whom I had saved from the
gallows; but it was all in vain. Finding persuasion useless,
she changed her tone and had recourse to threats; she pointed

out to him that he would be very likely to bring upon himself
the resentment of those in power, if he still persisted in refusing to assist a man who was so much and so deservedly esteemed by the Lord Lieutenant and the Council. She succeeded no better than before, and seeing the vessel under sail,
she determined to follow by land, and keep it in sight as long
as she could.

The weather was clear, calm and mild. The Captain proceeded to the Island of Durzey, and found my wife waiting
upon the promontory for the vessel to get opposite to it. She
made a signal with her apron tied to the end of a stick, and a
boat was dispatched to hear what she had to say. She had
taken the precaution of borrowing a speaking-trumpet, and
thus she was able to carry on conversation, from the cliff on
which she stood, with those who were in the boat below.
After a great deal of bargaining, and many difficulties being
raised and smoothed away, she at last persuaded them to
agree to my restoration to liberty upon the payment of £100
sterling. During this discussion I was stretched on my pallet
between decks, and I was in total ignorance of what was going
forward.

My wife went away to borrow the money, and the Privateer waited off the Island of Durzey expecting her to return
with it. She was unable to procure more than £30, the
greater part of which was from Mr. Boyd, to whom I had
paid it for rent only five days before we were attacked. Unable to raise more, she came back to the vessel with that sum,
accompanied by our son Peter, several of our tenants, and our
friend Mr. Hutchins of Bear Haven.

The Captain agreed to give me up on condition of his
having the £30 she had brought with her, and retaining one

of my sons as a hostage for the payment of the remaining
£70. He paid her many compliments upon the courage she
had displayed, and told her he looked upon her as a second
Judith.

She replied, " I should have felt more honored if you had
compared me to Deborah, but I am far from being surprised
that you should not be well versed in books that you are prohibited from reading."

My liberty was restored to me, but it was upon very painful conditions, and I felt melancholy indeed at having to leave
my poor boy in my stead.

When I left the ship, it was that traitor, of whom I spoke
before, Sullivan, who took me on his shoulders and climbed
up the rocks.   He had waited upon me all the time I was on
board the Privateer, for I was as helpless as an infant.   I reproached him with his ingratitude and treachery.   " How
could you find in your heart," said I, " after all that I had
done for you and yours, to act the part of guide to my enemies ?"

He replied, " I have not a word to say in excuse for my
conduct."

It was late on Monday night, almost Tuesday morning,
when I was ransomed by the exertions of my wife, and the
tenderness of my sons ; I say sons, because, though only one
was left, they were all equally anxious to have taken my place.
James could not be spared, he was old enough to look after
the farm, and take care of the few cattle remaining to us.
Peter, being next in age, would not hear of any one but himself being selected.

On the night of Tuesday, the eleventh day of October,
I slept at Bear Haven at the house of Mr. Hutchins, and the

next day I went in a boat to Bantry, in order to have the requisite surgical assistance, and in going there we passed near enough to have a view of our now desolate mansion.

My wife waited long enough to see me comfortably settled under the care of a skilful French surgeon, and she then went to Cork to endeavor to raise the £70, for the payment of which Peter had been retained as a hostage. The Bishop lent her twenty guineas, and she could easily have borrowed the remainder from other friends, but the merchants of Cork, upon hearing the particulars of the affair, set their faces against the payment of any thing more, and they assured her that our son would be liberated without it. Their reasoning on the subject was so convincing, that she returned to the Bishop what he had so kindly lent to her, and she declined borrowing any thing further. She also contrived to have a letter privately sent to Peter, exhorting him to keep up his courage, and have patience, and that she had no doubt he would soon be set at liberty, without ransom, but advised him to appear ignorant of it.

The Privateer hovered about the Island of Durzey for a long time, waiting for the money. Peter conducted himself remarkably well on board the ship, and evinced much more both of prudence and courage than might have been expected in so young a lad. The steadiness of his deportment attracted the attention of the Captain, who placed so much confidence in him as to give into his charge the key of the liquors, and this caused the whole crew to pay court to him.

While he was on board, the Privateer was one day chased by a British man-of-war; it was proposed to him to hide himself in the hold, which he declined; a musket was then offered to him that he might assist in the defence, but he said, " No, I

10*

would rather fight for the English than against them, for I regard them as my friends and countrymen."

The English vessel was inferior in point of sailing, and thus they escaped from her. The Captain had a son with him about the age of Peter, a vain, disagreeable boy, much disliked by the officers of the ship. He came to Peter one day, in a state of intoxication, and with a drawn sword in his hand, threatened to kill him. Peter seized a sword to use in self-defence, and succeeded in disarming the drunken boy, and lowering his importance, much to the satisfaction of the by-standers.

When they reached St. Maloes, the Governor of Brest condemned the Captain very much for his misconduct in bringing a hostage with him, contrary to the law of nations, and he would not suffer Peter to be landed and placed with the other prisoners.

The poor Captain was sadly perplexed, and nothing would have pleased him so much as that Peter should run away, and thus get him out of his dilemma, and he contrived to have it whispered to Peter that he was a great fool not to make his escape. He recollected the advice given to him in his mother's letter, and very properly considered that it would be an act of great folly to leave the vessel in a foreign country, when he had every reason to expect that he would be taken home again. After remaining a while at St. Maloes, the vessel went out on another cruise, Peter still in her.

CHAPTER XVI.

LEAVING Peter on his cruise, I will return to myself. As soon as I was well enough to mount a horse, I rode over to Kinsale with my son James, and two of the servants, and waited on the Chief Magistrate, and made an affidavit to the effect, that after capitulating upon terms with the express stipulation that we should have life and liberty, I had been forcibly carried off as a prisoner, and had only been released on the payment of £30, and leaving one of my sons as a hostage for the payment of the other £70.

The Governor, or commanding officer of Kinsale, as a retaliatory measure, immediately put all the French officers in irons who had been taken in the war, and were stationed there. He sent a copy of my affidavit to Plymouth, where there were numbers of French prisoners, and all these were likewise put in irons. You may suppose the letters of complaint from Kinsale and Plymouth were very numerous.

By the time the Captain got back a second time to St. Maloes, public feeling was much excited against him, and he was summoned to appear before the Governor of Brest, who wished to put him in prison, and even threatened to hang him. He made the most humble apologies, and was set at liberty only upon promising that he would convey Peter immediately to the place from whence he had taken him. Thus was our dear son restored to our arms, and that without our having to pay the £70, for which he was taken as a hostage.

I took all my family to Dublin except James, and it is unnecessary to say that we were in miserable plight.

I waited upon General Ingoldsby, one of the Council, and he presented me at once with an order for £100, which was the more acceptable as it was altogether unexpected. He had made an application for it as soon as he heard of my misfortunes, and that £100 was the sum demanded for my ransom.

I had made the acquaintance of this valuable friend only two months before our disaster. He had been deputed by Government to make a tour of inspection along the south-west coast of Ireland to select the most suitable harbor on which to erect a fortification. I went as far as Dunmannus to meet him, thirty-six miles from our house, where I invited him to sojourn when he came into the neighborhood.

He accepted my invitation, and he and his whole retinue remained with me three days, during which time I treated them as hospitably as I possibly could, making them welcome to the best the country afforded. Having had a little notice beforehand, we had time to make preparations, and I was able to have as many as fourteen or fifteen different dishes on the table every day, and a great variety of wine. He has been one of my best friends from that day to this. You may here notice once more the Providence of God, raising up for me, beforehand, a powerful friend against the day of need.

I determined to take up my abode for the future in the

city of Dublin, and to try to maintain my family by keeping
a school for instruction in Latin, Greek and French.

I found a house on St. Stephen's Green, that I thought
would answer our purpose extremely well. It had been
originally very well built, but was a good deal out of repair,
owing to its having been long without a tenant; and it had,
moreover, the reputation of being haunted by evil spirits. My
wife and I entertained no apprehension of being disturbed by
any unearthly visitors, so we were very glad to get this house
upon lower terms in consequence of the prejudice that existed.
I obtained a lease of it for ninety and nine years at £10 per
annum. It was a large house, forty feet square, it had good
substantial stone walls, and all the carpenters' work was of
oak. There was a yard and a garden attached to it three
hundred feet in depth, and the width of the house.

I was obliged to leave Dublin before we took possession
of the house, in order to prosecute my claim for damages,
upon the county of Cork, for injuries received at the hands of
Irishmen in the French privateer. By law, the county is
liable to make good all losses sustained by violence and robbery, provided the persons committing the act are natives and
not foreigners. I had given due notice to the High Constable
of the Barony, within the time limited by act of Parliament,
and all that remained for me now to do was to prove the facts
to the satisfaction of the grand jury of the county of Cork.
I took my son James and two servants with me as witnesses,
and I had no difficulty whatever in proving the robbery, and
also that there were many Irishmen among the assailants. I
presented an inventory of the property I had lost, particular-
izing those articles which had been carried away, and those
which had been destroyed by fire.

No one was more active in my behalf than Captain Cox, the son of Chancellor Cox, whom I have named before as accompanying the Duke of Ormond to the south of Ireland. It happened that I had made him a present of a handsome watch only three days before the privateer attacked us. The watch was a good time-piece, but it attracted his notice from having a miniature of the late Queen, wife of James II., at the back of it. He appeared to admire it so exceedingly that I gave it to him, and I was really glad of the opportunity of making him an acceptable present. I had received it in barter for some of my manufactured goods when I was living in Taunton. As soon as he heard of my losses, he proposed to return it to me, but I would not consent; for, if I had not given it to him, the pirates would certainly have carried it off.

The grand jury examined witnesses, and being fully satisfied that Irishmen had been concerned in the attack and robbery, they awarded me the sum of £800, to be paid by the county of Cork, in conformity with the provisions of an act of Parliament.

I gave my son James a power of attorney, authorizing him to receive the money, pay off all debts, and close my accounts at Bear Haven, and I returned to Dublin. My wife had been subject to some annoyance in my absence. I have said that the house I had taken was supposed to be haunted, and had remained unoccupied from superstitious fears. It appeared that it had been taken possession of by a party of vagrants, who were in the habit of alarming persons who attempted to occupy it, and thus arose the evil reputation of the house. When my wife went to it, these people told her they had been permitted to live in the house while it was untenanted, and begged to be allowed to remain a few days longer. It was not in her kind nature to refuse such a favor.

The first night neither she nor the children—they were all in one room—could get any sleep for the constant noises they heard. The old occupants were trying the game upon her which had been successful with others who had attempted to live in the house. She was very suspicious as to the noise being made by beings of flesh and blood and not by spirits. She bore it the first night, and, believing she had discovered the secret, she made her preparations accordingly for the second night.

She borrowed firearms and swords, called the inmates together before dark, and warned them to be sure not to leave their rooms if the noises should recur during the night, because she had provided herself with firearms, and she and her son had determined to make use of them against the evil spirit that made the disturbance ; therefore, they would see the propriety of keeping out of the way for fear they might be killed by accident. As may be supposed, the evil spirits were heard no more.

On my return, I made them all quit the premises : I had the house thoroughly repaired, made some alterations to fit it for a large family, and when all was completed, I found that it had cost me £450. In this house I have lived ever since. I have had a good school, taking both boarders and day-scholars ; and I have thus been able to give my children an education inferior in no respect to that bestowed upon the first nobles of the land. They have had masters for writing, drawing, dancing, and fencing ; and with me they have prosecuted their studies in Latin, Greek, geography, mathematics, and fortification. I have never spared any expense, either for boys or girls, by which I could give them greater opportunities of education and general improvement. My daughters have been instructed in drawing, and in every variety of ornamental needlework, in addition to the more solid branches of education.

Let us pause a moment for reflection upon the mercies and loving-kindness of our Heavenly Father, and our own short-sightedness. How distressing did it appear to me to lose, by the fisheries at Bear Haven, the property for which I had toiled year after year! When the final blow came by which we were so disastrously stripped of every thing, it appeared to be overwhelming; and yet without it, I should never, most probably, have had the means to clear myself of debt, and I should have been obliged to spend the residue of my days at Bear Haven, and have had to bring you all up in that desert, where it would have been absolutely impossible for me to have given you the excellent education you have received in Dublin; and from this I wish you to arrive at the conclusion, that God knows what is good for us much better than we do ourselves. If this becomes your settled conviction, there is no language equal to describing the peace of mind that it will cause. For my own part, I endeavor to receive with perfect submission every dispensation from the hand of my Maker; even though I see nothing but poverty, sorrows, and afflictions, grievous to the flesh, I can wait patiently his good time, for I know that in the end the result will be for the benefit of me and mine.

Here follows an incident quite to the purpose. General Ingoldsby, whose friendship for me was such that he was always on the look-out for something to benefit me, thought he had hit upon a plan that would be very agreeable to me. He had received orders to send all the half-pay officers, that were in Ireland, to Spain, and he entered the names of my sons Peter and John upon the list, without saying any thing to us until it was done. The boys were wild with joy at the idea of entering the army, and escaping from the drudgery of study.

I gave them but little recreation, it is true ; I tried, however, to make it easy by alternations from one employment to another so as to relieve the mind by variety. Latin and Greek were studies which they were obliged to attend to as tasks. I endeavored to make them look upon all the other things which they learned as relaxation and indulgence.

Mr. Secretary Dawson was not so favorably disposed, as General Ingoldsby was, towards us, and he refused to make out the commissions for my sons. He told the General that he had exceeded his powers by entering, upon the half-pay list, officers who had never served. Our kind friend was much chagrined at this unexpected obstacle, but he told us not to fret and he should probably yet have it in his power to serve us. The boys were most grievously disappointed ; I was not. I had felt unwilling to decline an offer that promised to be advantageous, and which my sons were themselves so desirous to accept, but at the same time I thought them fully too young to venture from the shelter of a parent's wing. I also preferred their continuing longer at study.

The half-pay officers embarked at Cork to go to Plymouth, there to join the fleet for Spain, my sons not of the number. On the passage, they were attacked by a French man-of-war, and though confessedly so inferior in size as not to warrant resistance, yet the officers of the army who were on board, being very numerous, would not consent to surrender without a fight—as mere passengers they should not have had a voice in the matter—and in the engagement which took place, one half were killed, almost all the remainder wounded, and they were obliged to surrender.

When the sad news reached us, I returned thanks to God with my whole heart for his having refused to me and mine what had been so ardently desired. Oh! my dear children, learn to place your trust in that Providence which will preserve you, even in spite of yourselves, if you will only trust in it. What a comfort it is to be able to realize that we are under the especial care of so wise, so powerful and so benevolent a Guide, one who only refuses to our prayers that which he knows would be prejudicial to us.

In the month of June, 1711, Peter was ready to enter college. Dr. Hall was to be his tutor, and he with the greatest kindness and generosity declined receiving the usual fees with him. He did the same by Moses and Francis when they went to college, by which I consider he made me a present of £35 or £36. In addition to this he procured a room for them free of rent and charges, which would have amounted to £27 more, and all this from pure benevolence and generosity, for we had never done any thing to deserve such kindness at his hands.

About this time, Lord Wharton being now the Lord Lieutenant of Ireland, an order was received instructing him to dispatch all the regiments that were in Ireland to Spain. In examining the troops, it was found that a great many sons of officers had been entered, who were mere children, therefore, before sending the regiments abroad, the Lord Lieutenant struck off the roll all under sixteen years of age, as too young for service. He was a little too fond of money, and he availed himself of the vacancies he had created, to add to his store, by selling the commissions for money.

John had set his heart upon being a soldier, and, by the advice of General Ingoldsby, I took the young man with me to wait upon Lord Wharton, to apply for a commission. I told him my circumstances would not allow of my purchasing one, I showed him some specimens of military drawings made by John. He was pleased with his appearance, and said it was a pity that one so handsome and so well formed should not have a commission, but still he did not promise to give him one, for he hoped to find purchasers for the whole.

I renewed my application from time to time, and at last, on the very eve of departure, finding that some of the commissions were unsold, General Ingoldsby went himself to the Lord Lieutenant and obtained an Ensign's commission for John, without our having to pay any thing more than the fees of office. The necessary expenses for his equipment amounted to £75. He was in the regiment commanded by Colonel Shawe, a cruel, avaricious man, a drunkard and a debauchee, who looked upon him with an evil eye, because he had entered the army through the favor of General Ingoldsby.

I leave John to tell his own story of his sufferings and mortification under such a Colonel, and of the severe illness he had in Spain. I feel myself bound, however, to acknowledge, in this place, the great goodness of God, in returning him to us safe and sound. He received several wounds himself and had wounded others, being often obliged to put his hand to his sword, but he never killed any body. I bless God, most especially for having preserved him amid dissolute companions, and scenes of temptation, from acquiring any vicious habit, and I earnestly beseech him to continue his fatherly protection.

In June, 1712, Moses and Francis entered college with great approbation from all the Professors.

Francis was very young, and small of his age, but he had excellent talents which he had most diligently cultivated. He had also enough of self-confidence to bring all his acquirements into play, and do himself full justice. He was the admiration of the whole college as long as he remained there, which was seven years and a half.

I purchased an apartment in the college, for the use of the three, and after painting, putting necessary articles of furniture in it, and making closets, it stood me in £42. They always had the use of this room without interruption or intrusion from any one, and when the two older ones left college, and Francis was there alone, I made interest that he should have no companion. My object was to avoid the possibility of their being corrupted by vicious companions, or drawn from their studies by idle ones, which very often happens to young persons whose principles are not firmly established. Thanks be to God, they preserved their purity of manners and holiness of life.

About two years afterwards, I entered Moses on the books of the Inns of Court. at the Temple, in London, because he intended to be a lawyer. He continued to study with great assiduity, and was well endowed in point of talent, but he had a most painful timidity and reserve. He went to London in 1715, and remained a year and some months; he then came home, and took his degree of Bachelor of Arts, for it was my wish that he should have it in his power to pursue the study of Theology, if he should hereafter find that he preferred it to law.

While Moses was in London, I went to the expense of en-

tering Francis also at the Temple. He was of a very quick and
ready turn, and had the gift of fluency of speech in a remarkable degree, which made me think he might choose the law
for his profession, but thanks be to God, he has chosen to dedicate himself to His service, and to prepare himself for the
holy ministry.

In the month of November, 1713, Captain Boulay, a French
gentleman, a half-pay cavalry officer, with whom I had not the
slightest acquaintance, called upon me to offer his grand-
daughter in marriage to one of my sons. She was his sole descendant, her father and mother were both dead, and she was to
inherit all his property. He told me he had heard an excellent report of my sons, that they had been well brought up,
and conducted themselves with propriety on every occasion,
being free from the follies and vices of the age, and this had
made him wish to secure one of them as a protector for his
grand-child when his head should be laid low. He said he
preferred in the husband of his child virtue without fortune,
to the largest property unaccompanied by the piety and discretion which he believed them to have. He was upwards of
eighty years of age ; his grand-daughter, Elizabeth Fourreau,
was about thirteen.

I thanked him very much for the flattering terms in which
he had made the proposal, and told him I thought the best
plan would be for him to send her to us, as though she were a
boarder, and then we might observe which of my sons liked
her the best, and for which of them she might feel a preference.

This plan met his views, and she came to live with us. We
found her to be a girl of very amiable temper, sweet disposition, and very fair natural talents, but her education had been
extremely neglected.

My sons consulted with each other about their feelings on the subject of the proposed marriage, and Peter, by the advice of his brothers, determined upon it.

Marriage articles were drawn up, and on the 29th March, 1714, the marriage took place with great privacy, because Peter had not yet taken his degree of Bachelor of Arts.

It was about this time that we began to turn our eyes towards America, as a country that would be most suitable for the future residence of the family.

John, the officer, was without employment, it was therefore determined that he should make a voyage to America, travel through every part where the climate was temperate, and purchase a plantation, in such situation as he judged would prove in all respects the most advantageous.

He landed in Virginia, travelled through that colony, as well as through parts of Maryland, Pennsylvania and New Jersey, to the town of New-York. He came to the conclusion that Virginia presented the most desirable circumstances, taking every thing into consideration; he purchased a plantation there, and also found a parish or benefice in the vicinity of his purchase, which he thought would suit Peter, and wrote to him to that effect.

Captain Boulay died in March, 1715, which made Peter the owner of £1000. He had taken his degree, and was ready to be ordained at the time he received John's letter. He accordingly went to London, and received ordination from the hands of the Bishop of London, who is also Bishop of all the British colonies.

In February or March, Moses conducted Peter's wife to join him in London; they embarked thence for Virginia, where they found John impatiently expecting them; and I have had the satisfaction of hearing from them that they are comfortably settled in their new home.

Moses remained in London, studying law with great diligence.

Francis was still at college, and a close student.

I was engaged all the time with my school; I had scholars enough to enable me to meet the heavy expenditure which had been going on, both in the maintenance of my family, and the education of my children.

I now felt that I had done for my sons all that was necessary; I ceased to feel anxious for them. They were all old enough to maintain themselves ; but I could not help feeling anxious about the future support of my wife and daughters. Should I be taken from them they would have nothing, for I had not been able to lay up any thing for them. My pension would cease at my death, and the school, of course ; so they would, to all appearance, be left destitute.

Lord Galway was now Lord Lieutenant of Ireland, and as he was my friend, I thought I might, through his aid, make an arrangement, by which my pension would be continued to my wife and daughters. I waited upon him, and explained to him my cause of anxiety, and begged that he would transfer my pension to my wife and daughters—one shilling a day to my wife, and two shillings each to my two daughters. He granted me the favor ; he had my name erased on the pension list, and the names of my wife and daughters inserted in the place, by which I had very nearly lost the pension altogether, without my wife and daughters gaining it.

The list which Lord Galway sent to London was not approved of ; and many persons were deprived of their pensions, under circumstances exactly similar to mine. The same

good God, whose providential care I have so often pointed
out to you, befriended me once more, and raised up for me
friends in Parliament, who spoke so warmly in my behalf,
when the subject came under discussion, that I was reinstated in my pension as before.

While this was going on, my eldest daughter, Mary Anne,
was married, with the consent of the whole family, on the
twentieth of October, 1716, to Matthew Maury, of Castel
Mauron, Gascony. He was a very honest man, and a good
economist, but without property. He had lived in Dublin for
two years, having come thither from France as a Refugee.

James was the next who went to Virginia. He sailed in
April, 1717, and took with him his wife and child, and his
mother-in-law. They had a very disastrous voyage; the vessel sprung a leak, and they were obliged to work the pumps
night and day, without intermission, for twenty-six days.
They arrived in safety at last. John met them, conducted
them to a house he had provided for them, where he had most
considerately laid up grain ready for their use.

In the same year, my son-in-law, Mr. Maury, went to
Virginia, and he was so much pleased with the appearance
of the country, that he took a portion of the land John had
purchased, made preparations for a small dwelling-house to
be erected upon it, and returned for his wife, and a son that
had been born to him during his absence. They left us in
the month of September, 1719.

In this year Moses became disgusted with the study of
law; he had some scruples of conscience about the practice
of it; and his natural diffidence was unfavorable to success.
I wished him exceedingly to study Theology, but I could not
persuade him. He said he knew that it would be impossible

John Fontaine

after an Original likeness by Kneller

G. P. PUTNAM & Co.

for him ever to speak in public. He made up his mind to be an engraver, which I did not approve of, after having given him an education to fit him for one of the learned professions. He would not do any thing without my consent, and he continued so resolute in his wish, that I was obliged to yield; and in the year 1719, he bound himself apprentice to an engraver. I am told he is a very good artist. It is certain that he evinced a decided talent for drawing, when he was instructed in the art as a boy. May God bless and prosper him in an employment which he allowed him to show so strong a preference for.

John returned to London from Virginia in the month of July, 1719, and he soon after came home to us, and remained more than a year, when he accompanied Francis to London. The latter had been devoted to study from infancy, and had determined to be a preacher of the Gospel. He had taken his degree of Master of Arts, and he was well skilled in the Oriental Languages, as well as in all the more usual branches of college education. The Archbishop of Dublin gave him a most particular letter of recommendation to the Bishop of London, from whom he received both Deacon's and Priest's orders, and many marks of kindness. He was married, in London, to Miss Mary Glanisson, a young lady of French parentage, the family originally from Jonzac, in Saintonge.

The Bishop of London furnished him with a letter of introduction to the Governor of Virginia, and he and his wife soon afterwards sailed for that colony. When he arrived, he was so much admired by all who heard him preach, that many parishes were desirous to have him for their pastor, and he gained the esteem and friendship of all who came in contact with him. He is settled in St. Margaret's Parish, King

11

William County, where he is so much beloved, that his parishioners have bestowed favors upon him, such as no previous minister had received from them. I have lately had the gratification of hearing from him that God has given him a son. John, becoming weary of passing his time without any settled occupation, has been learning the trade of a watchmaker, from his cousin, Peter Forestier, with whom he always boarded when he went to London. His reputation was great for making repeating watches. I find, by a late letter from John, that he has begun to work on his own account, which I am pleased to hear, for it will make him independent, in case he should be deprived of the half-pay which he has hitherto received.

I have now, my dear children, given you a brief statement of the present condition of each one of you, and I hope that you will add your individual histories to this, for the benefit of those who come after you.

My memoirs draw near a close. Your poor mother had suffered much from rheumatism for three years before John and Francis left us; this painful disorder continued to increase upon her till she was no longer able to go to church, and her spirits became much depressed under this privation. Finally, her complaint turned to dropsy, and she was unable to leave her bed. On the twenty-ninth of January, 1721, her sufferings were ended by death.

A melancholy day it was that deprived me of my greatest earthly comfort and consolation! I was bowed to the very dust, but it made me think of my own latter end, and gave me a wholesome warning to prepare myself to join her.

During her illness, our dear daughter Elizabeth supplied the place of all her brothers and her sister, who had left her alone to comfort and sustain her aged parents; she took the

greatest possible care of her mother, she never spared herself
in any way, but did every thing cheerfully that she thought
would be acceptable or beneficial.

Though I was sadly overpowered and much enfeebled, by
this great affliction, I continued to attend to the duties of my
school until the month of September, in the same year. My
health then became so bad that I broke up my school, dismissed the boarders as well as the day-scholars, in order that
I might be at leisure to prepare for the great and awful change
that I was assured could not be far distant. It was my wish
to withdraw from worldly care and die in peace.

After remaining some months in a deplorable state, suffering from constant low fever and other distressing symptoms,
given over by my physicians, and without the least expectation of recovery on my own part, I was severely attacked with
the gout, from which I had been free for eighteen months, and
this new disorder drove away all others. The fever disappeared, my appetite returned, and I have continued ever since
in a tolerable state of health, though suffering from debility,
finding it difficult to use my limbs, and walking with great pain.

Your sister Elizabeth has, all this time, given me constant
proofs of her affection and tenderness. She has never caused
me the least pain except by her tears, which she has not at
all times been able to restrain, and by the unceasing attention
to me, which has made me afraid her own health would suffer.
She has had a bad cold occasionally; but God, in his infinite
mercy, has preserved her to me, and I thank him for this very
great consolation. I recommend this dear daughter most
especially to the care of her brothers and sister. You must
remember, my dear children, she is the one who has smoothed
the downward path of life for her parents, and has performed

those tender offices which you all owe to them, but which your absence precluded you from performing.

I had written to John and Moses, to tell them I would send these memoirs to them, that they might make a copy for their own use before this was sent to Virginia. They replied that they would much prefer retaining the copy written with my own hand, and they would send that which they should write to Virginia. The expression of this most natural wish, has induced me to write a second copy with my own hand. God has prolonged my life, and given me leisure ; therefore I have felt it my duty to do it myself, as well to gratify them as to save them trouble, and prevent their being taken from their profitable employments to write it. I am sure those in Virginia will value this the more for being in my own handwriting. I have copied it word for word from the other, and have finished it this twenty-first day of June, 1722. If by any accident one copy should be lost, the other may be referred to.

I feel the strongest conviction, that if you will take care of these memoirs, your descendants will read them with pleasure, and I here declare that I have been most particular as to the truth of all that is herein recorded.

I hope God will bless the work, and that by his grace it may be a bond of union amongst you and your descendants, and that it may be a humble means of confirming you all in the fear of the Lord.

If our Heavenly Father, whose blessing I have implored upon the work, should vouchsafe to make use of it as an instrument for the advancement of His glory, and your eternal welfare, I shall think myself more than recompensed for all my trouble.   I am, my dear children,

Your tender father,

JAMES FONTAINE.

JOURNAL OF JOHN FONTAINE.

THE JOURNAL* commences on the 16th September, 1710, when he obtained an ensign's commission in Lord Shaw's regiment of foot. He was rather young to enter the service, only seventeen years old.

On the 1st February, 1710-11, the troops embarked at Cork, and put to sea immediately. The weather was very stormy, and one of the transports foundered at sea, having on board three companies under Colonel Chester. That on board of which John Fontaine was a passenger, arrived in safety at Plymouth on the 11th February. On the 26th March, the troops sailed for Spain, and encountered bad weather again, which caused them to put into Torbay. They anchored off Lisbon on the 22d April, and reached Barcelona on the last of May. There the troops were thinned by disease and violence. John observes: " There may be good laws in this coun-

* In the preceding narrative, there is mention made of a Journal kept by John Fontaine. This has been sent to me, with great kindness, by his descendants, who are now living in the neighborhood of London. I cannot refrain from expressing my admiration of the piety and excellence of my kinswomen, at the same time that I make my acknowledgments for their contribution towards the completion of our family annals. Their lives are in all respects such as one might hope and expect to find in those descended from a long line of pious ancestry.

try; but if there be, it is certain they do not put them in execution. And what is to be admired amongst these bigoted people is, that they do not punish murderers, but will rather protect them. If any man is murdered, it is commonly near a church; the murderer runs there at once, and then it is sacrilege to lay hands on him. He is protected from the law and the party offended, and also maintained, and furnished with a friar's habit, the better to hide his villainy; and passports are provided from convent to convent, until he is in a safe place."

" The country," he says, "seems to be very fruitful, but there are not people to cultivate the lands. All along the sea-shore, where there is the best land, places are not settled, because the Moors very often make descents, and carry away with them all they can get; and they make slaves of the people which they catch."

John appears to have been a very observing young traveller, his journal containing minute descriptions of what he saw in Barcelona, Terragona, Majorca, and Minorca, which I have not thought it worth while to give in this volume.

" The latter end of November, 1712, we had orders to embark; and as we were leaving Barcelona, the poor Spaniards, seeing they were left in the lurch, they called us traitors, and all the most vile names they could invent; and the common people threw stones at us, saying we had betrayed them into the hands of King Philip. It was with a great deal of difficulty we embarked."

The troops remained some time in the islands of Majorca and Minorca, and returned to England in the year 1713, without ever having had any engagement with the enemy. John went from Bristol to London by the stage-coach, which

at that time occupied three days.* He spent a short time
with his relations, the Arnaulds, in London, and then set
out for Ireland. He bought a horse, which carried him to
Chester in five days; and from there to Holyhead in three
days; and he crossed the Channel to Dublin in two days.

He spent some months at home, during which he employed
himself in studying navigation, preparatory to a voyage across
the Atlantic, which he contemplated making, in order to purchase land in some part of North America, to which it would
be suitable for the family to emigrate. He was entirely. at
leisure after his return from Spain, and was therefore glad to
make his taste for travelling subservient to the plans for the
future good of his brothers and sisters.

He proceeded to Cork to take passage for Virginia, and
after waiting from the 13th November to 3d December, 1714,
the ship Dove, of Biddeford, made her appearance in the harbor, and he engaged passage on board of her for himself and
four servants, for which he paid £25 sterling. He took out a
few goods as an adventure, and amongst them some Bibles,
Prayer-Books, and writing-paper, for account of Mr. Binauld,
a French Refugee, who had a printing establishment in Dublin.

A Journal of our intended voyage, by God's assistance,
in the Dove, of Biddeford, Captain John Shapley, commander.

7th Dec. 1714.—We embarked, and on the 10th the wind
proving fair, we set sail for the Virginias, with God's blessing.

    *   *   *   *   *   *

For the first week they had fair winds, and made respectable progress. Poor John was sea-sick for several days.

16th Dec.—Wind N.E., not very hard. We sailed five or

---

* The same journey is now accomplished by railway in three hours.

six knots the hour. We see many sea-hogs. We had no right observation. The method of taking an observation at sea :— You see first as high as you can the latitude you think yourself in ; then you fix your veins ; and then look for the horizon. You must observe that if the shade of the sun comes to the upper part of the slit of the horizon vein, and that the sun is at his full height, and that you see your horizon through the slit of the horizon vein, then you are assured of a good observation. You must begin to look before the sun is at his full height, that you may see him at the highest, and you must continue till you find him declining ; and when you find the sun declining, you must leave off observing. Then take off the degrees of the quadrant, and look in the table for the sun's declination, which you must subtract from your latitude by observation, and the remainder will be the latitude of the place you are in. *Now*, as the sun is going from us, we subtract, but when he comes to us, we must add.

*   *   *   *   *   *

20th Dec.—Wind S.W., very stormy ; and not being able to bear sail, we lowered our fore-sail and put a reef in our mainsail, and so lay under our mizzen, driving to the north-east all night. The weather thick, and in the morning rainy, which assuaged somewhat the winds ; but the greatness of the sea made us to continue under our mizzen-sail. We shipped some water, and see thousands of sea-hogs. We lay to the westward of the Azores, where, commonly, there is bad weather.

*   *   *   *   *   *

25th, Christmas.—Wind W. by N., very stormy and rainy. Not able to carry any sail, so we lay by under our mizzen. A mighty sea. Remained so all day and night, and made but an ordinary Christmas. Peas as hard as shot for breakfast.

Two fowls killed by the bad weather, for dinner, and stirabout for supper. In good health, God be praised.

26th, Sunday.—Wind W. by N. At 5 in the morning, not quite so stormy, but a great sea and much rain. We set our main-sail and fore-sail, and steered S. by E. at the rate of three knots per hour. Provisions scant, all our fowls dead.

27th.—Winds from N. W. to W. by S., very varying, rainy, cloudy, dismal and stormy, the sea great and raging, and we not able to carry any sail.

28th.—The wind at S. W., very stormy. We endeavored to scud before the wind, but the ship would not steer, so we were forced to bring to under our mizzen, driving at the mercy of the sea. The sea was extraordinary great. At the rising of the moon, a star rose close after and followed the moon, which the sailors said was a great sign of a tempest, and upon the like occasions that it commonly happens.

29th.—The wind rose and blew very hard in the morning, and increased continually till it blew a tempest. About 10 at night, we were obliged to take in our mizzen and lay under bare poles, and about two hours and a half after the wind blew so terribly in the rigging that it clapt one side of the ship under water, and the sea-water came in from the steerage door in such abundance, that had it continued long it would have filled the ship. The sailors were for cutting away the mainmast, but two went up and cut away the main-top-mast, and then the ship righted. The main-top-mast fell overboard, but all the ropes not being cut, the sea drove the mast with such violence against the side of the ship that we were afraid it would stave her through; but at last we got clear, and cut all the ropes which held, and were in hopes that we should receive no further damage, but that was not

11*

God's pleasure. Half an hour after one, the wind blowing most dreadfully, and the night dark as it possibly could be the sea looked like a fire, and foamed upon our deck ready to tear us in pieces. One wave came on board which tore away our bowsprit close to the foot of the fore-mast, and the shock was so terrible that we thought the ship was stove in pieces. What a terrible cry the people gave, expecting to go down every minute ; but it was God's will that nothing was broke but the bowsprit, which was striking, at every sea, violently against the ship's head. Two of our best sailors went up the fore-mast, to cut away the fore top-mast and the ropes that held the bowsprit. In the mean time we shipped another sea, which carried away the fore-mast, close by the board, and one of the men that was in the round top was carried with it into the sea ; the other man had his body bruised between the mast and the side of the ship, but not unto death, God be praised. He that fell in the sea, a rope had him by the leg, so that he fell into the sea, but got no farther hurt than that the rope hurt his leg. He got in safe, but had drank so much salt water, and worked himself so, that he was not able to stir. By the time these two were well in the steerage, another comes in that had almost cut off his left hand, as he was cutting the ropes to let the masts go clear. These three men were disabled, the best men that we had. What can be imagined more terrible than to see the head of the ship all under water, and the sea foaming amongst us upon the deck, and the men that remained almost disheartened, and those poor men that were disabled, grieving that they could not help themselves, and encouraging the rest to disengage the ship from the foremast and bowsprit, which were a thumping the ship to that degree, that we expected every minute the masts would come through. We were encompassed with death and horror within and without, and it would make the most brave to submit himself. What could we think, to see so many misfortunes, one after the other, but that it was God's pleasure we should perish, and be destroyed for our wickedness. But when we called upon him for relief, he helped us, and at last we got quit of our fore-mast and bowsprit without any damage to the sides of the ship.

How the Lord doth show us, that it is not by the arm of flesh we are preserved from the raging and terrible sea, but by his almighty hand and powerful outstretched arm. O Lord, we see that it is in thee alone we must trust, and have all hopes of relief from thee, and thou showest us this day, as our lives are witness of, that it is not in vain to humble ourselves before thee, and call upon our God and Saviour in the time of distress. Help us, therefore, O God, to perform what we have promised unto thee in our great distress. Thou hast granted unto us our lives, O strengthen us by thy grace to employ the remaining part to thy honor and praise, never forgetting how sweet thy help is, when no other can help. O Lord, it is not only on this occasion that thou hast been pleased to preserve my life to me in imminent danger, but several times; therefore, let me never forget these thy blessings. Make me to be thankful to thee, and help me to perform thy commandments to the uttermost of my power, until the end of my days. Amen.

30th.—We lay under our mizzen all the day like a log of wood, and suffered much by the greatness of the winds and sea, being most always under water. We comforted ourselves, seeing that through God's infinite mercy he had preserved us until now. The wind was at N. W. very showery and full of hail.

31st.—We lay a hull, with our mizzen-sail out. We shipped several seas, and were almost continually under water. The wind, God be praised, had somewhat fallen, as also the sea, but not being in a capacity for proceeding on the voyage to Virginia, for want of masts and sails,—we were then 400 leagues to the westward of Cape Clear in Ireland,—about twelve of the clock, we all consulted what was best and most proper, to continue on to Virginia, or to return to Europe. All the sailors with one consent, gave their voice to set sail for England or some part of Europe, lest by continuing on the voyage to Virginia, either for want of provisions or rigging, we should perish. The wind being at W. by N., we set our main-sail, and mizzen-sail before for a stay-sail, and steered our course for England, W. by S., but made little way. We were, by our reckoning, in the lat. 42° 20′, and were further westward than the Island of Flores, which is the most western island of the Azores.

We are setting our ship in as good order as we can, but she is miserably shattered. We hope God will continue the wind fair for Europe.

1714–15, *1st January.*—The wind at S. W. by S., something calmer, but the sea running very high. We lay by under our main-sail, but rolled miserably for want of masts and sails. We received several very dangerous seas that night, which we feared would founder us, but God was pleased to preserve us from all these threatening dangers. We made of our main-sail, a sprit-sail to make the ship steer; we also took down our mizzen top-mast, and fastened our main-mast, as well as we could, with our running tackle; and we are preparing sails, and contriving some posture to put the ship in, waiting for fair weather, when God will be pleased to send it.

We are almost wasted by the violent motion of the ship being without masts ; but we still trust in Thee, O God, and wait patiently for our deliverance by thy Almighty hand. Stretch forth thine arm to us, O Lord, and bear us up in this our distress, lest we sink and fall under the weight of our sins. Suffer us not to repine against thee in our trouble, but let us confess that we merit to be afflicted. Thou hast, O Lord, given for us thy only Son, our Lord Jesus Christ: to his merits we fly, and through him we hope for salvation. Do thou pardon us, O Lord, and accept of these our imperfect prayers, and if thou seest fit to take us to thyself, do thou also cleanse us, that we may be worthy of appearing before thee. All these thoughts come now before us, because we see death as if it were playing before our eyes, waiting for the sentence of Almighty God to destroy us. Nothing makes this sight so terrible as our sins, and it is our weakness and ignorance that makes us think more of death now than when we are at our own homes, and in our accounted places of security. If we rightly considered, we should think ourselves safer here than if we were in prosperity at home, for it is the devil's greatest cunning to put in our hearts that we are in a safe place, that we have long to live, and that a final repentance will be sufficient for our salvation. O God, give us grace that while we live, we may live unto thee, and have death always before our eyes, which most certainly will not cheat us, but come at last and take us out of this troublesome life, and if we are prepared for it, then we shall have our recompense for past watchfulness; therefore, let us cast off this world, so far as it may be prejudicial to our everlasting inheritance; and seek after thy laws, expecting mercy through the merits of our blessed Saviour and Redeemer. Amen.

2d Jan.—Wind S. by W. A fresh gale. By our observation, we found ourselves to be in the lat. 43° 00″; and that by our reckoning, we were 338 leagues to the westward of the Old Head of Kinsale.

All the mariners came to the master, and told him that if they proceeded on the voyage to Virginia, they were sure to perish by the way, and told him that they would not proceed but would return to Europe. The master would not consent to it without they made a protest against the ship, that she was not able to go to Virginia. I wrote the protest, they signed it, and we set our sails, and our course N. N. E. The wind being fair, and blowing fresh, we went at the rate of four knots per hour. About two of the clock in the morning we shipped two seas that we thought would have foundered the ship ; but, God be praised, we received no great damage. All our men are recovering of their wounds and bruises. I am, God be praised, in health. By the log we have made this last twenty-four hours 40 miles of our way homewards.

3d.—Wind hard at S. W., a great swell ; we steered our course N. E., and this twenty-four hours we made 58 miles. No observation. We shipped several seas, but not dangerous. The weather looks as if it would clear up. We saw some birds we call marline-spikes, mars, and rake-bats. We esteem ourselves by our dead reckoning to be in the lat. 45° 30″.

4th. Jan.—Wind S. by W., tolerable. We steered our course E. N. E. by N. This twenty-four hours we made 46 miles. No observation. We took out our mizzen-mast, and will put it in for a fore-mast as soon as the weather will permit. We are always wet upon deck, and the ship rolls most terribly. We reckon ourselves to be in the lat. 46° 00″.

5th.—Wind S. by W., blowing so hard that we could carry

no sail. We got a spare main-yard, which we put up for a mizzen-mast. We roll enough to tear the ship to pieces. The weather dark and hazy, always wet upon the deck as in the sea. No observation.

6th Jan.—Wind S. by E., stormy. We lay under a skirt of our main-sail, and so drove as the wind and sea carried us. The ship rolls enough to distract one, and is always shipping water. Give us grace, O Lord, to amend our lives by these warnings.

7th Jan.—Wind S. by E., stormy. A great sea, and we laying under a reefed main-sail. We shipped several seas. One carried away our main-tack, another came part in the steerage. We were forced to reef our main-sail, not able to bear any, the wind so stormy. We had but an indifferent observation, and think ourselves to be in lat. 49° 30″, and reckon ourselves to be 258 leagues to the westward of the Land's End. In a miserable condition for want of rigging.

8th Jan.—Wind S. by E., tempestuous. A terrible sea. About six of the clock in the morning, we were struck with a violent sea in the quarter and waist of the ship, and we all felt assured we should perish. We received several other seas, but not so terrible. No observation this day.

O God, be pleased to sustain us, for we are brought to nothing. Turn thy face towards us, look upon our afflictions, and take pity upon us, most miserable sinners.

9th Jan.—Wind S. by W. No observation. Weather thick, wind abated. We lay under our main-sail. The sea doth not break over us as it did, but there is still a great swell. We are in the lat. 50° 00″, and west from the Land's End 260 leagues.

10th Jan.—The wind S. W. by S., the weather fair and

the sea somewhat assuaged. We have an observation, and find
ourselves to be in the lat. 51° 21″, and by our reckoning distant west from the Land's End 220 leagues.

11th Jan.—Wind S. W. by S., very hard, and the sea
runs high. We esteem ourselves to be in lat. 51° 50.″ Cold.

12th Jan.—The wind about ten at night came from the
S. to W. by S., somewhat fair. We set our main-sail, and
made our course E. by S. until about nine of the clock in the
morning. Then the wind blew so hard that we were able to
carry no sail. It came to a storm. We shipped two seas,
but received no damage. No observation, but reckon ourselves to be in lat. 51° 30″. West of the Land's End in England 200 leagues.

13th Jan.—Wind W. N. W., abated, and about five of
the clock this morning we set our reefed main-sail. We sailed
about three knots per hour, and esteem ourselves to be in the
lat. 51° 10″, and distant from the Land's End 175 leagues.
About twelve of the clock in the night we shipped a sea that
broke our waist board, and afterwards another struck us in
the stern, but did us no great damage. We are securing our
bit of a fore-mast. Hazy and cold weather.

14th Jan.—Wind W. by S., and almost calm. Our course
steered S. E. We made between two and three knots per
hour. We had a good observation, and found ourselves in
lat. 51° 00″, and distant from the Land's End of England
160 leagues. The weather clears up, and the swell of the
sea is something abated. Our ship is as well rigged as we
can afford.

15th Jan.—Wind at S. by E., very hard, so that we can
carry no sail. It so continued for about nine hours, afterwards it cleared up, and was more moderate, so we set our

sails and steered our course W. by N.; went at the rate of three knots per hour. Thick weather, no observation, but esteem ourselves to be in lat. 51° 00″.

16th Jan.—The wind came about S. by E. to N. After several heavy showers of rain, we set our sails at about three in the morning, and made three knots and a half per hour. The wind moderate, but the weather thick, so that we had no good observation. We esteem ourselves to be in lat. 51° 00″, and west from Land's End 160 leagues. We saw a wild duck, which attempted several times to come on board, but at last fell into the sea by our side.

17th Jan.—The wind at N. W., a hard gale, but still we carried our main-sail, and steered our course S. E., and went by our log at the rate of five knots per hour. We had no observation, but by our reckoning we esteem ourselves to be in lat. 50° 50″, and distant from the Land's End 120 leagues.

By this day we may see that thy mercies are soon forgotten. Now that our miserable companions think they are out of danger, they forget all thy mercies to them, and bemoan their losses, repining against thy Providence for afflicting them. O Lord, give us grace to consider, that notwithstanding the wind doth not at this time blow hard nor the sea rage, yet we are still in thy hands, and we have deserved more afflictions than we have suffered.

18th Jan.—Wind W. by S. We steered our course S. E. by E., and went at the rate of four knots per hour, but not able to carry sail, being under our poles. Weather hazy.

19th Jan.—Wind W. by S., a good gale. Steered our course E. by S. We had an observation, and found ourselves to be in lat. 50° 24″, and westward from the Land's End of England 60 leagues.

Continue, O Lord, thy favors to us. Let thy Almighty hand be with us to conduct us to a place of safety.

20*th Jan.*—Wind S. by W. and S. W,; blew very hard. We lay under our mainsail. About seven of the clock, the wind fell and we set our sails.

21*st Jan.*—Wind at W. by S. ; a fair gale. About six in the afternoon we hove the lead, and found ground at sixty fathoms. The first the lead brought up was fine gray sand ; sounded again, and found gray sand mixed with shells, something reddish, and blue stones. About ten of the clock in the morning we saw a brigantine on our starboard quarter that bore N. N. E. of us. We made signals of distress to her, but she would not come to us, so we did not speak to her. At eleven we met with a sloop belonging to Cork, and spoke with her. She told us that Scilly bore from us 14 leagues E. ; but at twelve we had an observation, and found ourselves to be in the lat. 60° 41″ ; and by our reckoning Scilly bears of us about ten leagues E. by N. We steered our course E. Northerly, and ran at the rate of three and a half knots per hour.

22*d.*—Wind S. W. We ran at the rate of four knots per hour. At two of the clock we saw the Island of Lundy, and, at one, it bore of us E. Northerly ; at three we were up with the south end of the island, and the pilots came on board ; and at twelve at night we cast anchor in Clove Alley Road.

23*d.*—Weighed anchor at Clove Alley, and came over the bar of Biddeford. Though the weather was calm there was a great swell on the bar. We came over at three quarters flood, and in the shoalest place we found three fathoms water. I remained on board that night, and unbaled all Mr. Binauld's goods and distributed them amongst the sailors. I

wrote to my father and to Mr. Arnauld, and sent the letter
to the post by the master of the ship. I lay on board that
night, not well, but God be praised, delivered from the dangers of the sea. We cast anchor before Appledore, a handsome village.

24th.—In the morning I went ashore, where I met with the
son of Mr. Smith. I immediately hired a horse, and went to
Biddeford, where I met with Mr. Smith, the owner of the
ship. I spoke to him about the Bibles and paper, and inquired what he intended to do about the ship. He promised
me he would make her ready as soon as possible, and send
her immediately to Virginia. I went and took up my lodging
at the post-house, at the rate of seven shillings per week, for
diet and all. I was much out of order, so I went to bed immediately, and slept heartily.   *   *   *   *   *

The repairs of the vessel were completed in about a
month, and on the 28th February, she sailed a second time
for Virginia with the same crew; the sailors, after all their
hardships and dangers, consented to go again, relinquishing
all claim for wages for the three months spent at sea, and in
undergoing repairs.

We have the entire journal of the voyage, but nothing remarkable occurred upon it. On the 11th April they fell in with
two ships, of which the following mention is made: "We see
two ships, both under Turkish colors, which bore of us W. by
N. When within a league of us, one of them fired a gun,
and when within a mile, the other fired; they made us bring
to, then they hoisted out their boats and came on board of us,
and would have bought any thing of us, but the master was
afraid to trade with them. We found that they were Spaniards
come from the river De la Plata; they were laden with plate,

furs and skins. They had been three years out of Cadiz, in
Spain, and were now bound home. We told them the first
news of the peace, which rejoiced them. They were very
civil, and paid well for what little things they had of us. Each
galleon was about five hundred tons, and had forty guns a
piece mounted, and full of men. Their reckoning and ours
agreed very well together."   *   *   *   *   *   *

26th May, 1715.—About nine of the clock in the morning
we saw the land, about twelve we were up with Cape Henry.
I saw a ship bound for London, and sent a word by them to
my father to say I was well.

27th.—We continued, wind being fair, and before night we
passed over the horse-shoe, and by two in the morning
we came by the wolf-trap, and about ten we entered the
mouth of Potomac river, which is made by Virginia on
the west side, and Maryland on the east side. The rivers
here are the finest I ever was in ; all the borders are covered
with noble trees.

I have not been on shore as yet, but the planters, who
have been on board, inform me that there is not much tobacco
in the country this year.

28th.—In the morning, about ten of the clock, I landed
in Virginia, and walked about four miles to the Collector's,
one Mr. MacCartney, where I stayed till night, and then got
a permit to land my things, which cost me an English crown.
I inquired if my men would do well there, but I found no encouragement.

A guinea passes for twenty-six shillings, and all foreign
coin goes by weight. An ounce of silver passes for six shillings and threepence, and four pennyweights of gold for
twenty shillings.

29th, Sunday.—About 8 of the clock we came ashore, and went to church, which is about four miles from the place where we landed. The day was very hot, and the roads very dusty. We got to church a little late, but had part of the sermon. The people seemed to me pale and yellow. After the minister had made an end, every one of the men pulled out his pipe, and smoked a pipe of tobacco. I informed myself more about my own business, and found that Williamsburg was the only place for my design.

I was invited to dinner by one Mrs. Hughes, who lent me a horse, and the master of the ship another, and we went to her house, and dined there, and returned to the ship after dinner.

30th.—In the morning I went to one Captain Eskridge and bargained with him for a shallop to go to Williamsburg. I am to give him five pounds for the hire of her, and to maintain my people. I went with the sloop to the Dove, and loaded my goods, and made all things ready for this second voyage. I lay on board the ship, where we had several planters who got drunk that night.

31st.—This morning Captain Eskridge came on board our ship, and he agreed to receive his five pounds in goods, at 50 per cent. I gave him

One piece of linen, 20 yards, at 3s. 4d. .	£3	6	8
Eight pair of shoes, at 4s. . . .	1	12	0
One pair of gloves, ...	0	1	4
	£5	0	0

And so we left the ship, and went that day as far as a place called Cove, and here we remained the night, and had a gust, but it did no damage.

1st June.—Wind N. W. We set our sails, and came within three miles of Wicomico, and the wind fell calm.

2d.—Wind contrary and calm. We went a fowling, and killed two fishing-hawks, and went to see some of the planters, who treated us well.

3d.—We set sail, and made shift to get as far as New Point Comfort, where we cast anchor. A gust of rain, which wet us through.

4th.—We set sail, and came as far as Yorktown, and we landed at Gloucester, supped there, and lay that night. This town is on one side of York River, and Yorktown on the other side, opposite to it.

5th.—We set sail in the morning, had a fresh gale—as much as we could do to carry sail. About 12 we came to Queen's Creek, and about 3 to the landing of Williamsburg. I left the men in the sloop, and went up to the town, which is about a mile from the landing-place.

6th.—In the morning I hired two carts, and brought my goods up to town, and agreed for a lodging for myself, for diet and all, for twenty-six shillings per month. I hired a shop and a house for my people, and writ to my father.

7th.—I waited upon Governor Spotswood, and he assured me of all he could do. He invited me to dine, which I accepted of.

I remained in Williamsburg until the 6th September, and made several acquaintances. I also met with an old brother officer, Mr. Irewin. He did me a great deal of service.

9th November.—At eight of the clock in the morning, Mr. Clayton and I, we waited on Governor Spotswood, to tell him we were going to the Germantown, to know if he had any service there. We breakfasted with him, and at nine we mounted

our horses, and set out from Williamsburg—the roads very
good and level. About four of the clock we came to Mrs.
Root's, 25 miles from Williamsburg, where we crossed York
River to West Point. I reckon the river to be about one
mile and a half over at this place. This river of York di-
vides-itself here, where we landed, into two rivers, the north
branch called Mattapony River, and the south branch Pamunkey River. Both of these rivers are navigable for above
forty miles from the place where they fork. At a quarter
after five we mounted our horses, and rid about five miles farther, and came to one Mr. Austin Moor's house, upon Pamunkey River, where we were well entertained. We had
good wine and victuals. We made this day in all, thirty-one
miles and a half, the miles of the same length as those in
England, and the roads good.

10th. Sunday.—King William County.—We remained here all this day. I went to see Mr. Moor's improvements in the marsh, where, by draining, he hath very good
hay. We are very kindly received here. My horse is run
away.

11th.—Not being in any hopes of finding my horse, I borrowed one of Mr. Moor. About nine of the clock we sent the
horses over Mattapony River, in the boat, and at ten we took
our leave of Mr. Moor and his wife, and went in a canoe,
which is made of the body of a large tree that is about three
feet in diameter, which they saw off about twenty feet long,
and afterwards saw off a slab of it, and then dig it hollow.
Six or eight men may go in one of these canoes. As we were
going along the marsh, I saw the nest of a musk-rat. This
animal is about twice as big as a London rat, and the same
color as a beaver. It lives both in the water and on the

land. I went to his nest, which was made in the marsh, of reeds, and made about the bigness of a half hogshead. I pulled this building to pieces, and found that it was made two stories high, and four rooms in it—two of a floor—the rooms were in the form of a pair of spectacles, two underground, and two above.

We continued on to the other side of the river, which is King and Queen County. At eleven of the clock we mounted our horses, and went this day to Mr. Baylor's, where we put up, and were well entertained. He lives upon Mattapony River, and is one of the greatest dealers for tobacco in the country.

12th.—About seven of the clock we breakfasted; about nine, a servant of Mr. Moor's brought me my horse to Mr. Baylor's, and at eleven we took our leave, and continued on our way. The day very windy. We see by the side of the road an Indian cabin, which was built with posts put into the ground, the one by the other as close as they could stand, and about seven feet high, all of an equal length. It was built four-square, and a sort of a roof upon it, covered with the bark of trees. They say it keeps out the rain very well. The Indian women were all naked, only a girdle they had tied round the waist, and about a yard of blanketing put between their legs, and fastened one end under the fore-part of the girdle, and the other behind. Their beds were mats made of bulrushes, upon which they lie, and have one blanket to cover them. All the household goods was a pot.

We continued on our road, and saw several squirrels, and were on horseback till ten of the clock at night, and then arrived at Mr. Robert Beverley's house, which they reckon from Mr. Baylor's thirty miles. The roads very good. Here we were well received.

13*th.*—It being blowy and showery weather we remained
here. After breakfast we went to see Mr. Beverley's vineyard. This Beverley is the same that made the History of
Virginia. When we were in his vineyard we saw the several
sorts of vines which are natural, and grow here in the woods.
This vineyard is situated upon the side of a hill, and consists
of about three acres of land ; he assures us that he made this
year about four hundred gallons of wine. He hath been at
great expenses about this improvement. He hath also caves
and a wine press ; but according to the method they use in
Spain, he hath not the right method for it, nor his vineyard
is not rightly managed. He hath several plants of French
vines amongst·them.

14*th.*—The weather was very bad, and rained hard. We
were very kindly received. We diverted ourselves within
doors, and drank very heartily of the wine of his own making, which was good ; but I found by the taste of the wine,
that he did not understand how to make it. This man lives
well ; but though rich, he has nothing in or about his house
but what is necessary. He hath good beds in his house, but
no curtains ; and instead of cane chairs, he hath stools made
of wood. He lives upon the product of his land.

15*th.*—Blowing weather. Mr. Beverley would not suffer
us to go. He told me that the reason he had for making so
large a vineyard was, that about four years ago he made a
wager with the gentlemen of the country, who thought it impossible to bring a vineyard to any perfection. The following was the agreement : If he would give them one guinea
then, in hand, they would give him ten, if, in seven years'
time, he could cultivate a vineyard that would yield, at one
vintage, seven hundred gallons of wine. Mr. Beverley gave a

12

hundred guineas upon the above-mentioned terms, and I do not in the least doubt but the next year he will make the seven hundred gallons, and win the thousand guineas. We were very merry with the wine of his own making, and drank prosperity to the vineyard.

16th.—Mr. Beverley detained us, and we went out a hunting. We saw several deer, but could kill none. We shot some squirrels and partridges, and went round a great tract of land that belongs to him, and returned home. We passed the time away very agreeably, and so to bed.

17th, Sunday.—About ten of the clock, we mounted our horses, Mr. Beverley with us, and we went about seven miles to his Parish Church, where we had a good sermon from a Frenchman named Mr. De Latané, who is minister of this parish. After service, we returned to Mr. Beverley's house, and finished the day there.

18th.—Mr. Beverley's son hindered us from proceeding on our journey this day, by promising to set out with us the next morning; so we took our guns, and went a hunting. We killed some squirrels and partridges, but did no hurt to the wild turkeys nor deer, though we saw several. To-day we went to some of the planters' houses, and diverted ourselves for some time, and so returned to our friend's house, and passed away the evening merrily.

19th.—In the morning, about nine of the clock, we mounted our horses, and took our leave of Mr. Beverley. His son came along with us; it rained hard from eleven until twelve. About three we came to a place upon Rappahannoc River, called Taliaferro's Mount, from whence we had a feeble view of the Appalachian Mountains, and a fine view of the river, which is navigable for large ships, and has several fine islands in it.

When we had satisfied our sight, we continued on our journey, and about six we arrived at one Mrs. Woodford's, who lives upon Rappahannoc River, in a very agreeable place. This day we made thirty miles. This place is ten miles below the Falls of Rappahannoc River, and forty miles from the German settlement, where we design to go. We saw upon the river abundance of geese, ducks, and water-pheasants. We were kindly entertained.

20th.—At seven in the morning, we took our leave of Mrs. Woodford. The gentlewoman gave us provisions with us, and we put on our way, and at the distance of about five miles we came upon a tract of three thousand acres of land, which is in the disposal of Mr. Beverley, which he told me, when I was at his house, he would sell me at the rate of £7 10 per hundred acres. I rode over part of the land, and found it to be well timbered and good. It fronts upon the river of Rappahannoc about half a mile, where vessels of a hundred tons, or sloops may come. Five miles above it, I saw a small river which runs through the heart of the land, which river they call Massaponax, and is fit to set mills on. I would have agreed for this tract of land, but that Mr. Beverley would not dispose of it as commonly land is disposed of, but would have the deeds made to me for nine hundred and ninety-nine years, which I would not consent to, but insisted on having it for me and my heirs for ever ; so I did not buy the land of him.

We continued on our way until we came five miles above this land, and there we went to see the Falls of Rappahannoc River. The water runs with such violence over the rocks and large stones that are in the river, that it is almost impossible for boat or canoe to go up or down in safety. After we had satisfied our curiosity, we continued on the road. About five

we crossed a bridge that was made by the Germans, and about
six we arrived at the German settlement. We went immediately to the minister's house. We found nothing to eat, but
lived on our small provisions, and lay upon good straw. We
passed the night very indifferently.

21st.—Our beds not being very easy, as soon as it was day,
we got up. It rained hard, but notwithstanding, we walked
about the town, which is palisaded with stakes stuck in the
ground, and laid close the one to the other, and of substance
to bear out a musket-shot. There are but nine families, and
they have nine houses, built all in a line; and before every
house, about twenty feet distant from it, they have small sheds
built for their hogs and hens, so that the hog-sties and houses
make a street. The place that is paled- in is a pentagon, very
regularly laid out; and in the very centre there is a block-
house, made with five sides, which answer to the five sides of
the great inclosure ; there are loop-holes through it, from
which you may see all the inside of the inclosure. This
was intended for a retreat for the people, in case they
were not able to defend the palisadoes, if attacked by the
Indians.

They make use of this block-house for divine service.
They go to prayers constantly once a day, and have two sermons on Sunday. We went to hear them perform their service, which was done in their own language, which we did not
understand; but they seemed to be very devout, and sang the
psalms very well.

This town or settlement lies upon Rappahannoc River,
thirty miles above the Falls, and thirty miles from any inhabitants. The Germans live very miserably. We would tarry
here some time, but for want of provisions we are obliged to

go. We got from the minister a bit of smoked beef and cabbage, which were very ordinary and dirtily drest.

We made a collection between us three of about thirty shillings for the minister; and about twelve of the clock we took our leave, and set out to return; the weather hazy, and small rain. In less than three hours we saw nineteen deer. About six of the clock we arrived at Mr. Smith's house, which is almost upon the Falls of Rappahannoc River. We have made this day thirty miles. Mr. Smith was not at home, but his housekeeper entertained us well; we had a good turkey for dinner, and beds to lie on.

22d.—At seven in the morning we mounted our horses, and we met upon the road with two huntsmen; we went with them into the woods, and in half an hour they shot a buck and a doe, and took them on their horses. So we left them, and continued on our road, and about four of the clock we arrived at one Mr. Buckner's house, upon Rappahannoc River, where we tarried the night. We had good punch, and were very merry.

23d.—At eight in the morning breakfasted, got our horses, and continued on our road. About eleven we met with Mr. Beverley, and went with him to see a piece of land he had to sell, containing five hundred acres. It lies upon Rappahannoc River, and fronts one mile on the river, and on one side of it there is a large creek navigable for sloops, and an old house upon the land, with one hundred acres of cleared land about it; the other four hundred acres have wood growing on it, but all the large timber is cut down. He asked £50 per hundred for it, which I thought too dear, and we could not agree. We saw several wild turkeys in our way, but had no arms with us. About seven o'clock at night we arrived at Mr.

Beverley's house. We made, this day, about thirty-eight miles.

24th.—At eight in the morning, we got on horseback, and took our leave of Mr. Beverley and his son, who left us, and so we put on our journey till we came to Mr. Thomas Walker's house upon Mattapony River. Here we set up that night, and were well entertained, and made in all this day twenty-five miles.

25th.—My horse proving lame, I was obliged to leave him at Mr. Walker's. I hired a horse, and from thence we went to King and Queen Court House, where we dined and tarried till four in the afternoon, and were invited by Captain Story to his house. We went with him and tarried all night, and we had but indifferent entertainment.

26th.—In the morning we crossed York River ferry to the brick house. About one, we put up at Fourier's Ordinary, where we dined, and at two we set out from thence, and at five in the afternoon we arrived at Williamsburg.

This journey, going and coming from Williamsburg to the German settlement comes to 292 miles, besides ferriages, and cost me about £3 10.

Our Journalist appears to have remained quietly at Williamsburg until April, 1716, when he thus proceeds in his narration:

The Governor proposed a journey to his settlement, on Meherrin River, called Christanna.

April, 1716, *Williamsburg.*—The first day, Governor Spotwood and I set out from Williamsburg about eight of the clock in the morning, and we went to Jamestown in a four-wheeled chaise. Jamestown is eight miles from Williamsburg, and situated close upon James River. This town consists chiefly in a Church, a Court House, and three or four brick houses, it was the former seat of the Government, but now it is removed to Middle Plantation, which they call Williamsburg. The place where this town is built is on an island, it was fortified with a small rampart with embrasures, but now all is gone to ruin.

Our horses were ferried over before us; we left the chaise at Jamestown, and about ten of the clock we were in the ferry boat, and crossed the river, which they reckon to be about two miles broad at this place. When we arrived at the other side of the river, we mounted our horses, and set out on the journey. It rained all this day very fast, and we were well wet. About two of the clock we put into a planter's house and dined upon our own provisions, and fed our horses; and about three, we mounted our horses, and came to a place called Simmons' Ferry, upon Nottoway River. There was a great fresh in the river, so that we were obliged to swim our horses over, and to pass over ourselves in a canoe; then we mounted our horses and put on till we came to one Mr. Hicks' plantation, upon one of the branches of Meherrin River, called Herring Creek. The man of the house was not at home, so we fared but indifferently. We made in all this day 65 miles.

April, the 2d day.—We set out with a guide for Christanna, for this house is the most outward settlement on this side of Virginia, which is the south side. We have no roads here to conduct us, nor inhabitants to direct the traveller. We met with several Indians, and about twelve we came to Meherrin River opposite to Christanna Fort. We saw this day several fine tracts of land, and plains called savannas, which lie along by the river side, much like unto our low meadow lands in

England; there is neither tree nor shrub that grows upon these plains, nothing but good grass, which, for want of being mowed or eaten down by cattle, grows rank and coarse. These places are not miry, but good and firm ground; they are subject to inundation after great rains and when the rivers overflow, but there is seldom over six or eight inches of water, which might easily be prevented by ditching.

About half after twelve we crossed the river in a canoe, and went up to the Fort, which is built upon rising ground. It is an inclosure of five sides, made only with palisadoes, and instead of five bastions, there are five houses, which defend the one the other; each side is about one hundred yards long. There are five cannon, which were fired to welcome the Governor. There are twelve men here continually to keep the place. After all the ceremony was over, we came into the fort and were well entertained. The day proving wet and windy, we remained within doors, and employed ourselves in reading of Mr. Charles Griffin his observations on the benefit of a solitary life. We reckon that we made this day fifteen miles; in all, from Williamsburg, eighty miles.

The 3d day.—About nine in the morning we got up and breakfasted. Mr. Griffin, who is an Englishman, is employed by the government to teach the Indian children, and to bring them to Christianity. He remains in this place, and teaches them the English tongue, and to read the Bible and Common Prayers, as also to write. He hath been now a year amongst them, and hath had good success. He told the Governor that the Indian chiefs or great men, as they style themselves, were coming to the fort to compliment him. These Indians are called Saponey Indians, and are always at peace with the English: they consist of about two hundred persons, men,

women, and children; they live within musket-shot of the
fort, and are protected by the English from the insults of the
other Indians, who are at difference with the English; they
pay a tribute every year to renew and confirm the peace, and
show their submission. This nation hath no king at present,
but is governed by twelve of their old men, which have
power to act for the whole nation, and they will all stand
to every thing that these twelve men agree to, as their own
act.

About twelve of the clock the twelve old men came to the
fort, and brought with them several skins, and as soon as they
came to the Governor, they laid them at his feet, and then all
of them as one man made a bow to the Governor: they then
desired an interpreter, saying they had something to represent to him, notwithstanding some of them could speak good
English. It is a constant maxim amongst the Indians in general, that even if they can speak and understand English, yet
when they treat of any thing that concerns their nation, they
will not treat but in their own language, and that by an interpreter, and they will not answer any question made to them
without it be in their own tongue.

The Governor got an interpreter, after which they stood
silent for a while, and after they had spit several times upon
the ground, one of them began to speak, and assured the
Governor of the satisfaction they had of seeing him amongst
them, and of the good-will they had towards the English.
They said that some of the English had wronged them in
some things, which they would make appear, and desired he
would get justice done to them, that they depended upon him
for it: which the Governor promised he would, and he thanked them for the good opinion they had of his justice towards

12*

them ; whereupon they all made a bow, and so sat down on the ground all around the Governor.

The first complaint they made was against another nation of Indians called Genitoes, who had surprised a party of their young men that had been out a hunting, and murdered fifteen of them, without any reason. They desired of the Governor to assist them to go out to war with these Genito Indians, until they had killed as many of them ; but this the Governor could not grant. He told them he would permit them to revenge themselves, and help them to powder and ball, at which they seemed somewhat rejoiced. They also complained against some of the English, who had cheated them. The Governor paid them in full for what they could make out that they were wronged of by the English, which satisfied them, and afterwards he made them farewell presents, and so dismissed them.

About three of the clock, came sixty of the young men with feathers in their hair and run through their ears, their faces painted with blue and vermilion, their hair cut in many forms, some on one side of the head, and some on both, and others on the upper part of the head, making it stand like a cock's-comb, and they had blue and red blankets wrapped about them. They dress themselves after this manner when they go to war the one with the other, so they call it their war-dress, and it really is very terrible, and makes them look like. so many furies. These young men made no speeches, they only walked up and down, seeming to be very proud of their most abominable dress.

After this came the young women; they all have long straight black hair, which comes down to the waist ; they had each of them a blanket tied round the waist, and hanging down about the legs like a petticoat. They have no shifts, and most of them nothing to cover them from the waist upwards; others of them there were that had two deer skins sewed together and thrown over their shoulders like a mantle. They all of them grease their bodies and heads with bear's oil, which, with the smoke of their cabins, gives them an ugly smell. They are very modest and very true to their husbands. They are straight and well limbed, good shape, and extraordinary good features, as well the men as the women. They look wild, and are mighty shy of an Englishman, and will not let you touch them. The men marry but one wife, and cannot marry any more until she die, or grow so old that she cannot bear any more children; then the man may take another wife, but is obliged to keep them both and maintain them. They take one another without ceremony.

The 4th day.—In the morning I rid out with the Governor and some of the people of the fort, to view the lands, which were not yet taken up. We saw several fine tracts of land, well watered, and good places to make mills on. I had a mind to take some of it up, so I asked the Governor if he would permit me to take up 3,000 acres, and he gave me his promise for it. I went through the land I designed to take up, and viewed it. It lies upon both sides of Meherrin River, and I design to have it in a long square, so that I shall have at least three miles of the river in the tract. I am informed that this river disgorgeth itself into the Sound of Currytuck. This river, though large and deep, is not navigable, because of the great rocks it falls over in some places. There is a great deal of fish in this place; we had two for dinner—about sixteen inches long—which were very good and firm.

I gave ten shillings to Captain Hicks for his trouble in showing me the land, and he promises that he will assist me in the surveying of it. We saw several turkeys and deer, but we killed none. We returned to the fort about five of the clock.

The 5th day.—After breakfast, I went down to the Saponey Indian town, which is about a musket-shot from the fort. I walked round to view it. It lieth in a plain by the riverside, the houses join all the one to the other, and altogether make a circle ; the walls are large pieces of timber which are squared, and being sharpened at the lower end, are put down two feet in the ground, and stand about seven feet above the ground. These posts are laid as close as possible the one to the other, and when they are all fixed after this manner, they make a roof with rafters, and cover the house with oak or hickory bark, which they strip off in great flakes, and lay it so closely that no rain can come in. Some Indian houses are covered in a circular manner, which they do by getting long saplings, sticking each end in the ground, and so covering them with bark ; but there are none of the houses in this town so covered. There are three ways for entering into this town or circle of houses, which are passages of about six feet wide, between two of the houses. All the doors are on the inside of the ring, and the ground is very level withinside, which is in common between all the people to divert themselves. There is in the centre of the circle a great stump of a tree ; I asked the reason they left that standing, and they informed me it was for one of their head men to stand upon when he had any thing of consequence to relate to them, so that being raised, he might the better be heard.

The Indian women bind their children to a board that is cut after the shape of the child : there are two pieces at the bottom of this board to tie the two legs of the child to, and a piece cut out behind, so that all that the child doth falls from him, and he is never dirty. The head or top of the board is round, and there is a hole through the top of it for a string to be passed through, so that when the women tire of holding them, or have a mind to work, they hang the board to the limb of a tree, or to a pin in a post for that purpose, and there the children swing about and divert themselves, out of the reach of any thing that may hurt them. They are kept in this way till nearly two years old, which I believe is the reason they are all so straight, and so few of them lame or odd-shaped. Their houses are pretty large, they have no garrets, and no other light than the door, and that which comes from the hole in the top of the house which is to let out the smoke. They make their fires always in the middle of the house ; the chief of their household goods is a pot and some wooden dishes and trays, which they make themselves ; they seldom have any thing to sit upon, but squat upon the ground ; they have small divisions in their houses to sleep in, which they make of mats made of bullrushes ; they have bed-steads, raised about two feet from the ground, upon which they lay bear and deer skins, and all the covering they have is a blanket. These people have no sort of tame creatures, but live entirely upon their hunting and the corn which their wives cultivate. They live as lazily and miserably as any people in the world.

Between the town and the river, upon the river side, there are several little huts built with wattles, in the form of an oven, with a small door in one end of it ; these wattles are plaistered without side very closely with clay, they are big enough to hold a man, and are called sweating-houses. When they have any sickness, they get ten or twelve pebble stones

which they heat in the fire, and when they are red-hot they
carry them into these little huts, and the sick man or woman
goes in naked, only a blanket with him, and they shut the
door upon them, and there they sit and sweat until they are
no more able to support it, and then they go out naked and
immediately jump into the water over head and ears, and this
is the remedy they have for all distempers.

The 6th day.—The Governor sent for all the young boys,
and they brought with them their bows, and he got an axe,
which he stuck up, and made them all shoot by turns at the eye
of the axe, which was about twenty yards distant. Knives and
looking-glasses were the prizes for which they shot, and they
were very dexterous at this exercise, and often shot through
the eye of the axe. This diversion continued about an hour.
The Governor then asked the boys to dance a war dance, so
they all prepared for it, and made a great ring ; the musician
being come, he sat himself in the middle of the ring ; all the
instrument he had was a piece of board and two small sticks ;
the board he set upon his lap, and began to sing a doleful
tune, and by striking on the board with his sticks, he accompanied his voice ; he made several antic motions, and sometimes
shrieked hideously, which was answered by the boys. As the
men sung, so the boys danced all round, endeavoring who
could outdo the one the other in antic motions and hideous
cries, the movements answering in some way to the time of
the music. All that I could remark by their actions was,
that they were representing how they attacked their enemies,
and relating one to the other how many of the other Indians
they had killed, and how they did it, making all the motions
in this dance as if they were actually in the action. By this
lively representation of their warring, one may see the base

way they have of surprising and murdering the one the other, and their inhuman manner of murdering all the prisoners, and what terrible cries they have, they who are conquerors. After the dance was over, the Governor treated all the boys, but they were so little used to have a belly full, that they rather devoured their victuals than any thing else. So this day ended.

The 7th day.—After breakfast we assembled ourselves, and read the Common Prayer.* There was with us eight of the Indian boys who answered very well to the prayers, and understood what was read. After prayers we dined, and in the afternoon we walked abroad to see the land, which is well timbered and very good. We returned to the fort and supped. Nothing remarkable.

The 8th day.—About ten in the morning there came to the fort ten of the Meherrin Indians, laden with beaver, deer and bear skins, to trade, for our Indian Company have goods here for that purpose. They delivered up their arms to the white men of the fort, and left their skins and furs also. Those Indians would not lie in the Indian town, but went into the woods, where they lay until such time as they had done trading.

---

* The Rev. F. L. Hawks, D. D., has lent me a rare old book upon the colony of Virginia, by Hugh Jones, A. M., Chaplain to the Honorable Assembly, &c., 1724, from which I make the following extract:

" He (Governor Spotswood) built a fort called *Christanna*, which, though not so far back, yet proved of great service and use ; where, at his sole expense, I think, I have seen seventy-seven *Indian children* at a time at school, under the careful management of the worthy *Mr. Charles Griffin*, who lived there some years for that purpose. These children could all read, say their catechisms and prayers tolerably well. The *Indians* so loved and adored him, that I have seen them hug him, and lift him up in their arms, and fain would have chosen him for a *King* of the *Sapony* nation."

The Governor and I we laid out an avenue about half a mile long, which gave us employment enough this day.

The 9th day.—About seven in the morning we got a horseback, and were just out of the fort when the cannon fired. We passed by the Indian town, where they had notice that the Governor was returning, so they got twelve of their young men ready with their arms, and one of their old men at the head of them, and assured the Governor they were sorry that he was leaving them, but that they would guard him safe to the inhabitants, which they pressed upon him, so that he was forced to accept of it. They were all afoot, so the Governor to compliment the head man of the Indians lent him his led-horse. After we had rid about a mile, we came to a ford of Meherrin River, and being mistaken in our water-mark, we were sometimes obliged to make our horses swim, but we got over safe. The Indian Chief seeing how it was, unsaddled his horse, and stript himself all to his belt, and forded the river, leading his horse after him ; the fancy of the Indian made us merry for a while. The day being warm, and he not accustomed to ride, the horse threw him before we had gone two miles, but he had courage to mount again. By the time we had got a mile further, he was so terribly galled that he was forced to dismount, and desired the Governor to take his horse, for he could not imagine what good they were for, if it was not to cripple Indians.

We were obliged to ride easy, that we might not get before our Indian guard, who accompanied us as far as a river, called Nottoway River, which taketh its name from the Nottoway Indians, who formerly lived upon this river. The place was about fifteen miles from the fort. When we parted with the Indians the Governor ordered them to have a pound of powder and shot in proportion to each man. So they left us, and we crossed the river and rid fifteen miles further, until we came to a poor planter's house, where we put up for that night. They had no beds in the house, so the Governor lay upon the ground, and had his bear-skin under him, and I lay upon a large table in my cloak, and thus we fared until day, which was welcome to us.

The 10*th day.*—At five we got up, and at six we mounted our horses, and we took a guide who pretended to know the way, and bring us a short cut, but instead of that, he took us about seven miles out of our way. When we found that he was lost, we dismissed him; the sun began to shine out clear, so the Governor he conducted us, and about four of the clock we came to James River and took the ferry, and about six of the clock we mounted our horses and went to Williamsburg, where we arrived about eight of the clock. I supped with the Governor; and being well tired, I went after to my lodgings and to bed.

This journey, coming and going, comes to 160 miles.

Williamsburg, 20*th August,* 1716.—In the morning got my horses ready, and what baggage was necessary, and I waited on the Governor, who was in readiness for an expedition over the Appalachian mountains. We breakfasted, and about ten got on horseback, and at four came to the Brickhouse, upon York River, where we crossed the ferry, and at six we came to Mr. Austin Moor's house, upon Mattapony River, in King William County; here we lay all night and were well entertained.

21*st.*—Fair weather. At ten we set out from Mr. Moor's, and crossed the river of Mattapony, and continued on the road, and were on horseback till nine of the clock at night, before we came to Mr. Robert Beverley's house, where we were well entertained, and remained this night.

22*d*.—At nine in the morning, we set out from Mr. Beverley's. The Governor left his chaise here, and mounted his horse. The weather fair, we continued on our journey until we came to Mr. Woodford's, where we lay, and were well entertained. This house lies on Rappahannoc River, ten miles below the falls.

23*d*.—Here we remained all this day, and diverted ourselves and rested our horses.

24*th*.—In the morning, at seven, we mounted our horses, and came to Austin Smith's house about ten, where we dined, and remained till about one of the clock, then we set out, and about nine of the clock we came to the German-town, where we rested that night—bad beds and indifferent entertainment.

German-town, 25*th*.—After dinner we went to see the mines, but I could not observe that there was any good mine. The Germans pretend that it is a silver mine ; we took some of the ore and endeavored to run it, but could get nothing out of it, and I am of opinion it will not come to any thing, no, not as much as lead. Many of the gentlemen of the county are concerned in this work. We returned, and to our hard beds.

26*th*.—At seven we got up, and several gentlemen of the country, that were to meet the Governor at this place for the expedition, arrived here, as also two companies of Rangers, consisting each of six men, and an officer. Four Meherrin Indians also came.

In the morning I diverted myself with other gentlemen shooting at a mark. At twelve we dined, and after dinner we mounted our horses and crossed Rappahannoc River, that

runs by this place, and went to find out some convenient place
for our horses to feed in, and to view the land hereabouts.
Our guide left us, and we went so far in the woods that we
did not know the way back again; so we hallooed and fired
our guns. Half an hour after sunset the guide came to us,
and we went to cross the river by another ford higher up.
The descent to the river being steep, and the night dark, we
were obliged to dismount and lead our horses down to the
river side, which was very troublesome. The bank being very
steep, the greatest part of our company went into the water
to mount their horses, where they were up to the crotch in the
water. After we had forded the river and came to the other
side, where the bank was steep also, in going up, the horse of
one of our company slipped and fell back into the river on
the top of his rider, but he received no other damage than
being heartily wet, which made sport for the rest. A hornet
stung one of the gentlemen in the face, which swelled prodigiously. About ten we came to the town, where we supped,
and to bed.

27th.—Got our tents in order, and our horses shod.
About twelve, I was taken with a violent headache and pains
in all my bones, so that I was obliged to lie down, and was
very bad that day.

28th.—About one in the morning, I was taken with a violent fever, which abated about six at night, and I began to
take the bark, and had one ounce divided into eight doses, and
took two of them by ten of the clock that night. The fever
abated, but I had great pains in my head and bones.

29th.—In the morning we got all things in readiness, and
about one we left the German-town to set out on our intended
journey. At five in the afternoon, the Governor gave orders

to encamp near a small river, three miles from Germanna, which we called Expedition Run, and here we lay all night. This first encampment was called Beverley Camp in honor of one of the gentlemen of our party. We made great fires, and supped, and drank good punch. By ten of the clock I had taken all of my ounce of Jesuit's Bark, but my head was much out of order.

30th.—In the morning about seven of the clock, the trumpet sounded to awake all the company, and we got up. One Austin Smith, one of the gentlemen with us, having a fever, returned home. We had lain upon the ground under cover of our tents, and we found by the pains in our bones that we had not had good beds to lie upon. At nine in the morning, we sent our servants and baggage forward, and we remained, because two of the Governor's horses had strayed. At half past two we got the horses, at three we mounted, and at half an hour after four, we came up with our baggage at a small river, three miles on the way, which we called Mine River, because there was an appearance of a silver mine by it. We made about three miles more, and came to another small river, which is at the foot of a small mountain, so we encamped here and called it Mountain Run, and our camp we called Todd's Camp. We had good pasturage for our horses, and venison in abundance for ourselves, which we roasted before the fire upon wooden forks, and so we went to bed in our tents. Made 6 miles this day.

31st.—At eight in the morning, we set out from Mountain Run, and after going five miles we came upon the upper part of Rappahannoc River. One of the gentlemen and I, we kept out on one side of the company about a mile, to have the better hunting. I saw a deer, and shot him from my horse, but the horse threw me a terrible fall and ran away; we ran after, and with a great deal of difficulty got him again; but we could not find the deer I had shot, and we lost ourselves, and it was two hours before we could come upon the track of our company. About five miles further we crossed the same river again, and two miles further we met with a large bear, which one of our company shot, and I got the skin. We killed several deer, and about two miles from the place where we killed the bear, we encamped upon Rappahannoc River. From our encampment we could see the Appalachian Hills very plain. We made large fires, pitched our tents, and cut boughs to lie upon, had good liquor, and at ten we went to sleep. We always kept a sentry at the Governor's door. We called this Smith's Camp. Made this day fourteen miles.

1st. September.—At eight we mounted our horses, and made the first five miles of our way through a very pleasant plain, which lies where Rappahannoc River forks. I saw there the largest timber, the finest and deepest mould, and the best grass that I ever did see. We had some of our baggage put out of order, and our company dismounted, by hornets stinging the horses. This was some hindrance, and did a little damage, but afforded a great deal of diversion. We killed three bears this day, which exercised the horses as well as the men. We saw two foxes but did not pursue them; we killed several deer. About five of the clock, we came to a run of water at the foot of a hill, where we pitched our tents. We called the encampment Dr. Robinson's Camp, and the river, Blind Run. We had good pasturage for our horses, and every one was cook for himself. We made our beds with bushes as before. On this day we made 13 miles.

2d.—At nine we were all on horseback, and after riding about five miles we crossed Rappahannoc River, almost at the head, where it is very small. We had a rugged way; we passed over a great many small runs of water, some of which were very deep, and others very miry. Several of our company were dismounted, some were down with their horses, others under their horses, and some thrown off. We saw a bear running down a tree, but it being Sunday, we did not endeavor to kill any thing. We encamped at five by a small river we called White Oak River, and called our camp Taylor's Camp.

3d.—About eight we were on horseback, and about ten we came to a thicket, so tightly laced together, that we had a great deal of trouble to get through; our baggage was injured, our clothes torn all to rags, and the saddles and holsters also torn. About five of the clock we encamped almost at the head of James River, just below the great mountains. We called this camp Colonel Robertson's Camp. We made all this day but eight miles.

4th.—We had two of our men sick with the measles, and one of our horses poisoned with a rattlesnake. We took the heaviest of our baggage, our tired horses, and the sick men, and made as convenient a lodge for them as we could, and left people to guard them, and hunt for them. We had finished this work by twelve, and so we set out. The sides of the mountains were so full of vines and briers, that we were forced to clear most of the way before us. We crossed one of the small mountains this side the Appalachian, and from the top of it we had a fine view of the plains below. We were obliged to walk up the most of the way, there being abundance of loose stones on the side of the hill. I killed a large rattlesnake here, and the other people killed three more. We

made about four miles, and so came to the side of James
River, where a man may jump over it, and there we pitched
our tents. As the people were lighting the fire, there came
out of a large log of wood a prodigious snake, which they
killed; so this camp was called Rattlesnake Camp, but it
was otherwise called Brooks' Camp.

5th.—A fair day. At nine we were mounted; we were
obliged to have axe-men to clear the way in some places. We
followed the windings of James River, observing that it came
from the very top of the mountains. We killed two rattle
snakes during our ascent. In some places it was very steep,
in others, it was so that we could ride up. About one of the
clock we got to the top of the mountain; about four miles
and a half, and we came to the very head spring of James
River, where it runs no bigger than a man's arm, from under
a large stone. We drank King George's health, and all the
Royal Family's, at the very top of the Appalachian mountains.
About a musket-shot from the spring there is another, which
rises and runs down on the other side; it goes westward,
and we thought we could go down that way, but we met with
such prodigious precipices, that we were obliged to return to
the top again. We found some trees which had been formerly marked, I suppose, by the Northern Indians, and following these trees, we found a good, safe descent. Several of
the company were for returning; but the Governor persuaded
them to continue on. About five, we were down on the other
side, and continued our way for about seven miles further,
until we came to a large river, by the side of which we encamped. We made this day fourteen miles. I, being somewhat more curious than the rest, went on a high rock on the
top of the mountain, to see fine prospects, and I lost my gun.

We saw, when we were over the mountains, the footing of elks and buffaloes, and their beds. We saw a vine which bore a sort of wild cucumber, and a shrub with a fruit like unto a currant. We eat very good wild grapes. We called this place Spotswood Camp, after our Governor.

6th.—We crossed the river, which we called Euphrates. It is very deep; the main course of the water is north; it is fourscore yards wide in the narrowest part. We drank some healths on the other side, and returned; after which I went a swimming in it. We could not find any fordable place, except the one by which we crossed, and it was deep in several places. I got some grasshoppers and fished; and another and I, we catched a dish of fish, some perch, and a fish they call chub. The others went a hunting, and killed deer and turkeys. The Governor had graving irons, but could not grave any thing, the stones were so hard. I graved my name on a tree by the river side; and the Governor buried a bottle with a paper inclosed, on which he writ that he took possession of this place in the name and for King George the First of England.* We had a good dinner, and after it we got

* *Governor Spotswood,* when he undertook the great discovery of the *Passage* over the *Mountains,* attended with a sufficient guard, and pioneers and gentlemen, with a sufficient stock of provision, with abundant fatigue *passed* these *Mountains,* and cut *his Majesty's name* in a *rock* upon the highest of them, naming it MOUNT GEORGE; and in complaisance the gentlemen, from the Governor's name, called the mountain next in height *Mount Alexander.*

For this expedition they were obliged to provide a great quantity of horse shoes, (things seldom used in the lower parts of the country, where there are few stones;) upon which account the Governor, upon their return, presented each of his companions with a golden horse shoe, (some of which I have seen studded with valuable stones, resembling the heads of nails,) with this inscription on the one side: *Sic juvat transcendere montes;* and on the other is written the tramontane order.

This he instituted to encourage gentlemen to venture backwards, and

the men together, and loaded all their arms, and we drank
the King's health in Champagne, and fired a volley—the Princess's health in Burgundy, and fired a volley, and all the rest
of the Royal Family in claret, and a volley. We drank the
Governor's health and fired another volley. We had several
sorts of liquors, viz., Virginia red wine and white wine, Irish
usquebaugh, brandy, shrub, two sorts of rum, champagne, ca-
nary, cherry, punch, water, cider, &c.

I sent two of the rangers to look for my gun, which I
dropped in the mountains ; they found it, and brought it to me
at night, and I gave them a pistole for their trouble. We
called the highest mountain Mount George, and the one we
crossed over Mount Spotswood.

7th.—At seven in the morning we mounted our horses,
and parted with the rangers, who were to go farther on, and
we returned homewards; we repassed the mountains, and at
five in the afternoon we came to Hospital Camp, where we
left our sick men, and heavy baggage, and we found all things
well and safe. We encamped here, and called it Captain
Clouder's Camp.

8th.—At nine we were all on horseback. We saw several
bears and deer, and killed some wild turkeys. We encamped
at the side of a run, and called the place Mason's Camp. We
had good forage for our horses, and we lay as usual. Made
twenty miles this day.

9th.—We set out at nine of the clock, and before twelve we
saw several bears, and killed three. One of them attacked
one of our men that was riding after him, and narrowly missed

make discoveries and new settlements; any gentleman being entitled to
wear this Golden Shoe that can prove his having drunk *his Majesty's
health* upon MOUNT GEORGE.—*Hugh Jones*, 1724.

him; he tore his things that he had behind him from off the horse, and would have destroyed him, had he not had immediate help from the other men and our dogs. Some of the dogs suffered severely in this engagement. At two we crossed one of the branches of the Rappahannoc River, and at five we encamped on the side of the Rapid Ann, on a tract of land that Mr. Beverley hath design to take up. We made, this day, twenty-three miles, and called this Captain Smith's Camp. We eat part of one of the bears, which tasted very well, and would be good, and might pass for veal; if one did not know what it was. We were very merry, and diverted ourselves with our adventures.

10*th*.—At eight we were on horseback, and about ten, as we were going up a small hill, Mr. Beverley and his horse fell down, and they both rolled to the bottom; but there were no bones broken on either side. At twelve, as we were crossing a run of water, Mr. Clouder fell in, so we called this place Clouder's Run. At one we arrived at a large spring, where we dined and drank a bowl of punch. We called this Fontaine's Spring. About two we got on horseback, and at four we reached Germanna. The Governor thanked the gentlemen for their assistance in the expedition. Mr. Mason left us here. I went at five to swim in the Rappahannoc River, and returned to the town.

11*th*.—After breakfast all our company left us, excepting Dr. Robinson and Mr. Clouder. We walked all about the town, and the Governor settled his business with the Germans here, and accommodated the minister and the people, and then to bed.

12*th*.—After breakfast went a fishing in the Rappahannoc, and took seven fish, which we had for dinner ; after which Mr.

Robinson and I, we endeavored to melt some ore in the smith's forge, but could get nothing out of it. Dr. Robinson's and Mr. Clouder's boys were taken violently ill with fever. Mr. Robinson and Mr. Clouder left us, and the boys remained behind.

13th.—About eight of the clock we mounted our horses, and went to the mine, where we took several pieces of ore; and at nine we set out from the mine, our servants having gone before; and about three we overtook them in the woods, and there the Governor and I dined. We mounted afterwards, and continued on our road. I killed a black snake about five feet long. We arrived at Mr. Woodford's, on Rappahannoc River, about six, and remained there all night.

14th.—At seven we sent our horses and baggage before us; and at ten we mounted our horses; we killed another snake, four feet nine inches long. At twelve we came to the church, where we met with Mr. Buckner, and remained till two, to settle some county business; then we mounted our horses, and saw several wild turkeys on the road; and at seven we reached Mr. Beverley's house, which is upon the head of Mattapony River, where we were well entertained. My boy was taken with a violent fever, and very sick.

15th.—At seven my servant was somewhat better, and I sent him away with my horses, and about ten o'clock the Governor took his chaise, and I with him, and at twelve we came to a mill-dam, which we had great difficulty to get the chaise over. We got into it again, and continued on our way, and about five we arrived at Mr. Baylor's, where we remained all night.

16th.—My servant was so sick, that I was obliged to leave him, and the Governor's servants took care of my horses. At ten we sent the chaise over Mattapony River, and it being Sunday, we went to the church in King William County, where we heard a sermon from Mr. Monroe. After sermon we continued our journey until we came to Mr. West's plantation, where Colonel Basset waited for the Governor with his pinnace, and other boats for his servants. We arrived at his house by five of the clock, and were nobly entertained.

17th.—At ten we left Colonel Basset's, and at three we arrived at Williamsburg, where we dined together, and I went to my lodgings, and to bed, being well tired, as well as my horses.

I reckon that from Williamsbùrg to the Euphrates River is in all 219 miles, so that our journey, going and coming, has been in all 438 miles.

Williamsburg, 14th October, 1716.—I settled my business and left all my things in the hands of Major Holloway, designing with God's blessing for New-York. I went to dine with the Governor, and took my leave of him and of all my acquaintance.

15th.—Got all things in readiness, mounted, and rode down to Hampton, which is forty miles from Williamsburg. About six of the clock I arrived, and went to my friend, Mr. Irewin's, where I supped and lodged.

16th.—I sent away my horses to Williamsburg, writ to Major Holloway, went to see several of my acquaintances. Mr. Michael Kearney also designed for New-York, so we agreed about what provisions we should put in for our voyage, and I returned to Mr. Irewin's.

17th.—This town, Hampton, lies in a plain within ten miles of the mouth of James River, and about one mile inland from the side of the main river; there is also a small arm of the river that comes on both sides of this town, and

within a small matter of making it an island. It is a place
of the greatest trade in all Virginia, and all the men-of-war
commonly lie before this arm of the river. It is not navigable for large ships, by reason of a bar of land, which lies between the mouth, or coming in, and the main channel, but
sloops and small ships can come up to the town. This is the
best outlet in all Virginia and Maryland, and when there is
any fleet made, they fit out here, and can go to sea with the
first start of a wind. The town contains one hundred houses,
but few of them of any note, and it has no church. The inhabitants drive a great trade with New-York and Pennsylvania, and are also convenient to trade with Maryland. They
have the best fish and oysters of any place in the Colony, and
there is good fowling hereabouts. The town is not reckoned
healthy, owing to the great mud-banks and wet marshes about
it, which have a very unwholesome smell at low water. We
met at Mr. Irewin's, were very merry, supped well, and to
bed.

18th.—Mr. Kearney and I spoke to the master of the
sloop for our passage, and bought provisions for ourselves, and
sent our clothes on board. Took leave of my acquaintances,
and went to Mr. Irewin's, where I lay.

19th.—At eleven in the morning, the wind being N. E.
we hoisted our anchor. By one we had passed Point Comfort, which makes the entrance of James River, and were in
the Bay of Chesapeake. At four we were between the two
Capes of Virginia, Cape Henry and Cape Charles. Weather
fair. We kept within ten leagues of the shore, and so steered
our course all night.

20th.—Wind continued N. E., weather fair. We kept
within sight of the shore, and sounded, and found fourteen

fathoms water, white sand. We saw several flocks of ducks and geese going to the southward. A smooth sea, but great swell. There is no harbor all along this coast, from Cape Charles till you come to the mouth of the Bay of Delaware, which goes up to Philadelphia.

21st.—Wind N. E. till one of the clock, and then it came about N. W., and blew very hard, so we sounded, and found but ten fathoms water. The wind continued to blow, so we came to an anchor, and about four we saw a sloop coming from the sea. She came to an anchor by us. Here we remained all night, and the wind blew very hard, still in sight of the land, and somewhat to the northward of Delaware Bay. There are great banks of sand lie off here, which are very dangerous. We can see the breakers on them.

22d.—In the morning about seven of the clock we raised our anchor, and set our sails, wind at N. W., a stiff gale and great sea, and about 12 of the clock we split our jib and foresail. At three we were up with Sandy Hook, which is the cape land of New-York port. The land is low and sandy with few trees upon it. About sunset we came to an anchor under Sandy Hook, in seven fathoms water, and three miles from shore.

23d.—In the sloop at anchor under Sandy Hook. The weather was so foggy all day that we could not see the shore, nor landmarks, so we could not hoist our anchor, for this is a very dangerous bay to come up without one has fair weather to see the landmarks. There are several banks and shoals of sand which are very dangerous. There is a great deal of water fowl of all sorts on these shoals. I observe that the ducks and geese are sooner here than with us in Virginia.

24th.—Calm weather, but such a fog that we could not

see half a mile. We had a mind to go ashore, but the master and sailors were afraid that they could not find the sloop again with the boat, so we consented to remain on board. This fog is occasioned by the burning of the woods, for at this season the inhabitants set the woods on fire, and the Indians also about this time of the year go a fire hunting.

25th.—We are still at anchor, weather very foggy, so that the master will not venture up with his sloop. About twelve it cleared, so that we could see the land, and we got out the boat, and the men landed us in Staten Island. We were obliged to walk about four miles, not being able to hire any horses. This island is mostly high land and rocky, and that part of the land which is good is mixed with small stones. There are some good improvements here ; the inhabitants are mostly Dutch ; the houses are all built with stone and lime ; there are some hedges as in England. The chief increase is wheat and cattle, they breed large horses here.

About five of the clock we came to the Ferry between Long Island and Staten Island, which is about one mile broad. The main body of New-York River runs between these islands. We crossed the ferry and came upon Long Island, to a small sort of village, where, it being late, we put up at the house of a Dutchman, one Harris Hendrick. We were well lodged and had a good supper.

26th.—About eight of the clock in the morning, we hired two horses to go to New-York. It is about eight miles from this ferry by land, but not near so much by water. Long Island is generally very plain ground, bears extraordinary good grass, and is an excellent place for cattle. It produceth wheat and all English grain in abundance. The chief part of the inhabitants are Dutch, but there are some few French.

Amongst them there are several good improvements, and
many fine villages, the woods are mostly destroyed. Besides
the plentiful produce of the Island, there is every advantage
for fishing and fowling that can be wished. About eleven
o'clock we came to a fine village opposite New York, and we
crossed the ferry. The river is about a quarter of a mile
over, and runs very rapidly; there are good convenient land-
ings on both sides. As soon as we landed we went and
agreed for our lodgings with a Dutch woman named Schuyler,
and then I went to see Mr. Andrew Freneau at his house,
and he received me very well, after which I went to the
tavern, and about ten at night to my lodgings and to bed.

27th.—About nine I went and breakfasted at the Coffee-
House, and at eleven I waited upon Governor Hunter, who
received me very kindly, and invited me to dine with him.
After dinner I walked with him about the fort, wherein he
lives. It is a small square situated upon a height above the
town, and commanding it. The one side of it fronts the harbor, and hath a small curtain and two bastions; the land side
hath but two half-bastions to it, so that it is a square composed of two whole and two half-bastions. There is a ravelin
towards the land that lies on one side of the gate. It is but
a weak place, and badly contrived. There is a regiment
here, and the Governor always hath a guard, and this is all
the duty they have, which is very little.

From the Governor I went to see the Mayor of the town,
one Doctor Johnson, and was kindly received by him; thence
to Colonel Delorty, and at night I went to the tavern, and
was there with the Irish club until ten, and so to bed.

28th.—About eight in the morning, Mr. Kearney and I
we hired horses, and went about seven miles out of town to one

Colonel Morris's, who lives in the country, and is Judge or Chief Justice of this province, a very sensible and good man. We were well received by him, and remained with him all night; and we saw a great many fine improvements that he had made, and he showed us several rare collections of his own making. He lives upon the river that comes down to New-York.

29th.—About ten of the clock we left Colonel Morris's, crossed the river, and arrived at New-York at twelve. The roads are very bad and stony, and no possibility for coaches to go, only in the winter, when the snow fills up the holes and makes all smooth, then they can make use of wheel-carriages. There are but two coaches belonging to this province, because of the badness of the roads, though there are many rich people.

We were invited to dine at two with Mr. Hamilton and Mr. Lane. After dinner, I visited Mr. Freneau, and had a great deal of discourse with him about the trade of Virginia. From thence I walked round the town. There are three churches, the English, the French, and the Dutch Church; there is also a place for the Assembly to sit, which is not very fine, and where they judge all matters. The town is compact, the houses for the most part built after the Dutch manner, with the gable-ends towards the street; the streets are of a good breadth; the town is built close upon the river, and there is a fine quay that reigns all round the town, built with stone and piles of wood outside. There are small docks for cleaning and building small ships. At high-water, the vessels come up to the quay to lade and unlade. In winter the river is frozen, sometimes all over, and such abundance of ice comes down, that it often cuts the cables of ships, but cannot hurt

13*

those near the quay. The town is built on ground that gradually rises from the water, so it is amphitheatre like. The French have all the privileges that can be, and are the most in number here, they are of the Council and of the Parliament, and are in all other employments. The chief produce of this province is beef, flour, pork, butter, and cheese, which they send to the West Indies, and sometimes to Lisbon. They drive a great trade with the Northern Indians for skins and furs. There is plenty of all sorts of fish, oysters, and waterfowl. The climate is very cold in winter, a great deal of snow and frost for four months, and very hot in the latter part of the summer.

30th.—At ten of the clock, went to the Coffee-house, and at two of the clock to the Governor's to dinner. Thence I went to see Colonel Ingoldsby, and to the Irish Club, where I remained till ten, and so home to my lodgings.

31st.—At ten, went to the Coffee-house, and walked upon the Exchange, which is a small place that is planked, and hath pillars of wood all round, which support the roof and leave it open on all sides. I dined with Mr. Andrew Freneau, and remained with him till four of the clock, and then I went to the Coffee-house for an hour or two, and at six to the French Club, where they treated me, and at ten home and to bed.

1st November, 1716.—At eleven to the Coffee-house, dined at the tavern, from thence to Mr. Freneau, and went home at nine.

2d.—Breakfasted at the Coffee-house at nine, dined at the tavern at two ; thence went home and writ to my cousin Arnauld in London, and so to bed.

3d.—Breakfasted at the Coffee-house at eight, dined at one at the tavern, informed myself about one Maxwell, whom Mr.

Fooks recommended to me, and I was informed that he was very much in debt, and had been a long time in prison in New-York; but that he is now gone to South Carolina, and calls himself Joseph Mitchell, instead of his right name, James Maxwell. I writ to Mr. Fooks, in Dublin, about this Maxwell, and to bed.

4th, Sunday.—At ten I went to Mr. Freneau, and with him to church. I returned to his house and dined with him, and at half an hour after two we went to church again, which is after Calvin's way. The church is very large and beautiful, and within it there was a very great congregation. After service, I went home and to bed.

5th.—At ten in the morning, I carried Mr. Freneau a memorandum of the prices of goods. I dined at the Coffeehouse, and then went to the French Club at the tavern, where we drank loyal healths, and at ten went home and to bed.

6th.—About ten went to visit Mr. Delancy, and then Mr. Freneau. The Postmaster-General, Mr. Hamilton, invited me to dinner, and I dined with him. At three, I went to the Coffee-house, and at six, I went with Mr. Byerly, the Collector, and some others, to the tavern. where we remained till ten. Thence to bed.

7th.—At eight, went to the Coffee-house; at ten, waited on Governor Hunter, and drank tea with him; from thence I waited on Mr. Burchfield, Surveyor-General, and I dined with him; and when I took my leave, he made me promises of service if an opportunity should offer. At four, I went to the Coffee-house, where I met with Mr. Freneau, and at six we went to the French Club, and at ten to bed.

8th.—At ten, I waited upon Governor Hunter and breakfasted with him; I dined with him at two, and at four I took leave of him, went to my lodgings and supped there, and at eight to bed.

Friday, 9th November, 1716.—At five of the clock in the morning, got all our things in the ferry-boat, and set out for Amboy ; the wind was contrary, and it blew so hard that at nine we were forced back again. So, Mr. Kearney and I, we hired two horses, and went seven miles out of town to Colonel Morris's, where we dined, and returned at night to our lodgings in New-York.

10th.—At eight in the morning, I bought a horse of Mr. Lancaster Sims, and paid him £8 for it. We crossed the ferry from New-York to Long Island about ten, and mounted our horses. We passed by a fine village called Flatbush, and at twelve we reached Hans Hendrick's house. The ferryman endeavored to cross the ferry from thence to Staten Island, but had to put back, so we dined at Hendrick's. At three, we saw a ship called the Cæsar Galley run aground upon White Bank. At five, we got into the boat again, and with much difficulty crossed to Staten Island, then we mounted our horses and came to one Stuart's, an inn on the road, about seven miles from the ferry, where we supped, and lay all night.

Sunday, 11*th.*—At seven in the morning we set out from Stuart's, and at twelve of the clock, we came to one Colonel Farrier's house, where the ferry is kept, and we got ferried over to Amboy, which is a small village where the Governor hath a house and gardens. It is a very agreeable place, surrounded on two sides by the water. After dinner we went to church. The church is very small, and much out of repair. The wind blew so hard that we could not get our horses ferried over, so we were obliged to remain all night.

12th.—The wind continued blowing very hard at N. W.,

and we could by no means get over the ferry in the morning; so we took a walk abroad in the country about here, which is very agreeable. At two we returned to our inn and dined. We met with two gentlemen from New-York, both lawyers, Justice Johnson and Mr. Bickly. We drank till ten, and to bed.

13th.—At ten we crossed the ferry, and mounted our horses; we dined at two, and continued on our way from three until seven.. We made but thirty-two miles this day. We had bad entertainment.

14th.—At half an hour after seven we set out from our lodgings, and within one mile of Burlington I met with Mr. John Ballaguier. At eleven we came to Burlington, where we dined. It is a very pretty village, and there is a river passes through it navigable for sloops. At half an hour after twelve we set out for Philadelphia, the distance is twenty miles from Burlington. The roads are good here. At six we arrived at Philadelphia, and I waited on Mr. Samuel Perez and gave him Mr. Freneau's letter. He had no service for me.

15th.—At eight of the clock went to view the town, which is situated upon rising ground on Delaware River, and is built very regularly, the houses mostly of brick, after the English fashion. The streets are very wide and regular. There are many convenient docks for the building ships and sloops here. There is a great trade to all the Islands belonging to the English, as also to Lisbon and the Madeira Islands. The produce of the country is chiefly wheat, barley, and all English grain, beef, butter, cheese, flax, and hemp. The inhabitants are most part Quakers, and they have several good meetings, and there are also some English churches. There are all

sorts of trades established in this town. Money that is not
milled passes for six shillings and fourpence the ounce.

At twelve of the clock we left Philadelphia, and crossing
a ferry about two miles out of the town, we had a great
shower. The roads not good here. At five of the clock we
got to Harlem, a small village well situated on Delaware River,
sixteen miles from Philadelphia. Good entertainment.

16th.—At eight of the clock set out from Harlem. We
crossed two ferries, and at one of the clock came to New-
castle. After dinner I walked about the town, which has a
great many good brick houses, but is a place of no trade,
though situated upon Delaware River. We remained here
all this day, and were well entertained and lodged.

17th.—About eight of the clock we set out from New-
castle for Bohemia landing. About fifteen miles on the way
we came to the division line between Pennsylvania and Maryland. At three we reached Bohemia landing, and were disappointed at finding no sloop there, and were obliged to go
farther, for though there are two or three houses there, there
is no entertainment. After riding four miles farther we came to
Mr. Paterson's, a house of entertainment, where we remained
this night.

Sunday, 18th.—We remained all day at Paterson's, where
there is nothing to be seen but trees A fair day. We are
sixty miles from Philadelphia.

19th.—At eight of the clock set out from Paterson's
house, and at twelve arrived at the Court House of the County
of Kent, where we baited our horses, and had but indifferent
entertainment. About three Mr. Kearney and I went to his
brother's house in the neighborhood, where we put up and remained all night. We reckon that we made this day thirty-
three miles.

20th.—It being rainy we remained where we were, and had good entertainment. This gentleman hath an extraordinary good tannery, which turns to account.

21st.—At nine in the morning we set out from the house of Mr. Kearney's brother, and at one we came to one Sutton's house, about twenty-eight miles from Mr. Kearney's plantation, and dined at three. There were eight rogues drinking at the place, who resolved to fall upon us and rob us. My comrade went out, not expecting any thing, and was knocked down; he endeavored to defend himself with his sword, but they with their stakes broke it to pieces. They tried to serve me after the same manner, but being on my guard I defended myself and my friend, until we got to our horses, and with a great deal of struggle we got away from them, and put on forward on the road about six miles to avoid them, and stopped, it being dark, at a poor man's house. About ten o'clock at night they came to steal our horses, and endeavor to surprise us, but when they saw we were prepared for them, after some few injurious words and threats, they made off. This is Sussex County. We sat up all night on our guard.

22d.—Being threatened with an assault in the morning, we thought it convenient at two of the clock to get our horses and take a guide. By six of the clock we were twelve miles on our way, and stopped at one Duick's house, where we breakfasted, and at ten continued our journey to Indian Creek. This part of the country is hardly inhabited, and the few people who are here make it their business to rob all passengers. We were detained at the creek two hours for the want of a canoe; we got one at last, and swam our horses over. We mounted on the other side, and went three miles further until we came to one Pepper's house, where we lay all night.

23d.—At seven in the morning got on horseback; a fair day; we rid sixteen miles through the forest, no inhabitants all the way, and at the end of the sixteen miles we came to on Mumford's, where we ate a bit; at two we mounted again, and at five of the clock came to Snow Hill, being forty miles from Pepper's, where we lay last night. This is a small village, but few houses, and not one public house, so we put up at a private house. This village is situated upon Pocomoke River, navigable for sloops as far as this place. Bad beds and ordinary victuals.

24th.—At eight got on horseback, and when we were seventeen miles on our way, we called at one Mr. Pope's, where we took a guide, the ways being very intricate. At five of the clock we came to one Mr. Kemp's, which we reckon about thirty-five miles distant from Snow Hill. We paid our guide and dismissed him. We were very well entertained, and our horses well fed, and about ten we went to bed.

25th.—At ten we breakfasted, at eleven Mr. Kemp and I rode out and viewed a fine tract of land, and returned to his house to dinner at two. After dinner we went to see the shallop that we design to hire. The wind blew very hard at N. W. At ten we went to bed.

26th.—At ten Mr. Kearney and I agreed with the skipper of the sloop for a passage for ourselves, and our horses, to Rappahannoc River on the other side of the bay. We are to give him forty-four shillings for his trouble. We ordered him to ballast his sloop and be in readiness when the wind offered. At breakfast we drank of an herb called the golden-rod, the leaf is long, and it tastes and is of the color of green tea. We dined at four; after dinner we played at chequers, then supped and drank punch and diverted ourselves till twelve, and then to bed.

27th.—At ten we breakfasted—at twelve we ballasted the shallop, and hoisted the two horses in, and put all our things on board, as also liquor and provisions for the run. We were resolved to set out this afternoon, but neither wind nor tide would serve, and night drawing on we returned to our friend Mr. James Kemp, supped, and at ten went to bed. Wind at N. W., stormy.

28th.—At eight in the morning got up, breakfasted at nine, and took leave of Mr. Kemp, and went to one Sanford's before whose house the sloop lay. The wind blew hard, but we got a canoe, and with some difficulty we were put on board our shallop. At ten we hoisted the anchor, with the wind at N. and N. by E., a hard gale. At two we came to Egg Island, and at five, it being but half flood, we struck on Watts's shoals, where we remained, thumping for an hour. After we floated we came up to Watts's Island. At seven we cast anchor, and went ashore, to one Joseph Bird's house, where we supped on our own provisions, and for want of beds lay before the fire all night.

29th.—We got up at four in the morning, and went to the water, and called up the shallop-men ; we got on board, and by five weighed anchor, and hoisted our sails. The wind is at N. E., and a fresh gale, but the tide against us. At seven we see the Tangier Islands, and at nine of the clock, came in sight of Windmill Point, which makes the north side of Rappahannoc River, and Gwinn's Island, the south side. At one, we came abreast with Windmill Point, and the wind changed to S. W., and blew fresh, with a great sea ; we endeavored to weather Gwinn's Island, but we could not, in order to get to Queen's Creek in Piankatank River. We spoke a ship at three, she was from Barbadoes. At a quarter after three, finding the wind still freshen, we were obliged to put before it up Rappahannoc River. It became calm about six, so we put ashore at Mr. Churchill's plantation, and landed our horses with some difficulty. It was very dark, so we were obliged to lie at the negroes' quarters that night.

30*th*.—At eight mounted our horses, fasting; at ten we crossed Piankatank Ferry, and mounted again, but being strangers to the road, we came out of our way to Ivy River. We returned to the road, and passed by Gloucester County Court House. At three we came to Gloucester Town upon York River; we crossed the ferry and came to York Town; we went to Power's Ordinary, where we lay all night.

I accompted, and found that my journey to New-York and back again cost me twenty-four pounds.

Saturday, 1st December, 1716.—At nine in the morning set out, accompanied Mr. Kearney a mile from the town, and there took my leave of my fellow-traveller, and at eleven reached Williamsburg. I went and visited the Governor and my acquaintance.

3d December.—Set out from Williamsburg, and went to my plantation in King William County, and got together my servants and overseer, who had all run away, and put things into some order.

8*th*.—I returned to Williamsburg, and on the 11th, received news that my brother Peter had arrived at Hampton, and I went down to meet him, and on the 14th, he and his wife came up with me to Williamsburg, where we all took up our lodging, and in a few days my brother and I went to view the parishes and the plantations, and on the 29th got back to Williamsburg.

In February, 1717, Peter got a presentation to Roanoke

Parish, and preached there. We all removed there in the month of March, and lodged at Captain Harwood's. I became very sick of the fever and ague, which continued until the month of May, when being somewhat better, I returned to the plantation in King William County. I bought another servant, which cost me £11 5, sterling.

October, 1717.—My brother James and his family arrived at York Town, and though I was very sick, I went down to meet them, so we all came up together in the ship to Captain Littlepage's. The houses that I was building, not being quite finished, when my brother's family arrived, they lodged at one Mr. Sutton's near the plantation.

By the 7th November, every thing was completed, so that we brought all our things and came to live there.

In November, we also sheathed the ship, which had sprung a leak during the passage, and when she was repaired and well fitted out, we tried to sell her, but could not; so we afterwards freighted her for Bristol, and in January, 1718, she fell down the river.

When my brother James and his family were settled on the plantation, I bought twenty-one head of cattle, one horse, eleven hogs, and another servant, and left every thing to the management of my brother. I was very sick for about five months, and so was all our family, so we had a great deal of trouble.

27th March, 1718.—I received a letter from my brother-in-law, Mr. Matthew Maury, to say that he was at Captain Eskridge's house, with his goods; where he would wait for me. I was not well, and the weather was wet and rainy, but I set out immediately, and crossed the ferry at Mr. Baylor's, and rid afterwards seven miles in the rain, and about an hour after night I came to one Bridgeworth's, where I lay.

28*th.*—I got up very sick next morning, but set out fast-
ihg. The day was very windy. I got about eight miles on
my way, when my fever increased so much, and the pains in
my head and bones, that I could ride no farther, and was
forced to alight. At about ten of the clock I came to a
poor widow woman's house, where I was for about two hours
quite senseless. I was then taken with a violent vomiting,
and my fever abated something, so I got on horseback again
and rid to the ferry on Rappahannoc, where I lay that night
—badly entertained.

29*th.*—Crossed the river, and got to Captain Eskridge's
house at seven, and found that Mr. Maury was gone. Being
very sick, I remained until the 1st of April to recruit, and on
that day I mounted my horse and rid as far as Mr. Naylor's
house, where I lay.

2*d.*—Crossed the river in a small boat, and was in great
danger of being drowned. Got to Mr. Baylor's, where I lay
that night, and went home next day. I made upon this journey, in all, going and coming, 135 miles.

22*d April.*—I went down to Williamsburg to meet Mr.
Maury, who had come round there. We hired a flat to convey
his goods up the river. On the 25th, the goods were embarked, and we went to the Oyster Banks, and took in a great
many oysters to carry home with us. We went about six
miles up the river, and then we stopped for the night. We
came as close to the land as we could, and stuck an oar in the
mud, and tied our flat to it, and there we lay till it was day.
A cold place.

26*th.*—Took up our oar and rowed about four miles, the
wind at N. W., blew very hard. We were blown in on the
shore, and the sea was very high, and there was no possibility

of landing, so we were obliged to throw out all our oysters, to lighten the boat. We shipped a great deal of water, and having no anchor, we were like to drive on the mud and lose the flat. About two of the clock, the weather calming, we set out again, and made five miles, when the wind came to N. W., and such a violent storm, that we were obliged to put before the wind, and when we had gone back about a mile, we ran the flat ashore upon the strand, where we thumped mightily. The wind continued very high, but the tide being fallen, we unloaded the goods, expecting that when the tide would rise again, the boat would go to pieces. By twelve of the clock at night, we had all our goods on shore, but there being no house near, we lay upon the strand all night, and it rained very hard, so that we were wet to the skin. The wind abated a little, and as the tide rose, we drew up the flat nearer shore, and got her up as far as we could, and received no damage but being wet with both salt and fresh water.

27th.—We put the goods on board again, first thing in the morning, and the wind abated during the day, so that we were able to continue on our way, and we got to West Point about nine of the clock at night.

28th.—Came to Captain Littlepage's, and next day we got to Philip Williams his ferry, where we landed the goods.

I remained on the plantation till the 6th of June, and then went down to Williamsburg, and settled all my business with Mr. Irewin and Major Holloway. On the 16th, I spoke to Captain Bonnequil, and agreed with him for my passage home.

On the 17th of July, 1718, I made over the deeds of the land to my brother James, in order to go to England.

4th August.—I received a letter from Mr. Freneau to say that there was a ship coming consigned to me; so I got my things on shore, left my fowls with the master, and paid him twenty-two shillings for the charges I had put him to.* As soon as my goods were landed from the vessel, I came to York Town, thence to Williamsburg, and so to the plantation, which I reached on the 10th August.

19*th December*, 1718.—Received news of the arrival of the Henry and Margaret, consigned to me. I went immediately to her and entered her, landed the goods, and sold the most part of them, and kept the ship till the 7th June, 1719, when I set sail in her from James River, and on the 18th July, we came to Weymouth, on the 19th to Cowes, in the Isle of Wight, where I remained three days.

22*d.*—I left Cowes, and crossed the bay to Southampton.

23*d.*—I set out in the stage-coach for London, and arrived about eight of the clock. I took a hackney-coach, and went to Mr. Arnauld's, at Islington, where I remained until the 24th November, 1719, about the business of the cargo, and doing what I could for another voyage, but all to no purpose; so, on the 24th November, I left London. My horse tired at Coventry; so, on the 27th, I took the stage-coach, and came to Chester on the 29th. On the 30th, I hired three horses for Holyhead.

1*st December.*—I lay at Bangor; the 2d arrived at Holyhead, and went upon the top of the hill, from whence I could see Ireland. The 5th I embarked, and the 6th arrived in the Bay of Dublin. I took the wherry and landed by twelve, and came to Stephen's Green.

---

* I understood afterwards, that in going home this vessel foundered, and all on board perished; so that I have great reason to return thanks to God for my preservation at this time; for I was fully resolved to go with him, had I not been prevented by Mr. Freneau's letter, which came to my hands four days before Captain Bonnequil sailed for England.

INTERESTING FAMILY MEETING FOR RELIGIOUS PURPOSES.

THE next interesting item of family history, which we are able to bring to light, is the fact, that, after our ancestors emigrated to Virginia, they were in the habit of meeting annually, to hold a solemn religious thanksgiving, in commemoration of their remarkable preservation, when attacked by French privateers, in the south of Ireland.

The following sermon was preached on one of these occasions, by the Rev. Peter Fontaine. It bears the date upon it, and also a pencil memorandum of the Psalms and Lessons which he had selected as appropriate to the services of the day.

1st *June* 1723.
PROPER PSALMS XVIII., CIII., CXVIII.
I. LESSON. EXODUS xiv.
II. LESSON. EPHESIANS vi., from v. 14 to the end.

COLLECT.

Almighty and most glorious Lord God, who dost render ineffectual the most subtle devices and best concerted measures of wicked and haughty men, and didst as at this time with a high hand and lifted up arm deliver us from our inveterate enemies; and hast sundry times before and since

exerted thy power in our favor; grant that we may always
bear so grateful a sense of these thy mercies in our minds, as
may engage us to embrace all opportunities of worshipping
and glorifying and praising thee, with one mind and with
one mouth, through Jesus Christ our Lord, who taught us, &c.

SERMON.

ROMANS, chap. xv. v. 6.

That ye may with one mind and one mouth glorify God, even the Father
of our Lord Jesus Christ.

THE Apostle, after having spent the fourteenth chapter in general exhortations and directions to stronger Christians, concerning their behavior towards their weaker brethren, in
the use of their Christian liberty about things indifferent,
and in advising them neither to be censorious in judging, nor
yet to put a stumbling-block in the way one of another, proceeds in the former part of this chapter in the prosecution of
the same argument and design, enjoining their forbearance
from the example of our Blessed Lord, and concluding his
exhortations *and instructions with this short prayer to Almighty God, that they may with one heart, and one mind,
glorify him; that is, that whatever reason they may have for
small differences amongst themselves, they should lay them all
aside, but more especially when they are about to give God
glory.

I shall, therefore, upon this occasion, from these words
observe to you:

Firstly, The duty here enjoined, that is, to glorify God.

Secondly, The manner of performing it, that is, with one mind and one mouth. And,

Thirdly, Put you in mind of your high obligations to comply with this duty, not only because of the signal deliverance which we are met together to celebrate, but by reason of that infinite number which God hath vouchsafed to favor us with at other times, no less worthy our remembrance and thanks.

I begin with the duty here prescribed, and that is, to glorify God, by which we may not understand that we can add any thing to the glory and perfection of the divine nature, for that is not in our power ; for God is the same yesterday and to-day, and admits of no new accessions to his glory, by any thing we can say or do. The glorifying of God consists chiefly in these two things—in a high and honorable esteem and reverence for him in our hearts, and likewise in all outward expressions of honor, duty, and reverence towards him in our lives. The one is internal honor, whereby we are said to glorify God in our souls and spirits, the other is external, whereby we glorify him by our conversation and behavior.

I say, to glorify God is to have a high and honorable esteem and reverence for him in our hearts ; to entertain thoughts worthy of him, and have conceptions imprinted in our minds, suitable to the eminence and perfections of his nature, that is to apprehend him to be really as he is—superlatively good, wise, powerful, holy, and just ; to take him for our Maker and Preserver, and to own our absolute and entire dependence upon him, and pay him our homage and adoration accordingly. In such internal and devout acts of the mind, does the glorifying of God chiefly and principally consist ;

14

and without these it would be vain for any person to pretend
that he doth in any measure comply with the duty in the
text, though it doth not rest here, but manifests itself,

Secondly, In external acts and expressions of honor suitable to them. To have such high thoughts of his infinite
power and greatness, as to make us dread and stand in awe of
him ; such apprehensions of his justice as to make us fear of-
fending him ; such an esteem of his wisdom as to cause us to
admire him ; and such a sense of his goodness, as to put us
upon all acts of adoring and worshipping him, and to influence our whole behavior with regard to him and our neighbor.
This the Psalmist styles, the giving unto God the honor that
is due to his name, and worshipping him with a holy worship.
Now, as this duty cannot be any where performed with such
advantage as where the faithful are assembled together for
that purpose, let us, therefore, with the royal prophet, take
all opportunities to give thanks unto God, in the great congregation, and praise him among much people ; and not only so,
but let us, as we are in duty bound, and by promise engaged,
miss no opportunity of assembling ourselves together, upon
the days which we have set apart for returning our most
hearty and unfeigned thanks for the great deliverances vouchsafed to our family, and glorify, and thank, and praise God
with one heart and one mouth.

And this leads unto the *second* thing I proposed to speak
to ; to wit, the manner of performing this duty implied in
these words of the text, where we have the unanimity that is
to be observed in our devotions.   To excite and encourage us
to this, we have many precepts both in the Old and New Testament. Holy David calls upon the the people to worship the
Lord in the beauty of holiness ; that is, with a comely order

and harmony which will add a grace to it, and make it look fair and amiable. Elsewhere he wills them to serve and praise the Lord together, which refers in some measure to the unity of place, but more particularly to the unity of mind. that it be done with one heart, and with one consent.

In the New Testament we find our Saviour making our agreement in our petitions necessary to the success of them; saying, If two or more shall agree on earth touching any thing that they shall ask, it shall be done for them of my Father who is in heaven, for where two or three are gathered together in my name, there am I in the midst of them; where 'tis the harmony of our prayers, or the offering them up with one accord and one mind, that procures audience and acceptance of them; and therefore the last thing our blessed Lord prayed for in the behalf of his disciples and followers, was for this unity and harmony of mind: " That they all may be one; as thou, Father, art in me, and I in thee, that they also may be one in us; that the world may believe that thou hast sent me;" where he begs his Father to work the hearts of his followers to that temper of mind and affection that was between his Father and him, which would be the best argument to convince mankind of the truth of his mission and doctrine; for the world would sooner believe that God had sent him, if his disciples could agree together in what they desire, and in what they profess, rather than if they clash or differ in either, and pray without or against one another; for which reason St. Paul beseeches the Corinthians by the name of Christ, that there might be no divisions amongst them in those things, but that they may be perfectly joined together in the same mind and in the same judgment. In his Epistle to the Philippians he exhorts them to stand fast in one spirit and in one mind, striving together for the faith of the Gospel; and further, he beseeches them by all that is dear and sacred, to be like-minded, having the same love, being of one accord and of one mind, which is what our text here calls us to. And that this is a possible duty we find from many passages both in the Old and New Testament. Jerusalem, which in the Scripture phrase signifies the whole nation of the Jews, is expressly said to be at unity within itself, for thither the tribes went up, even the tribes of the Lord, to testify unto Israel, and to give thanks unto the name of the Lord, which the Psalmist declares as matter of great joy. " I was glad," says he, " when they said unto me, we will go unto the house of the Lord. Our feet shall stand in thy gates, O Jerusalem."

In the New Testament we read of the primitive Christians that they were all of one heart and of one mind; that they were continually together in the temple blessing and praising God; that they met together, in one place, with one accord, and with one mind; that they continued steadfast in the Apostle's doctrine and fellowship, in breaking bread, and in prayer; all which, and many more testimonies that might be cited, plainly show that blessed harmony and concord that was found among them in matters of religion and the worship of God, and that there was a time when men joined together with one mind to glorify their great Creator. The many precepts to unity show it to be a possible and a practicable duty, and the many sharp rebukes of divisions, and cautions against neglects of this kind, manifest that they are not unavoidable, else the precepts and rebukes would both be to no purpose.

Having now done with the duty here enjoined, as also the manner of performing it, there remains that we consider in the *third* place the particular obligations our family are un-

der of complying with it. Let us pass by those we are under
to Almighty God for our creation, preservation and redemp-
tion, and all the other blessings of this life, which are without
number, and which we enjoy in common with the rest of mankind, and let us turn our eyes upon that continued chain of
miracles which hath been wrought in our favor, and which are
sufficient to rouse the most stupid to a sense of the duty enjoined in the text. To date our relation as high as the deliverance of our parents out of the bondage of France, we will
find subject matter enough to make us cry out with holy
David, " O how great is thy goodness which thou hast laid up
for them that fear thee, which thou hast wrought for them that
trust in thee before the sons of men."

Several months was our parent obliged to shift amongst
forests and deserts for his safety, because he had preached the
word of God to a congregation of innocent and sincere persons, who desired to be instructed in their duty and confirmed
in their faith. The woods afforded him a shelter, and the rocks
a resting-place; but his enemies gave him no quiet until, of
his own accord, he delivered himself up to their custody.
They loaded his hands with chains, his feet stuck fast in the
mire, a dungeon was his abode, and murderers and thieves his
companions, until God, by the means of a pious gentlewoman,
whose kindness ought to be remembered by us even to latest
posterity, withdrew him from thence, and was the occasion
that his confinement was more tolerable.

His charge was preaching in the woods and praying aloud
in the prison; by the former they pretended that he perverted
the fidelity of the people towards their prince, and by the
latter interrupted their devotions at Mass, both which accusations, could they have been fairly made out, would have

proved matter of death, or at least long imprisonment; but
He, who blows upon the schemes of the wicked, and baffles all
their designs, had so contrived it that the witnesses should
mistake the date of the time that he preached, and the substance of the prayer, insomuch that he was released, to the
great satisfaction of his friends.

Alas! his sorrows for this time did not end here, but
rather this was the beginning of woe. During his confinement,
which had lasted nearly a year, his flock had either been van-
quished or scattered, there was scarcely any footsteps of them to
be traced.

The persecution grew warmer and sharper, and whosoever
would not bow the knee before Baal was cast into prison,
where soul and body were kept together merely that they might
endure the torment of a thousand deaths. The faggot and
sword, the wheel and the galleys, were employod in making
converts to that monstrous church.

There, O Rome! did thy emissaries glut themselves with
the spoils of the innocent, and wallowed in the blood of the
guiltless; there, if ever, wert thou satiated with cruelty and
revenge.

At that time our father, with his beloved and much-
lamented consort, our dear mother, was obliged to flee for
safety. They left friends and relatives, brothers and sisters,
lands and houses, and all they held dear, for the sake of Him
who once laid down his life for them. Human nature is incapable of more glorious conduct than theirs, which could have
been carried to no higher degree of perfection, unless God had
required them to seal their faith with their blood. Such
actions are above the conception and envy of the mean part of
mankind, and can fire none but the most generous souls. It

is the pious courage and divine resolution of our parents, that we, their descendants, with eagerness should desire to inherit a great measure of, in case God should think fit to lay upon us this heavy task. We may look back and see them, hand in hand, flying from the pestilential breath of the whore of Babylon, making their escape through difficulties and dangers, death pursuing close behind, until at last they were safely landed on the English shore. Thus, O Lord, didst thou exert thy mighty arm in behalf of our parents, and withdrew them from the slavery of Egypt. Thou broughtest them through the great and wide ocean, and placedst their feet on dry land in a place of safety.

This is but a short and imperfect sketch of the deliverance which God wrought in behalf of those who were immediately before us. What he did for our fathers in former days is not as yet come to my knowledge, but if I mistake not, some of them were favored with great and mighty deliverances.

As to ourselves, I need make use of no argument to persuade you that we have been the peculiar care of the Almighty, and that he hath delivered us sundry times from dangers and death. These were refreshed to our memories, after a very lively manner, in that good and pious discourse which was delivered to us this morning, and which ought not to fail of having a lasting effect upon our future behavior.

What I would endeavor to impress upon your minds is, that these mercies loudly call for our sincere thanks and humble acknowledgments, and that we must be highly insensible, if we cannot perceive the necessity of it.

Doth God vouchsafe to save and deliver in this miraculous manner, and can we forget? Can we scarcely be prevailed upon to spare two days in one year to meet together, and glorify him with one heart and with one mouth? When the fire and the sword, death and destruction stared us in the face, we would have been glad to compound for many days of hard and difficult service; nay, had God desired some great thing of us that we should have remembered these deliverances daily, we should not have thought it hard. But perhaps time, which consumes and devours every thing, hath blotted these mercies out of our minds and memories; or, our powerful Protector hath shortened his arm on some occasions since, and hath not proved the same God still, to save and deliver. No; surely it can be neither the one nor the other of these, for it is but nineteen years since the first, and fourteen since the last happened; and his wonders have been manifested sundry times since.

This neglect in some measure proceeds from the same infatuation which possessed the Israelites formerly, when God by his prophet Hosea reprimands them for their slothfulness and inconstancy. " O Ephraim, what shall I do unto thee? O Judah, what shall I do unto thee? for your goodness is as a morning cloud, and as the early dew it goeth away." God's favors are showered upon us abundantly, I may say, as the dew of the morning; but to what purpose, if we are unmindful of them, and suffer the cares of the world to stifle our gratitude? Can we be so unreasonable as to imagine that he will for ever give, if we continue to forget?

Common blessings, such as he dispenseth to just and unjust, he will not, perhaps, deprive us of. He will not make our inheritance dry, while he watereth that of our neighbor. But are these the only blessings we stand indebted for? Are these such as gave rise to the solemnity of this day in particular? Are we favored with no other distinguishing marks of his kind Providence and goodness? What, then, mean those

wonderful deliverances vouchsafed to our forefathers time out
of mind, those to our immediate parents, and those to ourselves without number?

Let these reflections, my brethren, be a spur to all noble
and generous exercises; and as God hath thought fit to distinguish us by his miraculous care and protection, and hath increased our family considerably, let us distinguish ourselves
by our virtue, and our zeal for his service. Let our eyes, instructed to survey higher objects, overlook the dazzling and
false grandeur of the world, pierce through the clouds and vapors which intercept, and fix upon the Sun of Righteousness
only. Let our hearts admit of no affections or passions to the
prejudice of those which are due to our great Deliverer, and
let the whole man, body and soul, be dedicated to his service.
Let us, as the Apostle in the text enjoins, with one heart and
one mind glorify God. Let us, upon no trivial occasion, omit
assembling ourselves together, for God, without exception of
one more than the other, in the day that our enemies pressed
sore upon us, delivered us all; and shall any of us be back-
ward to return him thanks? No, certainly; I hope better
things of you, my brethren, and that none of you can be so degenerate as to return his loving-kindness thus with ingratitude.

It is the joy and happiness of angels, and their continual
exercise by praise and thanksgiving, to glorify the Lord of the
whole universe. Why may not we take the opportunity to
imitate them, by joining our hearts and voices to the heavenly
chorus? Our deliverances have been wonderful and miraculous, and why may not our thanks be accompanied with
rapture? Praise the Lord, O my soul, and all that is within
me praise his holy name. Let the people praise thee, O God;
yea, let all the people praise thee. These should be upon all

14*

occasions our themes, and we should be delighted with these divine hymns. Could we once raise our souls to that pitch of devotion, the world and all its false splendor would pass by us unobserved, and its necessary incumbrances would seem to be only small lets and hindrances to our divine contemplations. Virtue and religion would be our chief study, and we should leave them as an inheritance to our children.

And since the only way to communicate the knowledge of the great deliverance of the Almighty to our families and children hereafter, is, to set apart certain seasons yearly to renew them to our minds and memories; let me beseech you by all that is dear and sacred, not to absent yourselves from these meetings upon any slender excuse, but that you be ready and willing at all times, with one mind and mouth to glorify God. Some may perhaps say, that this duty may be as well performed by each one in his own particular family; but I leave it to your own judgments, whether you think this will redound so much to the glory of God and the good of our souls. Nay, let me ask whether you have not been more deeply affected with the importance of this duty at those times when it has been our happiness, with one mind and one heart, to join in glorifying our great Creator? Has not your zeal and devotion been then carried to a greater height than at any other time; and at the conclusion of the day have you not felt more comfort and satisfaction from your performances? I am apt to think that you have all found an inexpressible difference. There is something in acknowledgment which is burdensome to a grateful soul, and requires to be communicated before it can be easy. It is this which makes the royal Prophet launch out into so great lengths, as to invite the most inanimate things to his assistance, when he is about to give God glory.

He says: Praise ye him sun and moon, and all ye stars of light. Praise the Lord from the earth, ye dragons, and all deeps; fire and hail, &c., &c.

For my part I feel a sensible accession to my joy in the presence of each one of you, and I cannot but think that every single person adds weight before the throne of grace to our reasonable petitions, and altogether harmony and beauty to our praises and thanksgivings, and invites a greater measure of the Holy Spirit. This is the way indeed to praise the Lord in the beauty of holiness, and to worship him with a holy worship.

We, whose duty it is to administer unto you in holy things, will not fail laying before you after the best manner we are able, the remarkable deliverances which have been performed in favor of our family, and put you in mind of your high obligations, nay, we will endeavor to go before you in the performance of this duty of thanksgiving by our example and instruction, and would to God that every one of you would strive not only to come after or keep up with us, but rather to excel us in these things.

Would to God that you would make it your business to teach them to your children, that they may be qualified to perpetuate them to infinite generations to come, and thereby engage the protection and draw down the blessings of the Almighty upon them. For God is not like Isaac who had no more than one blessing in store. He hath millions of millions to bestow upon them who love and fear him. He can bless in time of war, he can bless in time of peace, he can bless in time of sickness, he can bless in time of health,* he

---

* The ancient manuscript broke off here, and the sermon has been finished by a different hand.

can bless in the days of poverty and in those of prosperity.
Let us not faint, my brethren, if our Heavenly Father should
see fit to try our faith in the furnace of affliction. We have
his assurance that all things work together for good to them
that love the Lord. All things! What can be more com-
prehensive and encouraging? Let us then love the Lord and
trust in him. " Blessed is the man that trusteth in the Lord,
and whose hope the Lord is ; for he shall be as a tree planted
by the waters, and that spreadeth out her roots by the river,
and shall not see when heat cometh, but her leaf shall be
green, and shall not be careful in the year of drought, neither
shall cease from yielding fruit." " Trust ye in the Lord for
ever, for in the Lord Jehovah is everlasting strength." For
of him, and through him, and to him are all things, to whom
be glory for ever. Amen.

LETTERS OF MARY ANN MAURY.

• ⚫ •

September 2d, 1745.

DEAR SISTER:—I received your most cordial and affectionate letter, which I assure you was a sensible pleasure to me, though so far distant, that I have the opportunity of conversing with one who has been from infancy till now so dear to me.

I thank you for your kind wishes for my son James, and I hope they will be accomplished. He is now in his turn very edifying to us, please God he continues as he has begun. He and his wife are not gone to housekeeping yet, but their house will be ready for them at Christmas. The Lord send his blessing upon them. I dare say she will prove an industrious woman, for she hath been brought up to it. They have a son, with which she spares no pains that a loving mother is capable of. My son and she love each other tenderly, so I have great hopes of their being happy, which is a great pleasure to us. Thank God, my dear partner continues in good health, but dear Molly is always sickly. Aby is, thank God, very well.

As I believe you wish to know the state of all our families here, I shall begin with my brother James. His first wife is dead, and left four daughters and two sons. The youngest daughter, named Ann, has lived several years with my niece Mary Anne Winston, and I hope will turn out well. My brother is married again, but to who or what sort of a woman I cannot say. They live so far from us that we receive more intelligence from you than from him.

My brother Peter's first wife Lizzy was one of the love-liest creatures I ever saw. God had endowed her with all the virtues of a good Christian, a good wife, and a watchful mother. She never let the least thing pass in her children that had any appearance of evil in it, and was very tender of them. She was an obliging neighbor, charitable to the poor, beloved of all them that knew her, and most dear to us. The girl she left I brought up, named Mary Ann, and to my great comfort she inherits the character of her mother, as also does her brother Peter, so that they are loved and respected of all.

As to my niece, she is well provided for, she is married to a young gentleman named Isaac Winston, who hath a very good fortune, and a spotless reputation. They live very happily together, and have two sons.

My brother Peter's present wife is a lovely, sweet-tempered woman, and she, Mary Ann, and Peter have an unusual tenderness for one another; and I believe if they were her own children, she could not show more tenderness to them. My brother hath two children by her, a boy and girl. The boy is named Moses. I hope God will spare my brother's life to raise them, as he hath the other two, who are examples of piety and wisdom, and a great comfort to their parents and to us.

I wish it lay in my power to give you as pleasing a de-scription of brother Francis, but to my great grief I cannot express the dismal state of his family. As for his first wife she was, I believe, a good Christian, and very careful to instil good principles in her children; but she was not a fit wife for this country, so by that means, and by her ignorance of country business, my brother was almost ruined in his estate. She left one girl and three boys, and if it had pleased God to have taken them with her, it would have been a great blessing; for this woman he has married is a mighty housewife, but a cruel woman, and she has the entire dominion over her husband, so he has been induced to cast off all paternal duty to his first children. His eldest son Francis that was a boy of good parts, and was in the College, he bound to a carpenter, and when he was sick and in necessity he had no bowels of compassion for him. They are going to bind John to a carpenter. God in his great mercy hath lately taken the youngest son, named Thomas, from under her tyranny. As for poor Molly, the negro women she brought with her are more indulgently used than she is.

My brother has a boy and girl by her, and he spares no pains with the boy, who is about seven years old, who is *a wonder* for his age, while the others are castaways.

I did my best to get the poor girl away from her, but she was too serviceable.

I assure you, dear sister, it has been a great grief to me to see one I loved so well, one in his station, a shepherd to guide his flock, that he should be so inhuman to his own flesh and blood. He is grown an enemy to all our families here, to ours especially, because I reminded him of his duty to his children, for which good will of mine we are quite rejected, as are all others that do not like of her doings. She is his only lawgiver, a terrible exchange for that of his Maker.

This is the melancholy state of his family, which I pray God in his own good time to rectify. I desire you will show this relation to my brother John. The Lord preserve us all in a due sense of our duty in our several stations, so that no considerations whatsoever may induce us to offend our Maker, but that we may work out our salvation with fear and trembling, which is the hearty prayer of her who remains with all sincerity, dear sister,

Your most loving and affectionate sister,
MARY ANN MAURY.

Mr. Maury tells me that my brother John knows my brother Francis's wife very well, if he can remember. She is the daughter of one Brush, who was a gunsmith to Col. Spotswood. He used to clean the magazines and the Governor's arms at the same time my brother John was at the Governor's.

———

July the 17th, 1750.

DEAR BROTHER MOSES :—I cannot express the pleasure your pious and affectionate letter gave me, for by sister Torin's letter, I expected to hear I had lost a most dear and affectionate brother. The Lord be praised, who hath so graciously heard my prayers in your behalf. I may cry out with holy David on this, as well as on many other occasions, "What shall I render to the Lord for all his benefits."

I thank you, my dear brother, for your good wishes for the restoration of my health : nothing is impossible to our great Creator, who hath but to will it, and I shall be whole. But why should I be so presumptuous, at the age of sixty years, as to

expect a much longer continuance here? I ought rather to
prepare for eternity, for I am persuaded that these light afflictions, which are but for a moment, work out for us a far more
exceeding and eternal weight of glory. I still continue in
the same weakly condition; but thanks be to God, who ena-
bles me to bear it with patience and submission. His blessed
will be done, and give me grace to make a right use of my
suffering, looking beyond this corruptible to that glorious and
incorruptible state of glory, which God hath reserved for
them that love him, to which I hope, through the merits of
my Saviour, to come, and to which happy state I pray God we
may all arrive, where, of his infinite mercy, we shall enjoy
each other to all eternity. Dear brother, your Christian sentiments and exhortations are always most delightful to me. I
would have writ you a longer epistle if my weakness had permitted me. It is a trouble to me that I cannot entertain you
as usual with the state of our families here, but Mr. Maury
will inform you of it. All I can add at present is, to assure
you, dear brother, that I remain, unalterably till death.

Your loving and affectionate sister and servant to command,

MARY ANN MAURY.

April the 15th, 1752.

DEAR BROTHERS:—I have received your dear and affectionate letters, and am thankful to God that he hath in some
measure restored you to your healths again; may he be
pleased to continue it to you and yours whilst it is his good
pleasure, who knows what is best for us.

I suppose, dear brothers, my son James hath informed you
of the irreparable loss both to me and my children. I have

been deprived of the dearest partner of my joys and affections, and they of the most affectionate father. He made the most uneasy things tolerable to me, and though I knew we were mortal, and that we must soon part, yet by my continual indispositions, I thought my labors were the nearest at an end, and that God in his mercy would have hearkened to my prayers, and let me pass first out of this vale of misery, and that I should never feel the loss of such a dear and worthy partner, which was endowed with all the virtues of a good Christian, without ostentation, loved by all, and envied by none. If it were not that I soon expect a change, my life would seem intolerable; for I can say with holy Job, I would not live always.

Cruel self-love, that I should lament the happiness of that good soul which is gone before me, to attain the immortal crown of glory which God hath promised through the merits of our blessed Saviour, to them that trust in him. God's will be done! May he, in his great mercy, support and relieve me in this my weak and low condition, both of body and mind, and make me have a true sense of all his former blessings bestowed so undeservedly on me and mine, and also make me grateful for those he has in his mercy left me, which cannot be numbered. That he hath promised to be the protector of the fatherless and widow is my chief comfort, and it will be to my life's end, for I know that God will never forsake me, though my children may leave me; for, if it please God that I sojourn much longer in this state of trial, I must be deprived of their sweet company and assistance.

My dear James hath left me already, in hopes to advance his fortune, to the great regret of his flock. My dear Molly and her husband are going on the same account, which are great additions to my sorrows; first, to be deprived of the dutiful behavior and godly exhortations of James, and then of Molly, who is the most dutiful child as ever was, of the same happy way of thinking and behavior as her dear father, and beloved by all. Thank God, she is very happy in her husband.

As to my dear Aby, I may, in all probability, expect to have comfort in him while I remain on this side the grave; for, thank God, he is a youth of a happy temper, very dutiful, sober, chaste, honest, and sincere, hearkening to good counsel. He was, the 18th of last March, twenty-one years old. He hath left off the thoughts of following the Law, and doth intend, God willing, to follow merchandising, of which he has had a little insight. The Lord direct them all, and give them grace to walk in the steps of their dear father, who was charitable and just, one whose heart never coveted more than a moderate portion of worldly goods, the which God granted him by his industry to attain. He hath left to each of his children a moderate living; the Lord grant they may make a good use of it.

My dear brother Peter is very often attacked with the gout, and could not possibly be with me in my affliction. His son Peter is such a worthy youth, that he hath attracted the love and attention of all considerate men.

The Lord preserve you and yours, and reward all your Christian offices to me and mine, and shower his most precious blessings on you in this world, and at the last crown you with heavenly joys, is the prayer of her who with sincerity styles herself, dear brothers,

Your most afflicted and affectionate sister, and servant to command,

MARY ANN MAURY.

My hearty love to my dear sister and cousins.   I received
the ring from my son, the token of your loves.   I return you
my thanks for that and a great many more favors.   I do intend to leave the ring to my dear Molly.

LETTERS OF THE REV. PETER FONTAINE

OF WESTOVER, VIRGINIA.

VIRGINIA, *Nov. 4th,* 1749.

DEAR BROTHER MOSES:—Yours and brother John's letters dated March last, with Mr. Torin's, by way of London, through the care of Mr. Carey, merchant there, came safe to our hands some time in September last. It is putting brother Torin to trouble and some charge, sending the letters about, which may have a more quick passage by directing them in a cover to us to the care of Messrs. Joseph Farrell, senior and junior, merchants, in Bristol, who will further them to me by all opportunities, provided they are directed to Peter Fontaine, minister of Westover Parish, James River, Va., which you may do for the future.

I observe you have but an indifferent state of health, no more than myself. When we are turned of fifty, we must expect indispositions will creep upon such weak constitutions as ours. The rheumatism upon you, and the gout upon me, distempers near of kin and very sharp, which, as you well observe, we must bear with Christian patience and resignation. We are, nevertheless, allowed to struggle against these attacks by all lawful means, such as temperance in meats and drinks,

warm clothing, gentle exercise, especially taking the air frequently on horseback ; and though we cannot hereby make
our shattered tenements sound and strong, yet we may keep
them up for some time, until we have made our peace with
God, and served our generation as long as he, in his great
wisdom, shall see fit. For this reason, I shall give you my
bill of health, not any prescription of our doctors here, for
they are very ignorant, but my own observations, by watching
my constitution diligently.

I drink no spirituous liquors at all, no small beer ; but
when I am obliged to take more than ordinary fatigue, either
in serving my churches, or other branches of my duty, I take
one glass of good old Madeira wine, which revives me, and
contributes to my going through without much fatigue. I
walk much about the family business, and ride constantly
every morning all over my plantation, giving to my servants
their several employments, in all which I avoid, as much as
possible, wet either in my body or feet. I eat very little
meat of any sort, living chiefly upon bread and butter, greens,
pulse, and roots, especially Irish and Virginia potatoes, Scotch
barley, milk, and the like ; and by this regimen have made
shift to be my own overseer last year, and made a tolerable
crop. The gout seized me once by my right knee and foot,
but was entreated to let me get clear without giving me much
pain. If this be of use in my case, it may in yours, and my
tale will not appear long or impertinent.

It is natural to pass from the dying to the dead. Poor
brother Francis, after having labored under ill health for
some years, was seized a few months since with a nervous
fever, which in four or five days time deprived him of his life ;
and of his senses the very first day. He has left the disposal

of all to his wife, who governed him and his with a heavy hand. His eldest son, by this means, will have nothing, and his second son, and his daughter by his first wife, but what she thinks fit to give them.

Both Frank and John are carpenters, as good trades as any in this wooden country. Frank has been some years in disgrace, upon account of disobliging his step-dame, and never received one farthing but what his master obliged my brother to do for him by contract. Frank has been free about six years, and is married and has had three children, the eldest of which is dead. He lives at the town of New Berne, in North Carolina, where he and a fellow-apprentice of his, who is married to his wife's sister, have all the carpenter's business between them. His master has been to see them, and has been here this week. He gave me a very agreeable account of their behavior and circumstances. He is apprised that his father hath left him nothing, and hath sent a kind invitation to his brother to join him. With the blessing of God, I doubt not he will make a thriving man, he being honest and of good principles. I do not like the place, and dissuaded him from going thither; but he is capable of serving God in his family, and does so, I understand, and is very diligent and active. They are much beloved, and thrive fast, for even knaves choose rather to deal with such men, than their like.

As to Molly, she has been well brought up, so that if she can but light of a good match, her personal qualities alone may prove better than an ordinary portion. She is a very pretty girl, much resembling our dear deceased sister, whom you have seen, but of a more hardy constitution. She is now about twenty years of age.

James Maury, his son by this last wife, is a boy of fine parts, and I hear goes now to the college. If the vixen's over-fondness crush him not in the bud, he will, it is to be hoped, make an excellent man, for he knows more than any boy in the country of his age. His sister, the youngest of all, is a pretty girl, but so cockered, that it will not be the old lady's fault if she doth not spoil her quite. I hope better things, however, and that she may take more after poor Socrates than Xantippe.

May God preserve you, is the hearty prayer of your affectionate brother and servant,

PETER FONTAINE.

" VIRGINIA, 14th Feb. 1750–1.

DEAR BROTHER MOSES :—I received yours and brother John's kind letters by the Virginia Packet, Captain Aselby.

Since the middle of last August to the middle of November, we have had continual rain, which has done much mischief. As to myself and family, we have been troubled with continual colds and small fevers, but are now, thank God, pretty well recovered.

Cousin Francis Fontaine came from New Berne in North Carolina last November, to see us, and buy some tools which could not be had there, and to hire workmen—a journey of almost four hundred miles. He is well settled in that place, and has much business. He has taken his brother John and some other workmen out with him. He paid a visit to his step-mother, and though she boasts my brother Francis's estate was valued at £1500 Virginia currency, yet she neither gave nor offered him one sous. He has two children, a boy named Francis, about three years old, and a girl of fourteen months, named Mary, He has several lots in the town of New Berne, and 640 acres of land near it, which supplies him with timber for his business. He brought with him sixty pistoles, to purchase his tools and other necessaries. His step-mother offered to be his security if he wanted more goods, than he had cash to pay for, but he refused it, and the merchant he dealt with told her his own credit was sufficient, if he wanted to take the value of £500.

He only asked of her to see his father's will, and they parted contented on both sides, he with the pleasure of having his brother with him, and she with that of getting rid of him. She gave John, however, a negro boy, which he carried with him.

Frank was, by means of her cruelty, cast off without a rag to cover him; and we see how God hath taken him up, and hath been to him a most tender and kind Father. He came very decently dressed, and my wife observed by the neatness of his clothes, and the good sewing of his linen, that his wife must be a good seamstress and ingenious woman. I need not repeat what I said in my former, that he is beloved and respected.

I sent your kind letter to my son soon after I received it. He lives threescore miles, in the woods back from the river. I can send a letter to you in as short a time as to him. No post travels that way, and I have not heard from him at all this two months. He is now out in the forest surveying, if well, and I do not expect to hear from him till April or May. His wife has brought him a fine son, named John. My wife was up to see them last August, and she says he is the greatest boy of his age she ever saw. He was

15

then three months old. Please God to preserve him ; he will
have limbs and strength to scuffle through the woods, and
cope with his fellow foresters, whether human or brute.

Dear brother, feed much on soup and vegetables, and
good fruits; and in the winter good salad oil with endive,
dandelion, and other bitter salads at your meals, will help
digestion, cut the tough phlegm which engenders the pleu-
risy, make good blood, and keep the body in good order. I
know you eat little meat. Taking the air on horseback in
fine weather, and your employment in your garden, will keep
you healthy and cheerful, with God's blessing. Be pleased
with little things, such as the flourishing of a tree or a plant,
or a bed of flowers, and fret not at disappointments. Why
may not the growth of your trees afford you as much pleasure as the flourishing of a colony does to His Majesty, who
hath as many, God bless him! as you have trees. Excuse
this piece of quackery. I give you the same advice I follow
myself, and am with great sincerity, dear brother,

Your affectionate, humble servant,

PETER FONTAINE.

VIRGINIA, 15th April, 1754.

DEAR BROTHERS JOHN AND MOSES :—Just received your
kind letters of 30th November, 1753, dated from your castle,
with a hard name, and give you joy of your purchase, which,
if you have a fee simple in it, will be, with God's blessing, a
pretty revenue for you and one of yours, for many generations.

While our Merciful Father pours in his blessings upon us
through one channel, he afflicts through another. I heartily
condole with you, my sister, and the rest of our relations on

the other side of the water, upon account of the loss of our dear niece, your daughter.

This world is a kind of warfare, where we meet with good and evil, and both dispensed by the same kind hand, to loosen our affections from it, and remind us that we have no abiding place here, but are reserved for a better. May we all make it our chief study to prepare for a blessed change.

I very much approve of your wise disposal of your boys to good trades. Labor was ordained by our good Creator to quell the impetuosity of our passions, lest they should run into riot if left unsubdued and unemployed; for which reason, considering our present degenerate state, that part of Adam's curse which condemned him to labor, hath to him and his posterity proved a remarkable blessing ever since; and, if I may be indulged in one thought more, even his fall was of no small advantage to all those who will make right reason and divine revelation their guide, since the happiness of heaven infinitely surpasseth the bliss of Paradise, even in the state of innocence.

As age comes on, my distemper gains ground, and warns me to prepare for my change. Last fit of the gout confined me to my bed almost three months. I am but just upon the recovery, and still very weak, so that without any pretence to the spirit of prophecy, I may say, in all probability, this will be the last letter you will receive from me.

The rest of the grave, had not God some wise purpose for detaining me here, for my own good or the good of others, or both, would be preferable to my present state. For the greatest of earthly blessings, of which I must acknowledge I partake infinitely more than I deserve, in the prosperity of our families here and elsewhere, do not afford me the same pleasure they used to do. Though I am sincerely thankful for them, yet the lazy body which I drag about, and which is never free from pain in my best estate, nor hath been, I may truly say, for some years past, soon palls my joy, and makes me believe I have arrived at those days mentioned by Solomon, in which I can say, I take no pleasure except in the promises of the Gospel, which I have sincerely believed from my youth up until now, and in prospect of a blessed eternity, through the merits and mediation of my Blessed Redeemer. God is now my only comfort and stay; a comfort so powerful through his infinite goodness, that it affords me relief in my most violent agonies, and chases away all melancholy and desponding thoughts from my heart; a blessing I can never sufficiently thank him for.

I shall now give you some account of my family. My son Moses, the oldest by my second marriage, is going in his twelfth year. My daughter Sarah is going in ten. These two can read and write, and are beginning to cipher. My daughter Elizabeth, going in seven, can spell pretty well. My son Joseph is going in six, and my last, Aaron, is about four months old. Three days ago I received an account from Peter, that his wife was delivered of a third son, named William. My daughter Winston, hath three fine boys. Peter, a month older than my Moses; Isaac, about nine years old, and William, about six. Their father, Mr. Isaac Winston, is the very best of husbands, a man of strict honesty, and possessed of a very plentiful estate. With regard to my worldly estate, I am full; I abound with every valuable blessing my heart can desire or wish for.

I look upon a competency, I mean a small estate which will, with a man's industry, maintain himself and family, and

set him above the necessity of submitting to the humors and
vices of others, the most happy state this life affords. And
as we here in Virginia may be said to be all of one trade,
namely, planters, about one thousand acres of land will keep
troublesome neighbors at a distance, and a few slaves to make
corn and tobacco, and a few other necessaries, are sufficient.
This, God hath enabled me to leave to each of my younger
children, who you may perceive by what is before, are five in
number.

I would by no means add affliction to the afflicted, or give
advice when it is too late, but had you taken me into your
counsel when you were deliberating about marrying my deceased niece to so near a relation, I should have opposed it,
and advised you rather to a stranger for her, as I did in the
case of my own daughter being married to James Maury, all
friends here being very intent upon the match.

Marriage was the first divine institution, the only one with
regard to our neighbor in the state of innocence, and consequently the best; joining again by the strictest ties of love
and duty those who are separated in many degrees by descent
from our first ancestors; thus, though by generation we are
continually falling off one from another, yet the circle meets
again, and we become one flesh. You may perceive that, confining these alliances within our own family is straitening
this circle greatly, making a circle within a circle, a state
within a state, as the clans of Scotland and the west of Ireland, which is not only of pernicious consequence to the government, but contrary to the true spirit of Christianity, which
is the most diffusive of any, and would have every man look
upon himself, not as of this or of that nation, but as a citizen

of the world. This comes too late for what is past, but may
be a caution for the future.

As you desire to know something of sister Maury, I will
tell you. In the first place, my brother left her the house,
land, and stock, household furniture, and six working slaves
during her life, besides twenty pounds a year. She lives on
the mansion plantation, and wants nothing this world affords
except health, the greatest blessing of all; but age brings infirmities, and she is perfectly resigned to God's will. Her
youngest son, Abraham, lives with her, and is not yet married.
As far as I can learn, James has got a parish amongst the
mountains, and is concerned in the Ohio Company, who have
an entry on Halifax, beginning on the other side, or properly,
west side of the great mountains, upon the line between North
Carolina and Virginia, of eight hundred thousand acres of
land. His wife's uncle, Colonel Walker, is the chief person
in this scheme. They have it quite free for some years, and
sell it to settlers at £3 the hundred acres. They have about
thirty settlements upon it, if the French and their Indians
have not routed them lately

He has three sons, Matthew, James, and Walker, the latter a mountain hero, by report, and two daughters, Ann and
Mary, and his wife, a healthy young creature, who, in all probability, will have half a score more. His last letter to me
consists of three sheets, wrote on all sides, with a box containing a piece of antediluvian mud, petrified with the perfect
print of a cockle-shell upon it, taken from the top of one of
the Great Mountains, and a piece of sea-coal as good as any
in Whitehaven, taken out of a broken bank. They have excellent limestone, and many other materials for building on
the other side of the mountains, and want but salt to live

comfortably, which, no doubt, is in great plenty, if once discovered.

Have not room to say a word or two about Brother Frank's family and Molly Claiborne, but shall refer you to Moses' particular letter, having no more than is necessary to assure you that I am,

Your affectionate brother and servant,

PETER FONTAINE.

———

VIRGINIA, 17th April, 1754.

DEAR BROTHER MOSES:—'Tis kind in you to send me a line, though brother John's ample letter might have satisfied a moderate appetite that way.

The first thing I look at is the name at the bottom, and having found all things right, I read the rest with pleasure, more especially when yours to me are sealed with black wax.

Though my brother's loss is great in being deprived of his only daughter, in the bloom of her years, yet your two precious lives, and that of my sister, are of much more consequence towards directing and providing for the four hopeful boys under your management, who as yet are but young, and beginning to launch out into the world, an ocean full of rocks and shoals; to the inexperienced and unwary most dangerous.

May God preserve your lives, that you may have the comfort to see the youngest of them well settled in the world, and all of them in a fair way to provide for themselves.

I always correspond with all the family who will be so kind as to answer my letters, and have endeavored to instil the same maxim in my son Peter, and my nephews James Maury and Frank Fontaine, and I reap no small benefit from

it; for next to being with my friends is the pleasure of hearing from them, and knowing how matters go with them in this
inconstant and fluctuating world. I am highly pleased to
find my conduct approved in this particular by those I esteem
and love, and I hope by this means, when I am gone, there
will not be wanting some to brighten the chain between us
here and you in England, many years to come, an Indian but
very significant expression, signifying to renew the affection
or alliance between people of different nations, or friends, at a
distance one from another.

Francis Fontaine, my brother's oldest boy, lives at New
Berne, in North Carolina, has three children, two boys and a
girl. He and his brother John have all the business of the
town, they both of them being good joiners and carpenters.
John is lately married to a girl of good fortune and reputation, a thing somewhat scarce in those parts, as they have no
established laws and very little of the Gospel in that whole
colony. I hear from them once a year, and am put to it to
find conveyances to send my letters, or get any from them.
They live at least 400 miles from hence, and there are very
few opportunities by water, they having little trade to Virginia. In every letter I exhort them to come to Halifax or
Lunenburg, near to my son Peter, who hath it in his power to
help them to good land, and where they may be under the
protection of the laws as to property, and have their children
educated in the fear of God. James Maury Fontaine is a
charming youth; he is at our college here, and makes great
proficiency in his learning. He is son of my brother Francis
by his second wife, who is still living. Molly Fontaine I have
not heard from lately. She is whole sister to Frank and John
above-mentioned, and I believe lives with my brother's widow,

her mother-in-law, as yet unmarried, for what I know. Judith, the youngest of all my brother Frank's children, is with her mother.

Mr. Daniel Claiborne, who married my niece Molly Maury, sold his estate in King William County, and now lives near my son Peter in Lunenburg, where he has purchased a fine tract of land, and has carried with him a good number of slaves. He has had two sons, both of which he had the misfortune to lose, and hath now but one daughter about three years old. He is a very worthy man, and kind husband. I have not heard any thing this three years of brother James's family. They live in Northumberland Co., Virginia, and we can never hear from them.

Cousin Abraham Maury has a fine tract of land in Halifax, to which he will probably remove after my sister's death, my brother having ordered in his will the land she now lives on should be sold then, so that in all probability our relations here will in time be near one the other.

Thus have my poor gouty hands, but skin and bones, performed more than I expected when I began. Excuse blots and blurs.

May our good and gracious God shed on you all his choicest blessings, is the hearty prayer of, dear brother,

> Your most affectionate brother and servant,
> PETER FONTAINE.

March 2d, 1756.

DEAR BROTHERS :—Yours of the 30th October, 1754, came to hand the February following, when I was very ill of the gout, which confined me to the middle of April, and

took me again in September, but did not confine me so long.
Thus much with regard to my troublesome companion.

My sister came to reside with us in the beginning of last
October, but we had no long enjoyment of her company, for
she departed this life the last day of December, after a five
days' illness, which though very sharp, she bore with a truly
Christian patience and resignation to the Divine will, spending her last breath in prayers for all her relations and acquaintances, and in blessing me and my little family, one by
one, as we stood in tears around her.   The first thing she said
to me when she came to my house was: " Brother I am come
to die with you."   Her countenance was cheerful, and I was
in hopes that her words would not be so soon accomplished.
During the little time she was with us, she did me and my
family much good by her pious exhortations, and she instructed my little ones in commendable works they were unacquainted with before, which she was very capable to teach
them.   She had, after her duty to God, taken the excellent
daughter, Proverbs 31st chapter, the 18th verse to the end,
for her pattern ; and she kept all about her employed, and
would often wish she had strength to do more herself, and not
be the only lazy person in the family ; and yet in that short
time, besides her daily task in the Bible, four chapters and
the Psalms for the day, she had read the best part of " The
Persecutions of the Vaudois of Piedmont," a pretty large folio
by John Liger, a minister of that country.   She concluded her
labors here in the sixty-sixth year of her age, and by the truly
Christian manner of her death gave us great comfort, who
were eye-witnesses of it.   This being the last scene she acted
on this troublesome stage of life, I have transmitted it to you
faithfully, and I hope we may all imitate her faith and constancy.

As to news, you have a better account in the public papers than I can give you.

Hitherto we have been shamefully defeated by the enemy, not for want of men to carry on the war, but of money and proper military discipline.

The French as you observe are bad neighbors, and the Indians not one jot better, neither of which any treaties can bind, so that though a peace should be concluded at home, and you should reap the benefit of it, till the floating walls are unmanned and laid up, the enemy will make use of that cessation of hostilities to distress us. It would be no peace for us here, for, until the English colonies can, by exerting themselves, force the enemy to retreat from their borders, the people will be cut off piecemeal under pretence of an Indian war. The French will furnish the Indians with arms, ammunition, scalping-knives and leaders, to harass us continually; and may it not be of evil consequence to tie up our hands by a peace just now? Is not this delivering us over to the tyranny of fear, an imperious master more dreadful than a thousand deaths? No doubt peace is a jewel more to be desired than any thing else this world affords, could it be expected to be a real peace; but to put off the evil day, because you or I, who are old, may by that time be out of harm's way, and leave the conflict to our children, is not acting a generous, but a dastardly part.

The other evil you mention, our intestine enemies, our slaves, increase daily. The females are far more prolific than the white women, for, living upon a simple diet, upon bread, water, pulse, roots and herbs, seldom tasting meat of any sort, and drinking no strong drink, and being used to labor in the ground, they seldom miscarry, have strong healthy children, liable to no distempers. When our mother country shall vouchsafe to consider us a part of herself, she may perhaps not suffer such multitudes to be brought from Africa to pleasure a company, and overrun a dutiful colony.

May God preserve you, is the hearty prayer of your affectionate brother and humble servant,

PETER FONTAINE.

————

March the 30th, 1757.

DEAR BROTHER MOSES :—As I was obliged to take my consignments out of the hands of Hanbury and Farrell, it has occasioned some miscarriages and delays of our letters. Thomas Knox, Esq., in Bristol, and Robert Cary, Esq., in London, manage for me now. I am favored with yours, and brother and sister Torin's letters, dated December, 1756, and January, 1757, received the 11th March. Yours and our kind relations' prayers for me and mine, give me great comfort, as I am persuaded they have a favorable audience at the Throne of Grace. Dear brother, the best thing we can do for one another at this distance, is to send up our petitions continually to the centre of our hope, love, filial affection and fear, where they meet in an instant, join us to our Heavenly Father, to our blessed Redeemer, and one to another. Thus we shall be disposed to turn our faces now towards our heavenly rest, where we shall ere long meet, see one another, and by God's grace and mercy live for ever. When our thoughts take this direction the darkest scenes of life disappear, or are only noticed as small rubs on our journey thither. Oh! let us not be concerned at the measure or duration of afflictions sent to bring us back from our strayings. Let us not open our lips in complaints, but, with holy David, be dumb, and be content that all our affairs should be managed by Him whom our soul loveth, and who we are persuaded loveth us, and who saith to the sword and to the pestilence, what he formerly said to the sea, Thus far shalt thou rage, and no farther, and there shall thy proud waves be stayed.

Now, to answer your first query—whether by our breach of treaties we have not justly exasperated the bordering nations of Indians against us, and drawn upon ourselves the barbarous usage we meet with from them and the French? To answer this fully would take up much time. I shall only hint at some things which we ought to have done, and which we did not do at our first settlement amongst them, and which we might have learnt long since from the practice of our enemies the French. I am persuaded we were not deficient in the observation of treaties, but as we got the land by concession, and not by conquest, we ought to have intermarried with them, which would have incorporated us with them effectually, and made of them stanch friends, and, which is of still more consequence, made many of them good Christians; but this our wise politicians at home put an effectual stop to at the beginning of our settlement here, for when they heard that Rolfe had married Pocahontas, it was deliberated in Council, whether he had not committed high treason by so doing, that is, marrying an Indian Princess; and had not some troubles intervened which put a stop to the inquiry, the poor man might have been hanged up for doing the most just, the most natural, the most generous and politic action that ever was done this side of the water. This put an effectual stop to all intermarriages afterwards. Our Indian traders have indeed their squaws, alias whores, at the Indian towns where they trade, but leave their offspring like bulls or boars to be provided for at random by their mothers. As might be expected, some of these bastards have been the leading men or war-captains that have done us so much mischief. This ill-treatment was sufficient to create jealousy in the natural man's breast, and made the Indians look upon us as false and deceitful friends, and cause all our endeavors to convert them to be ineffectual. But here methinks I can hear you observe, What! Englishmen intermarry with Indians? But I can convince you that they are guilty of much more heinous practices, more unjustifiable in the sight of God and man (if that, indeed, may be called a bad practice), for many base wretches amongst us take up with negro women, by which means the country swarms with mulatto bastards, and these mulattoes, if but three generations removed from the black father or mother, may, by the indulgence of the laws of the country, intermarry with the white people, and actually do every day so marry. Now, if, instead of this abominable practice which hath polluted the blood of many amongst us, we had taken Indian wives in the first place, it would have made them some compensation for their lands. They are a free people, and the offspring would not be born in a state of slavery. We should become rightful heirs to their lands, and should not have smutted our blood, for the Indian children when born are as white as Spaniards or Portuguese, and were it not for the practice of going naked in the summer and besmearing themselves with bears' grease, &c., they would continue white; and had we thought fit to make them our wives, they would readily have complied with our fashion of wearing clothes all the year round ; and by doing justice to these poor benighted heathen, we should have introduced Christianity amongst them. Your own reflections upon these hints will be a sufficient answer to your first query. I shall only add that General Johnson's success was owing, under God, to his fidelity to the Indians, and his generous conduct to his Indian wife, by whom he hath several hopeful sons, who are all war-captains, the bulwarks with him of the five nations, and loyal subjects to their mother country.

As to your second query, if enslaving our fellow creatures be a practice agreeable to Christianity, it is answered in a great measure in many treatises at home, to which I refer you. I shall only mention something of our present state here.

Like Adam we are all apt to shift off the blame from ourselves and lay it upon others, how justly in our case you may judge. The negroes are enslaved by the negroes themselves before they are purchased by the masters of the ships who bring them here. It is to be sure at our choice whether we buy them or not, so this then is our crime, folly, or whatever you will please to call it. But, our Assembly, foreseeing the ill consequences of importing such numbers amongst us, hath often attempted to lay a duty upon them which would amount to a prohibition, such as ten or twenty pounds a head, but no Governor dare pass such a law, having instructions to the contrary from the Board of Trade at home. By this means they are forced upon us, whether we will or will not. This plainly shows the African Company hath the advantage of the colonies, and may do as it pleases with the Ministry.

Indeed, since we have been exhausted of our little stock of cash by the war, the importation has stopped ; our poverty then is our best security. There is no more picking for their ravenous jaws upon bare bones, but should we begin to thrive they will be at the same again. All our taxes are now laid upon slaves and on shippers of tobacco, which they wink at while we are in danger of being torn from them, but we durst not do it in time of peace, it being looked upon as the highest presumption to lay any burden upon trade. This is our part of the grievance, but to live in Virginia without slaves is morally impossible. Before our troubles, you could not hire a servant or slave for love or money, so that unless robust enough to cut wood, to go to mill, to work at the hoe, &c., you must starve, or board in some family where they both fleece and half starve you. There is no set price upon corn, wheat and provisions, so they take advantage of the necessities of strangers, who are thus obliged to purchase some slaves and land. This of course draws us all into the original sin and curse of the country of purchasing slaves, and this is the reason we have no merchants, traders or artificers of any sort but what become planters in a short time.

A common laborer, white or black, if you can be so much favored as to hire one, is a shilling sterling or fifteen pence currency per day; a bungling carpenter two shillings or two shillings and sixpence per day; besides diet and lodging. That is, for a lazy fellow to get wood and water, £19. 16. 3, current per annum; add to this seven or eight pounds more and you have a slave for life.

My last to you was in March, 1756. The 9th of April following I had a son born whose name is Abraham, a fine child, praised be God, the biggest I ever had; he has eight teeth.

I have had a severe fit of the gout this winter, and am just able to write.

We hear the Brest fleet is out, and Louis the 15th dead.

If they come to Virginia we must take to the woods and fight behind the trees. We have no other fortification but the Lord of Hosts, if he be on our side we shall give them a great deal of trouble. May he be your protection and ours, is the daily and sincere prayer of, dear brother,

Your affectionate, humble servant,
PETER FONTAINE.

———

April, 1757.

DEAR SISTER TORIN :—I did not desire in any measure to occasion affliction by giving you an account of our dear sister's Christian death, but rather comfort, and such I hope it hath been to you.

I am sorry to hear your indisposition prevails, as you are but young in comparison of me, and how often hath my distemper brought me to the gates of the grave, and yet have I lived to see these troublesome times, and for what end God only knows, unless it be to bring up these dear little ones, which he hath bestowed on me, in his fear and love, which I strive to do both by my daily prayers and endeavors.

All our infirmities are a warning to us, as you rightly observe, to prepare for our end, to set our faces, our hearts and affections towards that heavenly country, where we may hope, through the mercy of the Lord Jesus, to meet our friends and relations who are gone before us. In the mean time we ought to wait in patience for our release from these bodies, and cheerfully bear their burdens, not knowing what further service may be in the designs of God's providence for us yet to perform. This, dear sister, will keep us cheerful in the midst of trouble, and lessen the pains of our pilgrimage here.

May God take you in his most gracious care, may he be your comforter, your joy and your hope, is the hearty prayer of, dear sister,

Your affectionate brother and servant,

PETER FONTAINE.

This is the last letter of the Rev. Peter Fontaine, which has fallen into our hands. He died in the month of July of the same year.

Extracts from his last Will.

IN the name of God, Amen. I, Peter Fontaine, of the County of Charles City, Parish of Westover, being infirm of body, but of sound mind and memory, knowing it is ordained for all men once to die, do make and ordain this my last will and testament.

First, I commend my immortal soul into the hands of my Creator, to be disposed of according to the determination of his unerring wisdom, humbly hoping through the merits of my only Redeemer, the Lord Jesus Christ, that it will obtain favor in his sight, and the pardon of all my known transgressions. As to my body, I commit it to the earth, whence it was taken ; there to be purged of all rags of corruption through the blood of my merciful Redeemer, firmly believing it will be raised again to eternal life, summoned by the awful trump of doom, and be joined to my soul and live with it for ever.   *   *   *   *   *   *

My will and desire is that I may have no public funeral, but that my corpse may be accompanied to the ground by a

few of my nearest neighbors, that no liquors be given to make
any of the company drunk ; many instances of which I have
seen, to the great scandal of the Christian religion, and abuse
of so solemn an ordinance.   *   *   *   *

I desire none of my family to go in mourning for me.

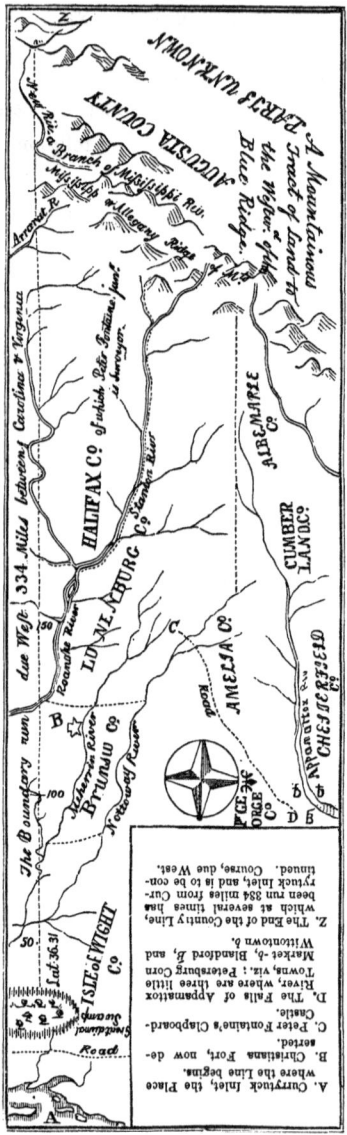

MAP OF THE VIRGINIA AND NORTH CAROLINA DIVIDING LINE.

(From a Draught at the head of the following Letter.)

LETTERS OF PETER FONTAINE, JUN.

OF ROCK CASTLE, HANOVER COUNTY, VIRGINIA.

———•◦•—◦—

LUNENBURG, VIRGINIA, *9th July*, 1752.

DEAR SIR :—I got not long since, your kind letter, by the hand of my father, bearing date 2d January, 1752, and take this opportunity of returning you my thanks for the many expressions of kindness it contains. We are all (God be praised) well, not only my family, but all our relations that I have lately heard from, except my good aunt Maury, who I hear has been very like to die, and is yet in a very low condition.

The kind curiosity you seem to have to know where I live, has put me upon sending you a sketch of that part of our country where I now reside, which I thought might be some entertainment to you, as you in your rambles with Colonel Spotswood, travelled over a good deal of the southern part of Virginia.

I find you have formed a very good judgment of the situation of these parts, for Lunenburg, as you imagine, joins (as you see by the plan) Carolina, though not so far now as it did before Halifax county, now on the head of it, was cut off from it by a late Act of Assembly. You judge very rightly that Meherrin River is in Lunenburg county. We live so high up Nottoway River that we have not any fish, as you imagine, but, thank God, a healthy air, fruitful soil, and good fresh range for stocks. I fancy you did not travel far enough southward to get acquainted with Roanoke River, which is a much finer stream than either Meherrin or Nottoway, and vastly larger, before it divides itself into two streams, called Stanton and Dan, near three hundred yards over, and either of the just mentioned branches of it are at least two hundred and thirty.

My district for surveying lies, i. e. the chief of it, in Halifax county, in the Fork of the river Roanoke, so that I now live out of my county, and by means of the indulgence granted me, of having assistants, I do not go at all in the woods, which indeed my weakly constitution is not fit for; yet, thank God, I have my health very well, when I am not obliged to undergo fatigue. Though my living a hundred and twenty miles from Williamsburg, forces me frequently to take very tedious rides, being sometimes called down in the heat of summer. But certainly, if any man in the world has reason to be thankful to the Great Giver of all blessings, I, who in a troublesome employment, am indulged to live at home at ease, ought to be all gratitude, and instead of murmuring at the trifling fatigues I undergo, should be thankful that I can reap a comfortable harvest without putting my hand to the plough.

You see, dear sir, that the regard you are so kind as to express for me, has made me so fond of myself, and so vain, as to trouble you with almost half a sheet full of my own history, and to imagine all the while that I am entertaining you agreeably.

My family is increased by the birth of a son, now two months old, whom we have named Peter. My wife joins me in tenders of hearty and unfeigned respect to you, my aunt, and all your good family. I have no more to add, but to beg on your part a continuance of the correspondence, which affords me so much real comfort, and to assure you that I am with my daily prayers for the health and welfare of you, and all our dear friends on your side the ocean,

Your very affectionate nephew and humble servant,

PETER FONTAINE, Jun.

To Mr. John Fontaine.

LUNENBURG, VIRGINIA, *7th June*, 1754.

DEAR SIR :—Your exceedingly kind letter of 30th November, 1753, is before me, and I am seated to return you my hearty thanks for that favor, and in a very talkative humor to perform my part in the only kind of conversation which the great distance between us will admit of.

Your kind acceptance of my little performance inclosed in my uncle John's letter for his and your perusal, has more than paid me for the trouble it cost me, and might induce me to make a draught of the country for your and his satisfaction, had I proper helps to assist me in those parts of it that I am less acquainted with than this, which the nature of my business in it has given me a tolerable knowledge of.

Your kind promise of embracing all opportunities of keeping up an epistolary correspondence with me, gives me the greatest pleasure, and renders the business I am now about a most agreeable one : as I have leave to expect that each epistle of mine will be rewarded with at least a few lines from you, the perusal of which affords me real satisfaction on many accounts, but on none more than the truly Christian disposition and open sincerity I conceive to be lodged in the heart that dictates them.

The indulgence that it has pleased God I have, by the favor of those who have the legislative power in their hands, enjoyed, has been of great service to my constitution. I pray God to enable me to express my gratitude, not with lips only, but a well-spent life and Christian conversation.

I have formed to myself a very agreeable idea of the situation of your present residence, as I imagine you live much retired; and being out of business, have great leisure for study and contemplation, to which I doubt not is added the pleasure of fine prospects, fertile soil, good gardens, and healthy air.

My father, whom I am preparing to visit on my way to Williamsburg (our metropolis), informs me by a letter I have received from him, that he has this past winter had a most severe fit of the gout, which affected his breast much and his head a little, symptoms that I fear forebode sorrows to those who can never part with him without regret; but, I thank God, he speaks of it as of a journey he shall undertake with joy, a circumstance which, I doubt not, will administer comfort to him and all his friends in time of need.

My wife assures you of her most hearty respect. Pray, my dear uncle, continue that good office of mentioning me and mine in your prayers to the throne of grace, and be persuaded that my poor petitions are frequently put up for blessings on you and all our dear friends on your side, and that I am, dear sir, your dutiful nephew, and

Very affectionate, humble servant,

PETER FONTAINE, Jun.

To Mr. Moses Fontaine:—Since the within, Colonel Washington, the commander of our three or four hundred men from Virginia, has, with a party of about forty men and some auxiliary Indians, by the intelligence of an Irish deserter, met with a party of about thirty-six French, who were in ambush in the woods waiting for him. Each party fired, and it has pleased God that we have killed or taken them all. There were thirteen killed and the rest taken. We lost only one man, and two wounded. The French seem to have a great mixture of Indian blood, and are sturdy fellows. The place in dispute is on the Ohio river, about two hundred miles back of our nearest mountains.   P. F.

LUNENBURG, VIRGINIA, *7th June*, 1754.

Dear Sir:—I return you hearty thanks for your very kind and most agreeable letter of the 30th Nov. 1753, and particularly acknowledge the favor of your having wrote me a longer epistle than I have ever yet received from your side of the water; for, I can with sincerity assure you, that my having more to read at once than I can at once remember, yields me great pleasure, as it sets me to reading again and again your kind letter, wherein I am in hopes, even to the tenth perusal, of finding something new, and never fail of meeting something very entertaining.

The encomiums your kindness has dictated on account of my little draught are, I am very sensible, more than it deserved, though I am very glad it has yielded you any satisfaction, as it has thereby fully answered its end.

I heartily condole with you upon the loss of my dear cousin, I believe, your only daughter. May God Almighty com-

16

fort you and your family, and him who cannot be less in want of it, my poor cousin, James Fontaine.

I congratulate you on your new purchase, by which, if I understand the matter rightly, you have turned your money to greater advantage than 4 per cent., and hope you will repair the loss sustained by the reduction on the interest prescribed by the Parliament while your money was in the Bank. I conclude that you lead a very happy life in your present country-seat, but must beg you will excuse me when I desire you will be so kind in your next as to let me know how the name of your castle is pronounced, for I observe it is spelt CWM, which, for want of vowels, I do not know how to pronounce, and which is, I fancy, the case in many Welsh words.

My present settlement does not answer the opinion you have conceived of it, being very little improved by art; for, as the only inducement I have hitherto had for residing at it is, its being the nearest tolerable neighborhood, I could find and purchase, to my business in Halifax, I have always been cautious of expending any thing considerable on it, being determined (God willing) to leave it when my business shall enable me to live in Hanover, a much more sociable part of the country, where I have upwards of five hundred acres of land very pleasantly situated, with good house and all other necessaries; though I am not so fond of my scheme but that I may perhaps sell my possessions below, and with the money purchase a larger quantity of land in these parts, since the increase of our family with which it has pleased God to bless me (having, thank God, three fine boys, John, Peter and William), may make it more expedient to spend our days near the frontier. However, I do not form, I hope I never shall form any other resolution than to endeavor to be contented in whatsoever station or situation it shall please God to place me, always striving for what appears the best.

Our neighborhood was, about eighteen months ago, rendered much more agreeable to us by the coming of Mr. Daniel Claiborne and his wife, my cousin, formerly Molly Maury, to reside about three quarters of a mile from us. They are both well, as is their daughter Molly, their only child. We live very happily together.

My aunt Maury is, I understand, somewhat better in health than usual, though but crazy. She lives where my uncle lived. Aby Maury is the only child she has with her. He acts the part of a dutiful son and a worthy young man. He carries on the business of a merchant.

My cousin, the Rev. James Maury, has removed from King William, and lives in Louisa County, in the upper parish; he is much beloved by his parishioners, and has a pretty income.

My sister, Mary Ann Winston, with her husband and three sons, Peter, Isaac and William, are well. Mr. Isaac Winston, her husband, is a wealthy planter, and what is much better, a tender husband and a good Christian.

The last time I heard from my cousins, Francis and John Fontaine, who carry on the carpenter's trade in New Berne, a town in North Carolina, they were well and in a thriving way. Francis is married. They live about one hundred and fifty miles from me. I need not tell you, that my cousins last mentioned are sons of my late uncle Francis. My aunt, his relict, lives in York County; her oldest son James, a fine, promising youth about fourteen years old, goes to the college. She has also a daughter with her. There is a kind of coolness towards her—I mean my aunt—in most of our family, on account of her treatment of my uncle's first children.

Ann Fontaine, sister to my cousin James, your son-in-law, lives with my sister Winston, who brought her up. She is a virtuous, good girl, and reaps the benefit of it even temporally, as my brother Winston has given her a little beginning, in case she should marry and leave him, and provides for her handsomely, as I dare say he will continue to do while she stays with him. I have not in a great while heard any thing of the rest of the family my uncle James left behind him. They live in the Northern Neck, 170 or 180 miles from me.

My father has by his last wife, my mother-in-law, five children, three boys and two girls, the oldest about twelve years old. He has made use of my opportunities as a surveyor to procure lands for them in Halifax County, where he has procured five tracts of land, amounting to about six thousand acres, which he designs, with near or about twenty slaves, to divide amongst them at his death.

And here I cannot help expressing my concern at the nature of our Virginia estates, so far as they consist in slaves. I suppose we have, young and old, one hundred and fifty thousand of them in the country, a number, at least, equal to the whites. It is a hard task to do our duty towards them as we ought, for we run the hazard of temporal ruin if they are not compelled to work hard on the one hand—and on the other, that of not being able to render a good account of our stewardship in the other and better world, if we oppress and tyrannize over them. Besides, according to our present method, which every body appears afraid to go out of, it seems quite necessary to lay most stress on that stinking, and, in itself, useless weed, tobacco, as our staple commodity, which is the reason that all other more useful trades and occupations are neglected, or professed by such as are not above half qualified for them; and every Virginia tradesman must be at least half a planter, and of course not to be depended upon as a tradesman.

I cannot help adding a piece of domestic news, which is, that the French on the back of us are disputing our title to the Mississippi lands, have built a fort to annoy our settlements, and have drove off about seventy families of my countrymen. The Assembly has enacted the levying of £10,000 currency to enable them to oppose the enemy. We expect every day to hear that about fifteen hundred men, levied in these colonies, have either settled on Mississippi and built a fort to countermine that of the French, or that they have, if opposed, engaged them. May God restore peace to our infant colony! I have but just room to add, that I beg you will excuse my writing in this manner on the back of my uncle Moses's letter, which I do under a notion of saving you postage, and that my wife joins in tenders of sincere respect to you and all your dear family. That you and yours may long enjoy here all temporal blessings, and in the regions of bliss everlasting happiness, is the fervent prayer of, my dear uncle,

Your obliged and dutiful nephew,

And very affectionate, humble servant,

PETER FONTAINE, Jun.

To Mr. John Fontaine.

———

CHARLES CITY COUNTY, VIRGINIA, *June 11th*, 1757.

DEAR SIR :—I have now an opportunity of returning you my hearty thanks for your kind mention of me and mine in yours of 8th Jan. 1757, to my father, and fulfilling your re-

quest so grateful to me. Impute not my silence to a want of
due regard to you, or an indifference in keeping up a correspondence with you. I have, since my last to you, removed
forty miles further southward than I then lived, which renders
my writing to you more difficult than formerly. But as the
motive that carried me thither, i. e., the keeping my place,
which is become, on account of our present troubles, of little
value, has no longer any weight in it, I have (*Deo volente*) determined (unless the times shortly change for the better,
which, from the appearance of things we have but little, and
from our own deserts no reason at all to hope) shortly to remove to my little seat in Hanover, where I propose to employ
my small abilities in the education of my three boys, which I
shall have the more leisure to attend to after having quitted
every kind of public business, and the many avocations which
are now a bar to such an employment; though I fear our dis-
tresses, unless it please God to put a speedy stop to them, may
prove an interruption to every occupation in every part of this
poor infant colony. We are here so utterly unacquainted
with military matters, that we all, from the legislator to the
meanest handicraftsman, are at a stand. All the measures we
have fallen upon seem ineffectual, and answer no other end
than to plunge us in debt, insomuch that the credit of the
country is almost sunk; and from the inexperience of the
managers, our expeditions have proved not only abortive, but
disgraceful. The miscarriages in all our enterprises have rendered us a reproach, and to the last degree contemptible in
the eyes of our savage Indian, and much more inhuman French
enemies.

Those of the Indians that call themselves our friends despise us, and in their march through our inhabited country,

when going to our assistance, insult and annoy us.   It is not above a month ago since a party of about a hundred and twenty Cherokees, in passing through Lunenburg, insulted people of all ranks.   About three weeks ago the Cattawbos behaved so ill in Williamsburg, that those in power were obliged to arm the militia, and the matter was near coming to extremities.   About fourteen days ago the same Cattawbos murdered a poor woman in Bartie County, in North Carolina, whom they met alone in the road.   It is said that for this last misdemeanor they are like to smart severely, as it is reported that four hundred men in arms are in pursuit of them (and they do not exceed one hundred), and are determined to avenge her death.

There is some hope that our affairs are better managed under the Earl of Loudon than formerly they were, as matters are conducted with great secrecy ; and it is presumed he has a good army.

The County of Halifax, in the mean time, is threatened by our Indian enemies, and the people in the upper part of that county, which by the late encroachments of our enemies is become a frontier, are in great consternation, and all public business at a stand.   The poor farmers and planters have dreadful apprehensions of falling into the hands of the savage, as indeed, considering the treatment those have had who have had the misfortune to be surprised by them, they have good reason.

We have among us two or three who have made their escape from the Shawnees (a tribe of Indians that live on the Ohio, to the westward of Halifax County); the Indians suspected that one of them, whose wife and children they had most inhumanly murdered, would attempt to escape, to pre-

vent which they cut deep gashes in his heels, and as soon as
the man was like to get well, and be in order to travel again,
they cut other gashes across the former, and by that means,
and at some other times searing his feet with hot irons, they
kept him a continual cripple. The man, however, being of an
enterprising spirit, contrived, by means of a piece of lighted
punk thrust into a barrel of gunpowder, to blow up a fine
French store in their town, for which, being after some time
discovered by the treachery of a fellow-prisoner, he was to
have been burnt alive by piecemeal, had he not very providentially made his escape. He gives most dreadful shocking
accounts of their treatment of our people, but more especially
of the poor women, upon whom they exercise all kinds of torture and brutality. In short, such cruelties do they practise
upon every one that falls into their hands, that all had rather
perish than be taken alive. I dare say I have by this time
tired you with the relation of our sufferings, and the bloody
triumphs of our enemies, which, though not perhaps as to the
minute particulars I have mentioned, you are no doubt in the
general well informed of from our public prints.

My family was, three days ago, when I left home, in good
health, as was also Mr. Claiborne and my cousin, Aby Maury,
who is his father's likeness both in person and all good qualities. I also saw a letter from my cousin, the Rev. James
Maury, the other day, by which I see he and his also enjoy
the same blessing.

I beg, my dear uncle, you will be so kind as to feast me
with a letter by the first opportunity, and that you will in the
mean time, think of me and mine in your approaches to the
throne of grace, and be assured that I am with the most profound respect, the most sincere affection, and daily prayers for

your well-being here, and everlasting happiness in that never-ending state of bliss, where I hope and trust we shall all, through the merits of the Redeemer, have a joyful meeting. My dear uncle, your dutiful nephew and most

Affectionate humble servant,

PETER FONTAINE, Jun.

This letter I believe to have been addressed to Moses Fontaine, it was without address, but endorsed in the hand-writing of Moses Fontaine. Received 23d September, 1757, answered 21st February, 1758.

———

ROCK CASTLE, HANOVER, VIRGINIA, *June* 9, 1760.

DEAR SIR :—It is so long since I have had the pleasure to receive a letter from you, that I am afraid something has happened on your part to prevent it, and yet I acknowledge you have seeming reason to doubt, to suspect my sincerity, when I tell you so, as I have been so long, so very long silent myself. But I am persuaded that you will make all possible allowance for a person who has had so much business on his hands, as I have had since I last wrote to you. The death of my dear father ; the business of his whole concerns falling into my hands, my own removal from Halifax and settling in Hanover, the late dismal prospect of our public affairs, with the almost continual sickliness of my own family, and the death of two dear children, and last of all, my having discontinued to ship tobacco home, which used to act as the monitor as well as offer opportunities of writing to you and my other friends on your side ; these, dear sir, have been the principal impediments in my way.

16*

As I have always understood that you are settled in South Wales, near my uncle John, I shall refer you to mine to him, for a particular account of my mother ; I hope, please God, all may end well at last.

Our public affairs have, through the merciful and almost miraculous interposition of kind Providence, taken quite another turn of late, and were it not that the Cherokee Indians have most perfidiously broken their treaty of peace, and fallen upon our frontiers, we should enjoy the sweets of peace again. But they have done considerable mischief in North Carolina on our borders, and some in our own Province ; several families, that had since the former troubles returned to their settlements on the frontiers, are again frightened and have left them—so that the county I lived in (Halifax), is as much confused, and as unfit, of course, for my business as when I left it. Our colonies are raising men to go against them. May the Lord of Hosts, the only giver of all victory, prosper the enterprise.

I, for my part, had, for the last two years I lived in Halifax, very little to do as a surveyor, nor should I, if I had continued till now. I there lived on rented land, at a smart expense, had houses, etc., here, suffering for want of me, and above all, had a longing desire to retire and live in private, where I might attend to the education of my boys, and had hopes that I could be, through the grace of God, thankfully contented with that competency with which his bounty had blessed me ; nor have I as yet, thank God, found myself in the least disappointed. I was always persuaded that a middle station was the happiest, in which condition it has pleased God in mercy to place me, with thousands of blessings—even in the midst of his chastisements—on my head, the least of which is more than I deserve.

As to perfect happiness, it is not, it ought not to be looked for in a valley of tears, or in a state of trial. Our good God has, in mercy, denied it to every station of life, lest we should anchor here, and not long for that better life, where tears and pain and want are strangers, and where friends are never parted. May the merits of our gracious Redeemer purchase for us all an inheritance, an estate for life eternal, in those happy mansions.

My wife and family join me in tenders of sincere regard and affection to you and all on your side the ocean. May temporal and eternal blessings attend you all. I am, dear sir,

Your affectionate nephew and humble servant,

PETER FONTAINE.

To Mr. Moses Fontaine.

————

To Messrs. Moses and John Fontaine and Mr. Daniel Torin.

FORKS OF PAMUNKEY RIVER, HANOVER CO., VA., 7 *Aug.* 1763.

MY DEAR UNCLES :—I take this opportunity by Mr. Harden Burnley, who is going home, to inquire after you all.

It is some considerable time since I had the pleasure of receiving a letter from you. I hope, please God, nothing has happened to interrupt that agreeable correspondence which has yielded me so much pleasure.

There has not any great alteration happened in the state of any of our relations' families here. I believe cousin Ann Fontaine, sister to cousin James (with you), was married when I wrote last to Mr. Thomas Owen. She has·two children.

But our public affairs are in a very bad situation at present, as all the Indians on the continent, i. e. between us and the Mississippi and St. Lawrence Rivers, have entered into a combination against us, resolved it seems to prevent our settling any farther than we have, viz., much about the main Blue Ridge of mountains; and in consequence of this resolution, they have, according to their manner, declared war against all our colonies, that is to say, all, or most of the tribes on our backs, divided themselves into proper parties, and fell upon our poor scattered unprepared frontier settlements, and have cut the throats of many of the inhabitants, whilst they were quite unaware that any mischief was intended them, and have carried a great number of women and children, as well as some men, and (for the first time too) a good many negroes, into captivity; indeed, 'tis said they have broke us more frontiers, come lower down to do us mischief, and killed as many people as in the last war.

I hope, my dear friends, you do not disapprove my manner of writing to you all together, as I direct for my uncle Torin, who after perusal, will be so kind as forward the letter to Wales. My family, I thank God, is at present in health. My youngest child is James, who I believe was born before I wrote last.

I long much to hear from you. I am in a more particular manner anxious to know how my dear aunt Torin and uncle Moses are, as I look upon them to be the greatest invalids, and of most crazy constitutions.

We all join in tenders of sincere respect and affection.

I am, my dear uncles, your most affectionate kinsman,

PETER FONTAINE.

The following memorandum endorsed upon the letter, in Mrs. Torin's handwriting.

I find he has not received mine, of 30th July, 1762, though it went by Mr. Sumpter, a friend of his, who went back with the Indian Kings.

It may be interesting to remark, that the James Fontaine, spoken of as an infant in the foregoing letter, in after life held a commission as Major of a volunteer regiment of cavalry from Kentucky, which composed part of the force which was sent against the Indians on our western frontier, after the close of the Revolutionary War. Owing to some indiscretion of the commanding officer, his regiment was surrounded by the Indians. Major Fontaine proposed to the troops to cut their way through them. There were but few who joined in this heroic attempt, which would probably have saved the greater part of the regiment, had the movement been executed by all, with the resolution which marked the brave few.

Major-Fontaine succeeded, but died almost immediately, from the numerous wounds he received.

To Mr. John Fontaine.

ROCK CASTLE, HANOVER CO., VA., *July* 8, 1765.

DEAR SIR:—Your very kind letter of 20th June, 1764, I just now received, for which, as for a most agreeable cordial, I return you my sincere thanks.

Your memento, my dear uncle, that you are now seventy-one years old, and that you are providing a substitute to act that kind part which you now fill yourself, after you shall leave the stage, though kind and reasonable, has yet raised in me that sorrow which is natural, at the thought of parting with a beloved friend. But it is a memorandum that I think we ought always to carry about us, that friends, the best of our worldly enjoyments, are liable to be taken from us every moment, or if not, we ourselves must some time or other be taken from them ; so that we ought to stand always prepared for the painful divorce, and not set our affections on the good things of this world, which are only intended by our good God as comforts and refreshments in our pilgrimage upon the journey to that other world, which is our proper home. May God grant, my dear uncle, that all of us may so run this short race, as that we may reap those joys which have no bitterness, and no bounds, in that everlasting world, to which you, that are seventy odd, and I that am forty odd, are equally hastening, and in which you only have a little the start; where I hope we shall not only be better acquainted with each other, k ow personally, and converse by word of mouth, and have no dangerous ocean of three thousand miles between us. But the very essence of all joy will be, that we shall know the Great Father of all our blessings and enjoyments, whom to know is eternal life.

As to public affairs here, we seem to have room to flatter ourselves that our cruel enemies the Indians, are, from some motive, more peaceably disposed towards us than formerly. And yet things wear but a gloomy aspect, for the country is so excessively poor, that even the industrious, frugal man can scarcely live, and the least slip in economy would be fatal. There is no money but the small remains of our paper currency, which is almost all returned to and burnt in the Treasury; and in the midst of this our poverty, our mother country, which seems to have contracted a dislike to some of our proceedings, is laying a tax (the forerunner we fear of others) upon us, which it appears impossible to pay, as I learn it is to be collected in silver, of which there is almost none in the colony; so that peace, the ardent wish ·of the poor wretch who is involved in war, seems to threaten us with as great, if not greater evils, than even the war itself. But I am not a politician, and the subject is disagreeable; therefore I will drop it, and in spite of alarming appearances, I will trust in Providence to send us better times, and to work a kinder disposition in our mother country towards us.

I saw my cousin, Mr. Abraham Maury, and his family, and Mr. Daniel Claiborne and his family, this spring, who were all well. I have also lately seen Mr. Isaac Winston and his family. They are well, except my sister, who is in but a low state of health.

My poor mother-in-law is now with Mr. William Mills, who married Elizabeth, her second daughter. Sally, the oldest, lives with us, unmarried. Moses, the oldest son, is in business in Charles City County. Joseph I have bound to a cabinet-maker, and he is like to do well. Aaron lives with Mr. Isaac Winston, and Aby, the youngest, is with his mother.

The Rev. James Maury I saw not long ago, and believe he and his family are well.

My cousin Mary, oldest daughter of my uncle Francis, is so unhappy as to have married an extravagant, careless man, who is quite unable to maintain her; and she now lives in the capacity of housekeeper, with a very worthy clergyman in North Carolina.

I willingly embrace your kind proposal of commencing an epistolary correspondence with your son, my cousin James Fontaine, but not as your substitute, for I trust in God (provided it be for your good to continue here) that I shall have the pleasure of receiving many kind letters yet, from the good friend of seventy odd, if not of eighty odd.

With hearty thanks for your kindness in favoring me thus far with your correspondence, and sincere prayers for your temporal and eternal welfare,

I am, dear sir, your very dutiful and affectionate nephew,

PETER FONTAINE.

To Mr. Moses Fontaine.

DEAR SIR:—Your kind favor of 20th June, 1764, now lies before me; and most sincerely am I obliged by the kind promise you make of continuing to give me this proof of your affection. When your annual letter arrives, it yields me much more substantial pleasure than is felt at the feastings on the return of a birth-day. The meltings of heart that I experience when I read your pious letters, leave impressions on my mind that are of real advantage to me. I am persuaded there is a kind of instinct in souls; for though I never saw with my bodily eyes either you or my dear uncle John, yet I am better acquainted with nobody. I indulge myself in forming ideas of you in my mind; and sometimes in an agreeable reverie, enjoy a kind of ideal conversation with you. I seem quite intimate with you both, and so closely united in familiar friendship, that nine-tenths of those I am personally acquainted with, are incapable of affording me half the satisfaction, in repeated interviews, that I reap from only poring over one of your letters once a year.

As to articles of intelligence, I have forestalled myself in my letter to my uncle John, to which I have only to add, that my family of children now consists of three sons, John, William, and James, and three daughters, Sarah, Mary Anne, and Judith, who with my wife, are, thank God, well. To avoid repetition, I refer you to the letter aforesaid. Indeed, I have learned to consider you and my uncle John, almost as one person, for I find you so united in your letters, your habitation in Wales, and in another warm habitation you have in my heart, that whatever I write to the one, always anticipates my thoughts to the other: I therefore conclude with hearty wishes for your health and happiness here and hereafter.

I am, dear sir, your dutiful and affectionate nephew,

PETER FONTAINE.

LETTERS OF THE REV. JAMES MAURY.*

———•♦•———

FREDERICKSVILLE PARISH, LOUISA COUNTY, *Aug. 9th,* 1755.

DEAR SIR:—I am always tardy. Your kind and agreeable letter of October last, now before me, ought to have been answered by my friend Knox's ship, from Pamunkey, which sailed some time in June, and should have been so, had the map come to hand in time, which it was necessary to have my hand upon, in order to answer some parts of it. I am sorry the engraver had not the most accurate copy. He has copied from that which was transmitted to the Board of Trade and Plantations, who, it seems, wrote so expressly for it, that the government thought proper to send them one before it had received the finishing touch; since that, the fuller draughts have been sent over sea by the compilers, as presents, one to the late pious Bishop of Man, Dr. Wilson, the other to a clergyman in Bristol. However, sir, incomplete as it is, you may form a tolerable guess, where each of our families is situated, by the directions which I am about to give you, whence you will also discover how the American branches of the Fontaine family are dispersed, and how seldom, of consequence, they can have the satisfaction of seeing one another,

* Son of Mary Ann Fontaine, who married Matthew Maury. He was ordained in London, in the year 1742.

though residents in the same colony. But it is some comfort that a time is coming, when we hope for a happy meeting with all who are dear to us, in a happier state, however separated at present by extensive tracts of land and sea.

But, to the map. My uncle Peter's habitation is in Charles City County, about two miles to the northward of James River, pretty near midway between Weynoke and Swineyards.

Mr. Isaac Winston, who married his daughter, resides in Henrico, on the south side of Chickahominy, about six miles from the meadow bridges.

My cousin Peter, with a view of reaping the full benefit of his place, has lately removed into a new county, called Halifax, between Stanton and Dan, the two main branches of Roanoke River, and lives close upon the southern bank of the former, some few miles above the mouth of Difficult, as near as I can guess about seven; for, as it is several years since I was on the spot, and only once, I am not perfect in the geography of that part of the country.

My brother Claiborne has seated himself among the Forks of Nottoway, in Lunenburg.

My mother lives among the head springs of Jack's creek, which empties into Pamunkey, on the north side.

As to myself, I am planted about two miles to the northeast of Walker's under the South West Mountains in Louisa, close by one of the head springs of the main northern branch of Pamunkey, which runs through my grounds—a very wholesome, fertile, and pleasant situation, where, I thank God, I enjoy more blessings and comforts than I deserve; and am as happy as a good member of society can be, while the society to which he belongs is in a suffering and calamitous condition, as you will perceive by my letter to my uncle John (to which I refer you) ours is at present. God only knows when it will be better with us ; as he only knows when and how the present contest between Great Britain and France will be decided, upon which depends the *all* not only of this, but of every other British plantation in America. And such seems to be the connection between the mother and children in this case, that the downfall of either must sooner or later be attended with that of the other.

Our people are loaded with debt and taxes. Money is much scarcer than it has been for many years. Our spring crops of wheat, barley, oats, and rye, have been ruined by an early drought. Our Indian corn, the main support of man and beast in this part of the world, has been so much hurt by a later drought, that I fear scarce enough will be made for the sustenance of our people, exclusive of our stocks, great numbers of which must in all probability perish this winter. Some of our neighboring colonies have likewise suffered in the same manner, and cannot assist us. So fertile, too, are our lands, that there is no such thing as a magazine for grain in all British America, which, as it has never known the want of bread, has never made any provision against it.

Our frontiers are daily ravaged by savages, and, worse than savages, papists, who, in conjunction with them, captivate and butcher our out-settlers, and have drove great numbers of them into the thicker inhabited parts, who, as they have left their farms and stocks, must be supported by us, who shall be scarcely able to support our own families. These, with many others that might be mentioned, are very melancholy and affecting considerations. However, dependence upon the supreme arbiter of all things, and resignation to the dispensations of infinite wisdom are, not only our duty and interest, but also our greatest comfort. Though storms and tempests rage without, it has been, and it shall be my study to keep all within calm and serene. Happy beyond expression are they who, when laboring under national or private calamities, can say with David's trust and confidence: *God is our refuge and strength, a very present help in time of trouble; therefore will we not fear though the earth be removed, and the mountains be cast into the midst of the sea.*

As to the controversy of the two crowns about limits, that perhaps has not so much alarmed us as it has many on your side of the Atlantic. It is true the balance is held by the Almighty, and he may elevate or depress which scale he pleases; but, were the race always to the swift, and the battle to the strong, our colonies would have little to apprehend from the exertion of all the power which France, especially in a general war, could spare to annoy us here on this continent. Her American strength, compared with ours, is quite contemptible in all respects but one, and that is, the wisdom and prudence with which it is directed. Canada is a very unfriendly clime; her soil in general unfruitful. Her inhabitants, in the year 1748, I am informed by persons who pretend to know, amounted to little more than forty thousand, and for that number the lands have never yet produced a sufficiency of bread. Slaves have never yet been found as industrious as the sons of liberty.

The British plantations, on the contrary, are both fertile and populous; so fertile, that even here in Virginia, where our main force is applied to the production of tobacco, the labor of one man in a tolerable year will feed eight, besides a competent number of hogs, sheep, horses, and cattle; and so

populous, that on the most modest calculation, His Majesty
has four hundred thousand men on this continent capable of
bearing arms, hardy and robust, and ready, whenever called
upon, to sacrifice life and fortune in his service and their
country's cause.   This strength wisely directed, would be
justly formidable to France.   But, it is our common misfortune, that there is no mutual dependence, no close connection
between these several colonies; they are quite disunited by
separate views and distinct interests; and like a bold and
rapid river, which, though resistless when included in one
channel, is yet easily resistible when subdivided into several
inferior streams and currents.   The Indians, though not very
polite, are politic enough to observe this defect in our polity,
and honest enough to tell us that we resemble a chain of sand.
A remedy for this evil, though obvious and practicable, and
recommended seriously by several of His Majesty's governors
here, the great men on your side of the water have not thought
proper to apply, from a principle in politics, which we on this
side of it think more obvious than wise or just.

The colonies, sensible of the manifest disadvantages of
their present unconnected state, have long wished for a coalition by means of a General Council formed by a certain number of deputies from each colony, to be presided over by a
person commissioned by His Majesty to act as his representative.   By this means, the whole strength of his subjects here
(who, except a small intermixture of papists, and some natives
of the northern part of your island, are behind none of their
fellow-subjects in loyalty) might be easily and successfully
exerted against any of the enemies of Great Britain in this
quarter of the world.

Though we are numerous, we are poor, and unable to raise

such large sums of money as would be required to defray the heavy expenses of war; and this is an evil which might also have been partly remedied, had not Great Britain chosen to buy of her European neighbors, her rivals in many respects, articles which she might have had from her children here, as good in kind, and at cheaper rates. But, poor as we are, we have already exerted ourselves to the utmost in the present dispute, and we still intend to do so, desirous to convince our common mother, that we are in truth, what we have often professed ourselves to be, her dutiful children. We want not men, but only money to pay them, and to pay for arms, ammunition, and a few engineers. We wish to see none of your officers, nor indeed regulars, unless they be better than what we have seen. As to any officers which may hereafter be sent over, officers of rank, I mean; if they make as free with the liberties of the people, and the constitutions of the several governments, as a late gentleman has attempted to do, and in some particulars has actually done, I am so far a prophet as to foretell, that neither your interests nor ours will be ever promoted by them. I believe it is the general opinion here, that, liberty and property once lost, a people have nothing left worth contending for. Had we been a people conquered and enslaved, a polite and generous conqueror would have treated us with less rudeness and insolence than the gentleman above hinted at (now no more) in the plenitude of his power, adventured to treat us Americans, which, I am almost confident nothing but an honest zeal to further by all means the common cause, prevented them from resenting in the same manner as they would the acts of a public enemy. But I will add nothing further on this head, lest I break through my above-mentioned resolve, of keeping all within calm and serene, which I am sensible would by no means recommend me to one of your calm and equable disposition.

You are already so well convinced what weight your opinion has with me, that, should I tell you, how much fonder I have been of that mode of instruction, on which I have providentially fallen, since it has obtained your approbation than I was before, I foresee, you would in your next charge me with saying what is superfluous. That, which you tell me you have so happily pursued in the education of my cousins, seems excellently calculated for answering all the good ends proposed. Although, perhaps, it may not be so proper for public instruction, especially in such extensive parishes as some in Virginia, yet I have so great an opinion of it for the education of a small community, that, God willing, I propose to make experiments of it in my own family, as soon as the winter evenings come on. I can well remember when it was my own misfortune to receive words without the proper ideas; which has doubtless been the misfortune of many others. And, in that case, as you remark, words are of but little use.

Hereabouts I thought to have closed, but remembering that I have not mentioned some places to my uncle John, which are either not set down in the map, or have received new names since the map was published, I imagine you will readily excuse the following directions.

In the map I perceive the name of a river erased, empty-ing itself into New River, and in its general tendency for some considerable distance, pointing towards the angle be-tween the south boundary of Pennsylvania and the west of Maryland, and thence through several meanders penetrating into the Alleghany mountains, between Spring Head and Laurel Thickets. The word erased I guess to be Yaughyaughgaine. If so, there was an error, which I imagine has been corrected here by the surviving compiler of the map. The river now described has since been discovered to be Monongahela, though wrongly planned off, for it discharges itself into the Ohio, in the latitude of about 30 deg. 48 min. N. On the point of land formed by the confluence of these, Fort Duquesne now stands, to the eastward of the latter, and the northward of the former. If you would have Monongahela correctly laid down, you are to erase the river, which I suspect is called Yaughyaughgaine, from about four miles below that branch of it which most directly points to the above-mentioned angle, quite down to New River, and then extend it in an almost straight course from where you began to erase quite down to the Ohio, in the above-mentioned latitude.

Yaughyaughgaine is a branch of Monongahela, and falls into it on the north side, lat. N. 39 deg. 43 min. and long. W. from Philadelphia 5 deg. 7 min., and, after having run about twenty-five miles almost east, divides into three branches called the Turkey Foot, one of which verges northerly, the other southerly, and the third easterly, but none reach so far as the main chain of hills. Between the branches of this and Monongahela, about forty miles back of the hills just mentioned, are the Great Meadows where our brave Washington was last year attacked by the French and Indians.

On the north side of Cohongoronto you will see Caicucktuck, since called Will's Creek, on the point of land formed by which and the river, on the western side of the creek, is built Fort Cumberland, from which the brave but unfortunate, and I believe I may add, imprudent General Braddock marched this summer against Duquesne, near which, my uncle John, as well as the public prints can inform you, how

17

shamefully he was defeated by a contemptible band of naked French and Indians.

As I believe you to be master of a good stock of patience, and as you have informed me of the extraordinary strength of your eyes, you will suspect I mean to put both to the test, if I go much farther; my pen, too, is almost foundered, my fingers cramped, and my stock of matter almost exhausted, so that, after desiring you to accept of our good wishes and respects, I shall take my leave of you for the present, with a declaration that I am, very sincerely, dear sir,

Your affectionate friend and dutiful nephew,

JAMES MAURY.

LOUISA COUNTY, FREDERICKSVILLE PARISH, *Jan.* 10, 1756.

DEAR SIR:—Your kind letter, bearing date 1st January, I have now sat down to answer, and must tell you I consider it as a New-Year's gift; and believe me, it is a very acceptable one.

It pleases me much that the directions sent you as to the habitations of our relations here, and as to some alterations requisite to be made in the map of Virginia to render it more complete had been intelligible. Had it not been for the present troubles, which have rendered it unsafe for our people to make such long peregrinations into the backwoods as they used to do before their commencement, many other inaccuracies would doubtless, ere this, have been discovered in the western parts of it, where the courses of many considerable streams, several ranges of hills, and other particulars, must have been laid down, partly on conjecture, and partly on but imperfect information, which will ever be the case with one who undertakes to publish a map of a country not yet thoroughly explored, or actually surveyed. Since the publication of that map, another has made its appearance in the world, much more extensive, as it comprehends all that part of the British American Empire that lies between Boston and the southern boundary of Virginia, the Territory of the six confederate Northern Indian nations, the river St. Lawrence almost from Quebec to its source, the various communications between that river and the lakes, and Ohio; also Ohio with its dependencies lower than the Falls ; and in short, the present scene of action as far as their Excellencies Shirley and Johnson are, and Braddoc was concerned, published by Lewis Evans, Esq., of Philadelphia, and engraven there, and therefore, in that respect clumsily executed. With it the author has published an instructive, curious, and useful pamphlet, explanatory not only of the map, but of many particulars, too, relative to the face and products, and natural advantages of the tract of territory which is the subject of it. The map is but small, not above half as large as Fry and Jefferson's, consequently crowded. Though both it and the pamphlet be liable to several exceptions, and I believe just ones, yet both are very useful in the main, and together, give an attentive peruser a clear idea of the value of the now contested lands and waters to either of the two competitor princes, together with a proof amounting to more than probability, that he of the two who shall remain master of Ohio and the Lakes at the end of the dispute, must, in the course of a few years, without an interposal of Providence to prevent it, become sole and absolute lord of North America, to which I will farther add as my own private opinion, that the same will one day or other render either Hudson's river at New-York, or Potomac river in Virginia, the grand emporium of all East Indian commodities. Marvel not at this, however surprising it may seem; perhaps, before I have done with you, you will believe it to be not entirely chimera.

When it is considered how far the eastern branches of that immense river, Mississippi, extend eastward, and how near they come to the navigable, or rather *canoeable* parts of the rivers which empty themselves into the sea that washes our shores to the east, it seems highly probable that its western branches reach as far the other way, and make as near approaches to rivers emptying themselves into the ocean to the west of us, the Pacific Ocean, across which a short and easy communication, short in comparison with the present route thither, opens itself to the navigator from that shore of the continent unto the Eastern Indies.

Before I go on, lest from the word *canoeable*, just now used, you should form but a contemptible idea of the navigation of a river which must be carried on by vessels slender and tottering as canoes, I must beg you will suspend sentence for a while, and give me time to inform you, that although one single canoe will carry but a small weight, yet nothing is more common than to see two of these tottering vehicles, when lashed together side by side with cords, or any other strong bandages, carrying down our upland streams eight or nine heavy hogsheads of tobacco at a time to the warehouses, rolled on their gunwales crossways, and secured against mov ing fore or aft by a small piece of wood drove under the bilge of the two extreme hogsheads; an almost incredible weight for such slender embarkations! But as they will bear such a burden, their slender contexture is an advantage; they draw but few inches water, move down a current with great velocity, and leave the waterman nothing but Palinurus's task to perform when going downwards; and when they return, two men will shove the canoes with poles as far against stream in one day, as four brisk watermen with oars can a boat that will carry the same burden, in two days. For this great improvement of inland navigation, we mountaineers are indebted to the late Reverend and ingenious Mr. Rose. But, to return: There are more than probable reasons for believing that the western branches of this river are no less extensive than its eastern branches. This is a common property of most rivers, and that it is of the Mississippi, I have the authority of one Mr. Cox, an English gentleman who, either some time before, or during the reign of King William III (in virtue of a charter granted by Charles I., if I remember right, for I speak without book, to his Attorney-General, Sir Robert Heath, constituting him the Lord-Proprietor of the lands and waters of the Mississippi, and afterwards transferred through several hands, till it fell into those of this gentleman), sailed up to its Great Falls near 1500 miles from its mouth, both took its soundings that whole distance, traced some of its most considerable branches on either side, and almost up to their sources, made a settlement and planted a colony upon it near midway that distance, if my memory fails me not, and published a map of it from his own and the Company's journals as far as those Falls; and above them, from what information he could collect from the savages. One of its western branches, he tells you, he followed through its various meanders for seven hundred miles (which, I believe, is called Missouri by the natives, or Red River, from the color of its waters), and then received intelligence from the natives that its head springs interlocked in a neighboring mountain with the head springs of another

river, to the westward of these same mountains, discharging
itself into a large lake called Thoyago, which pours its waters
through a large navigable river into a boundless sea, where,
they told him, they had seen prodigious large canoes, with
three masts, and men almost as fair as himself, if I mistake
not; for, as I have read a History of the travels of an Indian
towards those regions, as well as those of Mr. Cox, the reports
of the natives to both of them as to the large canoes are so
similar, that I perhaps may confound one with the other.
Mr. Cox's book, I imagine, is very scarce. I know of but one
copy in this colony, of which I had an accidental, and therefore a cursory view, about four years ago. It is a small
octavo volume, entitled Cox's Carolana, that country being
thus called from the Donor.

Now, sir, though this narrative hath in it something of the
romantic air of the voyager, yet the author's accounts of such
branches of that river, and such parts of that country, even as
high up as the latitude of Huron's Lake, and also his description of the extent, situation, shape, soundings and other pro-
perties of the Lakes now confessedly navigated by him, together with his character of the circumjacent lands, are said to
have been found just by late discoveries, as far as discoveries
have been made. And, if so, it is but reasonable to give
credit to what he tells us concerning others of its waters and
countries, into which, perhaps, no British subject has ever
since penetrated.

I presume the credit which Colonel Fry gave to Mr. Cox,
and his recommending these matters to the consideration of
the Governor and Council, gave birth to a grand scheme
formed here about three years ago. But this is only a conjecture, founded on my having seen that book at his house.

The scheme might have been formed in Great Britain, and was this. Some persons were to be sent in search of that river Missouri, if that be the right name of it, in order to discover whether it had any such communication with the Pacific Ocean: they were to follow that river if they found it, and make exact reports of the country they passed through, the distance they travelled, what sort of navigation those rivers and lakes afforded, &c., &c. And this project was so near being reduced into practice, that a worthy friend and neighbor of mine, who has been extremely useful to the Colony in the many discoveries he has made to the westward, was appointed to be the chief conductor of the whole affair, had, by order of their Honors, drawn up a list of all the necessary implements and apparatus for such an attempt, and an estimate of the expense, and was upon the point of making all proper preparations for setting out, when a sudden stop was put to the further prosecution of the scheme for the present, by a commencement of hostilities between this Colony and the French and their Indians, which rendered a passage through the interjacent nations with whom they are ever tampering, too hazardous to be attempted. This, I must observe to you, still remains a secret ; and to prevent its discovery to the enemy, in case the ship I write by should be taken, the person to whom I have recommended this packet has instructions to throw it overboard in time. However, you are at liberty to impart it to my uncle John, or to any other friend, of whose retentive faculty you can be as confident as I can be of yours. But to return once more. As there is such short and easy communication by means of canoe navigation, and some short portages between stream and stream, from the Potomac, from Hudson's River in New-York, and from the St. Lawrence to the Ohio, the two latter through the lakes, the former the best and shortest. As there also is good navigation, not only for canoes and batteaux, but for large flats, schooners and sloops down the Ohio into the Mississippi, should Cox's account be true of the communication of this last river with the South Sea, with only one portage, I leave you to judge of what vast importance such a discovery would be to Great Britain, as well as to her Plantations, which, in that case, as I observed above, must become the general mart of the European World, at least for the rich and costly products of the East, and a mart at which chapmen might be furnished with all those commodities on much easier terms than the tedious and hazardous, and expensive navigation to those countries can at present afford. This would supersede the necessity of going any more in quest of the North East passage, which, probably, if ever discovered, will also be productive of another discovery, that it lies in too inclement a latitude ever to be useful.

The discovery of a communication through this part of the continent with the South Sea, would not only be a nursery for our seamen, but would be instrumental in saving the lives of great numbers of them, under Heaven, the protectors of you and of us; who, poor fellows, drop off like rotten sheep by scorbutic disorders consequent upon such long voyages as that to the East Indies.

What an exhaustless fund of wealth would here be opened, superior to Potosi and all the other South American mines! What an extent of region! What a—! But no more. These are visionary excursions into futurity, with which I sometimes used to feast my imagination, ever dwelling with pleasure on the consideration of whatever bids fair for contri-

buting to extend the empire and augment the strength of our
mother island, as that would be diffusing liberty both civil
and religious, and her daughter Felicity the wider, and at the
same time be a means of aggrandizing and enriching this spot
of the globe, to which every civil and social tie binds me, and
for which I have the tenderest regard.

But, these pleasing expectations, if not entirely vanished,
are much weakened and suspended, till Heaven decide the
controversy between the two mighty monarchs now contending, in some sort, for the empire of the world.

Sir, as these lands now in dispute are so immensely valuable, what reason can you assign why most of the great men
with you, and why persons of the highest rank here, with very
few exceptions, either were, or seemed to be, quite unacquainted with its value till of late? I know the reason of it
here. Great men are too wise to be informed. They are too
indolent to look about them ; therefore their views and no-
tions of matters of this nature, are contracted within so nar-
row a compass, that they think nothing worth their inquiry
beyond their own reach. And, when men of inferior fortune,
but not therefore of inferior merit, have been animated by a
principle both of industry and public spirit, to search unknown forests and wilds, and made discoveries valuable and
important to the State, and imparted them to these epicurean
gods, they either discountenance, disregard, or discredit them.
This, in too many instances, has been the misfortune here,
though not in all, as you will perceive by the scheme communicated above, which is an instance to the contrary, provided
my conjecture be correct, that it was originally formed here.

On the other hand, our politic and sagacious, though turbulent neighbors, leave nothing unattempted to extend the

17*

territory, and heighten the glory of the Grand Monarch.
For, I am told that in Canada, to have made the tour of the
Lakes, and Ohio and Mississippi, is reckoned an essential
qualification, almost the *sine quâ non* to recommend young
gentlemen to any important posts, civil or military, under the
government, the advantages of which they are now reaping.
And happy would it have been for us if a tour of the same
nature had been an especial qualification for recommending
gentlemen to seats in the Supreme Court, while those regions
were equally accessible to us and to them. But now, these
gentlemen living in the lower parts of the country, within a
day's ride of Williamsburg, except one, and none of them
knowing any thing of the back country, our frontiers, from
this very reason, have been left thus naked and exposed.

Great are my hopes, that as the people both of Great
Britain and the Colonies seem now at length to be highly sensible of the mischiefs of our past lethargy and supineness, we
at last shall rouse, and let those bold intruders know they are
not thus insolently to encroach on the demesne of the British
Crown with impunity, nor peaceably allowed to wrest from us
a country, the present intrinsic value of which, together with
such future and contingent advantages as are in prospect, besides others out of view, of which yet the womb of time may
be productive, almost exceed the power of numbers to calcu-
late. Were I only to enumerate in a concise manner such of
the important benefits only of the country watered by the
Ohio, which is but one branch of the Mississippi, as occur
even to myself, who have not leisure to attend to matters of
that sort, my letter would swell to an enormous size. Your
own imagination, therefore, shall be permitted at leisure to
range this ample field which I have here been endeavoring to

open just to your view, or rather to bring you nearer the verge of. You will no doubt ruminate with some little satisfaction on the vast importance of that prodigious river Mississippi, which is said to take its rise on the south side of hills which empty the springs on their northern side into Hudson's Bay, which rolls its waters due south, through a great variety of latitudes, between those mountains and the Mexican Gulf, where it intermingles with the sea, and, in its course, waters a fat and fertile soil, which, from those various latitudes, with proper culture, is capable of bearing almost any of the productions of any climate or country.

Of this the French are well aware, as I collect from their insinuations to the various European powers, in order to weaken the interest of Great Britain among them, that the sole possession of North America which they apprehend would be the consequence of our keeping the Ohio and the Lakes without partner or rival, would put it in the power of England not only to grasp at, but seize universal monarchy in Europe, in process of time. And though I may be mistaken, yet I verily believe as much. However, I think the *Monsieurs* in this ship have been somewhat abandoned by their usual sagacity, since the powers of Europe, upon an impartial comparison of the past conduct of the two contending nations for some centuries back, may possibly form a conclusion but little favorable to them—a conclusion that should the English get such an opportunity, there is only a probability that they *might ;* but should the French get such an opportunity, there is an infallible certainty that they *would* make use of it ; and also that in the former case liberty, both civil and religious, but, in the latter, tyranny of both kinds would be more widely diffused and extensively propagated.

Your observations and criticisms, or rather hints on the probability of the children doing well without the parent, and on the coalition I mentioned in my last, appear to me extremely just, and have contributed to open my eyes. However, they are subjects that require to be treated with great delicacy, and like fenny lands, will only bear to be gently touched and slightly skimmed. God only knows the determinations of his own wise counsels, or what grand revolutions may be ripe for birth. Our business is patiently to wait their execution, and when executing or executed, humbly to acquiesce in them as wise, and just, and right, and best.

Our public affairs, as you will collect from mine to my uncle John, are not in such a state as blind mortals, who see but little beyond the present, would wish, or as a friend to his country, who attentively surveys them, any satisfaction.

You will therefore also see, that we are trying first one expedient and then another, to give them a more pleasing aspect, depending, I hope, on Providence, to crown them with success. For this purpose, several schemes have been recommended, and several projects seen the light, besides many more which probably have perished in their embryo state.

Among other adventurers of this sort in the aerial world who erect elaborate piles of building in the air, you will fear I have classed myself, from a letter which, at the request of some neighboring gentlemen, I wrote to one of His Majesty's Council here, of which I herewith send you a copy, with a view (since you seem inquisitive into our affairs) of letting you further into our present circumstances; from the contents of which, I imagine, you will discover what we think has certainly rendered them bad as they are, and what we believe to be the most effectual method to mend them. And in order to render that letter still more conducive to those purposes, I propose to add to it some explanatory annotations, if I can find time.

Although I have already given such a loose to my pen, I must not yet hold my hand. Your postscript enjoins me to give some certain directions where my mother lives. *Infandum jubes renovare dolorem!* Alas! she lives no more on earth! She, for several reasons, the most weighty of which was, to consult my brother's interest, determined to remove to Lunenburg, and spend the remainder of her days with him. But as he was not yet prepared for accommodating her there in a manner suitable to her age and many infirmities, she last fall accepted of an invitation from my uncle Peter, to make his house her home, while my brother was preparing for her reception. There, I doubt not, the great kindness of my aunt, and my uncle's vivacity, as well as agreeable and instructive conversation, contributed to her passing the time with much comfort and satisfaction for a while, that is, until the hour was come when she was summoned to remove home into a building of God, an house not made with hands, eternal in the heavens. That she now lives there, we have abundant reason to conclude, as from her deportment while in the body, so from the manner in which she relinquished that perishable tabernacle; of which my brother has given me some account in two letters. One informs me when, about three in the afternoon, on Tuesday the 30th of December last, after four days' illness; the other, how; the most important point, which please to take in his own words. "The manner of her death was much like my father's. She was first taken with an ague, which was followed by a fever, which, after three days' continuance, deprived her of the use of one side. When my aunt acquainted her she was dying, she lifted up her hands and thanked God that he had at length heard her prayers; and she spent her last moments in wholesome admonitions to all about her, and in blessing us her children and all that we have. Thus," adds my dear brother, " our dearest mother made a most glorious end ! which, God grant we may all have the happiness to make whenever we shall be called upon !" Amen ! say I; and so I am confident will you too. The grand business of life is to prepare for death, as that is preparing for eternity. Of all the acts of that piece, the last is the most important as well as the most difficult, and therefore requires spiritual succor to perform it well. My mother having performed her last act so well, is much comfort even in the midst of affliction. Death, it seems, was regarded by her in the true light, as a removal from a laborious and fatiguing post to a state of reward, for having so faithfully maintained it. This, surely, caused her consolations to abound and overflow in that hour of darkness, and has, I hope, had the same effect on her surviving friends, as far as self-love and other imperfections of human nature will permit.

The decease of a person of her character, if we listen to divine revelation and unbiassed reason, cannot be lamented on the person's own account, except we think it acting a rational and Christian part to grieve that the deceased has exchanged mortality and corruption for immortality and incorruption, and removed from the busy, perplexing and toilsome scenes of life to a permanent and immutable state of rest, and peace, and bliss. However, at first, it is true we are but too apt to do so ; prompted thereto partly by the tender affections of humanity, and partly by a very singular regard for ourselves, which makes us reluctant to part from the comfort and pleasure we used to enjoy in the conversation and society of the departed. But, though it is not avoidable to sorrow on such occasions, yet there are not only different degrees, but different kinds of sorrow, too ; and, were it not for the certain discoveries of life and immortality through the sacrifice of our Redeemer, which have been so clearly brought to light by the Gospel, the sorrow consequent on such a loss as we have sustained, in the death of that excellent and pious parent, must have been a sorrow destitute .of any alleviating intermixture of comfort. But, according to the tenor of the precious promises of the Gospel, and of her life, thanks be to the Adorable Trinity, we are not quite void of comfort, because thence we have hope, that she now rests in a much happier place than a changeable and fleeting world ; hope, that her felicity has no limit as to its duration, nor any as to its measure, except those of the enlarged capacity of such a creature as man in his glorified and exalted state ; and hope, that the virtuous soul is making a perpetual progress towards the perfection of its nature, going on from strength to strength, arriving from one degree of happiness to another, and shining for ever with still new accessions of glory and bliss ; in a word, we have hope, that we too, who are left behind, shall not therefore be excluded the heavenly Jerusalem, but though we may arrive somewhat later thither, shall, if our honest endeavors co-operate with our gracious Redeemer's all-sufficient merits, be at length admitted into God's presence, where alone is fulness of joys and pleasures for evermore. These are pleasing and triumphant considerations, and the basis of those glorious hopes which shoot enlivening rays of comfort through the blackest clouds, and dash even grief with some refreshing alloy of joy, but of a joy which perhaps it is easier to feel than describe,

and which, it may be, can be felt by none but those whose
minds have been happily tinctured with Christian principles,
and who, to a lively faith and hope in Christ have been taught
to add an absolute resignation to the will of God, our strictest
duty, our greatest wisdom, and truest magnanimity.

That in all the afflictions and adversities which may occur
in our passage through this vale of misery and tears, these
considerations and hopes may be your support and mine, and,
indeed, the support of all others who need it, is the constant
and fervent prayer of, dear sir,

Your dutiful nephew and affectionate friend,

JAMES MAURY.

P. S. I had like to have forgot to inform you, that, thank
God, myself and mine are all well, and that they unanimously
desire to be affectionately remembered to yourself, and every
branch of my uncle's family. I am glad to hear of the welfare of our relations in London; may the Lord continue it!

N. B. Evans's map, colored, together with the pamphlet,
were sold in Philadelphia at two Spanish dollars, 4s. 6d. of our
money.

To Mr. John Fontaine.

LOUISA COUNTY, FREDERICKSVILLE PARISH, *June 15th*, 1756.

DEAR SIR:—The receipt of your kind and agreeable letter
of 1st January, happened at a very seasonable juncture, as it
administered much comfort-where comfort was much wanting.
Comfortable and satisfactory, to the highest degree, it is;
when we cannot see, yet to hear from those with whom we are
connected by the endearing ties of blood and friendship, ties

which, I trust, mutually link our hearts together now, and will continue so to do, till we meet in that more perfect, and, as my uncle Moses terms it, that inseparable and immutable state, where all imperfections will be done away, and· every impediment to a more intimate intercourse be removed. Hopes and views of this sort are most reviving cordials to a mind laboring under the pressure either of public or private afflictions, and Providence has been pleased to afford me an opportunity of proving them to be so by my own experience in both.

The private affliction, named in my letter to my uncle Moses, is one in which you will both be no small sharers; which, though in truth very deep, is far from incurable, as the same Hand that gavè it has graciously furnished means of cure, and poured healing balsam into the wound.

As to the other kind of afflictions, they are still incumbent, and when they will be removed, God only knows. I hope I am resigned to the will of the great arbiter of all things, yet I cannot remain an unconcerned spectator of the calamities of my country. But, lest you should suspect me of being uneasy without just reason, I shall give you as just and succinct an account as I can of the present state of affairs in this once flourishing and happy colony.

You may remember, I told you last year, the drought had been of long continuance and threatened famine; but the wise and gracious Disposer of all things, who, in the midst of judgment remembers mercy, mitigated things so far as to afford a sufficiency of bread for the life of man, but, in general, very little more, so that vast numbers of stock, of all kinds, perished, notwithstanding the uncommon clemency of last winter.

Taxes on taxes are multiplied, and, though it be a necessary, it is a heavy burden.

Besides genteel presents to the officers who behaved well last campaign at Monongahela, and a gratuity of £5 per man to every common soldier of our own regiment who survived the action, and pensions or presents to the disabled and to the widows of the slain, which amounted to a round sum; and besides levying money to pay the owners for upwards of one thousand hogsheads of tobacco, burnt in the warehouses of Bolling's Point, £40,000 was voted for His Majesty's service and our own defence, then, and £65,000 more this spring. This, as little or no tobacco was made last summer, falls heavily on the lower ranks of people, especially, as tobacco is the only medium of raising money, and as they generally cultivate the meanest lands, so were their crops proportionally short. Of this the legislature has been so sensible, that an act, to continue in force one year, was last fall passed, indulging the people by allowing them to pay off their public dues to the secretary, the county court clerks, the clergy and other public creditors (which ever before had been payable in tobacco), in money, at the rate of two pence per pound. The current market value has, hitherto, been twenty-six shillings per hundred, so that the law saves to those who have tobacco to sell, four pounds thirteen shillings and four pence per thousand, while it deducts the same from the annual salaries and revenues of the creditors. In my own case, who am entitled to upwards of seventeen thousand weight of tobacco per annum, the difference amounts to a considerable sum. However, each individual must expect to share in the misfortunes of the community to which he belongs.

Furthermore, to enable people to pay their taxes and debts, paper money has been issued, which, in every colony where it has been recurred to, has been attended with many evils, one of which is draining out the remains of their specie.

Notwithstanding all this, our people pay their taxes with much more cheerfulness than could reasonably be expected from those whose necks were never heretofore accustomed to such a yoke, and who have had the mortification to see those contributions, large compared with their circumstances, surprisingly misapplied, and, through a complication of most egregious blunders, promotive of scarce one good effect to our country. Of these blunders, it may suffice to remark, that, notwithstanding the sums levied and expended, and the readiness of the people to pay their taxes and risk their persons in the defence of their country, and vindication of the insults offered to the crown, yet, ever since the tragical event last July, on the banks of the Monongahela, our frontiers have been ravaged and dispeopled, great quantities of the stock of the back inhabitants driven off by the French and their Indians to Duquesne. Fire, sword and perpetual alarms have surrounded them, persons of every age and sex have fallen a prey to the barbarians, and, in short, the most shocking outrages perpetrated on the western settlements of this colony, and our two next neighbors to the northward. By these means, our frontiers have been contracted in many places 150 miles, and still are drawing nearer and nearer to the centre.

To what secondary causes all this has been imputable, you will discover from a letter which the persuasion of some of my friends induced me to write to one of our honorables, early in the spring, of which I have sent my uncle Moses a copy; whence you will collect what methods we think most proper (and ours is the general opinion) for putting a stop to the further progress of those evils, and guarding against the like

in time to come. In furtherance of these ends, I drew up,
and, by means of my acquaintance, dispersed in the three frontier and five contiguous counties, petitions to the General Assembly before its last session, praying, that such a line of forts
might be built, and such an Indian factory established. To
these a favorable hearing was given, and a bill framed according to them, as far as relates to the chain of forts. But before
this bill had gone through the several formalities requisite to
constitute it a law, an unlucky clause was tacked to it, which,
it is to be feared, will destroy every good effect that we had
reason to hope for from it; a clause incorporating five hundred men, now levying for the construction and defence of
these forts, into the Virginia regiment; rather than submit to
which, where the character of the regiment is known, people
will pay any fines. The five hundred men are to be raised by
a draught upon the young men of each county, who, on refusal to go upon duty are obliged to deposit £10 on the drum-
head, by way of fine.

Such was the treatment which that unfortunate regiment
received last campaign from the commander in chief, that no
person of any property, family or worth has since enlisted in it,
and the Governor has filled up the vacant commissions and the
new companies with raw, surly and tyrannical Scots, several of
them mere boys from behind the counters of the factors here ;
thus, that regiment, from an exceedingly good one, has degenerated into a most insignificant and corrupt corps. Whence, I apprehend, the salutary purposes of that act will be defeated, as
the above complement of men will generally be made up of
worthless vagrants, servants just out of servitude, and convicts
bought with the fines paid by recusants ; men utterly unacquainted with the woods and the use of fire arms, and, for

these reasons, were there no other, unfit to be sent against
Indians.

Besides this, feuds and dissensions still subsist between
different branches of the legislature.

To crown our misfortunes, we have been informed that
such accounts of our temper and disposition in this colony
have been transmitted to England, by a certain person, that
the Ministry suppose we want nothing but ability and opportunity to attempt shaking off allegiance to the Most Gracious
Prince, that, peradventure, ever adorned the British throne.
This is a vile calumny, for the calumniator well knows that we
have shed our blood with the utmost cheerfulness, and we have
paid taxes freely and willingly in support of the common cause,
equally with any of our sister colonies, in proportion to our
numbers and wealth.

I fear nothing good will be done with all the money we
have raised, unless affairs shall take quite a different turn on
the arrival of the Earl of Loudoun, whom private letters, as
well as public prints, give us reason daily to expect in his government.

Besides augmenting our regiment to one thousand men, in
the fall, and endeavoring to augment it further, now, to fifteen
hundred men, levying monies and guarding our frontiers, the
Honorable Peter Randolph and the Honorable William Byrd,
two of the Council, have been sent ambassadors to the Cherokees, and have concluded a treaty between this government
and that nation; obliging us, on the one hand, to build and
garrison a good and sufficient fort in their country, for the
protection of their women and children, which a body of men
are now on their march to perform; and that nation, on the
other part, is to furnish us with five hundred warriors, this

summer. This will probably afford some security to our frontiers; and, it gives a general satisfaction, for all now seem sensible, of what only some few were sensible, till of late, that Indians are the best match for Indians.

It is a very pleasing consideration to observe the general spirit of patriotism, and the resentment against the common enemy, which seems to have diffused itself through every rank of men. The common people have lately given proof of it. This spring, upon advice that some thousands of French and Savages were approaching our frontiers, in their northern quarter, the government thought it necessary to make a draught of the militia of ten counties, contiguous to the three frontier counties, with orders to rendezvous at the town of Winchester, otherwise called Frederick, there to receive further orders from Col. Washington; and, although it was at a season of the year when men could least be spared from home, and, indeed, when a long continuance on duty must have blasted all expectations of a crop in those who had no slaves to labor for them; yet great numbers voluntarily offered themselves, and marched with the utmost alacrity to meet the enemy, till they had advanced as far as the place of rendezvous, where the alarm appeared to be false. I am fully convinced, had there been occasion, they would have followed *their own officers*, with the utmost spirit to Duquesne, or any other place; if I may form a judgment from what I then saw, for I was present, having, at the request of the detachment from this county, accompanied them as chaplain.

Upon its being determined, in a council of war, held there by Col. Washington and the militia field officers, that only a certain quota of the militia of each county should be left behind, amounting in the whole to only four hundred and four

men, the quota of each county to be commanded by a lieutenant, and two sergeants of its own; the bare suspicion that
some of the officers of the regiment were to act over them as
captains, had almost the same effect on the men as a spark of
fire on a train of gunpowder. It raised such a fermentation,
as Col. Washington's positive declaration that they should
not be commanded by any officers but these lieutenants, could
scarce allay.

Although I have already been so prolix in these two letters,
yet, lest you should have reason to charge me with harping only
on the elegiac string, I must further inform you, which I do
with great pleasure, that the bountiful Giver of all good things,
has been pleased to cheer our spirits, under our misfortunes,
with a prospect of almost unparalleled plenty and abundance
for the current year. The last year's scarcity has made us
much more provident than usual. Much larger fields of wheat,
barley and rye last fall, and of oats this spring, have been
sown, and much larger quantities of ground planted with Indian corn, than has ever, heretofore, been known. And, although it be too early in the season to form any judgment of
the latter, yet, as the former will, in a few days, call for the
sickle and scythe some weeks sooner than usual, which is an
eminent instance of divine goodness, we can form a very good
judgment of them; and unless some disaster befalls them between this and harvest, I may venture to say that more wheat,
barley, rye and oats will be made here this year, than perhaps
has ever been made in any two or three preceding years together; for, besides the quantities sown, the winter and spring
have been so unprecedentedly seasonable, that the earth produces
by handfuls. And as we have known the evil of a scarcity,
though not want of bread, it is to be hoped the approaching

plenty will inspire us with due sentiments of gratitude to Him who sends us rain from heaven and fruitful seasons, and makes the valleys stand so thick with corn, that, in the Psalmist's bold and significant metaphor, they laugh and sing.

The wise man's general remark, that, When goods increase they are increased that eat them, is applicable to my own particular case, my wife having lately increased our family with a daughter, whom we have named Elizabeth.

As to affairs in the north, they continue much as they were left after Sir William Johnston's victory over the Baron, in our favor on the whole, but not so much so, but that our miscarriage there would give a turn to the scales.

Should the forces expected in America with Lord Loudoun be destined for this quarter, and the officers who command them have learned, from General Braddock's disaster, not to be too conceited of their own ability, and not to form too contemptible an opinion of the enemy, I think, if they arrive safe, they, in conjunction with some Pennsylvania, Maryland and Virginia troops, might make a successful attempt against Duquesne this summer and fall, and thereby largely contribute to forward the success of the general plan.

With my hearty prayers for the welfare of the whole little community at Cwm Castle, I am, with very great regard, dear sir,

Your affectionate nephew,
JAMES MAURY.

To Mr. Moses Fontaine.

Louisa County, Fredericksville Parish, *June* 11, 1759.

Respected Sir:—Yours of the 14th September, 1758, with the glasses which you have been so kind as to procure for me, and also the pamphlets, came safe to hand some months ago. Accept of my sincere thanks for the trouble you have taken to oblige me herein.

I am glad the manuscript afforded you any satisfaction. My reason for not sending it to the press without consulting those gentlemen, was, that I had cause to believe their influence necessary to procure it a passage into the world, for want of which many useful things had been suppressed, and also a persuasion founded on their usual conduct and general character, that they would have readily undertaken and heartily engaged in the business. Had I not taken this for granted, I should at first have sent it to some other press, for at that time I imagined it might have some little tendency to open the eyes of such as wanted to see. But at present I know not of what service it could be.

Many persons who have had better opportunities of information in such matters than myself, and whose rank and station in life give more weight to what they recommend than any proposals of mine could be expected to have; have both here and with you, with invincible force of argument, recommended those, or such like measures for our mutual security against the French intrigues and encroachments in America, both at present and in time to come. And Providence has been pleased of late to give so favorable a turn to public affairs in almost every department of the war, that I am in hopes those salutary measures will be carried into execution,

18

if not before, yet immediately after the conclusion of a peace, and such an one as you mention, solid, honorable, and lasting, may be no very distant event. For, blessed be the only Giver of victory for it, affairs both on your side of the Atlantic and ours wear a face very different from what they did some time ago, and much more pleasing than perhaps the most sanguine of us all could then expect they would at the present time.

At our entrance on the war, we indeed seemed possessed of every advantage and means that could conduce to victory, and thence were willing to conceive hopes of seeing our enemy well nigh crushed, almost before completely prepared for combat. But yet our counsels, we had the mortification to observe, were all frustrate, our enterprises unprosperous, and our arms almost every where disgraced.

Near our own doors, a well-appointed army of disciplined troops fled before a contemptible band of savages and ragamuffins, and stained Monongahela's memorable stream with British blood ; and not far from yours, Mahon was wrested from the nation in a manner which will greatly surprise posterity. In short, every attempt to annoy the enemy or secure ourselves miscarried, notwithstanding a great inequality of strength in our favor in those quarters of the world where the war chiefly centred.

None, I believe, but David's fool, and such as he, will deny this to be the Lord's doing. And, although in many cases, his judgments, and the reasons of them are unsearchable and impenetrable by short-sighted mortals, yet here, methinks, they do not seem inexplicable. Had not too many of us, think you, been under the influence of that spirit which prompted Mezentius, in the poet, before combat

to boast, *Dextra mihi Deus et telum quod missile libro,* and
the proud Assyrian, in the prophet, after victory to vaunt.
*By the strength of my hand I have done it, and by my wis
dom?* If so, the Great Superintendent of the Universe
seemed concerned to exhibit some new proof that He doeth
according to his will, not only in the armies of heaven, but
also among the inhabitants of the earth.   Accordingly he chas
tised that insolent spirit in us, as he did in the two instances
just given; and as he sooner or later does in all others of
the like sort, consistently with that dreadful sentence, *Cursed
be the man who trusteth in man, and maketh flesh his arm,
and whose heart departeth from the Lord.* But whatever
were his reasons for chastising, he has now graciously interfered to rescue from destruction his heritage, humbled and
penitent, I hope, and sensible that without his blessing all
human force is vain; for our enemies, who then filled us with
terror, have since been themselves dismayed.   Our efforts
have reduced them, instead of an offensive, to act a defensive
part.   Their naval power has received severe and fatal checks.
Their commerce is not only greatly encumbered, but probably
well nigh ruined.   Their coasts have been perpetually alarmed
by repeated descents, and the horrors of war have been turned
loose to rage within their own borders, both in Europe and
here.   The armies of the Grand Monarch once, nay of late,
the terror of Europe, have been surprisingly mortified and reduced, nay, almost annihilated, as effectually, though not so
suddenly, as those of his brother Sennacherib.   The loss of
Mahon has been abundantly compensated by the acquisition
of Louisburg, which puts us in possession of the keys of Canada.   Frontenac, too, the gate from Canada into the lakes,
and their rich and extensive environs, is an important as it

was a cheap conquest. Niagara, too, the shortest and best communication between Canada and Louisiana, is said to be ours, though this I doubt cannot be depended on. However, it is confidently said Colonel Gage marched with two thousand men against it, upwards of two months ago, and has taken it.

Guadaloupe, too, in the West Indies, is no mean acquisition; and I am in hopes, at the present date, the British cannon, in the West Indies, on Lake Champlain, and up St. Lawrence, are venting the resentments of an injured nation against the fortresses of Martinico, Crown Point, and Quebec. May this series of successes produce in our hearts such effects as they ought! May they lead us to repent and constrain us to obey.

I can give you no account of our families here, only that my brother is concerned in victualling the troops stationed on the south-western frontier of this colony, and that by his prudence and activity, and his spirited conduct as Lieutenant of Halifax county, he has greatly contributed to keep the remote inhabitants from abandoning their habitations, and thereby done no small service to his country!—that my cousin Peter this spring lost a son with the nervous fever, and that my cousin James, son of my uncle Francis by his second marriage, has had the misfortune to lose a fine parcel of slaves, which came by his mother, taken from him by a suit at law.

The measles, now epidemic almost all over this continent, has gone through my family lately (only two or three having escaped), without any other inconvenience than retarding our plantation business so much at a critical season of the year, that our crops and harvest are likely to suffer. The smallpox, too, is near us in some places.

My wife and family desire to be respectfully remembered to you.

> I am, dear sir,
> > Yours affectionately and dutifully.
> > > JAMES MAURY.

———

To Mr. Moses Fontaine.

LOUISA COUNTY, FREDERICKSVILLE PARISH, *June 19th*, 1760.

DEAR SIR:—Yours from Cwm Castle of Nov. 30th came to hand some few days ago.

It has escaped my memory if you before advertised me of your intention to quit London.

My conjectures concerning the effect of your exchanging the gross air of that immensely populous city for the purer air you now breathe, I perceive were not quite without foundation. Indeed, they were in good measure built on what I have had occasion to observe here. Persons who have been either born in the mountainous country hereabouts, or resided in it long enough to acquire what we call a mountain constitution, on their removal to the flatter lands and the large rivers, are infallibly unhealthy there, however healthy and robust they used to be here, so that, in the course of a few years, an athletic habit degenerates and dwindles into one valetudinary and cachectic. But when driven thence to this part of the country again, which is beautifully diversified with Milton's grateful variety of hill and dale, you would be surprised to see how suddenly they recover their wonted strength and vigor. I suppose the great difference between the two airs to be the cause which produces these effects.

In the lower parts of the country, near the large rivers,
the lands are flat and the declivity towards the sea-coast much
more gradual than here. Hence, the water there descends
with less rapidity, and is not so pure ; hence, too, there are
many more stagnant collections of it, which may be considered
as so many seminaries of disease. On the rivers, too, are extensive tracts of marshy land, many parts of which are so miry
that, without exaggerating, you may with a light impulse of
the hand, bury a ten-foot rod in a perpendicular direction.
These are covered with a luxuriant growth of grass and weeds
in summer, and with a thick coat of dry sedge in winter ; so
that, except in the spring, when these places are set on fire,
they are utterly impenetrable to sun or air, excluding the salu-
brious blasts of the one and the purifying rays of the other,
and remain ever fraught with noxious and morbific particles.
Hence arise fogs, prodigiously dense, impregnated with unwholesome vapors, arising from these sloughs, and extremely
offensive to the smell, which often continue undispersed till
nine o'clock in the morning, by which probably the purity and
salubrity of the air is impaired. From the evils of these
treasuries of disease we mountaineers are happily exempt. The
descent of our lands is so quick, that morasses are scarcely
known among us, and the rapidity of our waters so great that
none of them have leisure to stagnate. Now, the difference
between the air of London and that of the country may possibly be as great as between that of a lowland and mountainous
situation here ; for, methinks it is highly probable, that the
smoke and filth of that prodigious city may infect and pollute
the air as much as the exhalations from our marshy grounds.
Whether these speculations be just or not, I, who never made
philosophy my study, will not undertake to decide, but it is

notorious that many constitutions, which had been so impaired
by the unwholesome air of the lower country, that the physician's art could neither mend nor restore, have surprisingly recovered their vigor by a change of situation. May your removal to rural retreats and sylvan scenes be attended with the
like happy effects!

A sound mind in a sound body, with a competent share of
the comforts of life, is doubtless the highest pitch of happiness
to which a reasonable man could aspire, till the desirable period arrive when He, who has so wonderfully connected and
interwoven in one frame two such different and heterogeneous
principles as flesh and spirit, shall think fit to dissolve the
union, in order to that more perfect and glorious re-union
which we expect to take place on that awful day, when this
corruptible shall put on incorruption, and this mortal, immortality, and when Death, that scourge of guilt and enemy of
our nature, shall be triumphantly swallowed up in victory.

Your command to let you know the distance and bearings
between the several branches of our family and Williamsburg,
and also between each other, I will execute as well as I am
able, without the assistance of a pair of dividers, which I have
not at present by me.

Mr. Fontaine, if I mistake not, lives near Bear Swamp,
close on the southern branch of the North Anna, a northern
branch of Pamunkey River, about 75 miles northwest from
Williamsburg, and about 56 miles almost due east from hence,
in the county of Hanover.

Mr. Claiborne is seated in the forks of Nottoway, in the
county of Lunenburg, between ninety and a hundred miles
distant from Williamsburg, by a course about two points to

the southward of west, and about the same distance hence in a direction somewhat to the eastward of south.

My brother, as well as I remember, lives on the waters of Difficult Creek, near the extremity of that point of land where the great river Roanoke is formed by the confluence of the Dan and Stanton, one hundred and twenty miles from the metropolis, in a course somewhat to the southward of west, in the county of Halifax, and a hundred miles at least from hence, a little to the westward of south.

The rector of Fredericksville is planted close under the southwest mountains, one hundred and thirty miles nearly northwest from Williamsburg.

To the article of public affairs, I have little to add to what has been said in my letters to uncle John and to Mr. Torin. However, it may not be unacceptable to subjoin, that General Stanwix, who last year commanded at Pittsburg, has, by his singular industry and application, and by prosecuting the works during the whole winter, as far as the rigors of the season would allow, completely finished a large and strong fortification there. Instead of wasting time in those pleasures and diversions which officers commonly indulge in during the winter, this gentleman continued at his post, and carried on the works with assiduity and vigor, and left not the wilds of Ohio till late in the spring, when he returned to Philadelphia in order to embark for Great Britain, where I hope his great merit will meet with the approbation, and applause, and grateful acknowledgment of his country and his Royal Master.

The command of the Southern army, since his departure, devolves on General Monkton, an officer, universally esteemed by those who have been witnesses of his spirited conduct on many occasions since the commencement of the war. At the time that the behavior of Braddock, and some other British officers, had caused very unfavorable ideas to be attached to the words—English officer—this gentleman, though only Lieu-tenant Colonel, was respected wherever he was known. By this date, I expect, he is on the point of embarking, either from Oswego or Niagara, on an expedition against Detroit, a French fortress, built on the western side of the strait, through which the upper lakes pay their constant tribute to Erie. This place is otherwise called Pontchartrain. Should he succeed, he is to advance to St. Sulpice, situate on the strait through which the Lake Michigan discharges its waters into Huron. Thence, if all go smoothly, and summer enough be left, a chain of forts is to be extended to the Mississippi, and all the most impor-tant portages and communications between the waters of the Mississippi, and the Lake Michigan, secured quite into Mis-sissippi. Whether this intelligence be authentic, I know not. The plan, however, seems to be good, pleasing at least to myself, as it exactly falls in with my own notion ; and, to me it appears practicable, as, without some uncommon disaster, the enemy, there, must submit to our superiority of strength. It is excellently calculated to prevent the augmentation of the French power here, to finish the glorious work of stopping up all the avenues of communication between their northern and southern settlements, and to open a most lucrative trade with nations scarce ever heard of by the American English. And. should the armaments, which, your prints tell us, are destined against their settlement of Louisiana, also triumph, Great Britain will then be in possession of what will one day prove a more copious source of wealth than all the Mexican and Peruvian mines.

The honorable and successful issue of the war, will, proba-

18*

bly, put it out of the power of any thing but our iniquities to hurt us; though, according to the course of things, it may minister material for cherishing those vices, which, alas! have already grown to a gigantic and enormous size. So that we may possibly, at length, fall under the Psalmist's malediction, and see those very things, which should have been for our wealth, by our own perverse abuse of them, unhappily converted into an occasion of falling. This is certainly an alloy that embitters the pleasure resulting from prospects of temporal greatness, to feel that all the enjoyments and possessions of this world carry in them, what, though not necessarily, yet, eventually, becomes a temptation to evil. And, therefore, you may believe that I, very heartily, join with you in praying that such a wonderful series of successes may not produce the unnatural fruits it sometimes does, but those, which in reason, and justice and duty it ought to do.

My family desires to be particularly remembered to you, and as for myself, I am, respected sir,

Your dutiful nephew and affectionate friend,

JAMES MAURY.

To the Rev. John Camm.

December 12th, 1763.

DEAR SIR:—Now that I am somewhat more at leisure, than when I wrote to you by Major Winston, from Hanover, some few days ago, I have sat down to give you the best account I can of the most material passages in the trial of my cause against the Collectors in that Court, both to satisfy your own curiosity, and to enable the lawyer, by whom it is to be managed in the General Court, to form some judgment

of its merits.   I believe, sir, you were advised from Nov'r
Court, that the Bench had adjudged the twopenny act to be
no law; and that, at the next, a jury, on a writ of inquiry,
were to examine whether the Plaintiff had sustained any damages, and what.   Accordingly, at December Court, a select
jury was ordered to be summoned; but, how far they who
gave the order, wished or intended it to be regarded, you may
judge from the sequel.   The Sheriff went into a public room,
full of gentlemen, and told his errand.   One excused himself
(Peter Robinson of King William) as having already given
his opinion in a similar case.   On this, as a person then present told me, he immediately left the room, without summoning
any one person there.   He afterwards met another gentleman
(Richard Sq. Taylor) on the green, and, on his saying he was
not fit to serve, being a churchwarden, he took upon himself
to excuse him, too, and, as far as I can learn, made no further
attempts to summon gentlemen.   These, you'll say, were but
feeble endeavors to comply with the directions of the Court
in that particular.   Hence, he went among the vulgar herd.
After he had selected and set down upon his list about eight
or ten of these, I met him with it in his hand, and on looking
over it, observed to him that they were not such jurors as the
Court had directed him to get, being people of whom I had
never heard before, except one, whom, I told him, he knew to
be a party in the cause, as one of the Collector's Securities,
and, therefore, not fit for a juror on that occasion.   Yet this
man's name was not erased.   He was even called in Court,
and, had he not excused himself, would probably have been
admitted.   For, I cannot recollect, that the Court expressed
either surprise or dislike that a more proper jury had not been
summoned.   Nay, though I objected against them, yet, as

Patrick Henry (one of the Defendant's lawyers) insisted they
were honest men, and, therefore, unexceptionable, they were
immediately called to the book and sworn.   Three of them.
as I was afterwards told, nay, some said four, were Dissenters
of that denomination called *New Lights*, which the Sheriff,
as they were all his acquaintance, must have known.   Messrs.
Gist and McDowall, the two most considerable purchasers in
that county, were now called in to prove the price of tobacco, and sworn.   The testimony of the former imported, that,
during the months of May and June, 1759, tobacco had cur-
rently sold at 50s. per hundred, and that himself, at or about
the latter end of the last of those months, had sold some hundreds of hhds. at that price, and, amongst the rest, one hundred to be delivered in the month of August, which, however,
were not delivered till September.   That of the latter only
proved, "That 50s. was the current price of tobacco that
season."   This was the sum of the evidence for the Plaintiff.
Against him, was produced a receipt to the Collector, to the
best of my remembrance in these words : "Received of Thomas
Johnson, Jun'r, at this and some former payments, £144, current money, by James Maury."   After the lawyers on both
sides had displayed the force and weight of the evidence, pro
and con. to their Honors, the jurors, and one of those who appeared for the Defendants had observed to them that they must
find (or *if they must find*, I am not sure which, but think the
former) for the Plaintiff, but need not find more than one farthing ; they went out, and, according to instruction (though
whether according to evidence or not, I leave you to judge), in
less than five minutes brought in a verdict for the Plaintiff, one
penny damages.   Mr. Lyons urged, as the verdict was contrary to
evidence, the jury ought to be sent out again.   But no notice

was, taken of it, and the verdict admitted without hesitation by
the Bench.   He then moved to have the evidence of Messrs.
Gist and McDowell recorded, with as little effect.   His next
motion, which was for a new trial, shared the same fate.   He
then moved it might be admitted to record, "that he had made
a motion for a new trial, because he considered the verdict contrary to evidence, and that the motion had been rejected ;" which,
after much altercation, was agreed to.   He lastly moved for an
appeal, which, too, was granted.   This, sir, as well as I can remember, is a just and impartial narrative of the most material
occurrences in the trial of that cause.   One occurrence more,
tho' not essential to the cause, I can't help mentioning, as a
striking instance of the loyalty, impartiality and attachment of
the Bench to the Church of England in particular, and to religion at large.   Mr. Henry, mentioned above (who had been
called in by the Defendants, as we suspected, to do what I some
time ago told you of), after Mr. Lyons had opened the cause,
rose and harangued the jury for near an hour.   This harangue
turned upon points as much out of his own depth, and that of
the jury, as they were foreign from the purpose ; which it
would be impertinent to mention here.   However, after he had
discussed those points, he labored to prove "that the act of
1758 had every characteristic of a good law ; that it was a
law of general utility, and could not, consistently with what
he called the original compact between King and people, stip-
ulating protection on the one hand and obedience on the other,
be annulled."   Hence, he inferred, "that a King, by disallowing
Acts of this salutary nature, from being the father of his
people, degenerated into a Tyrant, and forfeits all right to his
subjects' obedience."   He further urged, "that the only use
of an Established Church and Clergy in society, is to enforce

obedience to civil sanctions, and the observance of those which
are called duties of imperfect obligation; that, when a Clergy
ceases to answer these ends, the community have no further
need of their ministry, and may justly strip them of their ap-
pointments; that the Clergy of Virginia, in this particular
instance of their refusing to acquiesce in the law in question,
had been so far from answering, that they had most notoriously
counteracted, those great ends of their institution; that,
therefore, instead of useful members of the state, they ought
to be considered as enemies of the community; and that, in
the case now before them, Mr. Maury, instead of countenance,
and protection and damages, very justly deserved to be punished with signal severity." And then he perorates to the following purpose, "that excepting they (the jury) were disposed
to rivet the chains of bondage on their own necks, he hoped they
would not let slip the opportunity which now offered, of making
such an example of him as might, hereafter, be a warning to
himself and his brethren, not to have the temerity, for the
future, to dispute the validity of such laws, authenticated by
the only authority, which, in his conception, could give force to
laws for the government of this Colony, the authority of a
legal representative of a Council, and of a kind and benevolent and patriot Governor." You'll observe I do not pretend
to remember his words, but take this to have been the sum
and substance of this part of his labored oration. When he
came to that part of it where he undertook to assert, "that a
King, by annulling or disallowing acts of so salutary a nature,
from being the Father of his people degenerated into a Tyrant,
and forfeits all right to his subjects' obedience;" the more sober
part of the audience were struck with horror. Mr. Lyons
called out aloud, and with an honest warmth, to the Bench,

"That the gentleman had spoken treason," and expressed his
astonishment "that their worships could hear it without emotion, or any mark of dissatisfaction." At the same instant,
too, amongst some gentlemen in the crowd behind me, was a
confused murmur of Treason, Treason! Yet Mr. Henry went
on in the same treasonable and licentious strain, without interruption from the Bench, nay, even without receiving the
least exterior notice of their disapprobation. One of the jury,
too, was so highly pleased with these doctrines, that, as I was
afterwards told, he every now and then gave the traitorous de-
claimer a nod of approbation. After the Court was adjourned,
he apologised to me for what he had said, alleging that his sole
view in engaging in the cause, and in saying what he had, was
to render himself popular. You see, then, it is so clear a point
in this person's opinion, that the ready road to popularity here,
is, to trample under foot the interests of religion, the rights
of the church, and the prerogative of the Crown. If this be
not pleading for the "assumption of a power to bind the King's
hands," if it be not asserting "such supremacy in provincial
Legislatures" as is inconsistent with the dignity of the Church
of England, and manifestly tends to draw the people of these
plantations from their allegiance to the King, tell me, my dear
sir, what is so, if you can. Mr. Cootes, merchant on James
River, after Court, said "he would have given a considerable
sum out of his own pocket, rather than his friend Patrick
should have been guilty of a crime, but little, if any thing
inferior to that which brought Simon Lord Lovatt to the
block;" and justly observed that he exceeded the most se-
ditious and inflammatory harangues of the Tribunes of old
Rome.

My warmest wishes and prayers ever attend you. And

besides these there is little else in the power of, my dear Camm,

Your affectionate

J. MAURY.

———

To Mr. John Fontaine.

December 31, 1765.

—— But what hath given a most general alarm to all the colonists on this continent, and most of those in the islands, and struck us with the most universal consternation that ever seized a people so widely diffused, is a late Act of the British Parliament, subjecting us to a heavy tax, by the imposition of stamp duties on all manner of papers required in trade, law, or private dealings; on pamphlets, newspapers, almanacs, calendars, and even advertisements; and ordaining that the causes of delinquents against the Act, wheresoever such delinquents may reside, shall be cognizable, and finally determinable by any Court of Admiralty upon the continent, to which either plaintiff or defendant shall think proper to appeal from the sentence either of the inferior Courts of Justice or the superior. The execution of this Act was to have commenced on the first of the last month all over British America, but hath been, with an unprecedented unanimity, opposed and prevented by every province on the continent, and by all the islands, whence we have had any advices since that date. For this 'tis probable some may brand us with the odious name of rebels, and others may applaud us for that generous love of liberty which we inherit from our glorious forefathers, while some few may prudently suspend their judgment till they shall have heard what may be said on either side of the question.

If the Parliament indeed have a right to impose taxes on

the colonies, we are as absolute slaves as any in Asia, and consequently in a state of rebellion. If they have no such right, we are acting the noble and virtuous part which every freeman and community of freemen hath a right, and is in duty bound to act. For my own part, I am not acquainted with *all* that may be said on the one part or the other, and therefore am in some sort obliged to suspend my judgment. But no arguments that have yet come in my way, have convinced me that the Parliament hath any such right. The advocates for the Act, I observe, have alleged both precedents and arguments in support of the Parliament's right of taxation over the colonies. The precedents alleged are two Acts of Parliament; one establishing a Post-Office in America; the other, making some regulations with regard to the British troops sent hither in the late war; which are so very dissimilar from what they have been alleged to support, and therefore so foreign from the point, that instead of producing conviction, they really excite laughter. And of the arguments I have seen urged in behalf of this, till now unheard-of claim, the chief seems to be but a bare *ipse dixit*, an unsupported assertion that we, as British subjects, are virtually represented in the British Parliament, and consequently obliged by *all* its Acts. But, how some millions of people here (not a man of whom can, in consequence of his property here, either give a vote for sending a member to, or himself obtain a seat in, your House of Commons) can, in any sense, be said to be represented by that House, is utterly incomprehensible to an American understanding, or to any European understanding I have yet met with, which hath breathed American air. That we are subject to the jurisdiction of Parliament in matters of government that are of a nature purely external; subject, too, to such of its statutes as are of a date prior to the first migration of our ancestors hither, and to the first foundation of our government, is what seems to be generally granted amongst those I have conversed with. But taxation is an act of government purely internal, in which (allowing us to be freemen) we conceive a British House of Commons and a Parliament of Paris have an equal right to intermeddle. We flatter ourselves with a notion, that though we be subjects of Great Britain, and, we hope, as loyal as any others (and perhaps not less useful), we yet are freemen. All our charters declare (which we are not conscious of having ever forfeited) that all British subjects *dwelling and their children born here, shall have and enjoy all liberties, franchises and immunities to all intents and purposes, as if they had been abiding and born within the realm of England.* And if these charters have not been legally forfeited, as we trust they have not, are we not entitled to all the rights and liberties of Britons? If we be, we cannot, one would think, consistently with the principles of the British government, as ascertained in *Magna Charta*, be taxable without our own consent. We also conceive that the consent of no freeholder in America hath been given, or can possibly be given, in any constitutional mode, either personally or vicariously, to the Act in question, or to any other Act of taxation; because, not a man of us, as possessor of American property, can, as was before observed, vote for a member, or himself become a member, in that august House, whence all money bills, as far as their jurisdiction extends, must take their rise. We, moreover, consider ouselves, if you will allow me the expression for want of a better, as a *peculium* of the Crown. By charters from the Crown, that company was incorporated which first planted us. By the

Crown were those charters afterwards revoked. By the Crown, too, we are told, all the grants of liberties, all the charters which had passed from the company during its existence, to the colony, were, upon the revocation of the company's charters and its dissolution, confirmed and ratified to us. Under the immediate protection, direction, and government of the Crown have we been from that time to this. In short, thenceforward all the Acts of our Legislature either have, or constitutionally ought to have been, transmitted to Great Britain and subjected to the royal government, either to be disallowed, or ratified and confirmed by the ultimate sanction of the royal assent, previously to their having the force and validity of laws, without any parliamentary interposition whatever. So that the King, not as a branch of the British Legislature, but as a sovereign lord and absolute proprietor of the colony, in conjunction with his commissioner the Governor, his Council of State, and the people's representatives here, we suppose, form that aggregate Legislature, to the Acts of which alone, in all articles of internal government (of which taxation is a most important one) we owe obedience. To such alone, and to no other, have we paid obedience quite from our first establishment to this present day. And to such alone, in all such articles, particularly that of taxes, if I mistake not the sentiments of my countrymen, will they ever be disposed or prevailed on to pay obedience by any other argument than what some have called the *ultima ratio regum*, which may, for aught I know, be as convincing in matters of policy, as fire and faggot have been in those of religion. Besides all this, whenever the colony hath labored under any grievance which the branches of the Legislature here resident could not redress, or hath found it necessary to crave any indulgence or enlargement of privileges and immunities, their application has been always made to the King. And it doth not appear to me, that ever they have made any application to Parliament since King James I. took them out of the company's hands in 1624, on any occasion whatever, except once or twice when it was apprehended some bills, depending in Parliament, would pass into Acts, which would be prejudicial to their trade abroad, till they remonstrated against the Stamp Act. And, indeed, they have had very little encouragement to do so again, if what their agent hath told them be true; that their remonstrances against that bill (though modest as could be expected from men not sunk into the most abject slavery) were not so much as permitted to be heard. Such hath been the form of government under which we have lived from the year 1621, when our government was thoroughly established by charter from the company, to this present date. This we think a succession of years sufficient to establish that argument in support of our rights, had we no other, which is called prescription; for, during this whole period, no archives, records, or histories, that any here are acquainted with, or that any with you have cited, as far as I know, show, that ever the British Parliament attempted to tax us, or intermeddle in any matters relative to our interior government, till the date of this unhappy Stamp Act. All these rather prove the contrary. Nay, it appears that some Acts, even under an arbitrary Stewartine reign sent over hither with Lord Culpepper, when he came as Governor, were, by his Lordship's instructions, previously to their execution, to be subjected to the consideration of our General Assembly, in order to obtain their consent. It further appears, that they were so subjected and consented to by the Assembly, after the addition of two provisoes to one of them.   In a word, it is indisputable that, whenever the kings of Great Britain have wanted any aids either of men or money from this colony, the method of obtaining them hath been by letters requisitory, in the royal name, from a Secretary of State to the Governors, by whom those letters have been laid before the Assembly, who have levied the aids asked in such mode and by such ways and means as they thought most effectual and least oppressive, of which they surely are the best judges ; from all which premises the people of Virginia conclude, *the Parliament hath no right to tax them.*   But if they had, it is as steadfastly believed by most men here, as any article of their creed, that they have no right to deprive us of the inestimable privilege of being tried by juries.   This unconstitutional stretch of authority they are certain it is not their duty to obey.   The transition from subjecting us to be tried by Courts of Admiralty in civil matters to military government is so easy, that the thoughts of it almost reduce us to despair.   For these reasons, amongst many others, the people of this colony would not allow the stamped papers to be distributed, and forced the stamp-master to resign immediately on his arrival.   These reasons convince them that the moment they acquiesce under the Stamp Act, they commence slaves ; and the blood of their generous ancestors which flows in their veins, or some other cause, seems to have given them such an instinctive abhorrence of slavery that, were we to judge from appearances, they think any evil whatever more eligible than *that.*   How the affair will end, God only knows ! May his wise Providence prevent those tragedies, which my very heart even bleeds at the thoughts of !

But, put the case (which is the most favorable supposition that can be put) that the Colonies at last submit to the gall-

ing yoke, every friend to Great Britain must even then find
cause to detest and execrate the Act. For the execution of
it, or of any other Act of Taxation, will affect her in the tenderest points,—her manufactures, trade, and naval power.
The Colonies were poor before the war. They are much
more so since. Additional taxes must increase their poverty.
The poorer they are, the less of your manufactures can they
pay for and consume. The less demand there is for those
manufactures, the more of your manufacturers must want
bread. When we can no longer pay for your manufactures,
we cannot go naked. Necessity will set us upon improving
the natural advantages of our soil and climate, and manufacturing the products of it, flax, hemp, wool, and cotton, which are
to be had here in great plenty, as well as perfection. Besides,
it is said, some eminent merchants in London have computed
that one-third, others one-fourth, of your exports are brought
to the Colonies ; and have observed that those exports have
greatly diminished since this Act hath been on the carpet.
How just that computation or remark may be, I do not know.
But this I know, that the orders for goods from Great Britain have greatly decreased, wherever I am acquainted, as
well as the consumption of them, within these few months ;
that the number of wheels, looms, &c., have increased to an
amazing degree, and that only at one meeting in a neighboring Colony, upwards of two hundred merchants are said to
have bound themselves under most solemn engagements, not
to order any goods from Great Britain till that Act should
be repealed. In short, necessity will force every man of us to
employ his own labor and that of his slaves, so as may best supply his needs ; from which, I believe, nothing but some dragoons
at each man's door will prevent us. More need not be said to

prove this detestable Act productive of the most direful mischief, not only to the children, but to the mother island. For my own part, whatever the event may be, I comfort myself with the reflection, that every thing here below is subject to the control of irresistible power, directed by unerring wisdom and infinite goodness, &c. &c.

J. MAURY.

To the Honorable Philip Ludwell.

HONORABLE SIR :—However misbecoming it may in general be thought, in such as act only in a private station, to intermeddle in affairs of a public nature; yet when our country is in danger, to ward that danger off seems to be an object of common concern. Hence, I trust, any member of the community will be deemed pardonable, at least, in showing a readiness to forward the accomplishment of that desirable end. With this view then, I am about to take the freedom to offer to your Honor's consideration some few particulars with which, peradventure, the great distance between Williamsburg and those parts of the country which are most immediately affected by them, may have prevented some gentlemen, who share in the administration, from being so thoroughly acquainted, as, it is conceived, public utility, requires they should.

Not to mention the repeated acts of hostility and violence committed, on our fellow-subjects in the remoter parts of the Colony, by those bloody instruments of French policy, the Indians; nor the great extent of country on both sides the Alleghanies, now almost totally depopulated by them, which are facts long since notorious to all; I beg leave to in-

form you, that such numbers of people have lately trans-
planted themselves hence into the more southerly governments, as must appear almost incredible to any, except such
as have had an opportunity of knowing it, either from their
own observation, or the credible information of others.

From the waters of Potomac, James River, and Roanoke,
on the eastern side of the above-mentioned ridge of mountains,
nay, from the side of the Blue Ridge, hundreds of families
have, within these few months past, removed, deserted their
habitations, and conveyed themselves and their most valuable
movables into other governments.

By Bedford Court House, in one week, it is said, and I
believe truly said, near three hundred persons, inhabitants of
this colony, passed on their way to Carolina.   And I have it
from good authors, that no later in autumn than October,
five thousand more had crossed James River, only at one
ferry, that at Goochland Court House, and journeying towards
the same place; and doubtless great numbers have passed
that way since.   And, although all these had not been settled
in Virginia, yet a large proportion of them had.   From all
the upper counties, even those on this side the Blue Hills,
great numbers are daily following, and others preparing to
follow in the spring.   Scarce do I know a neighborhood but
has lost some families, and expects quickly to lose more.
What aggravates the misfortune, is, that many of these are
not the idler and the vagrant, pests of society, whom it is ever
salutary to a body politic to purge off, but the honest and industrious, men of worth and property, whom it is an evil at
any time to a community to lose, but is most eminently so to
our own in the present critical juncture.

Now, sir, as many have thus quitted fertile lands and

comfortable habitations, left behind them their friends, relations, and country, to all which they were attached by many powerful and endearing ties, we may conclude that weighty have been the reasons, at least these people have thought them such, which have already determined so many to act as these have done, and will determine others to follow their example. But, whether they be weighty in themselves or not, it is certain they are such as reduce the numbers of our inhabitants very fast, to the great detriment and loss of the public.

As I have had an opportunity of conversing with some of them upon the subject, and have thence discovered what considerations have influenced their conduct in this point, I shall take the liberty briefly and candidly to represent them to your Honor; after which, you may judge whether they have any weight or not; that, if they have, the gentlemen whose province it is to direct public affairs, may, if upon inquiry they find this information founded on truth, consider what will be the properest remedies for a timely prevention of the further progress of this consumption in our political constitution.

Although it be natural to suspect that the heavy taxes which the pressing exigencies of our country have rendered necessary, possibly may, and perhaps actually have, determined some to remove, yet, I know none who have been prevailed on to do so, purely and simply from that consideration. But, sir, an unhappy concurrence of various sinister events and untoward circumstances, preventing the Colony from reaping advantages from the sums levied and expended, adequate to those sums, together with a suspicion and dread that their persons and possessions are not sufficiently insured

19

against the cruelties and depredations of the savages, have been the prevailing and principal inducements to these people, thus, to their own private, as well as to the public detriment and loss, to become voluntary exiles.

Gentlemen in the administration may think, and I do believe they do think, that abundant provision has been already made for their protection and defence, as well by the several companies of Rangers sent out in the fall, as by the present expedition against the Shawanese. Whether the former of these measures has answered all the good ends, which, I presume, the Government had in view when it was resolved on, I undertake not to affirm or deny. And, whether the latter will, no man not endowed with the prophetic gift can foretell. However, I hope it will.

But this is foreign to my purpose, which is to inform your Honor of the sentiments and reasonings of those people who are daily seeking new habitations out of this Government. And they, sir, notwithstanding those measures, and all others which have yet been pursued with the same views, look upon our frontiers to be in so insecure and defenceless a state as to justify their apprehensions that the same bloody tragedies which were acted at the expense of their neighbors last summer, will, if they stay, be re-acted the ensuing at their own.

If only fifty Indians, which they believe to be as many as were upon our borders in the south-west last year, made such havoc and desolation, drove off upwards of 2,000 head of cattle and horses to support themselves and the enemy at Fort Duquesne, besides what they wantonly destroyed; if so contemptible a band depopulated and ravaged so large a tract of country, they suspect, much greater numbers, animated and tempted by the extraordinary success of those few, will, ere long, renew the same hostilities, and consequently, much greater and more extensive mischief will ensue. And, certain it is, should that be attempted and no effectual methods pursued to defeat the attempt, many parts of this Colony, now several miles within the frontier, will shortly become frontier in their turn.

As to the expedition under the command of Major Lewis, they regard it as a mark of the government's concern for their particular security, and of its attention to the welfare of the community at large. But yet, the success of it being uncertain, they think it not prudent to risk all that is dear in life, nay, life itself, upon such an uncertainty. They steadfastly believe, because it has been confidently affirmed by persons whom they judge worthy of credit, that the Shawanese have long since received intelligence of the march and destination of that party of Cherokees who are now to act in concert with the forces of this Colony, that are under the command of Major Lewis. And, hence, it is concluded, they have time either to augment their strength sufficiently to face us in the field, or else to retreat beyond the reach of our forces for awhile, in order, either when they shall be withdrawn thence, or even while they continue there in one body, to return on our back settlements by some one or other of those various passes through the Alleghany mountains, all which it will be utterly impossible for those forces in that united state to command or guard. And should this expedition, for these or any other reasons, succeed no better than some others have, what our remote inhabitants have heretofore suffered is judged but trifling, compared with what they would suffer in consequence of so disastrous an event; a dread of which, it is generally feared, would determine all the people beyond the Blue Ridge instant-

ly to abandon their habitations, and retreat to a place of greater
security; which they, as well as those who have already removed
thither, expect to find in the western parts of the Carolinas,
in the neighborhood and under the shelter of the Catawbas
and Cherokees; whither, it is supposed, the French Indians
will, at present, scarce think proper to make any inroads; for,
sir, in the present state of *our* frontiers, they must be sensible,
if they judge of the future from the past, that they may with
less trouble and hazard, get both scalps and plunder in Virginia, as valuable, nay, more valuable than they can well expect in the neighborhood of those two nations, our friends,
who are truly formidable to them, one for its martial and enterprising genius, the other for its numbers.

It is generally believed by the most prudent and discern-
ing in this part of the country, that during the present troubles, nothing will put a stop to this prevailing humor of removing southerly, because nothing will convince the people
they are safe, but a line of forts extended quite across the Colony, as a barrier against incursions of the barbarians; and
that this would, is quite probable, because a trifling fort on
Jackson River, a little below the mouth of Carpenter's Creek,
and another more trifling at the Drunkard's Bottom, on New
River, have, notwithstanding surrounding dangers, kept their
neighboring settlements tolerably well together, as yet. Sir,
if this be the case, it is submitted to superior judgments to
decide, whether or not it will be a prudent and necessary measure to have a chain of forts thrown across the Colony with
all convenient speed.

Should such a scheme be resolved on, the following line
might, perhaps, upon being viewed by proper persons, be
found to be not altogether inconvenient to build them on, to

wit: beginning near the head of Patterson's Creek on Potomac (for there is a fort already thirteen miles above its mouth),
continued up the western branch of Woppocomo, and down
Jackson River, and up Craig's Creek, crossing the Alleghany
Mountains to the Horse Shoe Bottom on New River, thence
up to the head of Reedy Creek, and extended down Holston,
quite to the latitude of our southern boundary. Each of
these forts might be built from other about thirty miles distant, more or less, as the natural situation of the grounds,
and some other requisite conveniences, would admit. Each,
too, might be garrisoned by a company of about fifty men, exclusive of officers, part whites and part Indians. As the
whole distance is somewhat upwards of 300 miles only, and
some few forts are already erected on or near this line, ten or
twelve at most, might be sufficient to serve our whole frontier, and six hundred men at most, Indians and whites together, to garrison the whole chain.

Should it be further determined that no person bear any
commission in these garrisons, except such as besides some
little fortune and a good character, are expert woodsmen, it
would still further insure the success of this matter.

As his Honor, the Governor, cannot be so well acquainted
with persons who may be best qualified to command these companies, as several gentlemen in the upper counties are, who
are themselves experienced woodsmen, and personally know
such as are most proper for such an office; both on this and
the other accounts just mentioned, would it be amiss, should
directions be given to the several courts of Augusta, Frederick, and Hampshire, Halifax, Lunenburg, Prince Edward
and Bedford, Albemarle and Louisa, Orange, Culpepper,
Prince William and Fairfax, each to recommend three or

four persons, the best qualified in their respective counties for
that business; out of whom his Honor might make choice of
such as he should think fit? Perhaps, too, it might be
thought necessary to appoint one general commander over all
these garrisons, who, upon any emergency, by drafting a certain quota from each, would be enabled more speedily and
more effectually to relieve any particular place in distress, as
well as to harass and intercept any parties of the enemy, daring enough to adventure within the line. Supposing these
fortresses built each from other at the distances mentioned above, the whole extent of country from north to south
might be daily ranged and explored, and a constant communication maintained between fort and fort; for each garrison
would bear dividing into six parties. Two might in regular
rotation be constantly employed in scouring the woods; one
about fifteen miles to the northward, the other about as far to
the southward of their own fort, while the remaining four continued at home, both for their own refreshment and for the
necessary guard and defence of their post. Each of the two
dividends upon duty might be obliged to range from their
own fort as above proposed to some distance, as nearly central
as may be, between it and that towards which they respectively patrol. The scouting parties of these two forts might
there meet each other in the evening, camp together that
night for mutual security, and before setting out for their several homes in the morning, make an appointment where the
two next detachments from the two same garrisons to be next
upon duty should meet and encamp on the evening of the
succeeding day; taking care, as frequently as may be, to
change their places of encampment, in order both to render
the passage of the enemy by night or by day more precarious,

and more effectually to guard against a surprise in the night, which might also be further guarded against were each party to have some few well-tutored and mettlesome dogs, the most vigilant of sentinels, whose antipathy against Indians is as strong as that of Indians against them. And by these parties thus frequently meeting, any intelligence might be easily transmitted from one extremity of this line to the other, or from any of the intermediate stations to either extremity, without any extraordinary trouble or expense. As all these garrisons might be under the same regulations, and detachments from each be daily ranging in the manner above-mentioned, the country thereabouts would be thoroughly searched and guarded, and yet the soldiers, through this alternate vicissitude of exercise and repose, not obliged to undergo any immoderate fatigue; for two-thirds of their time would be spent at their fort, and only one-third upon duty out of doors.

Now, sir, do not you think it highly probable that a scheme of this sort judiciously planned and faithfully executed, of which this may be considered only as an imperfect sketch, would render it extremely hazardous for the enemy, notwithstanding their celebrated activity and expertness in the woods, and the ruggedness and unevenness of those grounds, to make any inroads upon us with success? The diligence and activity that may be expected in officers thus cautiously chosen, and the garrisons under their command, having a proper intermixture of Indians no less subtle than the enemy, as bold, and equally well versed in all the barbarian arts and stratagems of war, would be much more formidable to those brutal ravagers, and embarrass them much more than many thousands of the best disciplined troops, and would either keep them at due distance, or, should they adventure within the barrier, se-

verely chastise their insolence and temerity. Such a measure,
too, besides affording the people in these quarters greater security than they have ever yet had, it is supposed will be less
expensive to the Government than any other that seems to
promise equal success. Good judges of work are of opinion
that each of these forts, together with its necessary buildings,
will not cost more than between £40 and £50, provided the
several companies be obliged to assist the undertaker in fell-
ing, hewing, sawing, and conveying into place the timber, in
digging the trenches for the stockades, and in other services
of that nature; and provided forts, built after the model, in
the manner, and of the dimensions of that of which you herewith receive a plan, be judged sufficient to answer the end.
Men, too, may be had to garrison them with very little bounty; many, perhaps, without any, provided the Government
would give them an assurance that they should not be obliged
to enter into any other service. When enlisted, they would
be less apt to desert than men are from corps of a different
denomination, and destined for services of a different nature.

Moreover, the Indians in these garrisons will certainly require less costly clothing, and perhaps be satisfied with lower
wages than soldiers are commonly allowed. The white men,
too, would be clothed as cheaply, perhaps more so, than soldiers regularly regimented. Several officers thought necessary in corps of this latter denomination, would here be needless; such as colonel, lieutenant-colonel, major, adjutant,
quarter-master, pay-master, commissary, and perhaps some
others. If I am not mistaken in the pay these several officers
receive in the Virginia Regiment, which, according to my calculation amounts to £177 10s. per month, the six hundred
men in these forts will be cheaper to the Colony by £2,130

per annum than the same number regimented, out of which, however, is to be deducted the pay of an officer to command the whole, which, rated at twenty shillings per day, a very bountiful and genteel allowance, leaves an annual clear saving to the Colony of £1,765.

As some of these forts will be convenient to the back inhabitants, the garrisons may be fed at much less expense than the Colony's troops at Cumberland can be, because the heavy charges of a long land carriage will be saved, savings which well merit the attention of a government, most especially when its treasury is well-nigh exhausted, and its subjects so little able to replenish it as our countrymen at present confessedly are.

But there is another very considerable expense which I had like to have forgotten, which this method of guarding our frontiers will render needless, and which therefore may be saved; for draughting the militia will probably hence be rendered unnecessary, which has frequently been done last year, and for aught that is known to the contrary, the Government may be necessitated to do the same the ensuing. And, should only six hundred of them be employed in defence of our frontiers, and stationed there only for one campaign, on the pay established by Act of Assembly, it would be such an addition to that load of debt and taxes under which the country at present labors, as, together with its unhappy circumstances in some other respects, must infallibly sink it beyond a possibility of emerging through a course of many years, how favorable a turn soever its present situation of affairs may take.

Such a chain of fortresses would also bring back the fugitives to their deserted plantations, would encourage others to prosecute anew their former schemes of seating the back lands,

19*

which these unhappy contests between the courts of London and Versailles have deterred them from executing, and would invite new settlers thither from several of the neighboring colonies, as well as from the crowded and interior parts of our own; hence, a considerable increase of people, which has ever been thought an augmentation of wealth and power. Industry, too, would revive, which in the remoter parts of the Colony, has for some time past been in a stagnant state, occasioned by the husbandman's uncertainty whether the returns of his labor were to support the enemies of his country or his own family. The people would cease to remove, as they would believe the Government had fallen upon the   [The remainder of this letter lost.]

Letter from John Fontaine to Rev. James Maury.

Jan. 2d, 1764.

DEAR NEPHEW MAURY:—The last letter we received from you was dated the 18th June, 1760, which was very acceptable to us, the which we answered the 24th Jan. 1761, and have received no letter from you since. Our great desire to hear from you will not permit us to be any longer silent, as the peace is now concluded so much to our advantage, and more especially so to all those who possess estates in North America, and that the French and Spaniards have ceded to us and put us in actual and quiet possession of more territory than the most sanguine could have expected, and that you are now sole lords of North America, bounded on the north by the north pole, on the south by the Gulf of Florida, and the west by the great river Mississippi. Nothing more can, we think, be wished for as to extent of territory, but to be thankful for this great enlargement, and the great deliverance from our powerful enemies the French and Spaniards, and from popery and idolatry, which in our opinion is as great, if not a greater blessing than any, or indeed all the others put together.

Now, thanks be to our great God for it, He may and will be worshipped without a rival from the north pole to the Gulf of Florida. It is impossible for you and me, without his especial assistance, to be sufficiently thankful for so many favors conferred on us and our posterity. A land flowing with milk and honey to inhabit, the pure and unadulterated doctrine brought down from heaven by our blessed Saviour and Redeemer to lead us to eternal life; these are blessings so complete that no more can be added to them.

The poor natural inhabitants still remain as thorns in your sides, lest you and we should forget the past deliverances. We pray to God to open their understandings, and make them one flock with us, obedient to the same God and Saviour. Whilst those Indians continue uninstructed in the principles of Christ's true religion, they will be cruel and treacherous. We are greatly concerned to hear of the horrible cruelties committed by those infidels upon your out settlers. We hope you will soon put a stop to their proceedings, and by a superior force bring them to reason, and convince them of the folly of such undertakings.

I received the Timothy grass you were so kind as to send me. I sowed some in my garden, and it grew well. I tried in the field, and the grass killed it. It would grow well in well cultivated lands if well weeded, and I think would produce a great crop; but I am too old and too feeble to undertake any thing, and I am often confined with the gout.

Your affectionate uncle,

JOHN FONTAINE.

*Letter from Colonel William Fontaine, after the sur-
render at York.*

RICHMOND, *Oct.* 26*th*, 1781.

DEAR SIR:—Major Penn gives me an opportunity, the first
I have met with since the glorious event, of congratulating
you on the surrender of York, which I do with all imaginable
cordiality. I had the happiness to see that British army,
which so lately spread dismay and desolation through all our
country, march forth on the 20th instant at three o'clock,
through our whole army drawn up in two lines at about
twenty yards distance, and return disrobed of all their terrors,
so humbled and so struck at the appearance of our troops that
their knees seemed to tremble, and you could not see a pla-
toon that marched in any order. Such a noble figure did our
army make, that I scarce know which drew my attention
most. You could not have heard a whisper or seen the least
motion throughout our whole line, but every countenance was
erect, and expressed a serene cheerfulness. Cornwallis pretended to be ill, and imposed the mortifying duty of leading
forth the captives on General O'Hara. Their own officers acknowledge them to be the flower of the British troops, yet I
do not think they at all exceeded in appearance our own or the
French. The latter, you may be assured, are very different
from the ideas formerly inculcated in us, of a people living on
frogs and coarse vegetables. Finer troops I never saw.

His Lordship's defence, I think, was rather feeble. His
surrender was eight or ten days sooner than the most sanguine
expected, though his force and resources were much greater
than we conceived. He had at least a fortnight's provisions,
and 1000 barrels of powder left, beside a magazine, that it is

supposed was blown up with design during the negotiation for
the surrender. The whole of the prisoners of war amount to
6,800, exclusive of sailors and marines, which, with the shipping, belong to the French, and the refugees, merchants and
followers of the army. The shipping of every sort is about
seventy sail, though a great many are sunk. Of brass ord-
nance we have taken eighty odd; of iron, 120; muskets, 7,313
fit for use, beside a great number in unopened boxes, and of
odd arms; of horse, about 300 accoutred; there must be more
horse accoutrements, but I have not seen a particular return
from Gloucester, where the horse lay. The military chest
amounts to only 800 guineas. Merchants' stores are subject
to the pre-emption of our army at a reasonable price for such
articles as suit them, the remainder they are allowed three
months to effect the sale of, then are to give their parole and
clear out. Tories are subject to be tried by our laws. The
20th of next month is appointed for that purpose. A small
proportion of officers are to remain with the prisoners, the rest
are to be paroled to New-York. A flag-ship is allowed Cornwallis to carry him to New-York; thence, I believe, he goes
home. His flag-ship is not to be searched. The officers retain their side-arms and baggage, and the soldiers their knap-
sacks. They marched out with drums muffled, and colors
furled and crossed. All property taken from inhabitants by
the British is liable to be claimed by them. In consequence,
Master Tarleton met with a most severe mortification the day
before yesterday. The hero was prancing through the streets
of York on a very fine, elegant horse, and was met by a spirited young fellow of the country, who stopped him, challenged
the horse, and ordered him instantly to dismount. Tarleton
halted and paused awhile through confusion, then told the lad

if it was his horse, he supposed he must þe given up, but insisted to ride him some distance out of town to dine with a French officer. This was more, however, than Mr. Giles was disposed to indulge him in, having been forced, when he and his horse were taken, to travel good part of a night on foot at the point of the bayonet; he therefore refused to trust him out of sight, and made him dismount in the midst of the street crowded with spectators. Many such instances have since happened on the road. The people who have been insulted, abused, nay, ruined by them, give them no quarter. I have not seen the articles of capitulation, but have given you the substance as well as I can recollect from such as have read them.

We are surely to have a garrison at York; whether French or American was not known when I left York, the day before yesterday. Some troops are to go to the southward. It is supposed the French fleet and most of their troops will go to the West Indies, though all is conjecture, and will probably remain so to all but the Count de Grasse and Gen. Washington. The General had been aboard the Admiral for some days past as I came away; something of consequence, I suspect, was projecting between them. The troops at Portsmouth are levelling to prevent the British taking post there. Nothing certain of a British fleet. They have lost, 'tis said Bengal and Madras in the East Indies, by the powerful exertions of Hyder Ali in favor of the French.

Cornwallis, I am well assured, previous to his surrender, acknowledged to the Secretary, that the capture of his army would put an end to the war. The same sentiment was expressed to me by two of his officers, and, I learn from an intelligent inhabitant of York, generally prevailed among them.

That General Lesly, with all the crew, perished in the passage from Wilmington to Charles Town in the Blonde Frigate *in ore est omnium.*

I certainly embark for Europe the soonest a passage can be had, perhaps three or four weeks hence, though I believe I shall be forced to take the West Indies in the way, and probably may winter there. My love to my good sisters and families. My best respects to Mr. Armistead, and all my relations and friends in your country. Farewell! farewell! the good Doctor, Parson Cole, and all.

I have commissioned a gentleman to get Mr. Holmes a hat from York. Mrs. Walker has recovered her two negroes, and my mother her one. The French fleet and all our troops were under sailing and marching orders. If Major Halston is with you, let him know Mr. Burrows, from his State, has his servant that he wrote about.

I enclose two yards of ribbon for my sister Sarah, and two for sister Mary, or in her absence, little Bess—trophies from York. Had the stores been opened, I would have dealt more largely, though they are strictly guarded, and general orders against any thing being sold till the army is supplied. All health and happiness to you and yours, and all with you.

Your affectionate friend and servant,

W. FONTAINE.

CONCLUSION.

———•••———

I have been at considerable pains to ascertain the present
condition of the descendants of the sons and daughter of
James Fontaine, who settled in Virginia; and the result of
my inquiry is, that, in regard to temporal circumstances, they
are chiefly in the condition so touchingly prayed for by Agur,
when he says :—" Give me neither poverty nor riches ; feed
me with food convenient for me : lest I be full and deny thee,
and say, Who is the Lord ? or lest I be poor and steal, and
take the name of my God in vain." I find scarcely any of the
family who are not earning a comfortable subsistence for
themselves and those who depend upon them, and at the same
time there are very few who can be called actually wealthy.

I am the more disposed to dwell upon this fact, from observing the very different condition of the descendants of
another Huguenot refugee, who, like our ancestor, left a written memoir for the use of his children. From this record I
learn that he had been a notary, and had been deprived of his
employment on account of his being of the Reformed religion.
He was a husband and a father. During the persecution
which preceded the actual revocation of the Edict of Nantes,
the dragoons visited his house, and behaved with their usual

brutality and insolence. They sent him away soon after their arrival, to procure for them, from the neighbouring village, some delicacies with which to pamper their appetites. While on the road, he was intimidated by hearing of the cruelty with which the dragoons had said they would treat him on his return home; and his informant, a kind neighbor, persuaded him to conceal himself in his house.

I think, that, whatever might have been his anticipations of suffering, it was most unmanly to desert his wife, and leave her alone with the dragoons, particularly from her state at the time, being in bed with an infant only three days old. As might have been expected, the dragoons vented all their malice upon the poor woman. When they found that her husband did not return, they dragged her out of bed, and threatened to roast her alive: they took it in turns to hold her close to a fire, which was so hot that each one could only bear to hold her for a short time. Death must soon have followed if she had not been rescued by the timely intervention of the village Curé, who accidentally heard what was going on, and persuaded them to desist, promising that he would make her recant. This was in the year 1681.

He went through various trials and vicissitudes during the four years following. His wife died, and her young infant also, and he was hunted from place to place; and at last in 1685, the memorable year of the Revocation of the Edict of Nantes, he proceeded to Rochelle, for the purpose of embarking for England. He was arrested and imprisoned there, and after much threatening, insult and abuse, he was induced to sign an act of abjuration. He was liberated immediately, but was more miserable than ever, full of remorse for the act he had committed when under the influence of fear. He still

hoped to escape from France, but it was more difficult to accomplish now that he had publicly abjured the Protestant
faith.   In the course of two or three years, however, he succeeded in getting away, but he left behind him a daughter,
eighteen years of age, for the sole purpose of trying to collect,
and turn into money, their few scattered resources, to bring
after him to England.   She was able to accomplish this end,
and to join him in about a year; which I think was more
than he had a right to expect; but we shall see that his
family were not much enriched eventually.

Observe; the memoir he wrote for his children has been
preserved and published; but how?   His descendants could
not read the manuscript, for it was in the French language,
and they, like ourselves, had become blended with another
nation.   English was with them, as with us, the mother
tongue, and they could read no other, for they were unedu-
cated.   The manuscript might have lain till now upon the
shelf of a miserable lodging-house in the heart of London,
had it not been brought to light by accident.   The owners
of it were in poverty, and applied for relief to a benevolent
Society, and one of the visitors, upon his charitable errand to
them, became acquainted with the existence of the manuscript.   He took it home to peruse, and undertook to have
it translated and printed, to be sold for the benefit of the
writer's descendants.

Now we come to the practical lesson which I draw from
contrasting the different condition of the descendants of these
two Huguenot refugees, and I desire to impress it upon our
minds. with the view of inducing us to aim at obtaining the
strong faith of our ancestor.

He believed that God would take care of him and his, if

he trusted in him ; he knew his promise, and that if he left house or parents, or brethren, or wife or children, for the kingdom of God's sake, he should receive manifold more in this present time, and in the world to come life everlasting. He therefore left all his worldly substance behind him, and fled to a land where he could worship God according to the dictates of his conscience. He waited not to sell houses and lands, and collect money for his support in a foreign country. He firmly believed the promises of God, he saw distinctly the path pointed out by duty to Him, he hesitated not, but followed on.

We know that he experienced many privations and hardships, but in the end he was able to maintain his family, and to give good educations to his children. His descendants have generally been able to do the same.

His manuscript record of his interesting and instructive life, instead of being a dead letter to his descendants like the one named above, has been perused and valued by each successive generation, as it has been handed down from father to son, as a precious and sacred inheritance.

In the other narrative we cannot but observe weakness of faith throughout. In his unmanly desertion of his wife, we first notice it, then in his signing the act of abjuration, and lastly in leaving his daughter in France to collect money for the support of the family.

My own mind is forcibly impressed with the conviction that *we* have reason to hope for the especial blessing which God has promised to the seed of the righteous. May we all strive to obtain the faith of our forefathers, and so to walk as not to prove degenerate scions from a worthy stock.

APPENDIX.

————•♦•————

THE KING'S EDICT.

Given at Nantes, April, 1598, and published in Parliament, 15 February, 1599.

Henry, by the Grace of God, King of France and Navarre. To all that are and shall be, greeting:

The most signal and remarkable mercy, among the infinite ones which it has pleased God to vouchsafe to us, is the having given us virtue and firmness sufficient to prevent our granting any thing under the influence of the dreadful trouble, discord and confusion which prevailed at the period of our accession to the throne. The kingdom was divided into many parts and factions, so many that the orderly portion was, perhaps, one of the smallest. We have been supported so as to withstand this great storm, we have overcome it, and now at last have reached the haven of safety and repose. Wherefore, to God's holy name be all the glory, and to us thankfulness of heart, in that he has been pleased to make use of our efforts, as his instrument for accomplishing the good work. It is plainly to be seen, that in view of so desirable an end, we have gone beyond what duty required of us, and have exposed ourselves with a freedom that at another time would scarcely have been consistent with the dignity of our position.

In the conflicting claims for pre-eminence amongst the various important and perilous affairs which pressed upon us, and which could not all receive attention at once, we resolved upon the following course. In the first place to deal with such as required to be

settled by main force, delaying for a while such as could be regulated by principles of reason and justice; as, for example, the
general differences amongst our good subjects, and some particular
hardships, complained of by the more healthy portions of the State,
which we believe may be the more effectually relieved by our having
first put an end to the civil war, which was one chief cause.

By the grace of God, we have happily so far succeeded that
hostilities have ceased throughout the kingdom. We hope for equal
success in composing those differences that yet remain to be adjust-
ed, and then will be accomplished the great object of our prayers,
and we shall be rewarded for all our labors, by once more behold-
ing peace and tranquillity within our borders. Amongst the most
important of said affairs, the consideration of which we were obliged
to postpone, were the complaints of various Catholic towns and
provinces that the Catholic Religion had not been universally re-established, in conformity with the Edicts formerly passed for the pacification of religious troubles; also, the petitions and remonstrances
of our subjects of the pretended Reformed Religion, complaining of
the non-performance of what had been promised to them by the
said Edicts, and begging for further enactments to secure to them
that liberty of conscience, personal safety and security of property
which the late disturbances have made them believe to be in jeop-
ardy, giving them reason to fear that plans were laid for their ruin.
We have put off from time to time the providing a remedy for these
grievances, partly, because we would avoid the burden of too much
business at once, and partly because the enactment of laws, be they
ever so desirable in themselves, can scarcely be compatible with the
din of arms. But, it having now pleased God to grant us the enjoyment of more tranquillity, we think we can make no better use
of it than in giving our attention to that which concerns the glory
of His Holy Name and service, and endeavoring to provide for the
religious worship of all our subjects, who, if they cannot yet join
in one form, we may at least hope, are actuated by one and the
same purpose, and therefore that by wise regulations all tumult and
strife may be put an end to, and that we and this kingdom may forever continue to deserve the glorious title of "Most Christian," that
title which was originally acquired by great merit and has been so
long possessed. We hope to be able so to regulate matters that
future trouble shall be avoided, on that subject which is of all others
the most delicate and searching, the subject of religion.

Being fully sensible of the great importance of this subject, and the necessity of bestowing deep consideration upon it, we have carefully looked over the folios of complaints from our Catholic subjects, and we have permitted our subjects of the aforesaid pretended Reformed Religion to assemble by deputy to prepare their list of grievances. We have conferred with both parties various times, and carefully examined all former Edicts, and now we have concluded that one general, clear, plain and absolute law must be enacted, for the government of all our subjects, and by which they shall be regulated in the settlement of all differences which have already arisen, or which may in future arise. With this, all must rest satisfied, as the best that the state of the times allows, we having, in our deliberations, had no other end in view than zeal for the service of God and a desire to see it manifested by our said subjects, amongst whom we hope to establish a firm and durable peace. We implore and look for the same blessing upon this, our effort, from the mercy of God that he has heretofore showered upon this kingdom from its earliest foundation to this day. We entreat him to send his grace upon our subjects, and to make them understand that in the observing of this our Ordinance, is laid the great foundation (after their duty to God and one another) of their union and tranquillity and the best prospect of a restoration of this State to its former splendor, opulence and strength. On our part, we promise to have it rigidly enforced, without any infringement.

Accordingly, with the advice and assistance of the Princes of the Blood, the Princes and Officers of the Crown, and other great and important personages of our Council of State, we have duly weighed and considered all this matter; and we have, by this perpetual and irrevocable Edict, said, declared and ordered, and we do say, declare and order,

1st.—That the memory of the past, on both sides, from the beginning of March, 1585, to the date of our accession to the throne, shall be buried in oblivion; and it shall be unlawful for our Attorney General, or any other person, public or private, at any time, or for any purpose whatsoever, to make mention of the former troubles in any process or law suit, in any Court or Jurisdiction whatever.

2d.—We forbid all our subjects, whatever may be their rank or condition, to revive the recollection of the past, or to attack, resent, injure or provoke by reproaches, under any pretext whatever; and they must not dispute, quarrel, outrage or offend one another, by word or deed, but must restrain themselves, and live in peace as brothers, friends and fellow citizens, upon penalty to the disobedient of being punished as disturbers of the peace.

3d.—We command that in all places of this our Kingdom and country of our obedience, where the exercise of the Apostolic Roman Catholic religion has been interrupted, it shall be re-established, to be there freely exercised without trouble or hindrance. We forbid expressly, all persons, of whatsoever rank, degree or condition, upon the above named penalty, to molest or disturb the clergymen in the celebration of Divine Service, the enjoyment and collection of tithes, first fruits and revenues from their benefices, or any other rights and duties appertaining thereto. All persons, who, during the troubles, became possessed of churches, houses, property and revenues belonging to the said clergymen, and who retain and occupy them, shall give up the same to the clergy, with the entire possession and peaceable enjoyment of all rights, privileges and securities which they had before they were seized upon. It is expressly forbidden, to those of said pretended Reformed religion, to preach or perform any service according to said religion in the churches, houses, or places of abode of said clergymen.

4th.—It shall be optional with the said clergymen to buy the houses and buildings erected upon unconsecrated ground occupied by them before the troubles, or to oblige the present possessor of the buildings to buy the ground; in either case the property to be valued by skilful persons, whom the parties shall agree to appoint. In default thereof, provision shall be made by the Judges of the places, reserving to the occupant a right of appeal. And wherever the said clergy shall constrain the occupant to purchase the ground, the estimated value shall not be paid to the former, but shall remain in the hands of the occupant, he being required to pay interest upon it at the rate of 5 per cent., until it shall be applied to the use of the church, which will be done at the expiration of one year. And when said time shall have expired, and the purchaser is unwilling to continue said rent, he shall be discharged therefrom, upon depositing the purchase money in the hands of a solvent person, authorized by the justice to receive it. Commissioners appointed without fail by us to see to the execution of the present Edict, shall give information as to the sacred places.

5th.—Notwithstanding, the ground, places and materials used

for repairing and fortifying the cities and places of our kingdom shall not be sold by the clergy or other individuals public or private, until the said fortifications shall be demolished by our Decree.

6th.—And in order to leave no opening for discord and divisions amongst our subjects, we have permitted and do permit those of the pretended Reformed religion to live and remain in all cities and places within this our kingdom and country of our obedience without being disturbed, vexed, molested or forced to do any thing against their conscience on the subject of religion, neither can their houses or places of abode be searched on that score ; provided that in all things they conform to what is contained in our present Edict.

7th.—We have also permitted all lords, nobles, and other persons, as well natives and others, professing the pretended reformed religion, in this our kingdom, having *"Haute Justice," or "pleint fief de Haubert," as in Normandy, whether in full ownership or merely usufruct, the whole, one-half, or the third, to have the exercise of the said religion in such of the houses of the said "Haute Justice" or fiefs as they shall name as the principal domicile, in the presence of our Bailiffs and Seneschals, each in his district ; and in the absence of the heads of the family, their wives and families, and parts of them, may have religious exercises. Though the right of "Justice" or "fief de Haubert" be disputed, yet the exercise of the said religion shall be allowed, provided that the above mentioned be in actual possession of the said "Haute Justice," even if our Attorney General be opposed. We permit also said religious exercises in their other houses of "Haute Justice" or "fief de Haubert" when themselves are present, but not otherwise. Such services may be not only for their own benefit, but their families, subjects, and all who shall wish to attend.

8th.—In the houses of the fiefs, where those of the said religion shall not have the said "Haute Justice" or "fief de Haubert," they may have religious exercises for their own families only, nevertheless, if other persons should be present, not exceeding thirty in number, on Baptismal occasions, friendly visits, or by invitation, they may attend said worship ; provided always that said fiefs are not

* Haute Justice. The jurisdiction of manorial courts where the judge takes cognizance of both civil and criminal suits, not affecting the Crown.

† Fief de Haubert. A tenure by Knight's service whose owner was bound to serve on horseback in complete armor. This tenure existed longer in Normandy, than any other part of France.

within Cities, Towns, or Villages, belonging to Catholic Noblemen, and where they have houses. In the latter case, the permission of said Noblemen must be given before religious worship can be had.

9th.—We also permit those of the said religion to continue the exercise of it in all cities and places under our government, where it was established and publicly practised at different times in the year 1596, and before the end of August 1597, notwithstanding any decrees or decisions to the contrary.

10th.—The said exercise shall likewise be established and restored in all cities and places where it was established, or had the right to be so, by the Edict of Pacification, passed in the year 1577, or by the secret articles and conferences of Nerac and Fleix, without the said establishment being prevented in places of the domain given in the said Edict, though they may since have been made over to Catholic persons. Let it then be understood that the said exercise may be always re-established in places of the said domain which have formerly been in the possession of those who professed the pretended Reformed Religion, in which it would have been placed in consideration of their persons, or because of their feudal rights, even if the said fiefs should now be possessed by persons of the said Apostolical Roman Catholic Religion.

11th.—Moreover, in each of the ancient Bailiwicks, Seneschal's jurisdictions, and governments taking the place of Bailiwicks and having jurisdiction independent of the Courts of Parliament, we ordain that in the faubourgs of a city besides those which have been granted to them by the said Edict, Articles, and Conferences, and where there are no cities, the exercise of the said religion may be publicly performed in any town or village, by all those who wish; though in the said Bailiwicks, Seneschal's jurisdictions and governments, there may be several places where the said exercise is now established, saving and excepting the towns in which there is an Archbishopric or Bishopric newly granted by present Edict; without for that reason depriving those of said pretended Reformed Religion of the privilege of demanding and naming as places for the said exercise, small towns and villages near to the said cities; except also the places and manors belonging to the Clergy, where we only mean that the said second place in the Bailiwick may be established, having them by special favor excepted and reserved. It is our intention, under the name of ancient Bailiwicks to designate those which, in the time of the late King Henry, our much honored Lord and Father-in-Law, existed as Bailiwicks, Senescha 's 'urisdictions and independent governments.

12th.—We do not mean by the present Edict to take any thing from the Edicts and Agreements heretofore made for the reduction to submission of any Princes, Lords, Nobles, or Catholic Towns within our jurisdiction, in what concerns the exercise of said religion, which Edicts and Agreements shall be kept and observed. Instructions to that effect will be given to the Commissioners who shall be appointed to execute the present Edict.

13th.—We expressly forbid any of the said religion having any religious exercise whatever, either ministerial, or for discipline or public instruction of children and others in this our kingdom; except in those places permitted and granted by the present Edict.

14th.—As also having any exercises of said religion within our Court and Suite, nor likewise in our lands and territories beyond the Alps, nor in our city of Paris, neither within five leagues of the said city: nevertheless, those of the said religion living in the said country beyond the Alps, and in our said city, and within five leagues around it, shall not be subject to espionage in their houses, nor compelled to do any thing on account of their religion against their consciences, if they in all things act in conformity with the provisions of the present Edict.

15th.—The public exercise of the said religion cannot be permitted in the army, except at the Quarters of those Generals who profess it, always excepting that occupied by our own person.

16th.—In conformity with the second article of the Conference of Nerac, we allow those of the aforesaid religion to build places for the exercise of the aforesaid, in the towns and places where it is allowed. Those places built by them formerly or the foundations of them, will be restored in their present condition, even in those places where said exercise is not allowed, if they have not been converted into other kinds of edifices. In which case, the present possessors of the said edifices shall give property equal to the former value, in the estimation thereof by skilful appraisers; reserving to the said proprietors and possessors the right of appeal.

17th.—We forbid all Preachers, Readers, and others who speak in public, using any words or discourse tending to excite sedition among the people, but on the contrary we enjoin upon them the practice of forbearance and meekness, saying nothing but what is for the instruction and edification of their hearers, and suited to the maintenance of that peace and tranquillity which we have established in our said kingdom, under penalties prescribed in former Edicts. We expressly enjoin our Attorneys General and their substitutes to give official information against those who violate it, under the penalty of being answerable for the same in their own names and persons, and being ejected from office.

18th.—We also forbid all our subjects, of whatsoever rank or condition, carrying off children by force, or persuasion, against the will of their parents of the said religion, in order to have them baptized or confirmed in the Apostolical Roman Catholic Church: the same prohibition extends to those of the said pretended Reformed religion, all being subject to exemplary punishment for such offences.

19th.—Those of the said pretended Reformed religion shall not remain bound by any abjuration, promise or oath which they may formerly have made, or any security given by them about matters concerning the said religion; and they shall be free from all disturbances or molestation on that account.

20th.—They shall be obliged also to observe all the appointed Festivals of the Apostolical Roman Catholic Church, and they may not on those days labor, sell, nor display in open shops their goods, and upon Festivals and other forbidden days, no artisan may work either out of his shop or within closed doors, at any trade the noise of which may be heard by passers by or neighbours. Nevertheless search shall not be made but by the officers of Justice.

21st.—Books relating to said pretended Reformed religion may only be publicly printed and sold in those cities and places where the public exercise of the said religion is permitted. And for the other books, which shall be printed in other towns, they shall be seen and inspected, as well by our officers as by Theologians, in the manner decreed by our Ordinances. The printing, publishing or selling any books or writings of an abusive, scandalous nature is forbidden under the penalties contained in our Ordinances. We enjoin it upon all our Judges and officers to attend to this.

22d.—We command that no difference or distinction shall be made on account of said religion in receiving pupils to be instructed in the Universities, Colleges and schools; or receiving the sick and poor into Hospitals, Infirmaries and Alms-houses.

23d.—Those of said pretended Reformed Religion, shall be

obliged to obey the laws of the Apostolical Roman Catholic Church, received in this kingdom, with respect to the Consanguinity and Relationship of parties making marriage contracts.

24th.—Likewise, those of the said religion shall pay all customary dues for the offices and employments conferred upon them, without being obliged to take part in any ceremony contrary to their said religion: and being called upon to take an oath they shall not be required to do more than hold up the hand, swear, and promise before God to speak the truth: shall not be obliged also to take a dispensation from the oath given by them, in making contracts and agreements.

25th.—We desire and command that all of the said pretended Reformed Religion, and others who have joined their party, of whatsoever rank or condition, shall be obliged and compelled in all proper and reasonable ways, and under the penalties contained in this edict, to pay tithes to the pastors and other clergy, and to all others entitled to them according to established usage.

26th.—Disinheriting or depriving of property, whether during life, or by will, solely from hatred or religious animosity, shall be null and void, for the past as well as the future.

27th.—In order the better to promote that union which we wish to see prevail amongst our subjects, and to take away all cause of complaint, we declare that all those who have made or shall make profession of the pretended Reformed Religion shall be eligible for all public offices or employments, whether Royal, Manorial, or Civic, in all parts of our dominions, and shall be impartially appointed thereto, our Courts of Parliament confining themselves in the matter to inquiries as to the piety, morality, and integrity of those nominated for offices, as much those of one religion as the other, without requiring from them any other oath than that they will faithfully serve the King and obey the laws. In case of vacancies occurring in any of said offices in our disposal, we shall without partiality appoint capable persons to such offices. Let it also be understood, that those of said pretended Reformed Religion can be admitted and received into all Councils, Assemblies, and Meetings, which follow from the aforesaid offices, without rejection on account of said religion.

28th.—We command our Officers and Magistrates, and the Commissioners appointed for the execution of the present Edict, in all the towns, &c., of the kingdom, to provide promptly convenient places for the burial of the dead for those professing said religion. And the cemeteries they formerly possessed, of which they were deprived during the troubles, shall be restored to them, unless occupied by any kind of edifices or buildings, in which case, others shall be provided gratuitously.

29th.—We enjoin it expressly upon our officers, to see to it that no scandal occurs at said funerals: and in fifteen days, at farthest, after a requisition has been made, they shall be obliged to provide a convenient place for the said interments, without any delay or procrastination, under a personal penalty of a fine of five hundred crowns. All said officers and others are forbidden to require any thing for conducting said dead bodies, under penalty of extortion.

30th.—In order that justice may be administered to our subjects without suspicion, hatred or favor, as a principal means of maintaining peace and good order, we have commanded and do command, that, in our Court of Parliament in Paris, a Chamber shall be established, consisting of a President and sixteen Councillors from the said Parliament, which shall be entitled the Chamber of the Edict, and shall take cognizance not only of the causes and lawsuits of those of the pretended Reformed religion who shall be within the limits of said Court, but also within the districts of our Parliaments of Normandie and Bretagne, according to the jurisdiction which shall be hereafter given to it by the present Edict, till similar Chambers shall have been established in each of said Parliaments to administer justice in those places. We command also that for the four offices of Councillors, in our said Parliament, remaining from the last establishment made by us, four discreet and competent persons of the said pretended Reformed religion shall be provided and received in said Parliament, namely, the first to be received in the Chamber of the Edict, and the other three, as soon as they can be received, in three of the *Chambres des Enquêtes*, and besides that, the two first offices of the Secular Councillors that shall become vacant by death, shall also be filled by two of the said pretended Reformed religion, and these received, shall be distributed also in the two other *Chambres des Enquêtes*.

31st.—Besides the Chamber formerly established at Castres, for the district of our Court of Parliament of Toulouse, which shall be continued as at present, we have for the same consideration commanded and do command that, in each of our Courts of Parliament of Grénoble and Bourdeaux, a Chamber shall likewise be established, consisting of two Presidents, one Catholic and the other of the pretended Reformed religion, and of twelve Councillors, of whom six shall be Catholic and the other six of the said religion, which Catholic President and Councillors shall by us be taken from and chosen out of the bodies of our said Courts. And as for those of said religion, there shall be a new President and six Councillors created for the Parliament of Bourdeaux, and one President and three Councillors for that of Grénoble, which, with the three Councillors of said religion now in said Parliament, shall be employed in the said Chamber of Dauphiny. The newly created Officers shall be entitled to the same emoluments, honors, rewards and dignities as the others of the said Courts. And the said sitting of said Chamber of Bourdeaux shall be held at Bourdeaux or at Nerac, and that of Dauphiny at Grénoble.

32*d.*—The said Chamber of Dauphiny shall have cognizance of the causes of those of the pretended Reformed religion within the jurisdiction of our Parliament of Provence, without requiring letters of appeal as in the Chancery Court of Dauphiny, in like manner those of said religion in Normandy and Bretagne shall not be required to take out letters of appeal or other preparation as in our Chancery Court of Paris.

33*d.*—Our subjects of the religion, of the Parliament of Burgundy, shall have the choice of pleading before the Chamber ordered in the Parliament of Paris or in that of Dauphiny. And they shall not be obliged to take out letters of appeal or other preparation as in the said Chancery Courts of Paris or Dauphiny, according to the choice they shall make.

34*th.*—All the said Chambers, composed as aforesaid, shall take cognizance and pronounce sentence definitively, without appeal, making decisions, to the exclusion of all others, upon suits and causes commenced and intended to be commenced, in which those of said pretended Reformed religion shall be principal or security, as plaintiff or defendant, in matters civil or criminal, whether the said complaint be made in writing or verbally, if it seems good to the said parties, and one of them shall demand it, before the commencement of the trial: excepting, always, all matters connected with Church Benefices, the possession of tithes not impropriated, clerical patronage and causes where the question turns upon the rights, duties or domains of the church, which shall all be treated and judged in the Courts of Parliament, without the said Chambers of the Edict having any cognizance thereof. It is also our will, that in deciding suits which may arise between the said Clergy and those of the said pretended Reformed religion, if the clergyman be defendant, the cognizance and judgment of the criminal suit shall belong to our Sovereign Courts, to the exclusion of said Chambers; and if the clergyman be plaintiff, and he of said religion defendant, the cognizance and judgment of the criminal suit shall belong to the said Chambers established, which shall give final decision, without appeal. During vacation, the said Chambers shall also have cognizance of matters referred, by the Edicts and Ordinances, to the Chambers established for the time of vacation, each within its district.

35th.—The said Chamber of Grénoble shall from this time forward be united and incorporated with the body of the said Court of Parliament, and the President and Councillors of the said pretended Reformed religion shall be nominated Presidents and Councillors of the said Court, and considered as of their number and of equal rank. And for these ends they shall first be distributed in the other Chambers; then selected and drawn from them to be employed and to serve in that which we shall order anew; always with the understanding that they shall attend, have a seat and vote in all the deliberations of the assembled Chambers, and shall enjoy the same emoluments, authority and dignities as the other Presidents and Councillors of said Court.

36th.—It is our will, and it must be understood, that the said Chambers of Castres and Bourdeaux shall be re-united and incorporated with those Parliaments, in the same way as the others, when required, and when the cause which has induced us to establish them shall cease and no longer be known amongst our subjects; and for these ends the Presidents and Councillors of those of the said religion, shall be named and appointed Presidents and Councillors of said Courts.

37th.—There shall also be newly appointed, in the Chamber ordered for the Parliament of Bourdeaux, two Substitutes for our Attorney and our Solicitor-General, one of whom shall be Catholic and the other of the said religion, for whom shall be provided ready money salaries from said offices.

38th.—The said substitutes shall be considered as substitutes only, and when the Chambers ordered for the Parliaments of Toulouse and Bourdeaux shall be united and incorporated with the said Parliaments, the said substitutes shall be furnished with the office of Councillors in them.

39th.—The copies of documents from the Court of Chancery of Bourdeaux, shall be made out in the presence of two Councillors of this Chamber, one of whom shall be Catholic, and the other of the said pretended Reformed religion in the absence of one of the Masters of Requests of our Hotel. And one of the Notaries and Secretaries of the said Court of Parliament of Bourdeaux shall reside in the place where the said Chamber shall be established, or else one of the ordinary Secretaries of the Court of Chancery, for the purpose of signing documents from said Court.

40th.—We desire and command that in the said Chamber of Bourdeaux there be two Clerks to the Registrar of the said Parliament, one civil and the other criminal, who shall discharge their duties under our Commission, and shall be called Clerks to the Court of Records, Civil and Criminal. The Registrars of the Parliament shall not have power to dismiss or recall them. The Clerks shall pay over to the Registrars all the fees of the said Registry, and they shall be paid by the Registrars as shall be deliberately resolved upon by the said Chamber. Moreover, Catholic doorkeepers shall be appointed, who shall be taken from said Court, or elsewhere, according to our pleasure : besides which there shall be two newly appointed of said religion, provided gratuitously, and the said doorkeepers shall all be regulated by the said Chamber, as well in regard to the fulfilment of their duties as in the allowance of perquisites to them. There shall also be a prompt appointment of a person to pay salaries and receive fines in said Chamber, if it be established elsewhere than in said city, to be approved of by us. The appointment formerly made, of a Paymaster to the Chamber of Castres shall take effect, and the duty of receiving fines in the said Chamber, shall be added thereto.

41st.—Good and sufficient assignments shall be made for paying salaries to the Officers of the Chambers ordered by this Edict.

42d.—The Presidents, Councillors and other Catholic Officers of the said Chambers shall be continued so long as shall seem to be for our benefit and the good of our subjects ; and when some are removed, others must be provided beforehand to take their places ; and during the time of service they must not be absent without the permission of those who shall have suits pending in conformity with the Ordinance.

20*

43*d*.—The said Chambers shall be established within six months, during which time (if it be so long before the establishment be made) the suits commenced and intended to be commenced, in which those of the said religion shall be parties, within the jurisdiction of our Parliaments of Paris, Rouen, Dijon and Rennes, shall be brought forward in the Chamber established for the present in Paris, in virtue of the Edict of the year 1577, or else in the Great Council, at the choice and option of those of the said religion if they require it: those who shall be of the Parliament of Bourdeaux, at their option, either in the Chamber established at Castres or at the said Great Council; and those who shall be of Provence in the Parliament of Grénoble. And if the said Chambers are not established within three months after our present Edict shall have been presented to them, those of our Parliaments which have refused, shall be deprived of all cognizance over and all right of judging the causes of those of the said religion.

44*th*.—The suits not yet tried of the above mentioned description, pending in the said Courts of Parliament and Great Council, shall be referred, in whatsoever state they may be, to the said Chambers, each in its proper district, if one of the parties of the said religion demand it within four months after the establishment thereof; and as for those which are suspended and not in a state for trial, the said persons of said religion shall be obliged to make their declaration on the first intimation and notice they shall have of the taking up of the suits; and the said time passed, it shall no longer be open to them to demand the reference.

45*th*.—The said Chambers of Grénoble and Bourdeaux, and the Chamber of Castres shall retain the forms and style of Parliaments, within the jurisdiction in which they shall be established, and those who sit in judgment shall be of equal numbers of each religion, unless the parties agree to the contrary.

46*th*.—All the judges to whom application shall be made for the execution of writs and orders from the said Chambers, and of Chancery letters, together with all constables and sergeants, shall be obliged to execute them; and the said constables and sergeants shall serve all subpœnas throughout the kingdom without asking *Placet, visa ne Pareatis*, under pain of suspension from their offices, and the risk of all costs and injuries to the parties, the cognizance of which shall belong to the said parties.

47*th*.—There shall be no removing of suits, the cognizance of which belongs to said Chambers, save in the case of the Ordinances, which shall be referred to the nearest Chamber established in conformity with our Edict. And the distribution of the suits of said Chambers shall be decided in the nearest, observing the orders and forms of said Chambers in which the suits shall be prosecuted; except for the Chamber of the Edict in our Parliament of Paris, where the suits commenced shall be distributed in the same Chamber by Judges who shall be nominated by us, in special letters to that effect, if the parties shall not prefer waiting the renewal of said Chamber. And if it happen that a similar suit be given to all the Mixed Chambers, the distribution shall be referred to the said Chamber of Paris.

48th.—The objecting to or challenging of the President and Councillors of the Mixed Chambers shall be allowed, to the number of six; to which number the parties must be limited, otherwise all shall proceed without regard to said objections.

49th.—The examination of the Presidents and Councillors newly appointed for the Mixed Chambers, shall be made in our Privy Council, or in the said Chambers, each in its own district when they shall be numerous enough; and nevertheless the usual oath shall be taken by them in the courts where the said Chambers shall be established, and on their refusal, in our Privy Council, excepting those of the Chamber of Languedoc, who shall take the oath before our Chancellor or in that Chamber.

50th.—We desire and command that the acceptance of our Officers of the said religion shall be decided in the Mixed Chambers by the plurality of votes, as is usual in other tribunals, without requiring a majority of two-thirds, according to the Ordinance, which in this respect is null and void.

51st.—And to these Mixed Chambers shall be referred all propositions, deliberations and resolutions appertaining to the maintenance of public tranquillity, and the private concerns and Police of those towns in which the Chambers shall be established.

52d.—The article upon the jurisdiction of the said Chambers, ordered by the present Edict, shall be followed and observed according to its form and tenor, equally in all that concerns the execution or non-execution, or infraction of our Edicts when those of said religion shall be parties.

53d.—The subaltern officers, Royal or otherwise, whose acceptance appertains to our Courts of Parliament, if they be of the said pretended Reformed religion, may be examined and received in the said Chambers: that is to say, those within the jurisdictions of the Parliaments of Paris, Normandy and Bretagne, in the said Chamber of Paris; those of Dauphiny and Provence, in the Chamber of Grénoble; those of Burgundy, in the said Chamber of Paris or of Dauphiny, at their option; those within the jurisdiction of Toulouse, in the Chamber of Castres; and those of the Parliament of Bourdeaux, in the Chamber of Guyenne; without any one being allowed to raise objection but our Attorneys-General and their substitutes, and those in said offices.   Nevertheless, the usual oath shall be taken by them in the Courts of Parliament, which shall not be able to take any action as to their admission; and if the said Parliament refuse, the said Officers shall take the oath in the said Chambers, after which ceremony, they shall be obliged to present the proof of their admission to the Registrars of the said Courts of Parliament, through a doorkeeper or notary, and also to leave a collated copy with the said Registrars: upon whom it is enjoined to record the said acts, upon pain of all costs and losses to said parties; and where the said Registrars shall refuse to do this, it shall be sufficient for the said Officers to report the fact of the said summons, dispatched by the said doorkeeper or notary, and the Registrar of the said district shall be obliged to make a record of it, for future reference, as occasion may require, under pain of prosecution and trial.   And as for those Officers whose admission has not usually been granted through our said Parliaments, in case that those, who ought to examine and admit them, refuse to do so, the said Officers shall apply for redress to the said Chambers, as they have a right to do.

54th.—The Officers of the said pretended Reformed religion who shall be appointed hereafter, to serve in our Courts of Parliament, Great Council, Court of Exchequer, Court of Excise or Treasury Bureau, and other financial Offices, shall be examined and admitted in the accustomed places; and in case of refusal or denial of justice, the matter shall be inquired into by our Privy Council.

55th.—The admission of Officers through the Chamber formerly established at Castres, shall be valid in spite of any Decree or Ordinance to the contrary.   We also declare to be valid, the admission of Judges, Councillors, Assessors and other Officers of said religion, by our Privy Council or by Commissioners appointed by us to act in case of the refusal of our Courts of Parliament, Excise and

Exchequer, all to be as valid as if they were admitted by the said Courts and Chambers, or by the other Judges, to whom the right of admission belongs. And their salary shall be paid without objection by the Court of Exchequer; and if any have been struck off the list, they shall be reinstated without requiring further orders than those contained in the present Edict, and without obliging any Officer to bring fresh proof of admission, notwithstanding Decrees to the contrary, which shall be null and void.

56th.—Until means arise from the payment of fines, for the expenses of justice in the said Chambers, a sufficient assignment shall be made to meet the expenses, without prejudice to the recovery of interest upon the property of condemned persons.

57th.—The President and Councillors of the said pretended Reformed religion formerly received in our Court of Parliament of Dauphiny, and in the Chamber of the Edict, incorporated with it, shall continue to have their seats and rank therein; that is to say, the Presidents, as they have enjoyed and do enjoy them, and the Councillors, in conformity with the decrees and orders obtained from our Privy Council.

58th.—We declare to be null and void, from this time forth, all sentences, judgments, arrests, prosecutions, seizures, sales and decrees made and given against persons, dead or alive of the said pretended Reformed religion, since the death of the late King, Henry II., our much honored Lord and Father-in-law, on account of the said religion, the tumults and troubles thence arising, together with the execution of those sentences and decrees. We command all of them to be erased and taken away from the Records of the Registrars of all Courts, superior and inferior. It is also our will that all marks, vestiges and monuments of said executions shall be entirely effaced and removed, as well as all defamatory books or acts injurious to their persons, their memory or their posterity; and that wherever injury or destruction of property took place from that cause, the same shall be restored in its present condition to the former proprietors, to enjoy and dispose of as they please. And generally, we declare null and void all prosecutions and informations laid for pretended High Treason and other crimes. In spite of any prosecutions, decrees and judgments implying resumption, incorporation and confiscation that may have passed, we command the restoration in full, of all property to those of the said religion, others who belonged to their party and their heirs, and that they be put in real and actual possession of the same.

59th.—All legal proceedings carried on, and all sentences and decrees passed, during the troubles, against those of said religion who bore arms, or who withdrew from our Kingdom, or entered within cities or countries of which they had the possession, on account of other affairs besides religion and the troubles; together with all non-suits, claims from right of prescription, as well conventional as customary, all manorial seizures made from having lapsed during the troubles, or gained by means of legal impediments caused by them, and of which the cognizance belongs to our judges, shall be considered as never having been made, given or occurred. And such we have declared and do declare them, and we make them void and of none effect, without appeal; but every thing shall be restored and reinstated, in spite of said sentences, and all shall be replaced on the same footing as before. The same course shall be pursued with respect to persons who were attached to the party of those of said religion, or who absented themselves from our Kingdom on account of the troubles. And, with regard to minor children whose parents, under the above named circumstances, died during the troubles, all shall be restored to them, free of expense, and without being obliged to pay any fines; it is, however, not to be understood that the decisions given by the Presidial or Inferior Judges against those of the said religion or their party should be null, if given by Judges holding their sittings in towns possessed by them, and to which they had free access.

60th.—The decisions shall be of none effect, which have been given by our Courts of Parliament, in matters whose cognizance belongs to the Chambers ordered by the Edict of the year 1577, and Articles of Nerac and Fleix, when the parties did not proceed voluntarily in said courts, that is to say, when they protested against the jurisdiction of the court in the case, or where causes have gone by default or foreclosure, as well in civil as in criminal suits, where, in spite of protest, the said parties have been compelled to go on. Such decisions shall be of no value. But with regard to decisions given against those of said religion who have not protested, but who have proceeded voluntarily, those shall stand. Nevertheless, without prejudice to the execution thereof, the parties may, if it seem good to them, ask for a revision before the Chambers ordered by this Edict, unless the time allowed by the present Edict shall have expired; and until the said Chambers and Courts of Chancery be established, a verbal or written appeal from those of said reli-

gion presented to the Judges, Registrars or Clerks, executors of the
sentences and judgments shall have the same force as if presented
by Royal Letters.

61st.—In all inquiries which shall be made for any cause in civil
suits, if the Examiner or Commissioner be a Catholic, the parties
shall be required to agree upon an associate, and where they cannot
agree upon one, the said Examiner or Commissioner shall select one
himself of the said pretended Reformed religion: and the same
practice shall be pursued, when the Examiner or Commissioner is of
the said religion, with regard to the selection of an associate, who
shall then be a Catholic.·

62d —It is our will and command that our Judges take cognizance of the validity of Wills, in which those of the said religion are
interested, if they require it, and appeals from said judgments may
be made, notwithstanding all custom to the contrary, even in Bretagne.

63d.—To obviate all differences which might arise between our
Courts of Parliament and the Chambers of those Courts ordered by
our present Edict, good and sufficient regulations shall be made by
us for the government of said Courts and Chambers, such as shall
secure to those of the said pretended Reformed religion, the full
benefit of said Edict: which regulations shall be recorded in our
Courts of Parliament, and kept and observed without regard to
precedents.

64th.—We prohibit and forbid all our sovereign and other
Courts of this kingdom to take cognizance and try any civil or
criminal causes of those of said religion, the cognizance of which by
this our Edict belongs to the said Chambers, provided that the
reference be demanded as is said in XL.* article aforesaid.

65th.—We desire also in the meanwhile and until otherwise
ordered, that in all suits commenced and intended to be commenced
in which any of said religion shall be plaintiff or defendant, principal or security, in civil matters in which our officers and Presidial
Courts have the power of final judgment, the privilege shall be
granted to them of requiring that two of the Chamber where the
suit is tried shall refrain from judging, which, without giving any
reason, shall restrain said two from judging, the Ordinance to the
contrary notwithstanding, which provides that judges shall not be

* It must be a misprint, and intended for Article LX.—TRANSLATOR'S NOTE.

challenged without cause: and in addition to this, the right of challenging others remains to them unimpaired. And in criminal suits,
in which also the said Presidial and other Royal Subaltern
Judges give final judgment, the arraigned parties, being of the said
religion, may require three of the Judges to refrain from trying the
cause, without assigning any reason. And the Provosts Marshal
of France, the Vice-Bailiffs, Vice-Seneschals, Lieutenants of the
Short Robe, and other officers of the same rank, shall judge in conformity with the ordinances and regulations heretofore given in the
case of non-residents (*vagabons*). And as for residents accused
and arraigned within the Provosts' jurisdiction, if they are of the
said religion, they may require that three of the said Judges who
have cognizance therein refrain from judging in their suits, and
they shall refrain accordingly, without any reason being assigned;
saving when, in the body where the suit is tried, there shall be found
the number of two in civil suits, and three in criminal suits, of the
said religion, in which case none shall be challenged without giving
a reason : which practice shall be mutually and commonly followed
with regard to Catholics, in the same form as given above for challenging the Judges, where those of the pretended Reformed religion shall be most in number ; not having it understood, however,
from what is here said, that the said Presidial Courts, Provosts
Marshal, Vice-Bailiffs, Vice-Seneschals and others who give final
judgment, shall take any cognizance of past difficulties. And as
for crimes and excesses arising from other causes than the troubles,
since the commencement of the month of March in the year 1585,
until the end of the year 1597, in cases of which they have cognizance, it is our will that appeals may be lawfully made from their
judgment to the Chambers ordered by the present Edict; the practice shall be similar for the Catholic participants and where those
of said pretended Reformed religion shall be parties.

66*th*.—We desire and command that henceforth in all preparations other than informations for criminal suits in the Seneschal's
Courts of Toulouse, Carcassonne, Rouergue, Loragais, Beziers, Mont-
pellier and Nimes, the Magistrate or Commissioner deputed to make
said preparations, if he be a Catholic, shall be obliged to take an
Associate who shall be of the said pretended Reformed religion,
upon whom the parties can agree, but if they shall be unable to
agree upon one, the aforesaid Magistrate or Commissioner shall select
for the office one of the said religion. In like manner, if the said

Magistrate or Commissioner be of said religion, he shall be obliged
to have a Catholic Associate.

67*th.*—Where the question shall be upon criminal prosecution
by the Provosts and their Lieutenants, of any one who is a resident
and is of the said religion, who is accused of crime within the jurisdiction of the Provosts' Court, if the said Provosts or their Lieutenants be Catholics, they shall be obliged to summon an Associate
of said religion, for the preparation of the suit, which Associate
shall be present, as well at the decision upon competency of jurisdiction, as at the final trial of the said suit. The question of competency can only be decided at the nearest Presidial Court, to which
all the principal officers of said Court, who can be found in the
neighborhood must be convened, under the penalty of the proceedings being null; unless the accused party should require the competency to be decided in the said Chambers, ordered by the present
Edict. In which case, with regard to those residing in the Provinces of Guyenne, Languedoc, Provence or Dauphiny, the substitutes
of our Attorneys-General in the said Chambers shall bring forward,
at the request of said residents, the charges and accusations laid
against them, for inquiry and decision as to whether the causes belong of right to the Provosts' Court or not, and afterwards, according to the nature of the crime, to be referred by the Chambers for
trial in the accustomed mode, or transferred to the Provosts' Court.
In either case the Chambers shall see that all is equitably done, in
conformity with our present Edict. The Presidial Judges, Provosts,
Vice-Bailiffs, Vice-Seneschals, and others who pronounce final
judgment, shall be respectively bound to obey implicitly all commands they shall receive from said Chambers, in like manner as
they have heretofore obeyed our said Parliaments, under penalty
of being deprived of their estates.

68*th.*—The proclamations, placards and public sale of estates,
under order from the Courts, shall take place in the customary
places and at the usual hours, so far as may be practicable, and consistent with our Ordinances; otherwise to be in the public market
place. If there be no market in the place where the property is
situated, the sale shall take place at the nearest market within the
district where the adjudication was made, and placards shall be affixed to the post of the said market-place, and at the entrance of
the Session House of the said place, and by this means the said
notices shall be deemed valid and sufficient, and the sale carried on

without delay from any plea of invalidity which might be raised on this account.

69*th.*—All title-deeds, papers, vouchers and documents which have been taken away, shall be returned and delivered up, equally by both sides to the rightful owners; even if the said papers or the castles and houses in which they were preserved have been taken and seized either by special Commission from the lately deceased King, our much honored Lord and brother-in-law, or others, or by command of the Governors and Lieutenant Generals of our Provinces, or on the other hand by authority of the Chiefs of the other party, or under any pretext whatsoever.

70*th.*—The children of those who quitted the Kingdom on account of religion and the troubles, after the death of our much honored Lord and Father-in law Henry II., even though the aforesaid children may have been born out of the Kingdom of France, shall enjoy all the rights and privileges of true native Frenchmen, and such we have declared and do declare them to be, and they shall not be obliged to take out letters of naturalization, or take any steps beyond the provisions of this Edict; notwithstanding all Ordinances to the contrary, which we have hereby annulled and do annul; only requiring that the said children, born abroad, shall take up their residence in this Kingdom within ten years after the publication of this Edict.

71*st.*—Those of the said pretended Reformed religion who shall have farmed any crown lands, fiefs, gabels, customs, or any other taxes belonging to us, from which they could not draw the income on account of the troubles, shall be discharged, and we do hereby discharge them from paying that which they did not receive from said taxes, or which they paid, without fraud, elsewhere than into our Exchequer, notwithstanding the obligations by which they were bound.

72*d.*—All places, cities and provinces of our Kingdom, all countries, territories and manors owing obedience to us, shall have full benefit and enjoyment of all privileges, immunities, liberties, franchises, fairs, markets, jurisdictions and Courts of justice of which they were possessed previous to the troubles, dating from the month of March, 1585, and preceeding, notwithstanding all Letters to the contrary. If any Courts were removed solely on account of the troubles, the said Courts shall be restored and re-established in the cities and places where they formerly existed.

73d.—If any prisoners are still in confinement or at the galleys, by judicial authority or otherwise, on account of the troubles, they shall be enlarged and set fully at liberty.

74th.—Those of said religion shall not, hereafter, be over-taxed or oppressed by the imposition of any tax, ordinary or extraordinary, beyond what is imposed upon Catholics, in proportion to their property and ability. The parties who complain of surcharge may apply for relief to the Judges who have cognizance thereof, and all our subjects, Catholics, and those of said pretended Reformed religion, shall receive equal justice, and shall be discharged from all impositions illegally laid on them by either party, together with all unpaid obligations, expenses incurred without consent of the parties, without, however, being able to recover the income which shall have been used for the payment of said charges.

75th.—It is intended that neither those of said religion, others of their party, nor the Catholics who remained in the towns and places occupied and retained by them, and who were laid under contribution, shall be prosecuted for the payment of subsidies, excise, city tolls, levies, land tax, quarters for soldiers, indemnities or other impositions and taxes laid during the troubles, before our accession to the Throne, whether by the Edicts and Mandates of the deceased Monarchs, our predecessors, or by the advice and legislation of Governors of Provinces, Courts of Parliament and others. We have discharged and do hereby discharge them from the payment of all such, in forbidding our Royal Treasurers, Receivers, General and Particular, their Clerks and Agents, and other Comptrollers and Commissioners of the Exchequer to inquire after, molest or disturb them, directly or indirectly, in any way whatever.

76th.—There shall be no claim upon the Chiefs, Lords, Knights, Nobles, Officers, Corporations, Societies, persons assisting them, or widows, heirs and successors of such as themselves took and collected, or by their decrees obtained money of any amount, whether belonging to the King's Revenues or to private individuals; rents, revenues, plate and sales of furniture belonging to clergy or laity; forest trees, royal or otherwise; fines, pillage, ransoms or any other kind of property, seized on account of the troubles beginning in March, 1585, and other previous troubles, up to our accession to the Throne. Those persons appointed to collect said funds, or who leased them, or procured them by their Ordinances, cannot be called to account for their proceedings now or at any future time, but shall forever remain free, they and their agents alike, from all inquiry about the management and administration of the said funds, on condition that they produce, before our Court of Parliament of Paris, within four months after the publication of the present Edict, receipts duly executed by the Chiefs of the said religion or by persons empowered by them to audit and close the accounts, or by the City Corporations who held power during the troubles. They shall remain equally free from disturbance on account of any acts of hostility, levying and leading troops, coining and valuing money, according to the orders of said Chiefs, casting or seizing upon artillery and ammunition, manufacturing gunpowder, seizing, fortifying, dismantling and destroying cities, castles, towns, &c., making attempts upon them, burning and otherwise destroying churches, houses, &c.; creating courts of justice, carrying out their sentences whether in matters civil or criminal, police regulations under them, journeys made, correspondence, negotiations entered upon, treaties and contracts concluded with foreign Princes and Governments, the introduction of foreigners within cities and other places in our Kingdom. In short, every thing is to be included within this general amnesty, that has been negotiated, arranged or completed, during the said troubles, by those of the said religion and their party, since the death of the late King, Henry II.

77th.—There shall no accusation be brought against any person of the said religion for holding General or Provincial Assemblies, as well that at Mantes as elsewhere, and since, up to this present time, together with Councils established and ordered through the Provinces, Deliberations, Ordinances and Regulations, made by said Assemblies and Councils; establishing and increasing garrisons, assembling troops, levying taxes, taking them out of the hands of our Receivers, Parish Collectors or others, in any way whatever, seizing salt, continuing or erecting new stage stations, toll houses, and receiving the tolls from them, even at Royan, and on the rivers Charente, Garonne, the Rhone and Dordonne; fitting out vessels and fighting with the same, together with any accidents or excesses arising from enforcing the payment of said tolls and other rates, fortifying cities, castles and other places, imposing taxes and forced labor (*corvées*) receipts from the same, deposing our Receivers, Farmers and other Officers, appointing others in their places; all combinations formed, dispatches sent and negotiations carried on within or without the Kingdom: in short, nothing done, discussed, written and ordered by said Assemblies, shall be inquired into, and those persons who advised, signed, executed, caused to be signed and executed the said Ordinances, Regulations and Resolutions, shall remain undisturbed, as also their widows, children and heirs, now and forever, even if the particulars of the case be not specially provided for herein. We impose perpetual silence on these subjects upon our Attorneys-General, their substitutes, and any others who may be interested therein, in any way whatsoever, notwithstanding all decrees, sentences, judgments, prosecutions or proceedings to the contrary.

78th.—We fully approve, authorize and pronounce to be valid, the accounts which have been audited, closed and examined by the deputies of the said Assembly. We desire that these, together with the receipts and papers which have been presented by the responsible parties, shall be taken to the Court of Exchequer in Paris, three months after the publication of the present Edict, and placed in charge of our Attorney-General, to be delivered to the keeper of the books and registers of our Chamber, to be ready when wanted for reference, at all times, without requiring said accounts to be revised, nor the parties responsible for them being obliged to appear or make correction, unless in the case of any thing received having been omitted, or in that of false receipts having been given. Our said Attorney-General must not raise any question with regard to deficient surplus, or formalities not carefully attended to. Officers of the Treasury, as well in Paris as in the Provinces where they are settled, are not to take cognizance of any such matters, in any way whatever.

79th.—With regard to accounts not yet given in, we wish them to be audited and closed by Commissioners who will be appointed by us for the purpose, who will make no difficulty in passing and allowing all items, paid by the said responsible parties, in virtue of the Ordinances of the said Assembly, or others possessing power.

80th.—All Collectors, Receivers, Farmers and all others, shall be fully and legally discharged from the payment of all funds of what nature soever, which they paid to the said Clerks of the said Assembly, up to the last day of this month. We wish to have every thing passed and allowed in the accounts presented to our Exchequer, purely and simply in virtue of the receipts which shall be borne upon them. If any shall be afterwards executed and delivered in, they shall be declared null, and persons who shall accept them or deliver them in, shall be condemned to the penalty, for presenting false accounts. And where there shall appear in accounts formerly given in to have been erasures made or entries introduced, the said parts shall be entirely restored as before, in virtue of these presents, without requiring special letters or any thing more than the production of an extract from the present article.

81st.—There shall be no claim upon Governors, Captains, Consuls, or persons appointed to collect funds for paying the garrisons of places held by those of the said religion, which our Parochial Receivers and Collectors, either by constraint or in obedience to command of the Paymasters, furnished by loan upon their notes or bonds, for the support of the said garrisons; as much as comes to what we concluded to place on the roll at the commencement of the year 1596, and the increase since granted by us. The said parties shall be free from all claim for what was paid for the above purpose, even if not expressly specified upon the notes and bonds, which shall be returned to them as null. And, in order to accomplish this discharge, the paymasters in each district shall make the individual Receivers of our taxes give receipts to the said Collectors, and the Receivers-general shall give receipts to the individual Receivers: for the release of the Receivers-general there will be the sums of which they will have kept account, as much as it is said to be, endorsed upon the orders issued by the Chancellor of the Exchequer, under the names of the Paymasters-General for the payment of the said garrisons, and where the said orders do not amount to as much as our said establishment of the year 1596, and the subsequent addition to it, we command that fresh orders shall be given for the amount necessary to release those responsible for it, and to recover said promissory notes and bonds, so that there may not hereafter be any claim upon those who gave them. All papers requisite for confirming the discharge of the accountable parties shall be executed in virtue of the present article.

82d.—Likewise, those of said religion must forbear and desist from all devices, negotiations and correspondence, as well within as without our kingdom; and the assemblies formed in the provinces must be dissolved immediately ; all leagues and associations formed, or to be formed, under any pretext whatsoever, contrary to our present Edict, shall be broken and annulled, as we do break and annul such ; we expressly forbid all our subjects from this day forth, holding clubs, raising money without permission, making fortifications, enlisting men, congregating and assembling otherwise than permitted by this Edict, and without arms, all of which we prohibit and forbid under pain of being severely punished, as despisers and breakers of our commands and ordinances.

83*d.*—All captures at sea, during the troubles, made in virtue of licenses, and those by land also, upon those of the opposite party, and which have been judged by judges and Commissioners of the Admiralty, or by the Chiefs of those of the said religion or their Council, shall be hushed under the provisions of our present Edict, without allowing any prosecution : neither the Captains nor others who have made the said captures, their securities, the said judges, officers, their widows or heirs, can ever be called to account or molested in any way whatever, notwithstanding any decrees of our Privy Council or letters of marque, and distraint, pending and not judged, of which we desire there to be full and entire replevin.

84*th.*—Likewise, there can be no inquiry made about those of said religion who, during, and even since the troubles, have hindered and opposed the execution of decrees and judgments obtained for the re-establishment of the Apostolic Roman Catholic Religion, in divers places within this kingdom.

85*th.*—And as for those who committed acts of hostility contrary to the regulations public or private, of Chiefs or Communities who held power in the Provinces, they may be prosecuted as the law directs.

86*th.*—Inasmuch, however, as if what was done contrary to the regulations on both sides, is indiscriminately excepted and reserved, from the general indemnity granted by our Edict, and allowed to be inquired into, there would be no military man exempt from disturbance, which would probably produce fresh troubles : on this account we wish and command that none but criminal cases shall be excepted from said indemnity, such as rape, burning, murder, theft committed by treachery, ambuscade out of the line of regular warfare to gratify private revenge, contrary to the laws of war, disregarding passports and safe conducts, murdering and pillaging without orders. Such to be the rule with regard to those of said religion, and others who have followed the party of their Chiefs, acting from private motives.

87*th.*—We command likewise, that punishment be inflicted for crimes and offences committed amongst persons of the same party, provided they were not acts ordered by the Chiefs of either party, in conformity with the necessities, usages and laws of war. For raising and exacting money, bearing arms and other warlike operations on private account, without authority, they shall be liable to prosecution according to law.

88*th.*—The cities, dismantled during the troubles, may be rebuilt and repaired from the ruins, at the expense of the inhabitants, and the (*octroi*) toll formerly levied upon provisions for this purpose may be continued.

89*th.*—It is our order, desire and pleasure, that all Lords, Knights, Nobles, and others of whatsoever rank and condition of the said pretended Reformed Religion and their party, be restored to, and effectually replaced in the full enjoyment of every and all their property, privileges, names, rights, and offices, notwithstanding judgments to the contrary procured during the troubles. We do declare all such decrees, seizures and judgments null and void.

90*th.*—Where those of the said pretended Reformed Religion, have become possessed of real estate belonging to the Church, in any other way than by grants from the deceased Kings our Predecessors, the title shall not stand good, but the Clergy shall be reinstated immediately and without delay, and be protected in the possession and actual enjoyment of the property alienated, without being obliged to defray the amount for which it was sold; and this notwithstanding deeds of sale, which we break and declare void; without however depriving the purchasers of the right to look for redress from the Chiefs, under whose authority the said property was sold. Nevertheless for the reimbursement of that which was truly and honestly paid, we shall execute Letters Patent giving permision to those of said religion, to claim upon them the amount of said sales, without allowing said purchasers to make any claim for damages from the loss of possession, but merely to content themselves with being repaid the sum actually paid by them for the property. If the property should have been bought at some unjust price below its value, a deduction of profits made from it must be allowed.

91*st.*—To the end that all Magistrates, Officers, and the rest of our subjects may perfectly understand our wishes and intentions, and that no ambiguity may arise from conflicting articles contained in former Edicts, we have declared, and we do now declare, to be null and void all former Edicts, Secret Articles, Letters, Declarations, Modifications, Restrictions, Explanations, Decrees and Records, as well as all Secret and other Resolutions formerly issued by us, or the Kings our predecessors, registered in our Courts of Parliament or elsewhere, upon subjects connected with the said religion, and the troubles arising therefrom in our Kingdom. To the abrogation herein contained, we add our declaration that by this our Edict we have broken, revoked, and cancelled all others; and we declare expressly, that we wish this our Edict to be steadfastly and inviolably kept and observed, by all Magistrates and Officers, as well as all our other subjects, eschewing every thing contrary to its provisions.

92d.—And for still further assurance, that this Edict be observed and carried out as we wish, it is our Royal will and pleasure that, immediately upon its reception, all Governors, and Lieutenant-Governors of our Provinces, all Bailiffs, Seneschals, and other Magistrates in our cities, shall swear to have it kept and observed, each within his District; as also the Mayors, Sheriffs, Capitouls, Consuls and Aldermen, annual or permanent, in our cities and towns. We also enjoin upon our said Bailiffs, Seneschals, or their Lieutenants, and other judges, that they call upon the principal inhabitants, indifferently of either religion, to swear to the maintenance of the present Edict immediately after its publication. We take all alike under our protection and safe-keeping, and desire all mutually to protect each other; and we make our officers liable to answer themselves in Court for any infraction of the present Edict by the inhabitants of the said cities, if they do not lodge a complaint against such offenders, and hand them over to the law.

We command our right entirely and well-beloved people, comprising our Courts of Parliament, our Courts of Exchequer, and Courts of Aids, under the penalty for causing Acts, that would otherwise pass, to be null and void, to let nothing intervene, but, immediately after receiving the present Edict, take the above oath and have the Edict published and registered in our said Courts, purely and simply according to the form and tenor of its contents, without modification, restriction, protest, or secret record, not waiting for any further order or command from us; and we require our Attorneys-General to exact and enforce the publication immediately without delay.

Therefore we lay our commands upon the members of our said Courts of Parliament, Court of Exchequer, Courts of Aids, our Bailiffs, Seneschals, Provosts, and all other Magistrates, whose duty it

21

may be, together with their Lieutenants, that they cause our present Edict and Ordinance to be read, published, and registered within their respective Courts and jurisdiction, and that they do all in their power to have it maintained and carried out in every point, giving the full and peaceable benefit thereof to all, putting a stop to every thing that could hinder or interfere with it. For, such is our Royal pleasure, in witness whereto, we have signed these presents with our own hand; and in order that it may be an established and settled thing for ever, we have affixed our seal.

Given at Nantes, in the month of April, year of Grace, one thousand five hundred and ninety-eight; and the ninth year of our reign.

Signed,   HENRI.

and below, the King being in his Council,

FORGET.

And at the side.   VISA.

And sealed with the great seal, with green wax upon cords of red and green silk.

Read, published and registered, the King's Attorney-General hearing and consenting thereto, at Paris, in Parliament, the twenty-fifth day of February, one thousand five hundred and ninety-nine.

Signed,   VOYSIN.

Read, published and registered, in the Court of Exchequer, the King's Attorney-General hearing and consenting thereto, the last day of March, one thousand five hundred and ninety-nine.

Signed,   DE LA FONTAINE.

Read, published and registered, the King's Attorney-General hearing and consenting thereto, at Paris, in the Court of Aids, the thirtieth and last day of April, one thousand five hundred and ninety-nine.

Signed,   BERNARD.

Secret articles, taken from the General ones, that the King granted to those of the pretended Reformed religion : which his Majesty did not wish to embody in the general articles, nor yet in the Edict made and drawn up from them, given at Nantes in the month of April last : and nevertheless it is the will of His said Majesty that they shall be as fully observed as those contained in the said Edict. And for this purpose they shall be registered in his Courts of Parliament and elsewhere as required, and all Declarations, Provisions and Letters, that be needed shall be dispatched.

ARTICLE 1st.—The sixth article of the said Edict relating to liberty of conscience, and permission to reside within this kingdom, granted to all his Majesty's subjects, shall be extended to, and include within it, all Ministers, Schoolmasters and others, who are or may be in future of the said religion, whether natives or foreigners, acting in all things in conformity with the provisions of said Edict.

2d.—Those of the said religion shall not be obliged to contribute towards the building or repairs of Churches or Chapels, nor to the purchase of Sacerdotal ornaments, Lights, casting of Bells, consecrated bread, hiring houses for Priests or Monks, nor any similar thing; except in cases where they themselves or their ancestors have made endowments.

3d.—They shall not be obliged to decorate their houses on Festivals when it is so ordered, they shall merely allow the official persons to do it, without contributing any thing towards it.

4th.—Those of the said religion shall not, when sick or dying, be obliged to receive exhortations from persons not of their own faith, and their own Ministers shall be permitted to visit and comfort them without hindrance. As for those who shall be under judicial condemnation, the said Ministers may visit and comfort them, but can only offer up public prayers in those places where the said religion is allowed free exercise.

5th.—The public exercise of the said religion shall be lawful at Pimpoul : and in the faubourg of Paulet for Dieppe ; and the said places of Pimpoul and Paulet shall be places for bailiwicks. As for Sancerre, the said exercise shall be continued as at present, save that for the establishment of it in the said town, the inhabitants must make it appear that they have the consent of the Lord of the Manor. Commissioners appointed by His Majesty for the execution of the Edict will attend to this. The free exercise of the said religion shall be re-established in the town of Montagnac in Languedoc.

6th.—The following plan has been decided upon, for the execution of the article upon bailiwicks. Firstly, for the establishment of the exercise of the said religion, in the two places granted in each Bailiwick, Presidency or Government, those of the said religion shall name two cities, in the faubourgs of which, the said exercise shall be established by the Commissioners, his Majesty shall appoint for the execution of the Edict. And in cases where the Commissioners shall not approve, those of the said religion shall name two or three villages near to the said cities, from which the Commissioners shall make choice of one. And if from war or pestilence, or other actual impediment, the religious exercise cannot be carried on in the appointed places, others may be named for use during the continuance of the impediment. Secondly, there shall only be two cities named within the government of Picardy, in the faubourgs of which the exercise of said religion may be allowed, for the Bailiwicks, Presidencies, and Governments dependent upon it: and where it may not be convenient to allow it in the faubourgs of the cities, two villages may be selected. Thirdly, in consideration of the great extent of the Presidency of Provence, and the Bailiwick of Viennois, His Majesty grants permission for the exercise of said religion in a third place, which shall be selected according to the above provisions, and shall be in addition to the places where the exercise already exists.

7th.—That which is granted by the said article, for the exercise of the said religion within the Bailiwicks, shall extend to the lands owned by the late Queen, the mother-in-law of His Majesty, and to the Bailiwick of Beaujolois.

8th.—In addition to the two places granted for the exercise of the said religion, by the private articles of the year 1577, in the Isles of Marennes and Oleron, two others shall be granted, for the convenience of the inhabitants: that is to say, one for all the Isles of Marennes, and one for Oleron.

9th.—The octroi or toll upon provisions granted by His Majesty, for the exercise of said religion in the city of Mets, shall take full effect.

10th.—It is the will and pleasure of His Majesty, that the 27th article of his Edict, relating to the eligibility for official Dignity of persons of the pretended Reformed religion, shall be understood and fully observed according to its form and tenor; notwithstanding edicts and grants formerly made for the reduction of any Princes, Nobles, or Catholic cities to obedience, which grants shall have no prejudicial bearing upon those of said religion, except in the matter of the public exercise thereof, which shall be regulated by the following articles; from which, instructions shall be drawn up for the Commissioners, whom His Majesty will appoint to put in execution the provisions of his Edict.

11th.—According to the Edict given by His Majesty, for the reduction of the Duke of Guise, the exercise of the said pretended Reformed religion, shall not be allowed within the cities or faubourgs of Rheims, Rocroy, Saint Disier, Guise, Joinville, Fîmes, and Moncornet in the Ardennes.

12th.—It shall not be allowed in the environs of the said cities, and places in which it was forbidden by the Edict of the year 1577.

13th.—And in order to take away all ambiguity that might possibly attach to the word *environs*, His Majesty declares that it is understood to apply to all places within the liberties, or the jurisdiction of the said cities, in which places the said religion shall not be established, except it should have been permitted by the Edict of 1577.

14th.—And inasmuch as by that, the said exercise was granted generally in the Fiefs belonging to those of the said religion, without excepting the said environs: His Majesty declares the same privilege shall still be possessed by those of the said religion holding such Fiefs, as is declared in the Edict given at Nantes.

15th.—According to the Edict given for the reduction of the Marshal de la Châtre, there shall be only one place granted for the exercise of the said religion, in each of the Bailiwicks of Orleans and Bourges, nevertheless the exercise may be continued where it is permitted by the Edict of Nantes.

16th.—The privilege of preaching in the Fiefs, shall be extended to the said Bailiwicks, in the way directed by the Edict of Nantes.

17th.—The Edict given for the reduction of the Marshal de Bois Dauphin shall be observed; and the said exercise shall not be permitted within any towns, faubourgs, or places brought by him into subjection to His Majesty. As for the environs of such, the Edict of 1577 shall be observed, even in the houses of the Fiefs, as directed by the Edict of Nantes.

18th.—There shall be no exercise of the said religion within the

cities, faubourgs and castle of Morlais, in conformity with the Edict
given on the reduction of the said city. The Edict of 1577 shall be
observed within the district, even in the Fiefs, according to the
Edict of Nantes.

19th.—In consequence of the Edict for the reduction of Quin-
percorantin, there shall be no exercise of the said religion within
the Bishopric of Cornouaille.

20th.—According also to the Edict given for the reduction of
Beauvais, there shall be no exercise of the said religion at Beauvais,
nor within the distance of three leagues around it. Nevertheless,
it may be established in the places permitted by the Edict of 1577,
even in the houses of the fiefs, in conformity with the Edict of
Nantes.

21st.—Inasmuch as the Edict given for the reduction of Admiral Villars was only provisional, and to be in force until the
King decreed otherwise, it is the will and pleasure of His Majesty,
that henceforth his Edict of Nantes shall regulate all cities and jurisdictions brought into subjection to His Majesty by the said Admiral.

22d.—According to the Edict for the reduction of the Duke de
Joyeuse, the exercise of said religion shall not be allowed in the
city of Toulouse or its faubourgs, or within four leagues around
it, nor any nearer than the cities of Villemur, Carmain and the
Isle in Jourdan.

23d.—It shall not be restored in the towns of Alet, Auriac and
Montesquieu; with the understanding, at the same time, that if
persons of the said religion within the said towns, shall petition for
a place where they can have the exercise of said religion, the Commissioners of His Majesty, or the officers of the place, shall assign
for each town some place of convenient and safe access for the said
exercise, to be not further than one league distant from the town.

24th.—The said exercise may be established according to the
provisions of the Edict of Nantes, within the jurisdiction of the
Court of Parliament of Toulouse; excepting, always, in the Bailiwicks, Presidencies &c. the chief town of which was brought into
subjection to the King by the said Duke de Joyeuse, where the
Edict of 1577 must be observed. It is to be understood that the
said exercise may be continued in the places where it existed at the
time of the reduction; and in the houses of fiefs as set forth in the
Edict of Nantes.

25th.—The Edict given for the reduction of Dijon shall be observed, and according to it, there shall be no religious exercises whatever but those of the Apostolic Roman Catholic Church, within the City or for four leagues around it.

26th.—The Edict given for the reduction of the Duke De Mayenne shall be likewise observed, and, in conformity with it, there shall be no exercise of the pretended Reformed religion within the towns of Châlons, and for two leagues around Soissons, for the space of six years, commencing from the month of January, 1596; after the expiration of which period, the Edict of Nantes shall extend there and be observed as through the rest of the Kingdom.

27th.—Persons of all ranks of the said religion shall be permitted to reside within the City of Lyons, and freely to go and come; and the same as regards other places within the Government of Lyonnois, notwithstanding prohibitions formerly made by the Syndics and Sheriffs of the said City of Lyons, and confirmed by His Majesty.

28th.—There shall be only one place in a Bailiwick for the exercise of said religion, within the whole Presidency of Poitiers, besides those in which it is now established. The fiefs to be regulated by the Edict of Nantes. The said exercise shall be continued in the town of Chauvigny: the said exercise shall not be re-established in the towns of Agen, and Perigueux, although by the Edict of 1577 it might be.

29th.—There shall be only two places in the Bailiwick for the exercise of the said religion, in the Government of Picardy, as has been said before; and the said two places may be given in the districts reserved by the Edict given on the reduction of Amiens, Peronne and Abbeville. The said exercise may be permitted in the houses of the fiefs, throughout the Government of Picardy, according to the Edict of Nantes.

30th.—There shall be no exercise of the said religion in the town and faubourg of Sens, and only one place in the Bailiwick shall be allowed within the district; without prejudice, however, to the privileges granted to the owners of fiefs, which shall be in accordance with the Edict of Nantes.

31st.—The said exercise shall not be allowed within the city or faubourgs of Nantes, nor in any place within three leagues around The houses of owners of fiefs excepted, according to the Edict of Nantes.

32*d.*—It is the will and pleasure of His Majesty, that his said Edict of Nantes be observed from this time forth, in all that concerns the exercise of the said religion, in all places where it was prohibited, until further orders, by the Edicts and grants given upon the submission of certain Princes, Nobles and Catholic cities. And where the prohibition was for a limited number of years, the Edict must be observed after that time is over.

33*d.*—A place shall be given to those of said religion for the city and precincts of Paris, within five leagues at the utmost, where the public exercise of said religion may be allowed.

34*th.*—In all places where the public exercise of the said religion is permitted, the people may be called together, even by the ringing of bells, and they may perform all acts and functions appertaining to said religion or its discipline, such as holding Consistories, Conferences and Synods, Provincial and National, with the permission of His Majesty.

35*th.*—Ministers, Elders and Deacons of the said religion shall not be compelled to appear as witnesses in a Court of Justice, with regard to matters made known in Consistory as questions for church censure, except it be in a matter bearing upon the safety of the State or the person of the King.

36*th.*—Persons of said religion who reside in the country, may lawfully go to towns or other places for the exercise of said religion, where it is publicly established.

37*th.*—It shall not be lawful for persons of said religion to keep public schools any where but in places where the said religion is publicly established: the provision heretofore granted for the erection and maintenance of Colleges shall be made good when required, and shall go into full operation.

38*th.*—It shall be lawful for persons making profession of the said pretended Reformed religion, to appoint such preceptors as shall seem good to them for the education of their children, and to substitute one or several, by will or codicil, or declaration made before a notary, or written and signed with their own hands. For the rest, the laws and ordinances of the Kingdom, as usually received, will be of full force in the giving and providing of guardians and protectors.

39*th.*—With regard to the marriages of Priests and Nuns which have already been contracted, it is, for various good reasons, the will of His Majesty that they shall not be disturbed or sought after, and he imposes silence upon his Attorney-General and other Officers in this matter. Nevertheless, His said Majesty declares that children, the issue of such marriages, shall only inherit the household goods and the earnings or acquisitions of their parents, and in default of such children the nearest relations are to inherit: and the wills, donations and other dispositions, made and to be made, by persons of said description, of the said household goods and earnings, are declared valid. His said Majesty declares that the said professed Monks or Priests and Nuns shall not succeed to any family inheritance directly or collaterally, except, only, they may take possession of what is left or shall be left to them by will, excepting, always, those by direct and collateral succession: as for those who made profession before the age stipulated by the Ordinances of Orleans and Blois, the tenor of said Ordinances shall be obeyed, each for the time of its being binding.

40th.—His Majesty's will and pleasure is, that persons of the said religion, who have contracted marriages or shall contract them, who are within the third or fourth degree of consanguinity, shall not be disturbed, nor the validity of the marriages called in question: in like manner, there shall be no dispute about the right of succession to property of the children born, or who shall be born from such marriages: and as for such marriages as shall have been already contracted between those of the second, or of the second and third degree, making appeal to the King, they shall be furnished with such grant or patent as shall be all-sufficient to protect them from molestation, and their children from disputed succession.

41st.—In order to judge of the validity of marriages made and contracted by those of the said religion, and to decide upon their legality, if the defendant be of the said religion, the Royal Judge shall have cognizance of the cause, and where the Catholic is defendant, the cognizance shall belong to the Ecclesiastical Judge. If both parties be of the said religion, the cognizance shall belong to the Royal Judges. His said Majesty's will is, that with regard to said marriages and differences growing out of them, the Ecclesiastical and the Royal Judges, together with the Chambers established by the Edict, shall respectively have the cognizance.

42d.—Gifts and legacies made, or that shall be made, by the last will of the dying, or the disposition of the living, towards the maintenance of Ministers, Doctors, Scholars or poor persons of the said pretended Reformed religion, or for other pious purposes, shall

21*

be valid and take full effect, notwithstanding any Judgments or Decrees to the contrary, without any prejudice, always be it remembered, to the rights of His Majesty or others in cases where the
said legacies and gifts fall in mortmain. All actions and prosecutions necessary for the recovery of said legacies and other-rights,
may be carried on by a Solicitor, in the name of the body and community of those of said religion who are interested therein, and if
it shall be found that the said gifts and legacies have been otherwise disposed of, such restitution as is practicable may be claimed.

43d.—His said Majesty permits those of the said religion to assemble before the Royal Judge, and by his authority to assess a tax
upon themselves and collect the same in sufficient sum to pay the
expenses of their Synods, and provide for the support of those who
are charged with the exercise of their said religion, of which they
will render an account to the Royal Judge : the copy of which shall
be sent every six months to His Majesty or to his Chancellor. The
said taxes and fines shall be levied, in spite of opposition or appeal.

44th.—Ministers of the said religion shall be exempt from guard
and patrol, or lodging soldiers or other assessments and imposts,
together with the guardianship of property seized under judicial
authority.

45th.—With regard to interments heretofore made in Ceme-
ries belonging to the said Catholics, it is the will of His Majesty that
no inquiry whatever shall be made, and this he enjoins upon his
officers to observe. With regard to the City of Paris, in addition
to the two Cemeteries which those of the said religion now have
there, that is to say, that of Trinity, and that of Saint Germain, a
third shall be given to them in a place convenient for the said interments, either in the faubourg St. Honoré or St. Denis.

46th.—The Catholic Presidents and Councillors, who shall serve
in the Chamber ordered by the Parliament of Paris, shall be chosen
by His Majesty from the list of officers of the Parliament.

47th.—The Councillors of the said pretended Reformed religion,
who shall serve in said Chamber, shall be present, if it seem good
to them, at the causes which are decided by Commissioners, and
they may have a deliberative voice, without having any part of the
funds deposited, although they have the privilege of being present.

48th.—The oldest President of the Mixed Chambers shall pre-
side in the meeting, and in his absence the second ; and the distribution of the causes shall be made by the two Presidents conjointly,
or alternately, by the month or by the week.

49th.—In case of vacancy in the offices to be filled, by those of said religion, by the Chambers of the Edict, the parties applying shall bring a certificate from the Synod or Conference to which they belong, attesting that they are of said religion, and persons of probity.

50th.—The indemnity granted to those of the said pretended Reformed religion by the 74th article of the Edict, shall extend to the seizing of all Royal funds, whether by breaking into the chests or otherwise, even including those which were taken on the river Charante, now, that they had been appropriated to private individuals.

51st.—The 44th article of the secret articles, given in the year 1577, touching the city and Archbishopric of Avignon, and earldom of Venise, together with the Treaty concluded at Nîmes, shall be observed according to their form and tenor : no *Letters of Marque* shall be given in virtue of said Articles and Treaty, but by the King himself, sealed with his great seal. Nevertheless, those who desire to obtain them, may, in virtue of this present article, appear before the Royal Judges, who shall inform themselves fully of the facts of the injustice complained of by those who desire said letters, and then send the information sealed to His Majesty, who will take such action as he pleases thereupon.

52d.—It is the will and pleasure of His Majesty, that Master Nicolas Grimoult shall be restored to the title and possession of the offices of Senior Lieutenant-General, both Civil and Criminal, in the Bailiwick of Alençon, notwithstanding the resignation made by him to Master John Marguerit, the reception of it, and the appointment obtained by Master William Bernard of the office of Lieutenant-General, Civil and Criminal, at the sitting of Exmes ; and the decrees given against the said Marguerit, to whom it was resigned during the troubles in the Privy Council, in the years 1586, 1587 and 1588, by which Master Nicolas Barbier is maintained in the rights and privileges of Senior Lieutenant-General in the said Bailiwick ; and the said Bernard in the said office at Exmes, the which His Majesty has reversed, and all else contrary to this. Besides this, His Majesty, for certain good and sufficient reasons, commands that the said Grimoult shall repay, within three months, the said Barbier, the sums that he has escheated for the office of Lieutenant-General, Civil and Criminal, in the Vicomté of Alençon, and fifty crowns for the expense ; empowering for that purpose the

Bailiff of Perche or his Lieutenant at Mortaigne. And the repay-
ment made or offered, though the said Barbier may refuse or delay
to receive it, it is His Majesty's will and pleasure that the said Barbier and the said Bernard shall not intermeddle any more with the
duties of the said offices, under pain of the punishment for perjury;
the said Grimoult shall be placed in full possession of these offices,
with the rights and privileges appertaining to them; and, by this
article, the suit pending before the Privy Council, between the said
Grimoult, Barbier and Bernard shall be terminated. His Majesty
forbids his Parliament to take any further cognizance, and also
forbids the parties themselves to agitate it again. Besides, His said
Majesty has taken upon himself to repay the said Bernard a thousand crowns escheated for his office, and sixty crowns for the *mare
d'or* * and expenses; having for this purpose now ordered good and
sufficient appropriations to be made, the collecting of which is intrusted to the diligence of the said Grimoult.

53d.—His Majesty will write to his Ambassadors to solicit for
all his subjects, even for those of the said pretended Reformed religion, that they may not be forced to do any thing against conscience,
nor be subject to the Inquisition, going, coming, travelling and
trading in foreign countries, the allies and confederates of this
Crown, provided, always, that they do not offend against the laws
of the country in which they may be.

54th.—It is the will and pleasure of His Majesty, that no inquiries be made about the collection of the taxes levied at Royan, in
virtue of the contract made with the Sieur de Candelay, and others
made in continuation of it. The said contract is declared valid in
all its items, until the eighteenth day of next May.

55th.—The outrages committed on the person of Armand Cour-
tines, in the town of Millaut, in the year 1587, and of John Reines
and Peter Seigneuret, together with the prosecutions of the suits
in consequence, by the Magistrates of the said Millant, shall be
quashed and consigned to oblivion, in virtue of the Edict, without
its being lawful for their widows or heirs, the Attorneys-General
of His Majesty, or their Substitutes, or any other person whatever,
to bring forward the case; notwithstanding, and without paying
attention to the Decree made in the Chamber of Castres on
the tenth of last March, which shall be null and void, together
with all proceedings begun on either side.

---

* A sort of entrance fee paid to the King before being installed in an office.—TRANS.

56th.—All prosecutions, suits, sentences, judgments and decrees given, as well against the deceased Sieur de la Nouë, as against the Sieur Odet de la Nouë, his son, since their imprisonment in Flanders, which occurred in the month of May, 1580, and the month of November, 1584, and during their constant occupation in the wars and service of His Majesty, shall be broken and annulled, and all else consequent upon them, and the defence of the said de la Nouë shall be received, and they shall be restored to the same state they were in before the judgments and decrees; without being obliged to defray any expenses, or deposit any fines, if any have been decreed, nor shall any non-suit, or proscription made during the time, be brought up against them.

Executed by the King, in Council at Nantes, the second day of May, one thousand five hundred and ninety-eight.

       Signed,

                 HENRI.

And below,   FORGET.

Sealed with the great seal with yellow wax.

Henry, by the grace of God, King of France and Navarre, to our right entirely and well-beloved people, holding our Court of Parliament in Paris, greeting. We executed, in the month of April last, our Edict, for the establishment of peace and good order amongst our Catholic subjects, and those of the pretended Reformed religion. And in addition, we have granted, to those of the said religion, certain secret and private articles, which we wish to have equal force and virtue, and to be observed and accomplished equally with our Edict. For this cause, we wish, desire, and most expressly command, by these presents, that the said articles, signed by our own hand, and attached hereto, under the counter seal of our Chancellor, be registered in the registers of our said Court; and that what is herein contained be maintained and observed in every point, the same as our Edict: ceasing, and causing to cease, all troubles and hindrances. For such is our pleasure.

Given at Nantes, the second day of May, year of grace one thousand five hundred and ninety-eight; and of our reign the ninth.

             Signed for the King.

                     FORGET.

And sealed on a simple label with yellow wax.

*Writ of grant from Henry the Great, to his subjects of the pretended
Reformed religion, the 30th April, 1598.*

This day being the third of April, 1598, the King being at
Nantes, wishing to gratify his subjects of the pretended Reformed
religion, and to help them to meet various great expenses which
they have incurred, has ordered and does order, that for the future,
to commence on the first day of the present month, there shall be
put into the hands of Monsieur de Vierse, appointed by His Majesty,
by his Treasurers, each in his year, assignments for the sum of forty-
five thousand crowns, to be employed in certain secret affairs which
concern them, but which His Majesty does not choose to specify or
declare ; which sum shall be assignéd from the general Receipts as
follows : that is to say, Paris, six thousand crowns ; Caen, three
thousand crowns ; Orleans, four thousand crowns ; Poitiers,
eight thousand crowns ; Limoges, six thousand crowns ; Bor-
deaux, eight thousand crowns. The whole amounting to the
said sum of forty-five thousand crowns ; payable quarterly
every year, out of the first and most available of the general
receipts, and no deduction shall be made for any falling short, or
any other cause. Which sum of forty-five thousand crowns shall
be furnished in ready money, which shall be put in the hands of the
King's Treasurer, which shall serve to pay the whole of the assignments. And whereas, for the convenience of the above-named, it
may be required to have some payments made from certain particular receipts ; the Treasurers and Receivers-General, shall be ordered
to make it, taking it from the assignménts of the said Royal Treasurers ; which shall afterwards be delivered by the said Sieur de
Vïerse to those persons who shall have been named to him, by
those of said religion, at the beginning of the year as the parties to
receive and dispense the funds received in virtue of this ; of which
they shall return a true account at the end of the year to the Sieur
de Vierse, with the receipts of the parties taking it, for the information of His Majesty as to the employment of the money. Neither
the Sieur de Vierse, nor those appointed to receive, by the authorities of said religion, shall be called to any account in any Chamber.
His said Majesty has commanded all necessary letters and instructions to be given, and to him the account is to be rendered, in virtue of this present writing, which he has signed with his own hand,

and had it countersigned by our Chancellor, in the Council of State
and Secretary for his commands.

Signed   HENRY.

and below,   Dè Neufville.

This day, the last of April, 1598, the King being at Nantes,
wishing to content his subjects of the pretended Reformed religion
as much as possible, and to grant all their requests to him, for such
things as they considered to be essential for the safety of their persons, property, and estates. And for the confidence that His
Majesty reposes in their fidelity, and their sincere affection, with
some other important considerations affecting the tranquillity of the
state ; His said Majesty, in addition to what is contained in the
Edict he has lately resolved upon, and which ought to be published,
for the regulation of what concerns them, has granted, and promised
to them that all places, cities, and castles, of which they had possession until the end of the month of August last, in which they
shall have garrisons, the list shall be drawn up and signed by His
Majesty, and shall remain in their keeping, under the authority of
His Majesty, for the space of eight years, to count from the day of
publication of the Edict. For other places which they hold, where
they shall have no garrison, there shall be no change or innovation.
His said Majesty does not mean it to be understood, that the towns
and castles of Vendôme and Pontorson be included in the number
of said places, left in the keeping of those of said religion. He does
not mean to include within the said number, the City, Castle and
Citadel of Aubenas, of which he wishes to have the free disposal,
without its being of any consequence, that if now in the hands of
one of the said religion, it shall. afterwards be appropriated to
another of said religion as in other cities granted to them. And as
for Chauvigny, it shall be restored to the Bishop of Poitiers, Lord
of the said place, and the new fortifications shall be razed and demolished. And for the support of the said garrisons, which are to
be maintained in the said cities, places and castles, His said Majesty
has granted the sum of one hundred and eighty thousand crowns,
without including those in the Province of Dauphiny, for which
there shall otherwise be provided the sum of one hundred and
eighty thousand crowns annually : promising and assuring, that appropriations shall be made of the most available and undoubted
nature, where the said garrisons are established. And if these shall

not be sufficient, the said sum shall be made up from other sources, and shall be completely paid. His Majesty likewise promises that when he makes up the list, or establishment for the said garrisons, he will call around him those of the said religion, to take their opinion, and listen to their complaints, before he gives his orders, which he will always do in a manner to be as satisfactory to them as he possibly can. And if during the eight years, it shall be necessary to make any changes in the said establishment, whether proceeding from His Majesty's judgment, or in answer to petition, he will observe the same plan as at first, in deciding upon it. And as for the garrisons of Dauphiny, His Majesty, in drawing out the establishments for them, will take the opinion of the Sieur de Lesdiguieres. And in case of the occurrence of any vacancies, amongst the Governors and Captains of the said places, His said Majesty promises and agrees to appoint none, but such as are of the pretended Reformed religion, and shall bring proof of being so from the Conference of the place where they live, and also the attestation to the fact of their being respectable men. He will content himself with requiring that he, for whom the writ has been made out, shall bring the certificate of the Conference, before the appointment is concluded, and the Conference shall be required to make their report without unnecessary delay, or if there be any delay, they must give their reasons for the same to His Majesty. And this term of eight years expired, although His Majesty's promise will be redeemed, and the places restored to him, yet he promises, that if garrisons shall be continued there, and Governors remain to command them, he will not dispossess those who shall be in office there, to appoint any others. He likewise declares that it is his intention, as well during the said eight years, as after them, to gratify those of the said religion, and to give them a share of the offices, governments and other honors that he will have to bestow ; and to distribute them without favor or partiality, according to the rank and merit of the persons, as to his other Catholic subjects ; without however, the places and cities which may be hereafter intrusted to their command, besides those they now have, being considered, in consequence of that, to be more particularly appropriated to those of the said religion. Also his said Majesty has granted to them, that those who are in charge of the magazines, munitions, powder and cannon of these cities, appointed by those of said religion, shall remain in charge of the same, upon receiving a commission from the Grand Master of

the Artillery, and the Commissary General. Which letters shall
be executed gratuitously, putting into their hands the list signed
in due form, of the magazines, munitions, powder and cannon;
without however allowing them, by virtue of these commissions, to
lay claim to any immunity or privilege. Their salaries shall be
paid out of the sums already appropriated for the support of the
garrisons, without being chargeable to his Majesty for any other
funds. And, inasmuch as those of the said religion have applied to
his Majesty, to know what he has been pleased to order, with regard to the exercise of said religion, in the town of Metz, inasmuch
as it is not clearly expressed in the Edict or Secret Articles; his
Majesty declares that he has dispatched Letters Patent, by which
it is directed, that the Temple, formerly erected in the said town
by its inhabitants, shall be restored to them, to take away the materials, or dispose of in any way they shall see fit; without its being
lawful however, for them to preach or have any religious exercises;
nevertheless, they shall be furnished with a convenient place, within the walls of the said town, where they may have public exercise
of said religion, without it being necessary to name it in the Edict.
His Majesty also grants, that notwithstanding the exercise of the said
religion is forbidden within his court and suite, yet the Dukes,
Peers of France, Officers of the Crown, Marquises, Counts, Governors and Lieutenants-General, Marshals of the Camp, and Captains
of the Guards of his said Majesty, who shall be of his suite, need
not fear any examination into what they do in their own homes,
provided that it be only in their own private family, with closed
doors and without singing Psalms aloud, or doing any thing to make
it known that there is a public exercise of the said religion; and
if his said Majesty shall remain over three days in any city or place,
where the exercise is permitted, the said exercise may be resumed
after that time, and continued just as it was before his arrival. His
Majesty declares that in the present posture of his affairs, he has
been unable to include his territories beyond the Alps, Bresse, and
Barcellone, in the permission given for the exercise of the said pre
tended Reformed religion. His Majesty, nevertheless, promises
that when these territories shall be reduced to obedience, he will
treat his subjects there, just as he treats those here, in all points
granted by the Edict to those of said religion, notwithstanding any
thing to the contrary in the Edict, and in the mean time they shall
remain as they are. His Majesty grants, that those of the said pre-

tended Reformed religion, who should be installed in the offices of
Presidents and Councillors, to serve in the newly created Chambers
ordered by the Edict, shall be installed gratuitously, and without
payment for the first time, upon the list which shall be presented
to his Majesty by the Deputies of the Assembly of Châtellerault:
as also the Attorneys and Solicitors-General, appointed by the same
Edict, in the Chamber of Bourdeaux: and in case of the incorporation of the said Chamber of Bourdeaux and that of Toulouse, in the
said Parliaments, the said substitutes shall be provided with the
offices of Councillor in those, also gratuitously. His said Majesty
will also cause Messire François Pitou to be appointed to the office
of Substitute to the Attorney-General, in the Court of Parliament
of Paris; and for this end there shall be a new office created, and
after the decease of the said Pitou, he shall be succeeded by a person of the said pretended Reformed religion. And in case of any
vacancy occurring from the death of the Master of Requests, in the
Hotel of the King, he will fill the first vacancies with persons of
the pretended Reformed religion, whom his Majesty will see to be
proper and suitable for the service: and also that they be persons
responsible for the value of the tax of the escheats. And, in the
meantime, it shall be ordered that there be two Masters of Requests
appointed in each quarter, to report upon the petitions of those of
said religion. His Majesty also permits the Deputies of the said
religion, assembled in the said city of Châtellerault, to remain together, to the number of ten, in the city of Saumur, for the purpose
of urging the execution of his Edict, until his said Edict shall be
verified in the Court of Parliament of Paris, notwithstanding that
the said Edict requires them to disperse immediately: without their
being allowed however to make any fresh demands, nor to intermeddle in any way other than urging the said execution, and completion
by the Commissioners who shall be ordered for this purpose. And
for all that is herein given, his Majesty pledges his word and faith
by this present writing, which he will sign with his own hand, and
have countersigned by the Secretaries of State, wishing it to have
equal force and value with what is contained in an Edict, verified
in his Courts of Parliament; hoping those of the said religion will
be contènted, and accommòdate themselves to existing circumstances, doing their best for the service of the king, by not pressing
to have this ordinance put in any more authentic form, having such
confidence, in the word and the kindness of his Majesty, as to believe

that he will cause them to enjoy the full benefit of it. Having for this purpose commanded that all the expedition and dispatch shall be made which is necessary for the execution of the above.

> Also signed,   HENRI
> And below,   FORGET.

The King's Proclamation, forbidding more than twelve persons to be present at the weddings and baptisms of persons of the pretended Reformed religion.

It having been represented to the King, in Council, that his having regulated the number of persons of the pretended Reformed religion who may attend at the funerals of those of said religion, they have made it a pretext for doing the same at marriages and baptisms, marching through the streets, pretending to be a numerous body going to their temples, contrary to all former usage, and which it is proper to provide against. The King, in Council, therefore decrees that in future not more than twelve persons, including the parents, shall be present at the marriages and baptisms of those of the said pretended Reformed religion, and no more shall walk through the streets, going to the said ceremonies, under penalty of forfeiting their privileges, &c., &c., &c.

Given in Council, at St. Germain en Laye, the ninth day of November, 1670.

> (Signed),   PHELYPEAUX.

Proclamation of the Sieur President and Lieutenant-General of Sedan, forbidding persons of the pretended Reformed religion to expose, retail or sell animal food or game on days when the use of it is prohibited by the Church.

It has been represented to us, by the King's Attorney-General, that an abusive practice prevails, without any authority but the having been established by the Ancient Princes, who were of the pretended Reformed religion. Butchers, as well Catholic as of the pretended Reformed religion, undertake to keep open the public butchers' shambles, and to expose and sell meat publicly, during Lent, and other days of fasting and abstinence ordered by the

Church, which proceeding causes scandalous disorders to religion, and is forbidden by the laws of the land, and is contrary to public decorum; for, as the said shambles are in the Grand Square, and have two large and two small doors, one large one opening upon the said Grand Square, on the road between the two streets leading from one gate of the city to the other, and forming the main entrance and exit to and from the Kingdom, the other large door of the said public shambles being exactly opposite to the Church of the R. P. Jesuits, strangers passing through the city on their first arrival in the Kingdom, or their departure from it, may well doubt if it be a Catholic place at all, perceiving indications like these of its being the contrary, which causes shame to decent people, and by which Catholics, French and foreign, are struck with horror, and the zeal and piety of a whole community is extremely scandalized, since it is the only city in the Kingdom where such an abuse is tolerated. Besides this, the inhabitants being part of them of the one religion and part of the other, having grown up together, lived and traded with one another, Catholics are to be found whose habits and manners partake of the same intermingling as their interests and their commerce, and they actually go, in the most unscrupulous manner, to the public shambles, they buy and they eat animal food during Lent and upon other prohibited days. The same scandal spreads to the Pork butchers, Poulterers, Pastry Cooks, Tavern-keepers, and others, who all sell meat, poultry and game, freely, openly and with impunity, in their shops or their houses at all times and to all sorts of persons, without distinction: which disorders having been provided against by Proclamations and Decrees of the Council of State which supersede the general laws throughout the Kingdom, and, in consequence, the said Attorney-General has applied to us to have them kept, observed, and executed within our jurisdiction: We, therefore, in conformity with this requisition, expressly forbid all Butchers, Pastry Cooks, Pork butchers, Poulterers, &c., alike Catholics or of the pretended Reformed religion, to expose, retail or sell meat or game of any kind whatever, either in the said public shambles or in their private shops during Lent, or on any other days when the use of meat is forbidden by the Church, making a reservation, only, for the sale of it privately to persons of the pretended Reformed religion, with the express understanding that they shall not be permitted to furnish or give the same to any Catholic, under any circumstances or for any pretext whatsoever. Nevertheless, it may be furnished, in the same private way to sick Catholics, who shall be obliged to send a note from the Sieur Curé of this city, every time they make a purchase, and the said Butchers, Pastry Cooks, Pork Butchers and others are forbidden to sell meat, pastry, poultry or game in any other way; and we command that they keep the Curé's notes very carefully during the week, and send them to us every Monday, under pain of forfeiting their stock and paying a fine of two hundred livres, one-third of which shall be the perquisite of the informer. Under pain of the above-named punishment, we forbid all Tavern or Hotel keepers to sell or furnish in any way whatever, any meat, poultry or game to persons who on the forbidden days shall eat, drink or lodge at their houses, be they Catholics or of the said pretended Reformed religion, residents, strangers or foreigners. We enjoin it upon all persons who shall know of any infraction of our present Ordinance, to give information within twenty-four hours, under pain of a fine of twenty livres, one-third to be the perquisite of the informer. This proclamation shall be read, published and posted up in public and frequented situations, in this city and faubourgs, also upon the four doors of the public shambles, &c., &c., &c. Given by the Honorable Joseph de Guillet de la Minardiere, Councillor of the King, Lieutenant-General and President, on the part of His Majesty, in the Sovereign Court of St. Manges.

ADAM
la Menardiere.

24th February, 1672.

Copy of Memorandum sent by Mr. Pelisson to various Bishops in Languedoc, dated 12th June, 1677.

Many conversions have been made in the valleys of Pragelas, through the instrumentality of Mr. de Grénoble, a company for the Propagation of the Faith and some Jesuit Missionaries, so that without the distribution of a larger sum than 2000 crowns in all, sent at various times, a certified list has been sent in, with the names of from 700 to 800 persons restored to the church. Several Bishops have done me the honor to write to me, and have said that they also could see the way to many conversions within their dioceses, if the money could only be sent to them. I replied, by order of the king, that it would be impossible to send funds to so many places; but that each one in his own sphere should work as best he could, and that they might furnish information when conversions were likely to be made in families of consideration, in order that his Majesty might think it over, and make the requisite provision. At the same time they should by no means neglect the opportunity of making conversions amongst the families of the people, for which very little would be required, as we have seen in these valleys, where for two, three, four or five pistoles, numerous families have been gained. I have even signified to them that they may go as high as 100 francs, though I have received no fresh order from his Majesty to pay the bills of exchange drawn upon me. This has been attended to most religiously in that respect by those to whom I had written of it. I said the same thing to Mr. Potel, Secretary to the Duke of Verneuil, who was going to the States of Langue-doc, in order that he might be prepared with information to give the Bishops assembled there, and I have confirmed to him by letter what I had already said, and that, the more cheerfully, because the King, animated by the great success, has just made a fresh appro-priation for the purpose, of one-third of the funds derived from the revenues of vacant Bishoprics, collected or to be collected from the month of December last, which funds are to be regularly laid aside for this use. It will only begin to be productive next year, but we may hope from that time to draw a regular supply for the future. Things remain yet in the state they were; even though the funds are not now available, means will be forthcoming to pay bills drawn upon me. But the following conditions must be strictly observed :—

1. That on no occasion must it be unknown, or little known persons, or persons without character, who draw upon me.

2. That each draft be accompanied by an abjuration, certified by the Bishop of the Diocese, the Intendant, or some other impor tant official personage, and also a receipt to be given to the Eccle siastic appointed by his Majesty to receive the temporalities of the Abbeys of Cluny and St. Germain des Prez, together with the third appropriated for the new conversions.

Still the sum of 100 francs may be given, though it is not in tended to give as much on all occasions, economy being most essen tial, first, in order to let this dew water as large a surface as possi ble, and also for the consideration that if 100 francs be given to insig nificant individuals, without families, how much larger would be the sums expected by persons in a higher position, and able to draw large families after them.

Prelates and others who are disposed to devote themselves to this charitable work, may rest assured that in no way can they better recommend themselves to the favor of the King, who sees all the lists, than by imitating what has been done in Grénoble, where the sum of 100 francs was scarcely ever paid, generally very much less.

Nevertheless, there is no objection to giving large sums to attain great objects, but the said large sums cannot be sent without submitting the case for his Majesty to decide upon himself.

Proclamation of the King forbidding those of the pretended Reformed Religion to act as Accoucheurs or Nurses.

Louis, by the grace of God, King of France and Navarre, to all who shall see these presents, greeting.

We have been informed that great abuses have arisen, in this our kingdom, from permitting the attendance of persons of the pretended Reformed religion upon women in childbirth, because, according to the principles of their religion, baptism is not absolutely necessary, and besides they not having the liberty to baptize, the administration of baptism being reserved to their ministers and to take place in their Temples, it happens that when children are dangerously ill, the absence of the minister, or distance from the Temple, makes it impossible to have them baptized before death. Likewise, when persons of said pretended Reformed religion are employed about Catholic women they do not give timely notice when they see life in danger, because they do not believe in the Sacraments of the Church, and death takes place without the administration of said sacraments. We wish to remedy this abuse, and also to provide against illegitimate children of Roman Catholic parents, whose birth is concealed, being brought up in the pretended Reformed religion, as they often are from the nurture and education being confided to those who attend upon the mothers. For these and other causes, by the advice of our Council and of our own free will, full power and royal authority, we say and declare that it is our royal will and pleasure, that henceforth no person of either sex, making profession of the pretended Reformed religion, shall be allowed to have any thing to do with the care of either Catholic women or those of the pretended Reformed religion in childbirth, under penalty of being fined to the amount of three thousand livres, &c., &c., &c.

Given at St. Germain en Laye, the Twentieth day of February, year of grace 1680, and the thirty-seventh of our reign.

Signed,   Louis.

[It would appear that the employment forbidden to Protestants by the above proclamation was one that had been followed by them with remarkable success, and even Roman Catholic women of high rank had more confidence in them than in those of their own faith, and were most anxious still to employ them, offering great and unusual remuneration for the risk to induce them still to attend. It is well known that the mind has much influence on the body at such times, and it was believed that the above proclamation caused the loss of many lives, not so much from want of skill in those assisting as in fright and want of confidence on the part of the patients.]

Declaration of the King to the effect, that children of the age of seven years may be converted from the Pretended Reformed Religion, &c.

Louis, by the grace of God, King of France and Navarre, to all who see these letters, greeting.

The great success which it has pleased God to give to the spiritual stirring up, and other reasonable means, we have employed for the conversion of our subjects of the said pretended Reformed religion, making it expedient for us to second the movement that God has commenced amongst our subjects, discovering to them the errors in which they were born, we ought to have resolved to annul our Declaration, of the first day of February, of the year 1669, by which children of said religion were in some sort excluded from conversion to the Catholic, Apostolical Roman Church, at the age of seven, when they are competent to exercise their reason, and make a choice upon a subject of so much importance as their own salvation, until the ages respectively of fourteen for males, and twelve for females, although the Edict of Nantes contained no such provision, which should have been required. Moved by these and other influential considerations, we have said and declared, and we do say and declare, by these presents, signed with our own hand, that henceforth, it is our will and pleasure that our said subjects of the pretended Reformed religion, as well male as female, having attained the age of seven years, may lawfully be received to abjure the said pretended Reformed religion, without permitting their fathers, mothers, or any other relation to put any impediment in the way, under any pretext whatsoever, annulling, for this purpose, as much as may be necessary of our said Declaration of the first day of February, 1669. It is our will also, that the newly converted children, of the age of seven years, shall have the full benefit of our Declaration of the fourteenth day of October, 1665, and, in conformity with that, they shall have free choice, after their conversion, either to return to their parents, and be maintained at home, or to go elsewhere, and require from them an allowance for support, proportioned to their condition and means, which allowance the said fathers and mothers shall be obliged to pay, quarterly, to their children, and in case of refusal, they shall be forced to do it, by all suitable and reasonable means. Whereas we have been informed, that several of our subjects, of the said pretended Reformed religion, have sent their children for education to foreign countries, where they may imbibe sentiments contrary to the fidelity due to us and to the State from their birth ; we enjoin it upon them expressly to send for their children home without delay. And for those who are possessed of real property, they shall forfeit the whole income the first year, and half of it, every year afterwards, until they recall their children. Those who have not real property, shall be fined in proportion to their means, and the said penalties of income and fine shall be in force year after year, until the children return home. We prohibit henceforth any of our subjects of said pretended Reformed religion, from sending their children to foreign countries, for education, under sixteen years of age, without our express permission, under pain of the punishments above-named.

This command is given to our trusty and well-beloved Councillors, &c., &c., &c.

Given at Versailles, this 17th day of June, and year of grace, 1681, and of our reign the 39th.

Signed,   LOUIS.

On the fold, By the King. COLBERT.

Sealed with the great seal with yellow wax.

22

Decree of the Council of State, forbidding private Individuals to re-
ceive the sick of the pretended Reformed religion into their
houses.

The King being notified, that various private individuals, as well
in the good City of Paris, as in other parts of his kingdom, have
taken upon themselves, under the pretext of charity, to receive sick
persons of the pretended Reformed religion into their houses, and
that in some places such accommodations for the sick have been
provided by the Consistories, and the intention of his Majesty being
that the said persons of the said religion shall be taken to the Hospitals, and there treated like the Catholics, and that those willing
to be converted, may avoid the danger of being hindered by being
in the said private houses, in the hands of persons of the said religion. His Majesty in Council expressly forbids all private individuals, of whatsoever rank or condition, from receiving, under
pretext of charity, the sick of the said religion into their houses, but
commands that they be taken to the Hospitals, to be there treated
like the sick Catholics. Under penalty to a private individual, who
infringes this law, of paying a fine of 500 livres, and forfeiting, to
the Hospital in the place, all the furniture and other articles used
about the sick persons; and to the Consistories who infringe the
law, the penalty will be a prohibition of all religious exercises in
the places where they have houses to receive sick persons of the
pretended Reformed religion.

His Majesty enjoins the publication of this Decree upon the In-
tendants, Commissioners, &c., &c.

Given in the Council of State of the King, His Majesty being
present, held at Versailles, the 4th September, 1684.

Signed,   COLBERT.

Edict of the King, which revokes that of Nantes, and all consequent
upon it, and forbids all public exercise of the pretended Reform-
ed religion in the Kingdom.

Louis, by the grace of God King of France and Navarre: to all
that are and shall be, greeting.

The King Henry the Great, our Grandsire of glorious memory,
desirous that the peace he had obtained for his subjects, after the

sufferings they had endured through a long period of domestic and foreign wars, should not be disturbed on account of the pretended Reformed religion, as it had happened during the reigns of the Kings his predecessors, endeavored by his Edict given at Nantes in the month of April, 1598, to make regulations with respect to those of said religion, the places where the exercise of said religion might be allowed; He also appointed Judges Extraordinary to administer justice on their behalf, and at length he even provided secret articles containing all that he deemed necessary for the maintenance of tranquillity in his Kingdom and lessening the hatred existing between those of the two religions, in order to place himself in a more advantageous position for laboring, as he had resolved he would, to re-unite to the Church those who had been so easily detached from it. And, as the intention of the King our Grandsire could not be carried out effectually on account of his untimely death, and that even during the minority of the deceased King, our much honored Lord and Father, of glorious memory, the execution of the Edict was interrupted by new enterprises of those of the pretended Reformed religion, which gave occasion to deprive them of various privileges which had been granted by the said Edict: nevertheless, the King, our said deceased Lord and Father, displaying his accustomed clemency, granted them yet another Edict at Nîmes, in the month of July, 1629, by means of which, tranquillity having been re-established once more, the said King, animated by the same spirit and zeal for religion that had filled the breast of the King, our said Grandsire, resolved to profit by this repose and try to put his pious design in execution, but foreign war broke out a few years later, so that from the year 1635 until the conclusion of the treaty, in the year 1684, with the Princes of Europe, the Kingdom being almost always in a state of agitation, it was impossible for him to do any thing for the benefit of religion but to lessen the number of exercises of those of the pretended Reformed religion, by forbidding whatever he found established contrary to the orders of the Edicts, and by dissolving the Mixed Chambers, whose establishment had only been provisional. God having at last permitted our people to enjoy perfect peace, and relieved us from the care of protecting them against foreign enemies, profiting by this treaty, we are enabled to give our entire attention to finding the best mode of carrying out successfully the intention of the Kings, our said Sire and Grandsire, which subject has occupied our thoughts, from the time of our succeeding to the Crown. We now behold, with due gratitude to God for it, that our exertions have accomplished what we proposed, since the greater part of our subjects of the said pretended Reformed religion have embraced the Catholic, and inasmuch as on this account the execution of the Edict of Nantes, and every thing else ordered in favor of the pretended Reformed religion becomes useless, we have resolved that we can do nothing better, with the view of destroying all memory of the past troubles, confusion and evils caused by the progress of this false religion in our Kingdom, which gave rise to this, and so many other preceding and subsequent Edicts and Proclamations, than to revoke entirely the said Edict of Nantes, and the secret articles granted after it, and all done since in favor of said religion.

1. Be it known, that for these causes, and others by which we are influenced, of our own certain knowledge, full power and Royal authority, we have by this perpetual and irrevocable decree repealed and revoked and we do repeal and revoke the Edict of the King our said Grandsire, given at Nantes in the month of April, 1598, to its full extent, together with the private articles issued on the 2d May following, and the Letters Patent executed upon them, and the Edict given at Nîmes, in the month of July, 1629. We declare them all null and void, together with all other concessions proceeding from these or other Edicts, Proclamations and Decrees to the people of the pretended Reformed religion, of any kind whatsoever, which shall all be as though they never had any existence, and consequently, it is our will and pleasure, that all places of worship belonging to those of the said pretended Reformed religion, situated within our Kingdom, Countries, Lands and Manors under our government, be demolished forthwith.

2. We forbid our said subjects of the pretended Reformed religion to assemble themselves together for religious exercises in any place or private house, under any pretext whatsoever, the same in bailiwicks and otherwise, even if the said exercises may have been sustained by decrees of our Council.

3. We likewise forbid all Lords of the Manor, of whatever rank they may be, to hold religious exercises in their houses or within their fiefs, be the fiefs what kind they may, under penalty to all our said subjects who take part in said exercises, of confiscation and imprisonment.

4. We enjoin all Ministers of the said pretended Reformed re-

ligion, who are not willing to be converted and to embrace the Apostolical Roman Catholic religion, to depart from our Kingdom and Territories within fifteen days after the publication of our present Edict, without being permitted to remain beyond that time, nor during the said fifteen days can they be allowed to preach, exhort or perform other functions, under penalty of the galleys.

5. We wish those of said Ministers who shall be converted, to continue in the enjoyment for life, and their widows after them, so long as they remain in the state of widowhood, of the same exemption from tax and the quartering upon them of soldiers that they enjoyed while performing the functions of the Ministry; and besides this, we shall order pensions to be paid to the said Ministers for life, amounting to one-third more than the sum they received as Ministers; the half of which pension shall be continued to their widows after their death, so long as they remain widows.

6. If any of the said Ministers desire to become Advocates or to take the degree of Doctor of Laws, we would have it understood that the three years of study prescribed by our Proclamations, shall be dispensed with in their case, and after having been submitted to examination in the usual way, and being judged competent, they may be received as Doctors upon paying only half the fees that are usually collected on such occasions in each University.

7. We prohibit private schools for the instruction of children of the pretended Reformed religion, and generally, every thing whatever that could be construed as a concession, in any sort of way, in favor of the said religion.

8. With regard to the children of those of the said pretended Reformed religion, we desire that henceforth they be baptised by the Curé of the Parish. We enjoin the fathers and mothers to send the children to Church for the purpose, under penalty of the payment of a fine of 500 livres, or more if it lapses; and afterwards, the children shall be brought up in the Apostolic Roman Catholic religion. We desire the Magistrates of the place to pay particular attention to this point.

9. And to evince our clemency towards those of said pretended Reformed religion who have gone out of our Kingdom and Territories before the publication of this, our Edict, we wish to have it understood that in case they come back within four months from the date of the said publication, they may, and it is quite open to them to resume possession of their property, and enjoy it as entire-

ly as if they had always remained in the country. On the contrary, with respect to those who do not return within the four months to our Kingdom, their property shall all be confiscated, in conformity with our Proclamation of the twentieth of last August.

10. We make express and reiterated declarations, that none of our subjects of the said pretended Reformed religion, they, their wives or children, shall be permitted to take away with them from our Kingdom and Territories any of their property or possessions under penalty of the galleys for men, and confiscation and imprisonment for women.

We wish it understood that proclamations issued against those who have relapsed shall be executed according to their form and tenor.

The remainder of those of the said pretended Reformed religion while waiting until it pleases God to enlighten them as he has done others, may remain in the cities and places within our kingdom and territories, and continue to follow commercial pursuits there, and enjoy their property in peace without being disturbed or hindered under pretext of the said pretended Reformed religion on condition as before said, that they have no religious exercises, no assembling for prayer or worship of any kind according to said religion, under the above-named penalty of confiscation and imprisonment.

Therefore we command our right trusty and entirely beloved people who compose our Courts of Parliament, Court of Exchequer, and Courts of Aids, Bailiffs, Seneschals, Provosts and other Magistrates and Officers, whose duty it may be, as well as their Lieutenants, to cause our present Edict to be read, published, and registered within their courts and jurisdiction, even in the time of vacation; and they must maintain it and cause it to be maintained, kept and observed in every point without contravention, and they must not permit it to be contravened in any way whatever. For such is our will and pleasure, and in order that the thing may be established and inviolable for ever, we have affixed our seal to these presents.

Given at Fontainebleau, in the month of October, year of grace 1685, and forty-third of our reign.

Signed,	LOUIS,
And on the fold visa,	LE TELLIER,
And at the side by the King,	COLBERT.

And sealed with the Great Seal with green wax, upon red and green silk cords.

Confession of Faith required to be subscribed to by converts from the Protestant Church; a very little modified, in the articles upon Purgatory and the Invocation of Saints, from that which was prepared under Pius IV. after the Council of Trent.

I, A. B., believe with steadfast faith, and acknowledge all and every one of the articles contained in this Creed used in the holy Roman Church, that is to say— * * * *

[Here follows the Nicene Creed.]

I believe and embrace steadfastly the Traditions of the Apostles and of the Holy Church, with all its constitutions and observances.

I admit and receive the Holy Scriptures according to and in the sense that the Holy Mother holds and has held, to whom belongs the right understanding and interpretation of the said Scriptures, and never will I receive or expound them otherwise than according to the common agreement and unanimous consent of the Fathers.

I confess that there are seven Sacraments truly and properly so called in the new Law, instituted by our Lord Jesus Christ, and necessary, but not all to every individual, for the salvation of mankind, which are Baptism, Confirmation, the Holy Eucharist, Penance, Extreme Unction, Ordination, and Marriage, and through these the grace of God is given to us; and that of them Baptism, Confirmation and Ordination cannot be repeated without sacrilege.

I believe also and admit the ceremonies adopted by the Catholic Church, and made use of in the solemn administrations of the said Sacraments.

I believe also and embrace every thing defined and determined by the Holy Council of Trent on the subject of original sin and justification.

I acknowledge that in the Holy Mass a true, fitting, and propitiatory sacrifice for the dead and the living is offered to God, and that the body and blood with the spirit of the Divinity of our Lord Jesus Christ is truly, really, and substantially in the very Holy Sacrament of the Eucharist, and that a conversion of the entire substance of the entire bread into the body, and the entire substance of the wine into the blood, takes place in it, which conversion is called Transubstantiation by the Catholic Church.

I confess also that we take and receive Jesus Christ whole and entire in one only of the two kinds in a true Sacrament.

I confess that there is a Purgatory in which the souls that are detained may be benefited by the good works and prayers of the faithful.

I avow that we ought to honor and invoke the blessed Saints, male and female, who are reigning with Jesus Christ and offering their prayers for us, and that we ought to venerate their holy relics.

As also that we ought to have and to retain images of Jesus Christ and of his blessed and always Virgin Mother, and the other Saints, male and female, rendering to them the honor and reverence that is their due.

I confess that Jesus Christ bequeathed to his Church the power of granting Indulgences, and that its use is very beneficial to Christian people.

I recognize the Holy Apostolic Roman Catholic Church as the Mother and Head of all Churches.

I promise and swear true obedience to the Pope and Holy Father of Rome, Successor of St. Peter, Chief and Prince of the Apostles, and Vicar of Jesus Christ.

I approve without any doubt, and I make profession of all that has been decided, determined and declared by the Holy Canons and General Councils, and especially by the Holy Council of Trent, and I reject, condemn, and anathematize all that is contrary to them, and all heresies condemned, rejected, and anathematized by the Church.

I, A. B., promise, vow, and swear, upon the Holy Evangelists, to persevere entirely and inviolably until I draw my latest breath, by the aid of God's grace, in maintaining this Catholic Faith, out of which there is no salvation and no one can be saved, and which now I make profession of without any constraint, and, as far as may be possible, I will cause to be held, kept, observed, and professed by all those over whom I have charge in my house and my station of life.

Therefore, God and the Holy Evangelists, on whom I swear and make oath, helping me, giving my hand to N., and in the presence of the undersigned witnesses, &c., &c., &c.

THE END

www.ingramcontent.com/pod-product-compliance
Lightning Source LLC
Chambersburg PA
CBHW072039020426
42334CB00017B/1323